# 14th Linguistic Annotation Workshop 2020 (LAW XIV)

Held online due to COVID-19

Barcelona, Spain
12 December 2020

ISBN: 978-1-7138-2831-0

# The 14th Linguistic Annotation Workshop

Proceedings of the Workshop

December 12, 2020

Barcelona, Spain (Online)

Copyright of each paper stays with the respective authors (or their employers).

# Introduction to the Workshop

The Linguistic Annotation Workshop (LAW) is organized annually by the Association for Computational Linguistics' Special Interest Group for Annotation (ACL SIGANN). It provides a forum to facilitate the exchange and propagation of research results concerned with the annotation, manipulation, and exploitation of corpora; work towards harmonization and interoperability from the perspective of the increasingly large number of tools and frameworks for annotated language resources; and work towards a consensus on all issues crucial to the advancement of the field of corpus annotation. These proceedings include papers that were presented at LAW XIV, held online in conjunction with the annual meeting of the Association for Computational Linguistics (ACL) in Barcelona, Spain, on December 12, 2020.

The series is now in its fourteenth year. The first workshop took place in 2007 at the ACL in Prague. Since then, the LAW has been held every year, consistently drawing substantial participation (both in terms of paper/poster submissions and participation in the actual workshop) providing evidence that the LAW's overall focus continues to be an important area of interest in the field, a substantial part of which relies on supervised learning from gold standard data sets. This year's LAW has received 33 submissions, out of which 17 papers have been accepted to be presented at the workshop, 7 as talks and 10 as posters. In addition to oral and poster paper presentations, LAW XIV also features an invited talk by Nils Reiter.

Our thanks go to SIGANN, our organizing committee, for its continuing organization of the LAW workshops, and to the ACL 2020 workshop chairs for their support. Also, we thank Luke Gessler and Adam Roussel, the LAW XIV publicity and publications chairs, for their invaluable help with these proceedings. Most of all, we would like to thank all the authors for submitting their papers to the workshop and our program committee members for their dedication and their thoughtful reviews.


## Special Theme: "Breaking the Mold"

This year's special theme is "Breaking the Mold", promoting novel or less studied types of annotations and data. This includes papers on less common annotations (for example metaphor, sense anaphora, gesture, humor); annotations in understudied settings or data types (new text types or novel collection methods); and annotation for languages other than English, especially beyond tagging/treebanking.

**Stefanie Dipper and Amir Zeldes**
Workshop chairs

**Program Committee Co-chairs**

Stefanie Dipper, Ruhr-Universität Bochum
Amir Zeldes, Georgetown University

**Publicity and Publications Chairs**

Luke Gessler, Georgetown University
Adam Roussel, Ruhr-Universität Bochum

**Organizing Committee**

Stefanie Dipper, Ruhr-Universität Bochum
Annemarie Friedrich, Bosch Research
Chu-Ren Huang, The Hong Kong Polytechnic University
Jena D. Hwang, Allen Institute for AI
Nancy Ide, Vassar College
Lori Levin, Carnegie Mellon University
Adam Meyers, New York University
Antonio Pareja-Lora, Universidad de Alcalá de Henares (UAH)/DMEG (UdG)/ATLAS (UNED)
Massimo Poesio, Queen Mary University of London
Sameer Pradhan, Boulder Learning, Inc.
Ines Rehbein, University of Mannheim
Nathan Schneider, Georgetown University
Manfred Stede, University of Potsdam
Katrin Tomanek, Google
Fei Xia, University of Washington
Deniz Zeyrek, Middle East Technical University
Heike Zinsmeister, Universität Hamburg

**Program Committee**

Ron Artstein, USC Institute for Creative Technologies
Nicoletta Calzolari, ILC-CNR
Emmanuele Chersoni, Hong Kong Polytechnic University
Kathryn Conger, University of Colorado, Boulder
Marie-Catherine de Marneffe, The Ohio State University
Jonathan Dunn, University of Canterbury
Richard Eckart de Castilho, UKP Lab, Technische Universität Darmstadt
Kilian Evang, Heinrich Heine University Düsseldorf
Federico Fancellu, Samsung AI Research Canada
Annemarie Friedrich, Bosch Research
Kim Gerdes, Sorbonne Nouvelle / Inria
Jena D. Hwang, Allen Institute for AI
Nancy Ide, Vassar College
Mikel Iruskieta, University of the Basque Country (UPV/EHU)
Sandra Kübler, Indiana University
John Lee, City University of Hong Kong
Els Lefever, LT3, Ghent University

Lori Levin, Carnegie Mellon University
Adam Meyers, New York University
Kemal Oflazer, Carnegie Mellon University in Qatar
Maciej Ogrodniczuk, Institute of Computer Science, Polish Academy of Sciences
Antonio Pareja-Lora, Universidad de Alcalá de Henares (UAH)/DMEG (UdG)/ATLAS (UNED)
Miriam R. L. Petruck, International Computer Science Institute
Massimo Poesio, Queen Mary University of London
Ines Rehbein, University of Mannheim
Michael Roth, University of Stuttgart
Nathan Schneider, Georgetown University
Manfred Stede, University of Potsdam
Bonnie Webber, University of Edinburgh
Michael Wiegand, Alpen-Adria-Universität Klagenfurt
Nianwen Xue, Brandeis University
Deniz Zeyrek, Middle East Technical University
Heike Zinsmeister, Universität Hamburg

# Table of Contents

# Conference Program
*All times are in Central European Time (CET)*

**Saturday, December 12, 2020**

14:00–14:10    *Introduction to the Workshop*
LAW XIV Chairs

14:10–15:00    *Invited Talk*
Nils Reiter

**15:00–15:20**    **Coffee Break**

**15:20–16:00**    **Session 1**

15:20–15:30    *Bayesian Methods for Semi-supervised Text Annotation*
Kristian Miok, Gregor Pirs and Marko Robnik-Sikonja

15:30–15:40    *Provenance for Linguistic Corpora through Nanopublications*
Timo Lek, Anna de Groot, Tobias Kuhn and Roser Morante

15:40–15:50    *A Sentiment-annotated Dataset of English Causal Connectives*
Marta Andersson, Murathan Kurfalı and Robert Östling

15:50–16:00    *A Novel Annotation Schema for Conversational Humor: Capturing the Cultural Nuances in Kanyasulkam*
Vaishnavi Pamulapati, Gayatri Purigilla and Radhika Mamidi

16:00–17:00    **Poster Session 1**

*Modeling Ambiguity with Many Annotators and Self-Assessments of Annotator Certainty*
Melanie Andresen, Michael Vauth and Heike Zinsmeister

*Representation Problems in Linguistic Annotations: Ambiguity, Variation, Uncertainty, Error and Bias*
Christin Beck, Hannah Booth, Mennatallah El-Assady and Miriam Butt

*Understanding the Tradeoff between Cost and Quality of Expert Annotations for Keyphrase Extraction*
Hung Chau, Saeid Balaneshin, Kai Liu and Ondrej Linda

*Cookpad Parsed Corpus: Linguistic Annotations of Japanese Recipes*
Jun Harashima and Makoto Hiramatsu

*Modelling and Annotating Interlinear Glossed Text from 280 Different Endangered Languages as Linked Data with LIGT*
Sebastian Nordhoff

17:00–17:30    *Coffee Break*

17:30–18:00    **Session 2**

17:30–17:40    *PASTRIE: A Corpus of Prepositions Annotated with Supersense Tags in Reddit International English*
Michael Kranzlein, Emma Manning, Siyao Peng, Shira Wein, Aryaman Arora and Nathan Schneider

17:40–17:50    *Supersense and Sensibility: Proxy Tasks for Semantic Annotation of Prepositions*
Luke Gessler, Shira Wein and Nathan Schneider

17:50–18:00    *Sprucing up Supersenses: Untangling the Semantic Clusters of Accompaniment and Purpose*
Jena D. Hwang, Nathan Schneider and Vivek Srikumar

# Bayesian Methods for Semi-supervised Text Annotation


**Kristian Miok[1,2], Gregor Pirš[1] and Marko Robnik-Šikonja[1]**

[1] University of Ljubljana, Faculty of Computer and Information Science, Slovenia
Email: {gregor.pirs, marko.robnik}@fri.uni-lj.si
[2] West University of Timisoara, Computer Science Department, Romania
Email: kristian.miok@e-uvt.ro



## Abstract

Human annotations are an important source of information in the development of natural language understanding approaches. As under the pressure of productivity annotators can assign different labels to a given text, the quality of produced annotations frequently varies. This is especially the case if decisions are difficult, with high cognitive load, requires awareness of broader context, or careful consideration of background knowledge. To alleviate the problem, we propose two semi-supervised methods to guide the annotation process: a Bayesian deep learning model and a Bayesian ensemble method. Using a Bayesian deep learning method, we can discover annotations that cannot be trusted and might require reannotation. A recently proposed Bayesian ensemble method helps us to combine the annotators' labels with predictions of trained models. According to the results obtained from three hate speech detection experiments, the proposed Bayesian methods can improve the annotations and prediction performance of BERT models.


## 1 Introduction

Recent successful applications of artificial intelligence in various fields, including natural language processing, are often due to long hours of human annotation when preparing datasets for machine learning. The annotation process transfers human knowledge to machine learning models but it is often done under time pressure and with inadequate instructions or with insufficiently trained annotators.Aiming to make the annotation process easier, we study the possibility of designing a data labeling process which requires less human supervision.

In practice, a fairly standard procedure in the annotation quality control is to recheck the labels that are wrongly classified by using several prediction models. As an alternative, Bayesian inference produces a distribution of possible decisions and can improve the selection of instances requiring reannotation (Miok et al., 2020). Most neural networks do not support the assessment of predictive uncertainty. The Bayesian inference framework can be helpful, however, most techniques do not scale well in neural networks with high dimensional parameter space (Izmailov et al., 2019). Various methods were proposed to overcome this problem (Myshkov and Julier, 2016), one of the most efficient being Monte Carlo Dropout (MCD) (Gal and Ghahramani, 2016a). Its idea is to use the dropout mechanism in neural networks as a regularization technique (Srivastava et al., 2014) and interpret it as a Bayesian optimization approach that samples from the approximate posterior distribution.

A common problem in text annotations is that annotators are not always sure about correct labels due to uncertainty in the text (Vincze, 2015; Szarvas et al., 2008). On difficult texts, annotators frequently give ambiguous labels and their annotations can be biased. Instead of asking annotators to label the raw text, it would be easier for them if they were proposed answers accompanied by probabilistic scores from an ensemble of predictive models. Ensemble methods produce robust models that frequently provide significantly better predictions than individual models. The key strength of ensembles is that they can overcome errors and shortcomings of individual ensemble members. However, diversity in combining different predictions and reliability of individual predictions need to be better understood and



1


*The 14th Linguistic Annotation Workshop*, pages 1–12
Barcelona, Spain (Online), December 12, 2020.

evaluated (Zhou, 2012). A recently published ensemble method Multivariate Normal Mixture Conditional Likelihood Model (MM) (Pirš and Štrumbelj, 2019) tries to understand the predictors on the distributional level and use Bayesian inference to combine them. In this work, we evaluate MM's performance when combining predictive models on the hate speech detection task. We show that our methodology can serve as a helpful tool in the data annotation process.

Recently, the most successful approach in text classification is to use transformer neural networks (Vaswani et al., 2017), pretrained on large monolingual corpora, and then fine-tune them for a specific task, such as text classification. For example, BERT (Bidirectional Encoder Representations from Transformers) (Devlin et al., 2019) uses masked language modeling and order of sentences prediction tasks to build a general language understanding model. During the fine-tuning for a specific downstream task, additional layers are added to the BERT model, and the model is trained on the data of interest to capture the specific knowledge required to perform the task.

The main aims of the paper is to propose methods that can save time and resources during the text annotation process and improve prediction performance. As a test domain we use hate speech detection in tweets, news comments and Facebook comments. We investigate two performance improving techniques which can be summarized as our main contributions as follows.

1. We remove instances with uncertain classifications from the training set and show that fine-tuning on the cleaned dataset improves the performance of the BERT model. Less certain classifications can be selected for reannotation.

2. We combine predictions of machine learning models using the MM probabilistic ensemble method. The approach is beneficial for predictive performance.

The paper consists of five further sections. In Section 2, we present related works on prediction uncertainty and hate speech detection. In Section 3, we propose the methodology for uncertainty assessment of deep neural networks using attention layers and MCD. In Section 4, we describe the tested datasets and evaluation scenarios. The obtained results are presented in Section 5, followed by conclusions and ideas for further work in Section 6.

## 2  Related Work

In this section, we introduce related work split into four topics. First, we present the work on semi-supervised learning that can be used in text annotation, followed by the related research on Bayesian learning for text classification. In the third subsection, we describe probabilistic ensemble methods and in the fourth, we outline the related work on hate speech detection.

### 2.1  Semi-supervised Learning for Text Annotation

The performance of supervised learning depends on the availability of a sufficient amount of labeled data. However, manual labeling is expensive and difficult to scale up to large amounts of data. Semi-supervised learning tries to utilize large amounts of unlabeled data available for many problems by combining them with small amounts of labeled data (Zhu, 2005). The goal of semi-supervised learning is to understand how combining labeled and unlabeled data can change the learning behavior, and design algorithms that take advantage of such a combination (Zhu and Goldberg, 2009). Most semi-supervised learning strategies extend either unsupervised or supervised learning to include additional information typical of the other learning paradigm. The transductive learning is related to the semi-supervised learning, but assumes that the test set is known in advance and its goal is to optimize the generalization ability on this (unlabeled) test set (Zhou and Li, 2010). In the non-transductive setting, Acharya et al. (2013) combine probabilistic classifiers. They take class labels from existing classifiers and cluster labels from a clustering ensemble. The consensus labeling is assigned to the target data.

### 2.2  Bayesian Methods for Text Classification

Although, recent works on prediction uncertainty mostly investigate deep neural networks, many other probabilistic classifiers were analyzed in the past (Platt, 1999; Niculescu-Mizil and Caruana, 2005; Zhang et al., 2013; Cao et al., 2015; He et al., 2018). Prediction reliability is an important issue for black-box models like neural networks as they do not provide interpretability or reliability information about their predictions. Most existing reliability scores for deep neural networks are contructed using Bayesian inference. The most popular exception is the work of Lakshminarayanan et al. (2017), who proposed to use deep ensembles to estimate the prediction uncertainty.

A computationally efficient simulation of Bayesian inference uses Monte Carlo dropout (Gal and Ghahramani, 2016a). The first implementation of dropout in recurrent neural networks (RNNs) was in 2013 (Wang and Manning, 2013) but further research revealed a negative impact of dropout in RNNs (Bluche et al., 2015). Later, the dropout was successfully applied to language modeling by Zaremba et al. (2014) who used it only in fully connected layers. Gal and Ghahramani (2016b) implemented the variational inference based dropout which can regularize also recurrent layers. In this way method mimics Bayesian inference by combining probabilistic parameter interpretation and deep RNNs. Several other works investigate how to estimate prediction uncertainty within different data frameworks using RNNs (Zhu and Laptev, 2017; Miok et al., 2019b), e.g., Bayes by Backpropagation (BBB) was applied to RNNs (Fortunato et al., 2017). Monte Carlo dropout was also introduced into variational autoencoders (Miok et al., 2019a; Miok et al., 2019c) and for estimating prediction intervals (Miok, 2018).

To our knowledge, Bayesian deep learning models were not yet used to detect less certain text classifications and remove them from a train dataset to improve the prediction performance.

## 2.3 Probabilistic Ensembles

Most methods used for text classification can produce probabilistic predictions which are rarely exploited beyond classification into a discrete class. As probabilistic predictions provide additional information compared to the discrete outcome, we use ensembles that can model predictive distributions. Ensemble methods can be divided into two main groups. The first group of methods estimates the performance of individual classifiers and weights them accordingly. The second group of methods learns the structure of predictions and bases their forecasts on it.

The first group of methods can be further divided into methods that are able to combine full posterior distributions and methods that only combine probabilistic point predictions. The advantage of the former is that they are more expressive, and a disadvantage is that they require inputs in the form of a full distribution, which is not always available. Bayesian model averaging (Hoeting et al., 1999) combines models by their marginal posterior probability. This method is suitable if one of the candidate models is the true data generating process, otherwise its performance decreases (Cerquides and De Mántaras, 2005). Bayesian stacking (Yao et al., 2018) is also useful in these cases. It is based on weighing the posterior predictive distributions of individual models by estimating their leave-one-out cross-validation performance. Linear opinion pool (Cooke, 1991) is a classical approach to combine classifiers and can be included into the second group of methods. It combines predictions as a linear combination of individual models by maximizing the likelihood. An example of Bayesian approach from the second group is the agnostic Bayesian learning of ensembles (Lacoste et al., 2014), which weighs the models by estimated probabilities of them being the best model; the estimates are based on holdout computation of generalization performance.

Methods that model the structure of predictions are especially useful in case of complex relationships between individual models' predictions and the response variable. Independent Bayesian classifier combination (IBCC) (Kim and Ghahramani, 2012) combines non-probabilistic predictions by estimating the probability mass of predictions with a categorical distribution, conditional on the true label. It provides probabilities for a new observation that are proportional to the probability mass of new inputs for each true label. Nazábal et al. (2016) has extended the IBCC to probabilistic predictions by using the Dirichlet distribution. Supra-Bayesian methods (Lindley, 1985) combine probabilistic predictions using the log-odds of probabilities and modeling them with the multivariate normal (MVN) distribution, conditional on the true label. They use the common covariance matrix over all true labels but vary the means.

Ensemble modeling has recently been studied also within the text classification area (Li et al., 2018; Silva et al., 2010; Kilimci and Akyokus, 2018), but not within the context of probabilistic ensemble models. In our work, we investigate Bayesian ensemble modeling for hate speech detection and how this can improve individual model predictions.

## 2.4  Hate Speech Detection

Analyzing sentiments and extracting emotions from the text are useful natural language processing applications (Sun et al., 2018). Being one of the wide range of applications where machines tend to understand human sentiments, hate speech detection is gaining importance with the rise of social media. We regard hate speech as written or oral communication that abuses or threatens a specific group or target (Warner and Hirschberg, 2012).

Detecting abusive language for less-resourced languages is difficult, hence, multilingual and cross-lingual methods are employed to improve the results (Stappen et al., 2020). This is especially the case when the involved languages are morphologically or geographically similar (Pamungkas and Patti, 2019). In our work, we investigate and compare hate speech detection methods for English, Croatian, and Slovene. English is by far the most researched language with plenty of resources (Malmasi and Zampieri, 2017; Davidson et al., 2017; Waseem and Hovy, 2016). Recently, hate speech detection studies were done also on neighbouring Slavic languages Croatian (Kocijan et al., 2019; Ljubešić et al., 2018) and Slovene (Fišer et al., 2017; Ljubešić et al., 2019; Vezjak, 2018).

Hate speech detection is usually treated as a binary text classification problem, and is approached with supervised learning methods. In the past, the most frequently used classifier was the Support Vector Machine (SVM) method (Schmidt and Wiegand, 2017), but recently deep neural networks showed superior performance, first through recurrent neural networks (Mehdad and Tetreault, 2016), and recently using large pretrained transformer networks (Mozafari et al., 2019; Wiedemann et al., 2020). In this work, we use the recent state-of-the-art pretrained (multilingual) BERT model.

## 3  Methods

We describe two approaches to the assessment of prediction reliability, Bayesian Attention Networks and Bayesian Probabilistic Ensembles.

### 3.1  Bayesian Attention Networks

The work (Miok et al., 2020) that introduce method named 'Bayesian Attention Networks' (BAN), proposes the dropout layers to be active also during the prediction phase. In this way, predictions are rather random and are sampled from the *learned* distribution, thereby forming an ensemble of predictions. The obtained distribution can be, for example, inspected for higher moment properties and it can offer additional information on the certainty of a given prediction. During the prediction phase, all layers of the network except the dropout layers are deactivated. The forward pass on such partially activated architecture is repeated for a fixed number of samples, each time producing a different outcome that can be combined into the final probability, or inspected as a probability distribution.

Monte Carlo dropout was adapted for the BERT model in the same way as for BANs. MCD can provide multiple predictions during the test time without any additional training (Gal, 2016). Training a neural network with dropout spreads the information contained in the neurons across the network. Hence, during the prediction, such a trained neural network will be robust; using the dropout principle, a new prediction is created in each forward pass, and a sufficiently large set of such predictions can be used to estimate prediction reliability. The BERT models are trained with 10% of dropout in all of the layers by default. Therefore, it allows for multiple predictions with the fine-tuned model. We call this model MCD BERT. A possible limitation of this approach is that during training a single dropout rate of 10% is used, while other dropout probabilities might be more suitable for reliability estimation. We leave this question for further work as it requires long and costly training of several BERT models.

### 3.2  Bayesian Probabilistic Ensemble

To alleviate the drawbacks of individual classification models, we propose the use of MM (Pirš and Štrumbelj, 2019), a Bayesian ensemble method suitable for combining correlated probabilistic predictions.

MM is an extension of IBCC (Kim and Ghahramani, 2012), which combines non-probabilistic predictions. The method is based on finding the latent structure of combined predictions and provides new probabilities based on its distribution. Let $m$ be the number of classes and $r$ the number of individual models we are combining. The main idea is similar to Supra-Bayesian ensembles (Lindley, 1985), as we first transform individual probabilistic predictions with the inverse logistic transformation (log-odds) to move from [0,1] space to the $\mathbb{R}$ space. We merge the transformed predictions of individual models and get a $(m-1)r$-variate distribution. We model this latent distribution with multivariate normal mixtures, conditional on the true label in a similar fashion as in the case of linear discriminant analysis. Let $\theta$ represent estimated parameters and $\theta_t$ the subset of parameters estimated for observations with true label $t$. Let $T^* \in \{1, 2, ..., m\}$ be the response random variable for a new observation and $u^* \in \mathbb{R}^{(m-1)r}$ the transformed and merged predictions for this new observation. Probabilistic predictions for unseen data can then be generated by calculating the densities of merged predictions for new data:

$$p(T^* = t|u^*, \theta) = \frac{p(u^*|\theta_t)(\gamma_t n_t)}{\sum_{i=1}^r p(u^*|\theta_i)(\gamma_i n_i)},$$

where $p$ is the MVN mixture probability density, $\gamma_t$ is the frequency prior for class $t$, and $n_t$ is the number of true labels in class $t$ in the training dataset. The method uses a regularization term, which increases the variance in any dimension that is difficult to model or has a detrimental effect on the results, effectively decreasing its effect. For a complete Bayesian specification and the derivation of the Gibbs sampler, we refer the reader to (Pirš and Štrumbelj, 2019). We used the same priors as proposed in this paper.

MM is well-suited for combining biased classifiers, or classifiers with systematic errors. It can serve as a calibration tool for an individual classifier by learning its latent distribution. Since BERT is usually accurate but less well calibrated, the MM method has the potential to alleviate miscalibration, while improving or at least preserving the classification performance.

## 4   Experimental Setting

We first introduce the three phases of our experiments, followed by the used datasets and implementation details. The experimental setting consists of three phases:

1. We categorize classifications to trusted and untrusted based on the uncertainty measure from MCD BERT. In this way, we can detect borderline classification that make a false impression of certainty.

2. We remove the instances with uncertain classifications from the *training set* to improve the dataset on which the BERT model is fine-tuned. This provides better quality data for training and shall improve the quality of the resulting prediction model.

3. We use Bayesian ensemble to combine automatic predictions with annotators' decisions to remove low-quality training instances.

### 4.1   Datasets

To test the proposed methodology in the multilingual context, we trained the presented classification models on three different datasets, summarized in Table 1.

1. The **English** dataset[1] is extracted from the hate speech and offensive language detection study of Davidson et al. (2017). We used the subset of data consisting of 5,000 tweets. We took 1,430 tweets labeled as hate speech and randomly sampled 3,670 tweets from the collection of the remaining 23,353 tweets.

2. The **Croatian** dataset was provided by the Styria media company within the EU Horizon 2020 EMBEDDIA project[2]. The texts were extracted from user comments in the news portal Večernji list[3].

---

[1] https://github.com/t-davidson/hate-speech-and-offensive-language
[2] http://embeddia.eu
[3] https://www.vecernji.hr

The original dataset consists of 9,646,634 comments from which we selected 8,422 comments of which 50% are labeled as hate speech by human moderators and the other half was randomly chosen from the non-problematic comments.

3. **Slovene** dataset is a result of the Slovenian national project FRENK[4]. Our dataset comes from two studies on Facebook comments (Ljubešić et al., 2019). The first study deals with LGBT homophobia topics while the second analyzes anti-migrants posts. We used all 2,188 hate speech comments, and randomly sampled 3,812 non-hate speech comments.

Table 1: Characteristics of the used datasets: type and number of instances, as well as the input embeddings for each of the datasets.

| Dataset | type | Size | Hate | Non-hate | LSTM embeddings |
|---------|------|------|------|----------|-----------------|
| **English** | tweets | 5000 | 1430 | 3670 | sentence |
| **Croatian** | news comments | 8422 | 4211 | 4211 | fastText |
| **Slovene** | Facebook comments | 6000 | 2188 | 3812 | fastText |

### 4.2 Implementation

The two Bayesian methods that were proposed in this paper to improve the annotation process have full implementation within their original papers. All of the particularities of how MCD BERT was implemented in PyTorch library[5] are presented in (Miok et al., 2020). The implementation details of the MM method are clearly explained in (Pirš and Štrumbelj, 2019) methods section and in this paper we provide full R code [6].

## 5 Results

In this section, we present three groups of results: removing uncertain instances from the training set, creating a cleaner training set, and improving annotations using he Bayesian ensembles.

### 5.1 Removing Uncertain Instances

Using MCD BERT, we obtain multiple predictions for each test set instance, and compute their mean and variance. Using the mean, we determine the classification (hate speech or not), while the variance reports on the certainty of the BERT for this specific instance. Based on the variance, we group classifications into certain and uncertain. Unsurprisingly, removing the uncertain test set instances improves the prediction performance as shown in Table 2, but also leaves a portion of borderline instances unclassified.

From Table 2 we can conclude that the variance of MCD BERT predictions is correlated with the performance of models: the more variance there is in the predictions the less accurate the model. Thus, removing the uncertain classifications can seemingly improve the performance of the test set. A practical benefit of this is that uncertain classification could be passed back to annotators to recheck them.

### 5.2 Creating Cleaner Training Sets

While the removal of uncertain instances from the test set might just sweep the problematic instances under the carpet, a more practical benefit is to use the uncertainty information to create a better training set. The test tweets/comments were removed based on how variate are their predictions. Thus, we repeatedly train the MCD BERT model on part of the dataset and use this model to obtain multiple predictions on the other part of the training dataset. In such a way, we collect multiple predictions for all original training tweets or comments and remove observations with the highest prediction variance. As a result of this procedure, 15 and 18 percent of the most uncertain predictions were removed for the English and Slovene dataset respectively. Croatian dataset contains a lot of comments with high variability in their predictions

---

[4] http://nl.ijs.si/frenk/ (Research on Electronic Inappropriate Communication)
[5] https://github.com/KristianMiok/Bayesian-BERT
[6] https://github.com/gregorp90/MM

Table 2: Performance of multilingual BERT model, after removing uncertain instances from the test set of 1000 comments.

| Language | Metric | Full dataset | 200 removed | 500 removed | 700 removed |
|---|---|---|---|---|---|
| EN | Accuracy | 0.91 | 0.96 | 0.996 | 0.997 |
| | Precision | 0.90 | 0.95 | 0.992 | 0.994 |
| | Recall | 0.89 | 0.95 | 1 | 1 |
| | F1 | 0.88 | 0.95 | 0.995 | 0.997 |
| CRO | Accuracy | 0.72 | 0.76 | 0.84 | 0.87 |
| | Precision | 0.68 | 0.71 | 0.80 | 0.85 |
| | Recall | 0.54 | 0.69 | 0.78 | 0.75 |
| | F1 | 0.61 | 0.70 | 0.79 | 0.83 |
| SLO | Accuracy | 0.71 | 0.76 | 0.83 | 0.87 |
| | Precision | 0.60 | 0.65 | 0.70 | 0.65 |
| | Recall | 0.56 | 0.64 | 0.66 | 0.54 |
| | F1 | 0.58 | 0.65 | 0.68 | 0.59 |

so for this dataset we removed around 35% of the most uncertain comments. The details of how many instances were removed for each of the three datasets are presented in Table 3.

Table 3: Sizes of the datasets before and after the removing: original number of instances, number of instances removed and final training data size.

| Dataset | Training Size | Number of removed | Final Size | Percent removed |
|---|---|---|---|---|
| English | 4000 | 719 | 3281 | 18 % |
| Croatian | 7422 | 2615 | 4807 | 35% |
| Slovene | 5000 | 731 | 4269 | 15 % |

Using prediction certainty to remove the uncertain instances from the training can improve the fine-tuning of BERT. For neural network models, during training or fine-tuning their performance is evaluated on a separate validation set. In Table 4, we can observe how the prediction accuracy on the validation set is improved with number of training epochs. We can see that fine-tuning BERT on the cleaner dataset improves its performance. We hypothesize that when the uncertainty due to unreliable labels is reduced, the decision boundary is easier to determine.

Table 4: Performance (measured using $F_1$ score) on the validation sets during training for original and cleaned datasets.

| | English | | Croatian | | Slovene | |
|---|---|---|---|---|---|---|
| | Original | Cleaned | Original | Cleaned | Original | Cleaned |
| Epoch1 | 0.92 | 0.98 | 0.68 | 0.77 | 0.70 | 0.64 |
| Epoch2 | 0.92 | 0.98 | 0.69 | 0.77 | 0.70 | 0.77 |
| Epoch3 | 0.92 | 0.98 | 0.68 | 0.78 | 0.71 | 0.79 |
| Epoch4 | 0.92 | 0.98 | 0.70 | 0.79 | 0.72 | 0.81 |

Results for the model fine-tuned on the cleaned dataset are contained in Table 5. Compared to the results in Table 2 (see the "Full dataset" column), the prediction results for Croatian and Slovenian datasets are improved while for the English dataset this is not the case. We explain this by the fact that the English dataset is well-annotated with high-quality predictions. On the other hand, we believe that the Croatian and Slovenian datasets are less clean and contain several questionable annotations. This can be confirmed for the Croatian dataset, which was created within the project we participate in, so we are well-informed about the annotation process.

Table 5: Test set performance ($F_1$ score) of the models trained on the cleaned datasets.

| Metrics | English | Croatian | Slovene |
| --- | --- | --- | --- |
| **Accuracy** | 0.87 | 0.74 | 0.72 |
| **Precision** | 0.88 | 0.73 | 0.62 |
| **Recall** | 0.81 | 0.60 | 0.55 |
| **F1** | 0.85 | 0.66 | 0.59 |

## 5.3 Improving Annotations using Bayesian Ensembles

We propose a Bayesian ensemble as a support method for the annotation process. As annotators can be distracted, biased, or influenced, we propose to use the MM method to provide them a hint of how shall they annotate the instances. From Table 6, we can observe that by combining probabilistic predictions of BERT, random forest, and support vector machines, we can further improve the predictive performance. The MM ensemble not only improves BERT's results but also provides better calibrated predictions as evidenced from Figure 1.

Table 6: The $F_1$ score of the hate speech classifiers and their ensemble.

| Method | English | Croatian | Slovene |
| --- | --- | --- | --- |
| **BERT** | 0.91 | 0.72 | 0.71 |
| **RF** | 0.83 | 0.67 | 0.65 |
| **SVM** | 0.86 | 0.71 | 0.69 |
| **MM** | **0.92** | **0.74** | **0.72** |

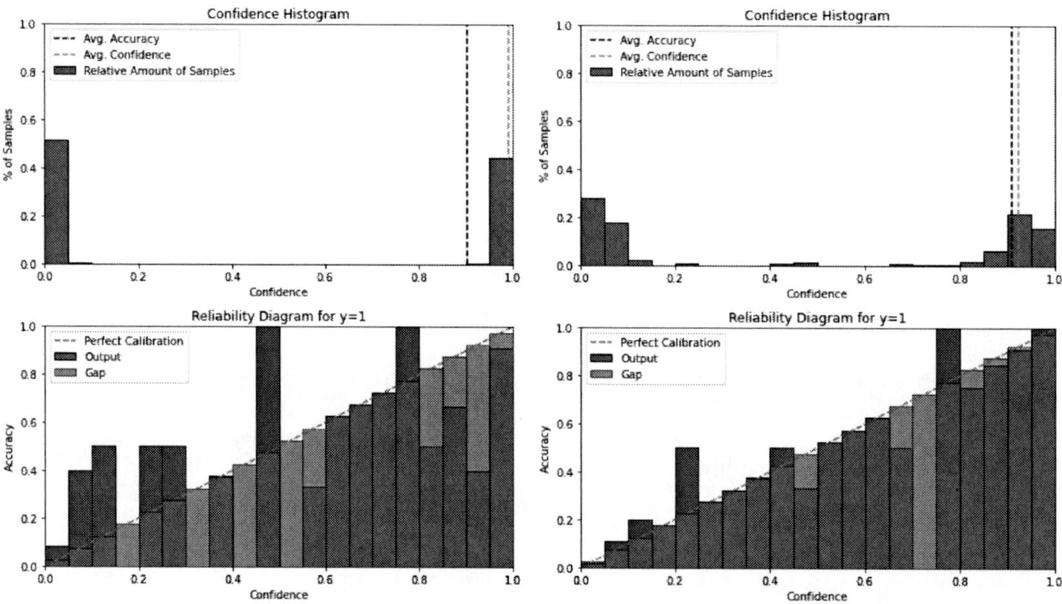

Figure 1: Calibration for the BERT predictions (left) and MM model predictions (right).

## 6   Conclusions and Further Work

A large amount of currently available textual data allows and requires modeling with machine learning methods. To apply the supervised methods, the text data has to be annotated, and effective learning requires accurate annotations, which may be expensive for organizers and difficult for human annotators. For this reason, the annotation process is often coupled with semi-supervised machine learning and classification reliability estimation.

We presented several machine learning approaches, based on Bayesian inference, that can improve the data annotation process. First, multiple predictions obtained with MCD BERT can identify instances with questionable labeling. Second, removing training instances with unreliable labels can improve the quality of the training set, making it more homogeneous and cleaner, thereby improving the predictive performance of BERT models. Third, probabilistic ensemble combinations can help annotators to better label the data by providing more accurate and better calibrated prediction probabilities. In conclusion, Bayesian methods can improve the annotation process and shall be further investigated and improved for this task.

In further work, we will focus on improving our method on how to remove uncertain instances. We will construct and test a workflow for semi-supervised text annotation in a real-world setting. Testing different dropout levels in the BERT model may provide a better understanding of its uncertainty and calibration.

## Acknowledgements

This paper was supported by European Union's Horizon 2020 Programme project EMBEDDIA (Cross-Lingual Embeddings for Less-Represented Languages in European News Media, grant no. 825153). The research was supported by the Slovenian Research Agency through research core funding no. P6-0411, project CANDAS (Computer-assisted multilingual news discourse analysis with contextual embeddings, grant no. J6-2581), and Young researcher grant (Gregor Pirš).

## References

Ayan Acharya, Eduardo R Hruschka, Joydeep Ghosh, Badrul Sarwar, and Jean-David Ruvini. 2013. Probabilistic combination of classifier and cluster ensembles for non-transductive learning. In *Proceedings of the 2013 SIAM International Conference on Data Mining*, pages 288–296. SIAM.

Théodore Bluche, Christopher Kermorvant, and Jérôme Louradour. 2015. Where to apply dropout in recurrent neural networks for handwriting recognition? In *2015 13th International Conference on Document Analysis and Recognition (ICDAR)*, pages 681–685. IEEE.

Keyan Cao, Guoren Wang, Donghong Han, Jingwei Ning, and Xin Zhang. 2015. Classification of uncertain data streams based on extreme learning machine. *Cognitive Computation*, 7(1):150–160.

Jesús Cerquides and Ramon López De Mántaras. 2005. Robust Bayesian linear classifier ensembles. In *European Conference on Machine Learning*, pages 72–83. Springer.

Roger Cooke. 1991. *Experts in uncertainty: opinion and subjective probability in science*. Oxford University Press on Demand.

Thomas Davidson, Dana Warmsley, Michael Macy, and Ingmar Weber. 2017. Automated hate speech detection and the problem of offensive language. In *Eleventh international AAAI conference on web and social media*.

Jacob Devlin, Ming-Wei Chang, Kenton Lee, and Kristina Toutanova. 2019. BERT: Pre-training of deep bidirectional transformers for language understanding. In *Proceedings of the 2019 Conference of the North American Chapter of the Association for Computational Linguistics: Human Language Technologies, Volume 1 (Long and Short Papers)*, pages 4171–4186.

Darja Fišer, Tomaž Erjavec, and Nikola Ljubešić. 2017. Legal framework, dataset and annotation schema for socially unacceptable online discourse practices in slovene. In *Proceedings of the first workshop on abusive language online*, pages 46–51.

Meire Fortunato, Charles Blundell, and Oriol Vinyals. 2017. Bayesian recurrent neural networks. *arXiv preprint arXiv:1704.02798*.

Yarin Gal and Zoubin Ghahramani. 2016a. Dropout as a Bayesian approximation: Representing model uncertainty in deep learning. In *International Conference on Machine Learning*, pages 1050–1059.

Yarin Gal and Zoubin Ghahramani. 2016b. A theoretically grounded application of dropout in recurrent neural networks. In *Advances in Neural Information Processing Systems*, pages 1019–1027.

Yarin Gal. 2016. Uncertainty in deep learning. *University of Cambridge*, 1:3.

Lirong He, Bin Liu, Guangxi Li, Yongpan Sheng, Yafang Wang, and Zenglin Xu. 2018. Knowledge base completion by variational bayesian neural tensor decomposition. *Cognitive Computation*, 10(6):1075–1084.

Jennifer A. Hoeting, David Madigan, Adrian E. Raftery, and Chris T. Volinsky. 1999. Bayesian model averaging: a tutorial. *Statistical science*, pages 382–401.

Pavel Izmailov, Wesley J Maddox, Polina Kirichenko, Timur Garipov, Dmitry Vetrov, and Andrew Gordon Wilson. 2019. Subspace inference for bayesian deep learning. *arXiv preprint arXiv:1907.07504*.

Zeynep H Kilimci and Selim Akyokus. 2018. Deep learning-and word embedding-based heterogeneous classifier ensembles for text classification. *Complexity*, 2018.

Hyun-Chul Kim and Zoubin Ghahramani. 2012. Bayesian Classifier Combination. In *International Conference on Artificial Intelligence and Statistics*, pages 619–627.

Kristina Kocijan, Lucija Košković, and Petra Bajac. 2019. Detecting hate speech online: A case of croatian. In *International Conference on Automatic Processing of Natural-Language Electronic Texts with NooJ*, pages 185–197. Springer.

Alexandre Lacoste, Mario Marchand, François Laviolette, and Hugo Larochelle. 2014. Agnostic Bayesian learning of ensembles. In *International Conference on Machine Learning*, pages 611–619.

Balaji Lakshminarayanan, Alexander Pritzel, and Charles Blundell. 2017. Simple and scalable predictive uncertainty estimation using deep ensembles. In *Advances in neural information processing systems*, pages 6402–6413.

Ming Li, Peilun Xiao, and Ju Zhang. 2018. Text classification based on ensemble extreme learning machine. *arXiv preprint arXiv:1805.06525*.

Dennis V. Lindley. 1985. Reconciliation of discrete probability distributions' in Bernado. *JM, DeGroot, MH, Lindley, DV, and Smith, AFM, Eds., Bayesian Statistics II. North Holland, Amsterdam*, pages 375–391.

Nikola Ljubešić, Tomaž Erjavec, and Darja Fišer. 2018. Datasets of slovene and croatian moderated news comments. In *Proceedings of the 2nd Workshop on Abusive Language Online (ALW2)*, pages 124–131.

Nikola Ljubešić, Darja Fišer, and Tomaž Erjavec. 2019. The FRENK datasets of socially unacceptable discourse in Slovene and English. In *International Conference on Text, Speech, and Dialogue*, pages 103–114. Springer.

Shervin Malmasi and Marcos Zampieri. 2017. Detecting hate speech in social media. *arXiv preprint arXiv:1712.06427*.

Yashar Mehdad and Joel Tetreault. 2016. Do characters abuse more than words? In *Proceedings of the 17th Annual Meeting of the Special Interest Group on Discourse and Dialogue*, pages 299–303.

Kristian Miok, Dong Nguyen-Doan, Marko Robnik-Šikonja, and Daniela Zaharie. 2019a. Multiple imputation for biomedicaldata using monte carlo dropout autoencoders. In *7th IEEE International Conference on E-Health and Bioengeneering (EHB)*. IEEE.

Kristian Miok, Dong Nguyen-Doan, Blaž Škrlj, Daniela Zaharie, and Marko Robnik-Šikonja. 2019b. Prediction uncertainty estimation for hate speech classification. In *International Conference on Statistical Language and Speech Processing*, pages 286–298. Springer.

Kristian Miok, Dong Nguyen-Doan, Daniela Zaharie, and Marko Robnik-Šikonja. 2019c. Generating data using monte carlo dropout. In *2019 IEEE 15th International Conference on Intelligent Computer Communication and Processing (ICCP)*, pages 509–515. IEEE.

Kristian Miok, Blaz Skrlj, Daniela Zaharie, and Marko Robnik-Sikonja. 2020. To ban or not to ban: Bayesian attention networks for reliable hate speech detection. *arXiv preprint arXiv:2007.05304*.

Kristian Miok. 2018. Estimation of prediction intervals in neural network-based regression models. In *2018 20th International Symposium on Symbolic and Numeric Algorithms for Scientific Computing (SYNASC)*, pages 463–468. IEEE.

Marzieh Mozafari, Reza Farahbakhsh, and Noel Crespi. 2019. A BERT-based transfer learning approach for hate speech detection in online social media. In *International Conference on Complex Networks and Their Applications*, pages 928–940. Springer.

Pavel Myshkov and Simon Julier. 2016. Posterior distribution analysis for bayesian inference in neural networks. *Advances in Neural Information Processing Systems (NIPS)*.

Alfredo Nazábal, Pablo García-Moreno, Antonio Artés-Rodríguez, and Zoubin Ghahramani. 2016. Human activity recognition by combining a small number of classifiers. *IEEE journal of biomedical and health informatics*, 20(5):1342–1351.

Alexandru Niculescu-Mizil and Rich Caruana. 2005. Predicting good probabilities with supervised learning. In Luc De Raedt and Stefan Wrobel, editors, *Proceedings of the 22nd International Machine Learning Conference*. ACM Press.

Endang Wahyu Pamungkas and Viviana Patti. 2019. Cross-domain and cross-lingual abusive language detection: A hybrid approach with deep learning and a multilingual lexicon. In *Proceedings of the 57th Annual Meeting of the Association for Computational Linguistics: Student Research Workshop*, pages 363–370.

Gregor Pirš and Erik Štrumbelj. 2019. Bayesian combination of probabilistic classifiers using multivariate normal mixtures. *J. Mach. Learn. Res.*, 20:51–1.

John C. Platt. 1999. Probabilistic outputs for support vector machines and comparisons to regularized likelihood methods. In *Advances in large margin classifiers*, pages 61–74. MIT Press.

Anna Schmidt and Michael Wiegand. 2017. A survey on hate speech detection using natural language processing. In *Proceedings of the Fifth International Workshop on Natural Language Processing for Social Media*, pages 1–10.

Catarina Silva, Uros Lotric, Bernardete Ribeiro, and Andrej Dobnikar. 2010. Distributed text classification with an ensemble kernel-based learning approach. *IEEE Transactions on Systems, Man, and Cybernetics, Part C (Applications and Reviews)*, 40(3):287–297.

Nitish Srivastava, Geoffrey Hinton, Alex Krizhevsky, Ilya Sutskever, and Ruslan Salakhutdinov. 2014. Dropout: a simple way to prevent neural networks from overfitting. *The journal of machine learning research*, 15(1):1929–1958.

Lukas Stappen, Fabian Brunn, and Björn Schuller. 2020. Cross-lingual zero-and few-shot hate speech detection utilising frozen transformer language models and axel. *arXiv preprint arXiv:2004.13850*.

Xiao Sun, Xiaoqi Peng, and Shuai Ding. 2018. Emotional human-machine conversation generation based on long short-term memory. *Cognitive Computation*, 10(3):389–397.

György Szarvas, Veronika Vincze, Richárd Farkas, and János Csirik. 2008. The bioscope corpus: annotation for negation, uncertainty and their scope in biomedical texts. In *Proceedings of the Workshop on Current Trends in Biomedical Natural Language Processing*, pages 38–45.

Ashish Vaswani, Noam Shazeer, Niki Parmar, Jakob Uszkoreit, Llion Jones, Aidan N Gomez, Łukasz Kaiser, and Illia Polosukhin. 2017. Attention is all you need. In *Advances in neural information processing systems*, pages 5998–6008.

Boris Vezjak. 2018. Radical hate speech: The fascination with Hitler and fascism on the Slovenian webosphere. *Solsko Polje*, 29.

Veronika Vincze. 2015. *Uncertainty detection in natural language texts*. Ph.D. thesis, szte.

Sida Wang and Christopher Manning. 2013. Fast dropout training. In *International Conference on Machine Learning*, pages 118–126.

William Warner and Julia Hirschberg. 2012. Detecting hate speech on the world wide web. In *Proceedings of the second workshop on language in social media*, pages 19–26. Association for Computational Linguistics.

Zeerak Waseem and Dirk Hovy. 2016. Hateful symbols or hateful people? predictive features for hate speech detection on twitter. In *Proceedings of the NAACL student research workshop*, pages 88–93.

Gregor Wiedemann, Seid Muhie Yimam, and Chris Biemann. 2020. Uhh-lt & lt2 at semeval-2020 task 12: Fine-tuning of pre-trained transformer networks for offensive language detection. *arXiv preprint arXiv:2004.11493*.

Yuling Yao, Aki Vehtari, Daniel Simpson, Andrew Gelman, et al. 2018. Using stacking to average Bayesian predictive distributions. *Bayesian Analysis*, 13(3):917–1007.

Wojciech Zaremba, Ilya Sutskever, and Oriol Vinyals. 2014. Recurrent neural network regularization. *arXiv preprint arXiv:1409.2329*.

Xunan Zhang, Shiji Song, and Cheng Wu. 2013. Robust bayesian classification with incomplete data. *Cognitive Computation*, 5(2):170–187.

Zhi-Hua Zhou and Ming Li. 2010. Semi-supervised learning by disagreement. *Knowledge and Information Systems*, 24(3):415–439.

Zhi-Hua Zhou. 2012. *Ensemble methods: foundations and algorithms*. CRC press.

Xiaojin Zhu and Andrew B Goldberg. 2009. Introduction to semi-supervised learning. *Synthesis lectures on artificial intelligence and machine learning*, 3(1):1–130.

Lingxue Zhu and Nikolay Laptev. 2017. Deep and confident prediction for time series at Uber. In *IEEE International Conference on Data Mining Workshops (ICDMW)*, pages 103–110.

Xiaojin Jerry Zhu. 2005. Semi-supervised learning literature survey. Technical report, University of Wisconsin-Madison Department of Computer Sciences.

# Provenance for Linguistic Corpora Through Nanopublications

**Timo Lek[1], Anna de Groot[1], Tobias Kuhn[1], Roser Morante[2]**
[1]Department of Computer Science, Faculty of Science, Business Web and Media
[2]CLTL Lab, Faculty of Humanities
Network Institute, VU Amsterdam
{timolek97,annagrotius}@gmail.com, {t.kuhn,r.morantevallejo}@vu.nl

## Abstract

Research in Computational Linguistics is dependent on text corpora for training and testing new tools and methodologies. While there exists a plethora of annotated linguistic information, these corpora are often not interoperable without significant manual work. Moreover, these annotations might have evolved into different versions, making it challenging for researchers to know the data's provenance. This paper addresses this issue with a case study on event annotated corpora and by creating a new, more interoperable representation of this data in the form of nanopublications. We demonstrate how linguistic annotations from separate corpora can be reliably linked from the start, and thereby be accessed and queried as if they were a single dataset. We describe how such nanopublications can be created and demonstrate how SPARQL queries can be performed to extract interesting content from the new representations. The queries show that information of multiple corpora can be retrieved more easily and effectively because the information of different corpora is represented in a uniform data format.

## 1 Introduction

The availability of annotated linguistic corpora is crucial to develop Natural Language Processing (NLP) systems (Chiarcos, 2012; Van Son et al., 2018). In the past couple of decades, many linguistic resources have been released, which contain different types of annotations, from morphosyntactic to semantic and discourse level annotations. However, they often lack structural and conceptual interoperability (Chiarcos, 2012). The former is related to the data format of annotations, such as XML-standoff or RDF representations, while the latter refers to the possibility of exchanging information in a consistent and mappable way. Diverging annotation guidelines, the structure of annotated output, and the different amounts of annotations created per corpus pose a challenge in organizing the provenance of corpora.

Often, annotation projects run on (subsets of) existing text corpora, which are thereby annotated with multiple annotation layers. Unfortunately, the format for linking annotations to the texts is mostly not standardized and these links therefore are often not fully precise or directly interoperable. This makes it challenging for a researcher to figure out the data's exact provenance and to integrate annotations from several corpora. Integrating different annotations is valuable because it can help scholars study and understand the different interdependencies between annotation layers (e.g. semantic parsers usually take syntactic structure in consideration).

Moreover, often the annotations follow idiosyncratic guidelines that pursue a specific annotation goal. The need to organize the various existing annotations has been recognized by the corpus linguistic community (Chiarcos, 2012; Kilgarriff, 2001). While a number of solutions to improve linguistic Linked Data have been presented in the past, we propose here a novel approach that uses the Linked Data format of nanopublications to represent annotated corpora in a more fine-grained semantic format, with the aim of boosting the interoperability of linguistic corpora and facilitating the automatic integration of annotations in a reliable and transparent manner.





*The 14th Linguistic Annotation Workshop*, pages 13–23
Barcelona, Spain (Online), December 12, 2020.

Our research is motivated by the empirical analysis on 20 event-annotated corpora presented in (Van Son et al., 2018), which highlighted the challenges, as well as the opportunity, of event corpora interoperability. Existing event annotation standards range from annotations about the participants, timing/temporal order, factuality, and entity coreference relation, making a standardized description of an event difficult. This is where nanopublications as a fine-grained and provenance-aware data format could provide transparency and interoperability for computational linguistic research.

For our case study, we have chosen to focus on integrating annotations from two corpora, FactBank (Saurí and Pustejovsky, 2009) and PARC 3.0 (Pareti, 2016). In PARC, attribution relations and their components (Cue, Content, Source) are annotated, while in FactBank events and their factuality values (i.e. the certainty of the occurrence of an event) are annotated. It is interesting to combine the two annotation layers in order to extract, for example, which events occur in the content of attribution relations and what are their factuality values. Figure 1 presents the same sentence annotated in PARC and FactBank.

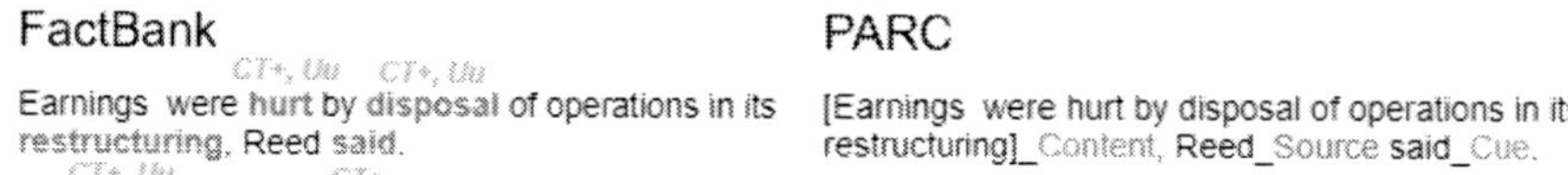

Figure 1: An example sentence with its annotations in FactBank and PARC.

Our main contributions thereby are (1) providing a fine-grained and interoperable Linked Data representation of annotated linguistic corpora in the form of nanopublications, (2) analysing the main interoperability problems that we encountered and solved with our nanopublication-based approach, and (3) demonstrating how the concrete annotations from our case study of two corpora can be integrated with nanopublications and queried with SPARQL.

We describe below how we converted these corpora into nanopublications and then report on the interoperability challenges faced and solved with our approach by representing the data in a uniform manner using nanopublications. Finally, we discuss based on our results the extent to which nanopublications can be seen as a viable alternative for improved linguistic corpora interoperability.

## 2   Linked Data, Data Provenance and Nanopublications

Linked Data is about connecting and publishing data in a structured way on the web, often on the basis of an ontology using the Web Ontology Language (OWL) (McGuinness et al., 2004). The data is often structured in triples using the Resource Description Framework (RDF). By using unique URIs for each entity of information, these entities can be interlinked in order to create an entire web of data (Bizer et al., 2011).

Several projects were already performed to create linked linguistic data. Since 2012, six series of Linked Data in Linguistics (LDL) workshops have been hosted to gather and discuss contributions promoting linking linguistic data. After the second workshop, one of the presented efforts was the Linked Linguistic Open Data (LLOD) cloud.[1]While creating the LLOD cloud, a lot of linguistic data was already available, which were mostly represented using RDF. One example is WordNet, which is also part of the Semantic Web (Gangemi et al., 2003; Chiarcos et al., 2013). Furthermore, Chiarcos proposed to represent linguistic corpora into OWL and RDF to interlink all of the different resources of corpora. In this way, the annotations of the corpora could be linked using terminological resources like standardized annotation formats (Chiarcos, 2012).

Existing approaches that aim to represent the structure and content of natural language and its annotations include the Ontology Lexicalisation and the Ontologies of Linguistic Annotation (OLiA) (Villegas and Bel, 2015; Buitelaar et al., 2011; Bosque-Gil et al., 2015). OLiA focuses on annotations of linguistic corpora and can be seen as a source that references to the 'annotation terminology' that can be used in combination with the LLOD to capture all of the information of the annotations in the LLOD in a similar format (Chiarcos and Sukhareva, 2015).

---

[1] https://linguistic-lod.org/

Since all different texts and annotations in a corpus may have a different origin, i.e. provenance, provenance ontology PROV[2] can be used for this. This ontology contains different classes and properties that represent the provenance information in different contexts, thereby usable for keeping track of the provenance information of linguistic corpora. The PROV ontology has been shown to be applicable to a diversity of fields to track provenance information in a general manner (Lebo et al., 2013).

Even though the RDF language is not optimized for this, the NLP Interchange Format (NIF)[3] makes it possible to represent texts and their elements in RDF, primarily by using strings. With the NIF ontology, a context, sentence, phrase, or word can be represented into RDF triples. It is also possible to have references between different levels, so a word can reference to another part of the RDF scheme that is the sentence from where it was derived. In a study by Menke et al. it was suggested to improve the reprensentation of the provenance information of the annotations in the NIF ontology by introducing a new ontology called MOND, which uses the PROV ontology to include provenance information in the NIF ontology (Menke et al., 2017).

Moreover, many annotation guidelines exist and each is usually represented in a different structure, increasing the difficulty in creating a standard model to transform annotations into RDF. The Web Annotation Vocabulary (Sanderson et al., 2017), for example, provides a possible solution with relations such as 'motivatedBy' and 'hasTarget', making it possible to structure annotations in an interoperable way.

Nanopublications are a format for small data publications based on RDF triples, consisting of three parts: the assertion, provenance, and publication information (Kuhn et al., 2013). The assertion contains the main content of a nanopublication, for example stating in a formal way the link between a gene and a disease. The provenance part states how this assertion came to be, by linking to the study that was performed or the paper from which the assertion was extracted. The publication information part, finally, records information about the nanopublication itself, such as by who and when it was created (Groth et al., 2010). In a previous work, a Java library for nanopublications was created, which can also be used as a command line tool (Kuhn, 2015). Nanopublications can be given *trusty URIs* as identifiers, which include a hash value of the complete content, and thereby make nanopublications immutable and verifiable (Kuhn and Dumontier, 2014). Such nanopublications can then be reliably and redundantly published to the existing distributed server network (Kuhn et al., 2016). Each of these servers contains all nanopublications, making it possible to retrieve the nanopublication from another server when one server is down. Nanopublications also allow for precise and reliable versioning, as well as the definition of incremental datasets by defining nanopublication indexes (Kuhn et al., 2017). Such indexes are represented as nanopublications themselves that contain links to other nanopublications and thereby defining sets of nanopublications.

## 3  Methodology

In this section we introduce our methodology to address the above-mentioned problems of interoperability and provenance of text corpora by applying the concept and techniques of nanopublications. To demonstrate and evaluate this methodology, we then present a case study. We introduce a number of questions on the combined annotations that can be answered in an integrated and automatic manner through SPARQL queries. Through the SPARQL queries we will show that data of multiple corpora can be retrieved using a single query, solving the interoperability issues.

### 3.1  Nanopublication Model for Text Corpora

In Figure 2, we present a general scheme for representing text corpora and their annotations as a network of interconnected nanopublications. This model ensures that new information from other corpora could easily be linked to existing nanopublications, through the addition of more nodes to the network. The nanopublications that form this general structure can be divided into four groups depending on what they represent: text, annotation, corpus, and index nanopublications.

---

[2]https://www.w3.org/ns/prov
[3]http://persistence.uni-leipzig.org/nlp2rdf/ontologies/nif-core

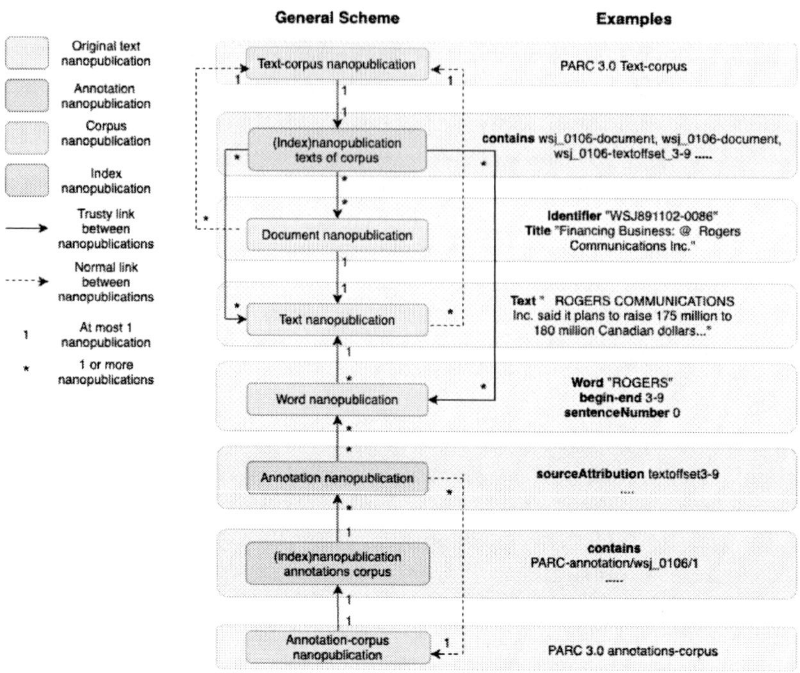



Figure 2: General nanopublication scheme with examples.

First, at the top of the figure the text-corpus nanopublication can be found. This nanopublication contains the information regarding the text corpus, which is the set of original texts. It is linked to an index nanopublication which points to all document, text, and word nanopublications which are part of the corpus. The document and text nanopublications can be part of multiple corpora and thus multiple index nanopublications. These document nanopublications contain all of the metadata on the actual texts, namely the provenance information, title, and identifier. Furthermore, the document nanopublications have a link to the nanopublication containing the actual text corresponding to the metadata. Both the document and the text nanopublication also contain a back-reference to their corpus nanopublication.

Additionally, word nanopublications are created, as words are the typical targets of annotations. They contain the word string, sentence number, and the offset values with respect to the text, and possibly other word-level information (e.g. their part-of-speech value). Thereby, each word gets its own URI as identifier, which is constructed from the text URI and the word's offset values. From the bottom, annotation corpora are pointing to these words. Similar to the text corpora, a corpus nanopublication of an annotation corpus contains the general corpus-level information, most importantly a link to an index nanopublication pointing to all annotation nanopublications. Their concrete content depends on the type of annotation, but they all point to the words they are annotating via the URIs as described above. For convenience, they are also pointing back to the overall annotation corpus nanopublication.

Modeling these elements as small self-contained entities has also the advantage that differences in licenses can be defined and handled on a fine-grained level. Often, annotations have a different, sometimes more permissive, license than the texts they annotate. For this, we introduce the nanopublication type `ProtectedNanopub` that we use to mark nanopublications that cannot be openly published due to license reasons. We updated the nanopublication client and server code such that an error is raised if a user accidentally tries to publish such a protected nanopublication to the server network.

Lastly and importantly, our approach is open for anybody to publish further annotations or texts as nanopublications. These wouldn't be directly included in the datasets, as the index nanopublications don't point to them, but they can be found by querying the nanopublication network, and included if desired in a given situation. Moreover, a new version of a corpus can include such "third-party" contri-

| | Question |
|---|---|
| Q1 | Who talked about an event, and what is the factuality value of that event? |
| Q2 | Which events have multiple factuality value annotations? |
| Q3 | What are the different factuality values expressed per document, and which values appear the most? |
| Q4 | How often are certain annotation values used? (e.g. the count of different factuality values represented or the count of different sources) |
| Q5 | How many of the annotated FactBank events are labelled with a specific attribution component? |
| Q6 | Where in the corpus is a specific word (or lemma) assigned a specific attribution label (e.g. where is the verb 'to surprise' annotated as Cue? |

Table 1: Case study questions.

butions, thereby making them a proper part but also clearly attributing the third-party contributor, which is defined in the provenance and publication info parts. This also allows for corrections to be published by anybody who finds something that is wrong.

## 3.2  Case Study Design

The case study workflow has 3 main components: (1) obtain and analyze original and annotated corpora; (2) convert these into nanopublications; and (3) assess the usefulness of the nanopublication representations. We evaluate on two event-related linguistic corpora, FactBank and PARC 3.0. For PARC, we process 34 annotation files that provide annotations on Wall Street Journal Corpus (WSJ) documents. For FactBank, we process 194 documents, which provide annotations on WSJ, New York Times (NYT), Associated Press Writer (APW) documents, and documents from several other sources. Thus, we use the intersection of 34 WSJ documents for which both corpora provide annotations for investigating the extent to which nanopublications indeed facilitate automated merging and interoperability.

The PARC corpus provides annotations about attribution relations, which are made up of three components a Source, a Content, and a Cue. The original annotations are made at the token-level and are presented in XML format. The FactBank corpus includes annotations about events and their factuality values. FactBank adopts event annotations from the TimeML annotations (Saurí et al., 2006), while it defines event factuality with a value that represents how certain or true an event is according to a source present in the text. FactBank has six primary factuality values present in its annotations. These annotations are contained in a set of 20 tables, each written in a separate text file. We refer the reader to (Saurí, 2008) and (Pareti, 2015) for detailed explanations of each annotation scheme, and we will elaborate below on their interoperability challenges.

For this case study, we came up with six general questions that somebody who would like to use the above annotations might want to ask. These questions are shown in Table 1. One of our goals is answering questions that show the merging capabilities and efficiency of nanopublications. For example, the answer to Q3, depending on the factuality values it outputs, might suggest how certain the content of the text is. An answer to Q6 might help an annotator clarify doubts during the annotation process, and Q5 demonstrates how FactBank events can be related to PARC attribution relations. Some questions ask only for information from one corpus, while others are more complex by requiring information from both corpora. We will use these general questions to make them automatically executable with our integrated nanopublication model and the SPARQL query language.

## 4  Case Study

We applied the nanopublication-based approach to the case study in order to address the problem of interoperability and provenance. Different types of nanopublications were created to represent the chosen corpora. As introduced above, nanopublications consists of an assertion, provenance, and publication info part. In these nanopublications the publication info part is similar for all our nanopublications, containing the date of creation, license, ORCID identifiers of the creators, and sometimes further comments and website links. All the text and word nanopublications, as well as the annotations of FactBank, are also marked as protected, due to their private licences. The remaining nanopublications are public and can therefore be published to the server network for public accessibility. The dataset of all public nanopublications can be found online.[4]

We defined four corpus nanopublications for our case study: one for the text contained in the corpus and one for the annotations contained in the corpus, for each of the two existing corpora (PARC and FactBank). They contain basic information about the corpus and link to their content via an index nanopublication, as can be seen in this example (abbreviated here and below for readability):

```
sub:assertion {
  corpus:parc-annotations a pvcp:AnnotationCorpus;
    dct:title "PARC Annotation corpus";
    rdfs:seeAlso <https://www.aclweb.org/anthology/L16-1619.pdf>;
    dcat:distribution indexnp: .
}
```

Via their index nanopublications, they point to 194 document nanopublications, which contain the document metadata. This is an example:

```
sub:assertion {
  sub:document a foaf:Document;
    dct:title "Financing Business: @ Rogers Communications Inc.";
    dct:created "1989-11-02T00:00:00"^^xsd:dateTime;
    dct:creator <http://dbpedia.org/resource/The_Wall_Street_Journal>;
    pvcp:hasText textnp:text .
}
```

These document nanopublications link to the actual text using `pvcp:hasText` to point to the text nanopublication. An example of the latter is shown here:

```
sub:assertion {
  sub:text a nif:OffsetBasedString, dct:Text;
    rdf:value """   ROGERS COMMUNICATIONS Inc. said it plans to raise 175 million to 180 million Canadian dollars (US$148.9
        million to $153.3 million) through a private placement of perpetual preferred shares. ... He declined to discuss
        other terms of the issue. """ .
}
```

The word nanopublications point back to the text nanopublication and provide word-level information including the word string, the offset of this string with respect to the text, and the sentence number. They can also contain lemma and part-of-speech information. As this word level depends on tokenization, there can be differences in how different annotation corpora define word boundaries. For this reason, our approach allows for the generation of new word nanopublications on demand. This creates an identifier for the word based on the URI of the text nanopublication and the offset of the word, thereby assuring that words introduced several times by different annotation corpora get the same identifier and are therefore immediately interoperable. In our case, we have 6,362 word nanopublications defined from PARC and 7,784 from FactBank. This is an example of the former:

```
sub:assertion {
  textoffset:3-9 a nif:OffsetBasedString, nif:Word;
    nif:beginIndex "3"^^xsd:int;
    nif:endIndex "9"^^xsd:int;
    nif:anchorOf "ROGERS";
    nif:lemma "rogers";
    olia:POS "NNP";
    pvcp:hasSentenceNumber "0"^^xsd:int;
    pvcp:isPartOfText textnp:text .
}
```

The annotations can now link to these words. We have 136 annotation nanopublications for PARC, that associate words with content, cue and source annotations, as can be seen in the example below:

```
sub:assertion {
  sub:annotation a oa:Annotation;
    dct:isPartOf corpus:parc-annotations;
    pvcpp:hasContentAnnotatedWord textoffset:101-106, textoffset:107-114, ...;
    pvcpp:hasCueAnnotatedWord textoffset:30-34;
    pvcpp:hasSourceAnnotatedWord textoffset:10-24, textoffset:25-29, textoffset:3-9 .
}
```

For FactBank, we have annotation nanopublications that declare events (7,784) and separate ones annotating their factuality values (10,948), with a similar structure as the PARC nanopublications above.[5]

We have focused above only on the assertion part, but all these nanopublications also come with specific provenance and publication information, for example describing that the PARC annotations were created at a different time by a different person than the nanopublications themselves.

---

[4]`https://github.com/ucds-vu/provcorp-model`

[5]The complete set of nanopublications can be found here: `https://github.com/ucds-vu/provcorp-model`

| | Addressed Challenge | corpus | abs. | rel. |
|---|---|---|---|---|
| 1. | Incompatible text offsets | PARC/FactBank | 194 | 100.0% |
| 2. | Metadata included in sentence number count | FactBank | 194 | 100.0% |
| 3. | Insufficient sentence splitting information | FactBank | 64 | 33.0% |
| 4. | Missing headline | FactBank | 33 | 17.0% |
| 5. | Inconsistent use of text tags | FactBank | 23 | 11.9% |
| 6. | Absence of text tags to structure the document | FactBank | 17 | 8.8% |
| 7. | Unknown journal / source | FactBank | 16 | 8.2% |
| 8. | No attribution relations for the document | PARC | 4 | 2.0% |
| 9. | Incompatible sentence splitting at semicolons | PARC/FactBank | 2 | 1.0% |
| 10. | Annotations on the headline | FactBank | 1 | 0.5% |

Table 2: Overview of addressed interoperability challenges, including their absolute and relative frequencies in the 194 documents of our case study corpora.


## 5 Results

In this section we analyze the interoperability challenges we faced and addressed with our approach and assess the extent to which we can automatically answer the questions we introduced above.

### 5.1 Analysis of Addressed Challenges

With our case study as described above, we encountered a number of interoperability challenges. We managed to resolve almost all of them in our manual conversion work as described above. However, we had to exclude ten documents of FactBank due to the fact that sentence numbers were skipped when a sentence ended with a double quote ("), and we did not have enough information to correct this mistake. In Table 2, we show an overview of the challenges we successfully addressed on the remaining 194 documents. This highlights the nature and extent of interoperability problems that come with the current way how such corpora are published but would be resolved if our approach was followed, i.e. if they would be published as interoperable nanopublications from the start.

The first issue on the list are text offsets. PARC and FactBank locate words in a text differently: PARC uses byte counts, whereas FactBank makes use of sentence and token numbers. Token numbers are tokenizer-specific, so FactBank's method is quite sensitive and difficult to replicate. FactBank's sentence numbers are moreover confusing as they also count the metadata fields, such as text headings, and not just the text content (which is challenge number 2). PARC, on the other hand, also has its quirks, such as including the six characters of the initial <TEXT> tag in the offset count. In our nanopublications, we use text offsets that unambiguously link to the text string of the content, and thereby ensure precise and interoperable text references.

For FactBank's sentence and token number approach to refer to words in the text, it is crucial to know where a sentence ends and a new one starts. This sentence splitting, similar to tokenization mentioned above, is sensitive to the used algorithm. This is why text corpora like WSJ provide us with this sentence splitting information by saving each sentence on a separate line in the provided file formats. However, the documents from NYT and APW didn't have this information and so these sentences had to be checked manually for the correct splitting (challenge 3). Moreover, sentences containing a semicolon in PARC are annotated as one sentence while they are considered two sentences in FactBank (challenge 9).

Challenges 5 and 6 point to the fact that text tags were used inconsistently. The main text is included in <TEXT> tags, but these were missing for 17 documents. Moreover, WSJ documents use <HL> and <DATELINE> tags for the headline and date, respectively, while NYT and APW documents use <HEADLINE> and <DATE_TIME>. Some documents moreover, did not contain tags at all, and we had to add them manually.

Normally, headlines are not annotated, but there is an exception in document APW19980213.1380, which includes an annotation of a part of the headline (challenge 10). Upon encountering this situation, we extended our model to also allow for headline annotations. Lastly, in some cases metadata was missing. Some documents did not have a headline (challenge 4) or did not include a journal or source (challenge 7). In PARC, there were also four documents that did not contain any attribution relations (challenge 8).

| question | short query description | count | time |
|---|---|---|---|
| Q1 | list source and factuality value per event | 656 | 0.206s |
| Q2 | list events with more than one factuality value | 1,050 | 0.092s |
| Q3 | list factuality values per document | 194 | 0.058s |
| Q4 | count of FactBank source values | 425 | 0.029s |
| Q5 | count of FactBank events with PARC source attribution | 6 | 0.033s |
| Q6 | list all occurrences of "surprise" as cue | 1 | 0.048s |

Table 3: SPARQL query results and average execution times to answer the general questions Q1 to Q6

In summary, all documents were affected by at least two challenges, and there seems to be a long tail of infrequent exceptions or small inconsistencies that one has to take into account in order to process such corpora correctly.

## 5.2 Query Results

In order to assess the practical benefits of our approach we implemented the general questions presented in Table 1 as queries in the SPARQL language so we could use a triple store (Virtuoso in our case) to automatically answer them. The resulting SPARQL queries can be found online[6]. They demonstrate that our nanopublication approach effectively merges the two corpora and allows for information to be extracted together in a practical and efficient way. Table 3 shows the average amount of time it took to run a query, as well as the number of rows it outputs. We managed to represent all these questions in SPARQL, and thereby to make them automatically executable.

The listing below shows an example of a SPARQL query to answer one possibility for question Q4 ("How often are certain annotation values used?") retrieving the count of words annotated as events from FactBank per PARC annotation attribution type:

```
prefix pvcpp: <https://w3id.org/provcorp/vocab/parc/>
prefix pvcpf: <https://w3id.org/provcorp/vocab/FactBank/>
prefix oa: <http://www.w3.org/ns/oa#>

select ?Attribution (count(distinct ?word) as ?Count) where {
  ?event pvcpf:hasEID ?eventid.
  ?event oa:hasTarget ?word.
  ?annotation ?Attribution ?word.
  values ?Attribution { pvcpp:hasContentAnnotatedWord pvcpp:hasCueAnnotatedWord pvcpp:hasSourceAnnotatedWord }.
} group by ?Attribution
```

The concrete result for this query is:

```
Attribution                     Count
pvcpp:hasSourceAnnotatedWord       3
pvcpp:hasContentAnnotatedWord    284
pvcpp:hasCueAnnotatedWord        130
```

This thereby demonstrates how FactBank and PARC are conceptually merged and can be queried in an integrated fashion.

As another example, the query representing question Q1 ("Who talked about an event, and what is the factuality value of that event?") gives us this result (only the first four rows are shown):

```
textID                   eID   eventWord     factValue relativeSource    sourcePhrase
https://.../wsj_0026...#text e1    said          CT+       AUTHOR            The White House
https://.../wsj_0026...#text e11   requested     CT+       AUTHOR            Timex
https://.../wsj_0026...#text e123  beneficiaries CT+       officials_AUTHOR  U.S. trade officials
https://.../wsj_0026...#text e123  beneficiaries Uu        AUTHOR            U.S. trade officials
...
```

This shows again how the annotations from both corpora can be queried simultaneously. The result is very informative for the file wsj_0026. The content of the columns, in order of appearance from left to right, is: the text identifier in the form of its nanopublication URI with the suffix #text, the event identifier of the event annotation, the word that is annotated as the event, the factuality value of the event, the source of the event (according to FactBank annotations), and the string in the document's text that represents the source (as annotated in PARC). As such, the query's result contains information from PARC (the source) as well as information from FactBank (the factuality value and event). Moreover, the output of the query allows us to see that an event can have two different FactBank sources who

---

[6]https://github.com/ucds-vu/provcorp-model/tree/master/queries

each give a different factuality value to the annotated event. This is seen in the last two rows where the event 'beneficiaries' has two different factuality values, one which was given by the AUTHOR (the writer of the text document) and another given by the 'officials' (a source talked about in the text document). The different conception of 'source' in FactBank and PARC can also be noted here, which shows that although annotations can be merged, the annotation schema of each corpus should always be considered when analyzing the results. This is also useful to reveal the representation of a corpus's data more easily. For example, we can see that an event from FactBank always has an AUTHOR source.

This demonstrates how we can use the power of query languages like SPARQL to access corpora in an integrated and fully automated way. Because the two corpora of our case study and the annotations are now formally linked, they are interoperable and can conceptually be seen as a single resource. Also, the results can be exported in a variety of formats, including CSV tables and JSON files, and be loaded and processed in other tools. It is then straightforward to write conversion tools to other formats, such as the CoNLL format (Buchholz and Marsi, 2006), a common practice data format used by computational linguists. This approach ensures that the data is interoperable from the start, and then format conversions are relatively easy as the range of nasty interoperability challenges is already taken care of.

## 6 Discussion and Conclusion

Nanopublications have been mostly used with scientific data, such as data from the biomedical domain (Kuhn et al., 2013). In this work, we show that linguistic corpora can also benefit from the fine-grained and provenance-aware structure of nanopublications. The collection of nanopublications presented here contains information from event annotated corpora. It is demonstrated that when these data is modelled in a homologous way, each unique corpus can be automatically merged in order to produce valuable data combinations that were not easily attainable prior to the merging. Specifically, our dataset can provide attribution annotation insight about events from FactBank.

Moreover, our nanopublications suggest the prospect of linguistic data fitting into the Linked Data ecosystem. During the dataset creation, we were able to reuse multiple existing Linked Data vocabularies. Linguistic data becoming more linked would also allow it to be connected more easily with already existing linguistic Linked Data sources from LLOD. Nevertheless, the data format of the original annotated corpora is extremely variable, which shows in the multiple textual challenges faced during production. While this project only focused on two corpora, there was inconsistency in annotation format not only between the corpora, but also within a corpus itself. Thus, the conversion of existing linguistic corpora into a Linked Data scheme can expect tedious pre-processing efforts. Even in our dataset, several documents needed to be excluded for the final version. Another aspect that makes it challenging to fit linguistic corpora in the Linked Data ecosystem relates to copyright availability. For example, this caused us to only be able to represent part of the PARC corpus.

In this paper, interoperability issues in linguistic data, specifically event annotated corpora, are discussed and nanopublications are proposed as a solution to resolve them. When one set of annotation guidelines is used to produce annotations on one corpus, that same corpus might already have other annotations that could be useful for the researcher. However, currently it is very difficult for a researcher to know or retrieve the version or provenance of these existing annotations due to poor documentation and variable annotation formats. Aspects of nanopublications that make them useful for annotated corpora are that they are able to be written in different formats, they can represent versioning, and they can track provenance. Also, they follow LLOD principles of using URIs for identification and RDF representation as output. Above all, they seem useful for merging linguistic annotation data. A successful model for translating existing event corpora into nanopublications is significant not only for computational linguistics, but also for the field of Linked Data.

## Acknowledgements

This research has been supported by the Academy Assistants Program from the Network Insitute from the VU Amsterdam. We are grateful to Silvia Pareti for making the PARC corpus available.

# References


Christian Bizer, Tom Heath, and Tim Berners-Lee. 2011. Linked data: The story so far. In *Semantic services, interoperability and web applications: emerging concepts*, pages 205–227. IGI Global.

Julia Bosque-Gil, Jorge Gracia, John McCrae, Philipp Cimiano, Sander Stolk, Fahad Khan, Katrien Depuydt, Jesse de Does, Franscesca Frontini, and Ilja Kernerman. 2015. The ontolex lemon lexicography module. *W3C Community Group Final Report*.

Sabine Buchholz and Erwin Marsi. 2006. CoNLL-x shared task on multilingual dependency parsing. In *Proceedings of the Tenth Conference on Computational Natural Language Learning (CoNLL-X)*, pages 149–164, New York City, June. Association for Computational Linguistics.

Paul Buitelaar, Philipp Cimiano, John McCrae, Elena Montiel-Ponsoda, and Thierry Declerck. 2011. Ontology lexicalisation: The lemon perspective.

Christian Chiarcos and Maria Sukhareva. 2015. Olia–ontologies of linguistic annotation. *Semantic Web*, 6(4):379–386.

Christian Chiarcos, Philipp Cimiano, Thierry Declerck, and John P McCrae. 2013. Linguistic linked open data (llod). introduction and overview. In *Proceedings of the 2nd Workshop on Linked Data in Linguistics (LDL-2013): Representing and linking lexicons, terminologies and other language data*, pages i–xi.

Christian Chiarcos. 2012. Interoperability of corpora and annotations. In *Linked Data in Linguistics*, pages 161–179. Springer.

Aldo Gangemi, Roberto Navigli, and Paola Velardi. 2003. The ontowordnet project: extension and axiomatization of conceptual relations in wordnet. In *OTM Confederated International Conferences" On the Move to Meaningful Internet Systems"*, pages 820–838. Springer.

Paul Groth, Andrew Gibson, and Jan Velterop. 2010. The anatomy of a nanopublication. *Information Services & Use*, 30(1-2):51–56.

Adam Kilgarriff. 2001. Comparing corpora. *International journal of corpus linguistics*, 6(1):97–133.

Tobias Kuhn and Michel Dumontier. 2014. Trusty uris: Verifiable, immutable, and permanent digital artifacts for linked data. In *European semantic web conference*, pages 395–410. Springer.

Tobias Kuhn, Paolo Emilio Barbano, Mate Levente Nagy, and Michael Krauthammer. 2013. Broadening the scope of nanopublications. In *Extended Semantic Web Conference*, pages 487–501. Springer.

Tobias Kuhn, Christine Chichester, Michael Krauthammer, Núria Queralt-Rosinach, Ruben Verborgh, George Giannakopoulos, Axel-Cyrille Ngonga Ngomo, Raffaele Viglianti, and Michel Dumontier. 2016. Decentralized provenance-aware publishing with nanopublications. *PeerJ Computer Science*, 2:e78.

Tobias Kuhn, Egon Willighagen, Chris Evelo, Núria Queralt-Rosinach, Emilio Centeno, and Laura I Furlong. 2017. Reliable granular references to changing linked data. In *International Semantic Web Conference*, pages 436–451. Springer.

Tobias Kuhn. 2015. nanopub-java: A java library for nanopublications. In *Proceedings of the 5th Workshop on Linked Science 2015 — Best Practices and the Road Ahead (LISC 2015)*, volume 1572. CEUR-WS.

Timothy Lebo, Satya Sahoo, Deborah McGuinness, Khalid Belhajjame, James Cheney, David Corsar, Daniel Garijo, Stian Soiland-Reyes, Stephan Zednik, and Jun Zhao. 2013. Prov-o: The prov ontology. *W3C recommendation*.

Deborah L McGuinness, Frank Van Harmelen, et al. 2004. Owl web ontology language overview. *W3C recommendation*, 10(10):2004.

Peter Menke, Basil Ell, and Philipp Cimiano. 2017. On the origin of annotations: A module-based approach to representing annotations in the natural language processing interchange format (nif). *Applied Ontology*, 12(2):131–155.

Silvia Pareti. 2015. Attribution: a computational approach.

Silvia Pareti. 2016. Parc 3.0: A corpus of attribution relations. In *Proceedings of the Tenth International Conference on Language Resources and Evaluation (LREC'16)*, pages 3914–3920.

Robert Sanderson, Paolo Ciccarese, and Benjamin Young. 2017. Web annotation vocabulary. *W3C recommendation*.

Roser Saurí and James Pustejovsky. 2009. Factbank: a corpus annotated with event factuality. *Language resources and evaluation*, 43(3):227.

Roser Saurí, Jessica Littman, Bob Knippen, Robert Gaizauskas, Andrea Setzer, and James Pustejovsky. 2006. Timeml annotation guidelines. *Version*, 1(1):31.

Roser Saurı. 2008. Factbank 1.0 annotation guidelines. *Ms., Brandeis University*.

Chantal Van Son, Oana Inel, Roser Morante, Lora Aroyo, and Piek Vossen. 2018. Resource interoperability for sustainable benchmarking: The case of events. In *Proceedings of the Eleventh International Conference on Language Resources and Evaluation (LREC 2018)*.

Marta Villegas and Núria Bel. 2015. Parole/simple 'lemon'ontology and lexicons. *Semantic Web*, 6(4):363–369.

# A sentiment-annotated dataset of English causal connectives


**Marta Andersson[*], Murathan Kurfalı[†], Robert Östling[†]**
[*]English Language Department, Stockholm University, Stockholm, Sweden
[†]Linguistics Department, Stockholm University, Stockholm, Sweden
`marta.andersson@english.su.se`
`{murathan.kurfali,robert}@ling.su.se`



## Abstract

This paper investigates the semantic prosody of three causal connectives: *due to*, *owing to* and *because of* in seven varieties of the English language. While research in the domain of English causality exists, we are not aware of studies that would cover the domain of causal connectives in English. Our claim is that connectives such as *because of* link two arguments, (at least) one of which will include a phrase that contributes to the interpretation of the relation as positive or negative, and hence define the prosody of the connective used. As our results demonstrate, the majority of the prosodies identified are negative for all three connectives; the proportions are stable across the varieties of English studied, and contrary to our expectations, we find no significant differences between the functions of the connectives and discourse preferences. Further, we investigate whether automatizing the sentiment annotation procedure via a simple language-model based classifier is possible. The initial results highlights the complexity of the task and the need for complicated systems, probably aided with other related datasets to achieve reasonable performance.


## 1 Introduction and background

Examination and extraction of sentiment (*sentiment analysis*, SA) from text traditionally rely on the coarse distinction between positive and negative polarity. The mainstay of the current methodologies is the idea that a text contains a single sentiment about one single topic, as in (1) below (Benamara et al., 2017; Mohammad, 2016). However, it is now generally acknowledged that sentiment within one topic should be considered at several levels of granularity, as in (2):

(1) *Out of Africa* is a fantastic movie.

(2) *Out of Africa* is a fantastic movie but a boring book.

This simple concessive construction in (2), which conveys both a positive and a negative sentiment about the same topic, demonstrates that the same word can be assigned different polarity labels dependent on the domain and context (cf. *terrible thriller* and *terrible weather* (Zitoune et al., 2016)), or on the nature of other discourse phenomena present in its close textual environment (cf. *You must read this paper* and *I believe you must read this paper* — in the latter case the negative polarity is reduced by the hedging effect of the verb *believe* ). Observations of this kind have spawned interest among SA researchers to tackle phenomena such as semantic gradation or context/domain influence on evaluation; however, an approach to sentiment detection which would allow for a theoretical characterization of text phenomena from the linguistic point of view, is much needed in the field (Mohammad, 2016).

One domain that is both challenging and useful for sentiment detection is causality — notoriously difficult to analyze (in spite of being regarded as one of so-called "semantic primitives" (Wierzbicka, 1998)), as it operates both at the level of factual events in the real world, and at the level of "meta-causality" — i.e. the speaker's reasoning and exchange between interlocutors (e.g. conclusions and



24    ·


*The 14th Linguistic Annotation Workshop*, pages 24–33
Barcelona, Spain (Online), December 12, 2020.

speech acts; see (Sweetser, 1990) and the literature on computational methods to detect causality, e.g. (Kang et al., 2017)). One example of a relation that conveys causality at the level of the speaker's reasoning is (3) below:

(3) the publications themselves are a kind of poetic transformation *due to* the finely crafted nature of them (Jamaican Eng.)

Both the causal argument (2nd clause) and the result argument (1st clause) convey the speaker's opinion, i.e. not a result based on a cause in the physical world. While such relations are very common in discourse, producing this type of deep causal explanation is beyond the capability of the existing systems (Kang et al., 2017). Attempts have been made in the field to capture causal explanations as, first of all, temporal sentiment analysis to predict causal relations (Kang et al., 2017; Preethi et al., 2015), and sentiment analysis and causal rule detection (Dehkharghani et al., 2014; Siganos et al., 2014). Some studies also utilize discourse connectives as predictors of discourse relation types, for instance, Wang et al. (2012) and Mukherjee and Bhattacharyya (2012), and indicate that discourse particles such as *but*, *since*, or *although* can be used to improve sentiment classification accuracy. Importantly, several linguistic studies have proved that discourse connectives prime or at least support the intended discourse interpretations as real-world consequences or meta-linguistic effects such as conclusions, opinions or speech acts (Andersson, 2019; Kamalski et al., 2008; Scholman and Demberg, 2017).

Since causality is basic to both human cognition and discourse coherence, our paper intends to further explore the nature of causal explanations and the role of discourse connectives in relation disambiguation by focusing on three causal connectives in English — *due to*, *because of* and *owing to* — from the point of view of their semantic prosodies. Semantic prosody has been described at several levels of abstraction (e.g., affective meanings of a given node with its typical collocates) (Sinclair, 1998; Stubbs, 2001), the discussion of which would be beyond the scope of this paper. The view adopted in the following is that semantic prosody is a feature of the node word that dictates the general environment which constrains the preferential choices of this word. As a result, it can affect wider stretches of text and so the words often tend to co-occur with either 'negative' ('bad', 'unpleasant') or 'positive' ('good', 'pleasant') collocates (Partington (2004), see also Xiao and McEnery (2006)). A related idea is colligation, i.e. the relationship between a node and grammatical categories. This feature is, however, excluded from our analysis based on the observation that all the investigated connectives follow the standard syntactic pattern: connective + NP in their target senses (Xiao and McEnery, 2006), for instance:

(4) Afghanistan and Iraq today is a bloody mess **because of** the Westminster's style of diplomacy. (British Eng.)

In order to detect the sentiment of the analyzed connectives, our first step was to investigate their general collocational behavior. To this end, we started our study by consulting the Oxford English Dictionary (OED).[1] While the connectives all have synonymous surface senses, their meanings and functions in natural discourse can be perceived as either negative, positive or neutral. According to the OED, the etymologies of the expressions that the connectives stem from can be assessed as quite negative for both *due to* and *owing to* (i.e. "indebted or beholden" for *owe* and "debt or obligation" for *due*), and neutral for *because* ("for the reason that"). However, the target senses we are interested in (i.e. the connective as a compound preposition followed by an NP), are all described as relatively neutral: while *because of* means "by reason of; on account of"; *due to* is defined as: "as a result of, on account of, because of"; and the target meaning of the connective *owing to* has been described as: "in consequence of, on account of, because of". We can therefore assume that our connectives are intrinsically neutral. This assumption is important in a study of semantic prosody, since words that have clear negative or semantic prosodies are hard to investigate given their context-neutralizing function (e.g. the verb *alleviate* remains positive even if accompanied by a clearly negative phrase, such as *suffering* (Lin and Chung, 2016)).

The conclusion to draw from this part of the investigation is twofold — while the analyzed connectives indeed seem to have quite neutral senses, given their complex etymologies and quite specific semantics

---

[1] https://www.oed.com/

(as opposed to that of multi-functional connectives such as *so*), it can be assumed that they will show tendencies to occur with either favorable or unfavorable events. Based on the previous studies within the domain of causality that have indicated that the verb *cause* has a negative semantic prosody (e.g. Stubbs (1995)), which has been demonstrated to prime experimental subjects to think about the same event as negative if preceded by this verb (Hauser and Schwarz, 2016), it can be assumed that at least some of the connectives in question will exhibit negative collocational behaviour. Needless to say, language users may quite flexibly establish the linguistic environment of any phrase (connectives included), based on their communicative and rhetorical purposes (cf. Lin and Chung (2016), on the prosody of the word *challenge*).

In order to establish the type of semantic prosody related to the analyzed connectives, we investigated their immediate linguistic environments and assessed whether the node item occurs with favourable or unfavourable meanings. While the underlying idea was that a specific word/phrase would be found in the context as governing the positive or negative flavour of the sentence, we analyzed at least a whole clause preceding and following the connective.

Apart from the practical use of our computational method for automatic annotation of the sentiment of discourse connective arguments, our investigation gives us a more detailed understanding of the differences between these near-synonymous connectives in English. Our aim has also been to use such differences as a proxy to investigate pragmatics-level language change, by making quantitative comparisons between different English varieties. The same methods could be applied to diachronic studies, given a corpus with sufficiently comparative text over a suitable time span. This goes beyond the scope of the current project.

## 2  Research Questions

While our main contribution in this paper is the annotated resource as such, the original motivation for performing the annotation work is to answer a number of questions on semantic prosody of causal connectives.

1. Do the different connectives in our study (*because of*, *due to* and *owing to*) display differences in their semantic prosodies? Our working hypothesis is that their discourse functions/preferences will differ and so, based on these differences, the connective can serve as a predictor of the sentiment.

2. Do the semantic prosodies of causal connectives differ between varieties of English? In particular, certain corpus observations prior to this study suggested that the negative connotations of *due to* may be less pronounced in some Asian varieties. We therefore intend to check the extent of usage flexibility, which may affect the predictive power of the connective.

3. Are the connotations of each connective more closely connected with one argument than the other? This would show us a non-even distribution between negative-cause/positive-effect and positive-effect/negative-cause uses, and allow a more fine-grained way of studying the use and evolution of causal connectives.

## 3  Corpus

### 3.1  Collection of dataset and Method

Randomly collected samples of the Global Web-Based English (GloWbE; (Davies, 2013)) corpus were annotated using PDTB Annotator (Lee et al., 2016). GloWbE contains about 1.9 billion words of text from twenty different countries. While the texts in the corpus consists of informal blogs (about 60% of corpus) and other web-based material, such as newspapers, magazines, and company websites, our study excludes the blogs, as they were available only in two of the analyzed varieties. It should also be noted that this usage of discourse connective is an extension to some approaches to discourse which require connectives to link two sentences (e.g., PDTB). In contrast, the connectives under study often connect a sentence to an NP.

As pre-processing, for each connective, the context of 250 words from left and right was extracted automatically. A random subset of word tokens has been erased from the GlobWbE corpus due to copyright reasons, so we only consider instances where the full context is present. We also discard all instances where a connective occurs more than once.

The following section describes the details of the annotation method and the decisions made in the process of corpus coding. [2]

## 3.2 Annotation Guidelines

Our annotation task can be regarded as sentence-level annotations of causal sentiment similar to Rosenthal et al. (2015) and Mohammad et al. (2016), who framed the task as "is this sentence positive, negative or neutral?" However, as mentioned, our idea is that the choice of discourse connective to signal a specific causal event type is governed by the presence of a discourse entity(ies) (underlined in the following) that can be coded as positive or negative based on its semantic nature. Such an entity may be but does not have to be an entire clause/sentence. For instance:

(5) When the examiners award you the degree at the end of your viva and you emerge out into the street near to tears **because of** tension/tiredness/relief (...) (British Eng.)

The two annotators of the AmE samples of the connective *because of* consistently (see Section 4.1 below) agreed that the underlined is a minimal text span both needed and sufficient to be identified as an antecedent/postcedent of the connective (in this case – both negative). This is consistent with the PDTB manual on the connective annotation, according to which "only as many clauses and/or sentences should be included in an argument selection as are minimally required and sufficient for the interpretation of the relation" (Prasad et al., 2007). Many naturally produced examples are, however, less straightforward and involve conceptually more complex arguments. Consider:

(6) It's very good to accomplish this **due to** the fact you'll remain present and understand what your choices are (Nigerian Eng.)

Why such relations are more difficult to analyze is because it is the entire event (and consequently, the whole clause) that should be treated as an antecedent or/and postcedent of the connective. This differs from the straightforward context of (5) with NPs as ante-/postcedents. Interestingly, (5) and (6) demonstrate that the analyzed connectives can signal both clearly negative and also clearly positive events. The question therefore arises on how to treat relations where each argument evokes different event type/includes different antecedent type. Consider:

(7) He's cognizant to make sure the proper people are credited this time **because of** what he went through last time (Malaysian Eng)

While the argument following the connective clearly implies a negative experience, the preceding argument conveys a positive outcome. This presents a methodological problem of how to annotate the nature of the whole event — in some approaches, the argument of an explicitly marked relation (as opposed to juxtaposed sentences) are maximally interpretable only in the context of another argument (Blakemore and Carston, 2005). This means that both arguments contribute to the interpretation of the relation. While this is a plausible hypothesis, which would explain the presence of the intrinsically neutral connective *because of* in this context, we believe that such claims have to be supported by experimental evidence (e.g. acceptability judgements). We have therefore decided to annotate the arguments separately and assess the prosody based on one argument being either positive or negative. However, most relations include either two arguments of the same type or one that appears neutral:

(8) My son's cat became diabetic and was told by his vet that they are seeing more cases **due to** cats being fed dry food. (British Eng.)

---

[2] The corpus is available at https://github.com/MurathanKurfali/sentimental-causal-connectives

|            | because of | due to | owing to | Sum  |
|------------|-----------:|-------:|---------:|-----:|
| American   | 99         | 97     | 97       | 293  |
| Australian | 98         | –      | –        | 98   |
| British    | 99         | 89     | 97       | 285  |
| Indian     | 99         | 94     | –        | 193  |
| Jamaican   | –          | 96     | 60       | 156  |
| Malaysian  | 95         | 97     | –        | 192  |
| Nigerian   | –          | 91     | 97       | 188  |
| **Sum**    | 490        | 564    | 351      | 1405 |

Table 1: Number of annotated relations per connective and per English variety.

While feeding animals dry food is not negative *per se*, in the context of its resulting in diabetes, the event becomes negatively tinted. This example is thus suggestive as to interpreting discourse entities at face value.

Nevertheless, as mentioned in Section 1 above, detecting causal explanations from texts is a complex task. Particularly difficult to analyze are relations that involve the speaker's emotional state, sarcasm and ridicule, rhetorical questions etc., see e.g. Mohammad (2016). Yet, our corpus material seems to consist mostly of relations that can be regarded as "neutral reporting of valenced information" (Mohammad, 2016), as (8) above. This means that it may be hard to judge whether the events should be regarded as neutral reporting or rather a negative emotional state, since the speaker does not provide any indication of her own emotional state. In (8), is the speaker just reporting on the course of events or upset about the situation? Since there are no overt signals of the speaker's emotional state, it seems that even more sophisticated methods of relation extraction would have difficulties assigning sentiment to (8). As a solution to this problem, we followed (Mohammad, 2016) simple sentiment questionnaire and annotated such relations as "the speaker is neither using positive language nor using negative language".

One final remark is that the rather neutral nature of the causal relations in our corpus samples may be related to both the nature of the corpus, which consists of web-based materials, such as: company websites, newspapers, magazines etc., which are not the primary site of the speaker's subjective opinions, and also to the very nature of unambiguous English connectives, which have been demonstrated to be used for very specific purposes (Andersson, 2019). Based on the semantics of the connectives analysed here, we assume that they are mostly used to signal factual event types. Yet, more research should be carried out to confirm this hypothesis.

### 3.3 Annotation Statistics

Each connective was annotated in at least four varieties of English to capture any possible differences in terms of the contexts they occur in (see Table 1). Our aim has been to code 100 relations for each connective, although in most cases a small number of examples was excluded because there was insufficient context to perform annotations. In one case, "owing to" in JmE, the number of annotations is significantly lower, since only 60 examples were found in the corpus.

Note that in the following, we will refer to the effect as *argument 1* and cause as *argument 2* (and order them as such when labels are paired). This choice reflects the default order of events in English, but inversion of the clauses is frequent in actual use. We then adhere to our convention by annotating *argument 2* as preceding *argument 1*.

## 4 Analysis

### 4.1 Inter-Annotator Agreement

To test the annotation guidelines, *because of* instances in the US corpus is annotated blindly by two annotators additional to the main annotator, out of whom the second annotator is more experienced than the third one annotating more files in total. We have selected *because of* for inter-annotator agreement (IAA) as our initial hypothesis is that it is more likely to occur in both negative and positive contexts

| | | | | | **due to** | | | | | |
|---|---|---|---|---|---|---|---|---|---|---|
| Variety | neg/neg | neg/neu | neg/pos | neu/neg | neu/neu | neu/pos | pos/neg | pos/neu | pos/pos | TOTAL |
| American | 44 | 11 | 3 | 4 | 17 | 1 | 2 | 6 | 9 | 97 |
| British | 41 | 15 | 3 | 8 | 7 | 1 | 2 | 8 | 4 | 89 |
| Indian | 52 | 16 | 1 | 6 | 5 | 3 | 1 | 4 | 6 | 94 |
| Malaysian | 42 | 19 | 2 | 13 | 9 | 0 | 2 | 7 | 3 | 97 |
| Nigerian | 44 | 11 | 0 | 9 | 11 | 5 | 1 | 5 | 5 | 91 |
| Jamaican | 42 | 15 | 2 | 7 | 11 | 2 | 2 | 9 | 6 | 96 |

| | | | | | **because of** | | | | | |
|---|---|---|---|---|---|---|---|---|---|---|
| Variety | neg/neg | neg/neu | neg/pos | neu/neg | neu/neu | neu/pos | pos/neg | pos/neu | pos/pos | TOTAL |
| Indian | 25 | 20 | 0 | 13 | 7 | 4 | 4 | 17 | 9 | 99 |
| British | 38 | 17 | 3 | 12 | 9 | 3 | 3 | 10 | 4 | 99 |
| Malaysian | 21 | 15 | 3 | 7 | 15 | 4 | 3 | 15 | 12 | 95 |
| Australian | 21 | 19 | 0 | 16 | 24 | 7 | 1 | 6 | 4 | 98 |
| American | 33 | 8 | 5 | 8 | 14 | 5 | 5 | 7 | 14 | 99 |

| | | | | | **owing to** | | | | | |
|---|---|---|---|---|---|---|---|---|---|---|
| Variety | neg/neg | neg/neu | neg/pos | neu/neg | neu/neu | neu/pos | pos/neg | pos/neu | pos/pos | TOTAL |
| American | 29 | 17 | 3 | 4 | 19 | 3 | 1 | 5 | 16 | 97 |
| Jamaican | 16 | 11 | 0 | 5 | 11 | 2 | 1 | 6 | 8 | 60 |
| British | 39 | 19 | 3 | 6 | 14 | 2 | 1 | 6 | 7 | 97 |
| Nigerian | 46 | 11 | 2 | 4 | 8 | 6 | 2 | 4 | 14 | 97 |

Table 2: Distribution of labels in our annotated data. For instance, the category neg/neu means that the label of argument 1 (effect) is *neg*ative, while argument 2 (cause) is *neu*tral.

| Annotation | 1-2 | 1-3 | 2-3 |
|---|---|---|---|
| 1st argument (effect) | 0.816 | 0.569 | 0.609 |
| 2nd argument (cause) | 0.648 | 0.348 | 0.345 |
| Combined | 0.788 | 0.544 | 0.537 |

Table 3: Inter-annotator agreement for the sentiment annotations of each argument individually, as well as of the whole pair counted as one unit between all annotators.

than the others, hence more challenging to annotate. We calculate the IAA on each argument separately as well as on the whole relation using linearly weighted Cohen's Kappa (McHugh, 2012) between each annotator pair.

Table 3 shows that for each case, IAA results between the most experienced annotators are $\geq 0.6$ which is regarded as substantial (Cohen, 1960).

The lower level of inter-annotator agreement between the third annotator and the others indicates the complexity of the analyzed relations and highlights a need for a training period. Yet, the IAA scores alone fail to provide any insight about the nature of agreement between annotators, hence we also analyze how the annotators disagree which each other. As can be seen in Figure 1a to Figure 1c, the disagreements are overwhelmingly between *Neutral* and one of the polarities. There are only few instances where annotators assigns opposite polarities.

## 4.2 Differences Across Varieties and Connectives

Our preliminary observations indicated that *due to* may have less negative connotations in Asian Englishes, represented in our sample by Indian and Malaysian English. We are therefore interested in testing this hypothesis, as well as the more general question of whether there are differences in general between the English varieties with respect to the different connectives.

For the specific question of *due to*, we define a *negative context* as any relation with at least one negative and no positive argument, i.e. negative/negative, negative/neutral or neutral/negative. We also define *non-negative contexts*, consisting of all relations with no negative argument. We compare two groups: *Asian* (Indian and Malaysian) English, and the *major* (American and British) English varieties. Using these definitions, we see that contrary to our hypothesis, the major varieties have a somewhat *smaller* (70%, 123 of 176) proportion of negative uses than the Asian varieties (80%, 148 of 185). This difference is statistically significant, but only marginally so ($\chi^2$ test, $p = 0.04$).

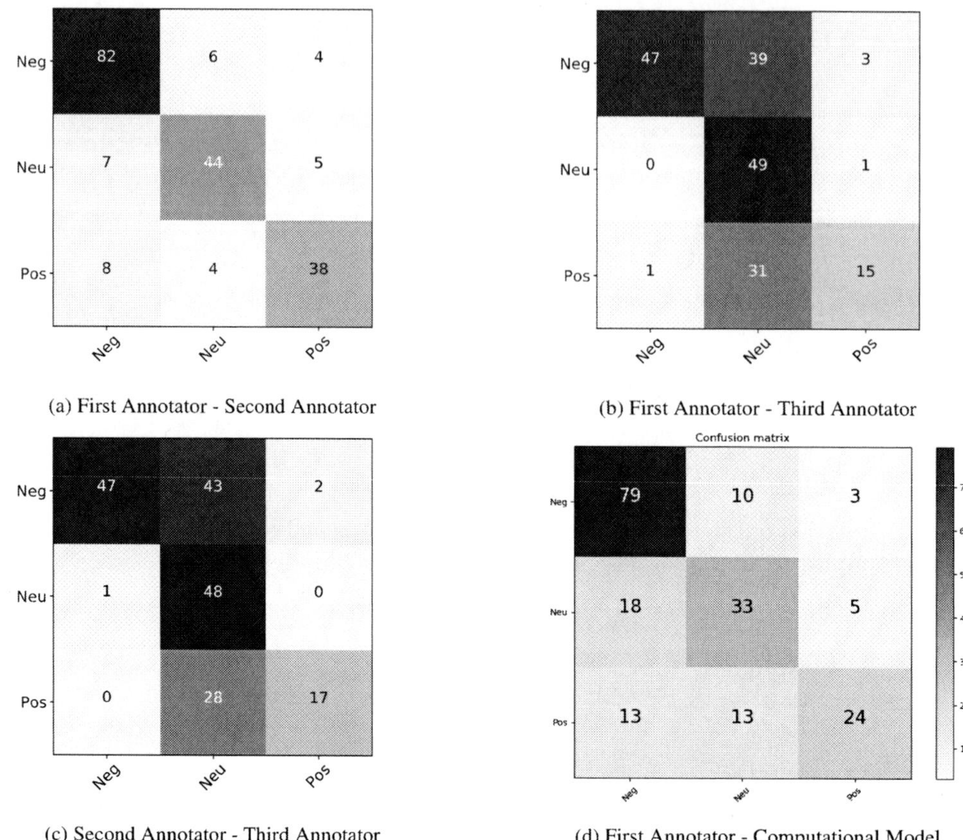



(a) First Annotator - Second Annotator

(b) First Annotator - Third Annotator

(c) Second Annotator - Third Annotator

(d) First Annotator - Computational Model

Figure 1: Confusion matrices between each annotator pair as well as between the first annotator and the computational model.

For the more general question, we compare all varieties that have been annotated for a given connective, with respect to three categories: *positive* (positive/positive, positive/neutral, neutral/positive), *neutral* (neutral/neutral), and *negative* (negative/negative, negative/neutral, neutral/negative). We find that there is no significant difference ($\chi^2$ test, $p = 0.26$) for *due to*, whereas both *because of* and *owing to* display significant differences between varieties (both have $p < 0.001$).

Although some differences are statistically significant, they are relatively small. Below, we summarize the annotation statistics (available in their entirety in Table 2):

- *due to*: large majority of negative (64–80%) uses, some neutral (5–18%) and positive (11–18%) uses.

- *because of*: majority of negative (48–72%), some neutral (7–25%) and many positive (18–35%) uses.

- *owing to*: majority of negative (54–69%), some neutral (9–20%) and many positive (16–27%) uses.

The ranges within parentheses indicate the minimum and maximum proportion of instances for that particular category, across the varieties for which we have annotations.

## 4.3 Differences Between Arguments

As shown in Table 4, cases where the arguments are of opposite polarity (negative/positive and positive/negative), are quite rare. Across all 1405 annotated relations, only 30 (2.1%) are annotated as

|            | neg/pos | pos/neg |
|------------|---------|---------|
| due to     | 11      | 10      |
| because of | 11      | 13      |
| owing to   | 8       | 5       |
| **Sum**    | 30      | 28      |

Table 4: Number of relations with arguments of opposite polarity.

negative/positive, and 28 (2.0%) as positive/negative. These have been left out in the comparisons in Section 4.2, because it is not straightforward to classify the whole relation as either positive or negative. However, these rare cases provide an opportunity to test our third research question: are the connotations of each connective more closely connected with one argument than the other?

We find that both opposition pairs (negative/positive and positive/negative) are about equally well-represented for each of the connectives, speaking against the hypothesis that predicts a much stronger connection of the connective to one argument over the other. However, more corpus research would be needed to verify/discard this hypothesis more reliably. See also the discussion on example 7, which has been annotated as positive/negative.

### 4.4 Computational Model

Along with the manual annotations, we also explore the automatic means to annotate sentiments of the arguments. To this end, we model the problem as a sentence classification task and fine-tune a pre-trained language model, BERT (Devlin et al., 2018),[3] which has become the standard procedure in NLP. As the task here is to predict the sentiment of an argument, we only pass the annotated text spans to BERT. The computational model is implemented using Huggingface's Transformers library.[4] As fine-tuning procedure is known to suffer from high variance, the model is run 5 times and we report test results of the run with the median development performance.

To test the performance of the classifier, we allocated the *US English because of* annotations as the test data and train the classifier on the remaining annotations.[5] In order to understand how well the classifier performs, we report the IAA scores between the classifier and each annotator in Table 5.

| Annotation           | Ann1  | Ann2  | Ann3  |
|----------------------|-------|-------|-------|
| 1st argument (effect) | 0.504 | 0.529 | 0.300 |
| 2nd argument (cause)  | 0.507 | 0.376 | 0.235 |

Table 5: Inter-annotator agreement (Cohen's Kappa) between the computational model and the annotators.

The results show that the classifier cannot match the human performance. When the divergences between the predicted labels and first annotator's coding (according to which the classifier is trained) are examined, we see that the nature of these disagreements is different from that of human annotators (see Section 4.1), as the model is less likely to label the arguments as *positive*. Yet, the total number of disagreements between opposite polarities is almost the same (compared Figure 1a and 1d), which suggests that the computational model does not make extremely precise predictions.

In almost all cases, however, the model's agreement with the experienced annotators are moderate, with Kappa $\geq$ 0.4, which we find promising given the limited number of the annotations available for training.

---

[3] We use bert-large-cased model.
[4] https://github.com/huggingface/transformers
[5] which consists of 2612 instances in total

## 5   Conclusion

The main finding of our study is that the three causal connectives analyzed, *due to*, *because of* and *owing to*, are all associated with predominantly negative semantic prosodies. Other than this general trend, the distributions of usages do not significantly differ between the connectives, between the analyzed regional varieties of English, or between the arguments (cause and effect).

We investigated the possibility of automating sentiment annotations for this project in Section 4.4 and our results indicate that the computational model achieves moderate agreement with the annotators despite the limited training data, suggesting that the procedure can benefit more annotations and have potential to be automatized to a good extent after a certain amount of manual annotation. The topics for future work are to involve more human annotators and develop more precise guidelines based on their observations and, also, investigate whether other, larger, sentiment-related resources can be exploited for this task.

## References


Marta Andersson. 2019. Subjectivity of english connectives. *Empirical Studies of the Construction of Discourse*, 305:299.

Farah Benamara, Maite Taboada, and Yannick Mathieu. 2017. Evaluative language beyond bags of words: Linguistic insights and computational applications. *Computational Linguistics*, 43(1):201–264.

Diane Blakemore and Robyn Carston. 2005. The pragmatics of sentential coordination with and. *Lingua*, 115(4):569–589.

Jacob Cohen. 1960. A coefficient of agreement for nominal scales. *Educational and psychological measurement*, 20(1):37–46.

Mark Davies. 2013. Corpus of global web-based english: 1.9 billion words from speakers in 20 countries (glowbe). *Available online atcorpus. byu. edu/glowbe/. RetrievedDecember*, 15:2015.

Rahim Dehkharghani, Hanefi Mercan, Arsalan Javeed, and Yucel Saygin. 2014. Sentimental causal rule discovery from twitter. *Expert Systems with Applications*, 41(10):4950–4958.

Jacob Devlin, Ming-Wei Chang, Kenton Lee, and Kristina Toutanova. 2018. Bert: Pre-training of deep bidirectional transformers for language understanding. *arXiv preprint arXiv:1810.04805*.

David J Hauser and Norbert Schwarz. 2016. Semantic prosody and judgment. *Journal of Experimental Psychology: General*, 145(7):882.

Judith Kamalski, Leo Lentz, Ted Sanders, and Rolf A Zwaan. 2008. The forewarning effect of coherence markers in persuasive discourse: Evidence from persuasion and processing. *Discourse Processes*, 45(6):545–579.

Dongyeop Kang, Varun Gangal, Ang Lu, Zheng Chen, and Eduard Hovy. 2017. Detecting and explaining causes from text for a time series event. *arXiv preprint arXiv:1707.08852*.

Alan Lee, Rashmi Prasad, Bonnie Webber, and Aravind K Joshi. 2016. Annotating discourse relations with the pdtb annotator. In *Proceedings of COLING 2016, the 26th International Conference on Computational Linguistics: System Demonstrations*, pages 121–125.

Yen-Yu Lin and Siaw-Fong Chung. 2016. A corpus-based study on the semantic prosody of challenge. *Taiwan Journal of TESOL*, 13(2):99–146.

Mary L McHugh. 2012. Interrater reliability: the kappa statistic. *Biochemia medica: Biochemia medica*, 22(3):276–282.

Saif Mohammad, Svetlana Kiritchenko, Parinaz Sobhani, Xiaodan Zhu, and Colin Cherry. 2016. Semeval-2016 task 6: Detecting stance in tweets. In *Proceedings of the 10th International Workshop on Semantic Evaluation (SemEval-2016)*, pages 31–41.

Saif Mohammad. 2016. A practical guide to sentiment annotation: Challenges and solutions. In *Proceedings of the 7th Workshop on Computational Approaches to Subjectivity, Sentiment and Social Media Analysis*, pages 174–179.

Subhabrata Mukherjee and Pushpak Bhattacharyya. 2012. Sentiment analysis in twitter with lightweight discourse analysis. In *Proceedings of COLING 2012*, pages 1847–1864.

Alan Partington. 2004. " utterly content in each other's company" semantic prosody and semantic preference. *International journal of corpus linguistics*, 9(1).

Rashmi Prasad, Eleni Miltsakaki, Nikhil Dinesh, Alan Lee, Aravind Joshi, Livio Robaldo, and Bonnie L Webber. 2007. The penn discourse treebank 2.0 annotation manual.

Peter G Preethi, Vilma Uma, et al. 2015. Temporal sentiment analysis and causal rules extraction from tweets for event prediction. *Procedia computer science*, 48:84–89.

Sara Rosenthal, Preslav Nakov, Svetlana Kiritchenko, Saif Mohammad, Alan Ritter, and Veselin Stoyanov. 2015. Semeval-2015 task 10: Sentiment analysis in twitter. In *Proceedings of the 9th international workshop on semantic evaluation (SemEval 2015)*, pages 451–463.

Merel Scholman and Vera Demberg. 2017. Crowdsourcing discourse interpretations: On the influence of context and the reliability of a connective insertion task. In *Proceedings of the 11th Linguistic Annotation Workshop*, pages 24–33.

Antonios Siganos, Evangelos Vagenas-Nanos, and Patrick Verwijmeren. 2014. Facebook's daily sentiment and international stock markets. *Journal of Economic Behavior & Organization*, 107:730–743.

John Sinclair. 1998. The lexical item. *Amsterdam Studies In The Theory And History Of Linguistic Science Series 4*, pages 1–24.

Michael Stubbs. 1995. Collocations and semantic profiles: On the cause of the trouble with quantitative studies. *Functions of language*, 2(1):23–55.

Michael Stubbs. 2001. *Words and phrases: Corpus studies of lexical semantics*. Blackwell Publishers Oxford.

Eve Sweetser. 1990. *From etymology to pragmatics: Metaphorical and cultural aspects of semantic structure*, volume 54. Cambridge University Press.

Fei Wang, Yunfang Wu, and Likun Qiu. 2012. Exploiting discourse relations for sentiment analysis. In *Proceedings of COLING 2012: Posters*, pages 1311–1320.

Anna Wierzbicka. 1998. Anchoring linguistic typology in universal semantic primes.

Richard Xiao and Tony McEnery. 2006. Collocation, semantic prosody, and near synonymy: A cross-linguistic perspective. *Applied linguistics*, 27(1):103–129.

Farah Benamara Zitoune, Nicholas Asher, Yvette Yannick Mathieu, Vladimir Popescu, and Baptiste Chardon. 2016. Evaluation in discourse: A corpus-based study.

# A Novel Annotation Schema for Conversational Humor: Capturing the cultural nuances in Kanyasulkam

**Vaishnavi Pamulapati**     **Gayatri Purigilla**     **Radhika Mamidi**

Language Technologies Research Center
International Institute of Information Technology
Hyderabad, India
`vaishnavi.p@research.iiit.ac.in`
`gayatri.purigilla@research.iiit.ac.in`
`radhika.mamidi@iiit.ac.in`


## Abstract


Humor research is a multifaceted field that has led to a better understanding of humor's psychological effects and the development of different theories of humor. This paper's main objective is to develop a hierarchical schema for a fine-grained annotation of Conversational Humor. A prominent 19th century play from Telugu, *Kanyasulkam*, is annotated to substantiate the work across cultures at multiple levels. Based on the Benign Violation Theory, the benignity or non-benignity of the interlocutor's intentions is included within the framework. Under the categories mentioned above, in addition to different types of humor, the techniques utilized by these types are identified. Furthermore, the inter-annotator agreement is calculated to assess the accuracy and validity of the dataset. An in-depth analysis of the disagreement is performed to understand the subjectivity of humor better.


*Keywords:conversational humor, Benign Violation Theory, multicultural, hierarchical schema*

## 1   Introduction

Humor and its dependence on society and culture have been the focus of research since times immemorial (Raskin, 1979). From finding theories to define humor (Raskin, 1985; Meyer, 2000; Attardo and Raskin, 1991) to an analysis of the perception of humor in jokes (Raskin, 1979), humor studies have been proved to be an essential aspect of linguistic as well as sociological, psychological and philosophical research. Many papers discuss types of humor (Dynel, 2009; Alexander, 1997; Behrens, 1977), but this paper stands apart. It focuses on creating an annotation schema for conversational humor with a stage play as the medium of analysis while claiming that this schema can be used across languages. Conversational humor is the spontaneous or pre-constructed interactional humor. The interlocutors intend to amuse the listener directly or shift to a humorous frame where there is humor beyond what the literal verbalizations convey (Dynel, 2009). Stage play is chosen as the medium of analysis since 'conversational humor' is an umbrella term that covers various semantic and pragmatic types of humor that occur in interpersonal conversation, both real-life and fictional (Dynel, 2009).

There are key differences between plays and other forms of discourse, like transcribed recordings of actual conversations or novels, justifying our use of stage play in the paper. The differences include but are not limited to pauses, pause fillers, and discourse markers as essential features of characterization in a play, unlike their use in actual conversations. In a play, there is more character-character interaction than in novels, which have more narration from one point of view (Wareing and Thornborrow, 1998). But the annotation schema presented here does not restrict its application on plays alone but can also cover novels, TV shows, movies, etc; essentially any genre that involves a premeditated conversation. This paper also focuses on how humor's form and function are influenced multiculturally by annotating one of the most famous plays of the Telugu culture, *Kanyasulkam*. Studies show that culture plays a vital role in conversational humor in some distinct ways like the need for shared knowledge and standard references, and others more indirect, like how the importance given to language awareness by any culture

---






*The 14th Linguistic Annotation Workshop*, pages 34–47
Barcelona, Spain (Online), December 12, 2020.

dictates the preference for wit and linguistic play (Mullan and Beal, 2018). *Kanyasulkam* is a play set in the 19th century Vijayanagaram which uses humor to talk about the social evils prevalent in the society. However, while the author talks about child marriages, widow re-marriage, and the Nautch question, we also see him discuss customs and traditions, superstitions, use of English and the fascination towards it, etc. Thus, making it culturally relevant and further justifying the use of *Kanyasulkam* in validating the role of culture on humor. Persona identification is an important application of the schema proposed. For instance, if character A has a tendency to sarcastically tease character B on most occasions, we gain an insight into A's sense of humor (SOH) as well the social function performed by A. While there have been several studies that suggest that an SOH indicates positive personality traits such as self-actualising, self-acceptance, and others (Maslow, 1954; Allport, 1961), the social function performed by A also provides an understanding of A's overall role in the story, therefore the character's persona.

## 2   Related Work

Interest in the study of humor has faced steady growth since 1970 (McGhee P.E., 1989). This interest in humor studies has led to a great deal of research on humor types and functions. In his paper on the issues in conversational joking, Neal R. Norrick (2003) talks about the structure of humorous discourse, the forms of conversational humor and its interpersonal functions, i.e., aggression vs. rapport. Two of Marta Dynel's studies, one based on a popular English sitcom, Friends (2011) and another on the sitcom, House (2013), are deemed relevant to this study. While the former analyses cultural references, the latter attempts to extract universal communicative phenomena that cause humor. Dirk Delabastita (2005) presents in her work, an overview of the humorous scenes with bilingual and translation-based situations from Shakespeare's plays. Levisen (2014) uses Natural Semantic Metalanguage to compare the Danish concept of 'sort humor' (a highly culturally specific way of Danish communication) and the English, 'black humor.' To recognize humor and irony in tweets, Antonio Reyes et al. (2012) analyze humor and irony to recognize these concepts in tweets. Agnese Augello et al. (2008) have worked on building a chatbot that recognizes and generates humorous expressions. There have been continuous efforts in the field of computer science for the comprehension (Binsted et al. 2006), detection (Taylor, 2009), production (Hempelmann et al., 2006), and recognition (Mihalcea et al., 2006) of conversational humor.

## 3   Data and Annotation

The full text of the Telugu play, *Kanyasulkam*, is annotated by two people, A1 and A2. For the pre-processing of the data, the whole text was split first by each character's dialogue, and each utterance by the character was further split into single sentences/segments. In the presence of poems, lists, etc. the utterance remains as is, and this final output is used for annotation giving a total of 6645 segments to be annotated. After developing the gold standard corpus (can be found here), 2710 utterances were classified as humorous, 1782 were given the tag *dialogue*, 1881 *conversational*, and 892 *benign*. The annotation was done with appropriate checkpoints after every 2000 segments to identify any new techniques or revise the schema.

## 4   Annotation Schema

**Types:** Teasing(T), Retort(R), Banter(Ba), Schadenfreude(S)
**Techniques:** Dramatic Irony(DIrn), Sarcasm(Src), Satire(Str), Fallacious Reasoning(FR), Exaggeration(Ex), Use of foreign language(FL), Allusion(A), Profanity(P), Other stylistic figures(O) (refer to Table 5).
*Note:* A segment can be annotated with more than one technique.

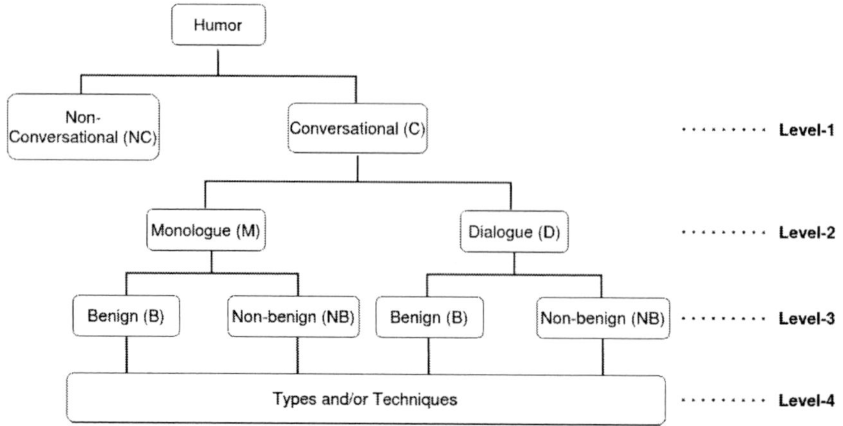

Figure 1: Hierarchical schema for Conversational humor

### 4.1 Level-1: Non-Conversational (NC)/ Conversational Humor (C)

This study uses Dynel's (2009) conceptualization of conversational humor. As the dataset used here is a play, it is of primal importance to note that the speaker's intent may not be to cause humor. However, a third-party present, or the metarecipients of the conversation, the audience/readers, may find it humorous. It is a common phenomenon to make the audience laugh at the expense of a fictional character. This study makes a distinction between conversational and non-conversational humor. In the latter, the humor does not exist in the realm of verbality but rather in the domain of the situation (slapstick humor, a character's trait such as miserliness, stupidity, etc.) For example, when a cowardly character is badmouthing his rival and the latter appears just then.

### 4.2 Level-2: Monologue (M)/ Dialogue (D)

The notion of "dialogue" is taken in the Socratic dialogue sense: a conversation between two or more people. In contrast, there are several definitions and types of monologues present: Dramatic monologue (Finch, 2010), soliloquy (Shea, 1963), and inner monologue (Neuse, 1934). This study defines a monologue as "utterances by a single person/character in real-life/fictional with the assumption by the speaker that there are no listeners present to hear their thoughts". The distinction between humor found in a dialogue and a monologue is made because it is recognized that if a person speaks to themselves with no listeners present, it gives rise to certain types and techniques of humor compared to those occurring in a dialogue. Take *retorts*, for instance. A retort is a sharp or witty remark in response to another's utterance (Sacks, 1992 [1972]). Hence, for this type of conversational humor, the first turn in an adjacency pair must transpire (Sacks, 1992 [1972], 419).

### 4.3 Level-3: Benign (B)/ Non-Benign (NB)

The Benign Violation Theory examines the intersection at which the listener perceives a violation in a joke as benign (McGraw, 2010). A joke is not a passive entity but is expressed by a person and perceived by another. Hence, the relationship between the joke-teller, the joke, and the joke-listener must be explored (Kant and Norman, 2019). In conversational humor, there is no notion of a "joke" ("canned joke" in Dynel (2009)). Humor is caused by the interlocutor's spontaneous speech that may or may not be humorous to the listeners present. For instance, in derision, reprimands, or put-downs, the speaker or listener may not find it humorous; instead, a third-party present (or an audience) may find the utterance humorous. In this study, it is important to note that the relationship between the author of the play and the audience is not examined, but the latter is given the role of a passive listener.

karata: *bAvA yIsammaMXaM ceswe nI koVMpaki aggeVtteswAnu.*

agni: *vIlYlammA SiKAwaraga, prawIgAdixakoVdukU wiMdipowullAga nAyiMtajeri nannanevAlYle*

**Translation:**

Karata: Brother-in-law, if you agree to this proposal, I will set your house on fire.

Agni: (An expletive directed at Karata's mother), every son of a donkey, comes to my house to eat like a glutton and ends up criticizing me.

**Context:**

Here, the interlocutors present in the scene do not find Agni's utterance humorous as he only intends to ridicule Karata and Venkamma. However, the metarecipients, the audience, are bound to find it amusing (Dynel, 2009). This study augments the BVT by modifying the factors by which a joke can be labeled as benign: (a) two contradictory norms of the relevant culture (b) a weak commitment to the violated norm, or (c) the social distance between the interlocutors and the content of what is uttered (d) the intention of the humor causer understood by the listener whether benign or not (Weiner 1993, 2009). By these four conditions, the above example is labeled non-benign as it goes against the salient norm of respecting a guest, and there exists no norm that states to insult a guest in the Telugu culture blatantly. Furthermore, Agni's intention is to solely deride his guest's behavior.

### 4.4    Level-4: Types of conversational humor

### 4.4.1    Teasing (T)

In this study, teasing is considered to transpire when the speaker intends to be playful, to only nip at the present listener non-aggressively. The main objective is to develop/strengthen the bond between the speaker and the listener(s). Other than this benevolent intention, the speaker also uses an element of "pretense" to tease (Clark, 1996; Dynel, 2009).

maXu: *anyAyaM mAtalu AdakaMdi, Ayana yaMwa caxuvukunnAdu, Ayanaki yaMwapraKyAwi vuMxi!*

*nedorepo goVppa vuxyogaM kAnEyyuMxi.*

**Translation:**

Madhu: Don't be unfair. He is a very learned man. He has a lot of fame as well. Very soon, he'll land himself a good job.

**Context:**

Madhu teases her client Ramappanthulu by praising another client of hers, Girisam. Rama detests and is jealous of Girisam. Knowing this, Madhu seeks to elicit a reaction by exaggerating (a common technique used in teasing) Girisam's strength playfully.

### 4.4.2    Retort (R)

A retort takes place at the second turn in an adjacency pair where the purpose is to out-challenge or outwit the other interlocutor(s) (Dynel, 2009) of the conversation by making a quick comeback (utilizing the other's behavior, personality, past, etc.) In this definition of retort, the speakers do not aim to collaborate and engage in conversation jointly, rather undermine (non-benign) or challenge (in some cases, benign) the listener (Holmes and Marra, 2002).

lubXA: *mAmagAru hAsyAnikaMtunnArugAni, ninnoVxulwArA?*

[...]

rAma: *alAgaddi peVttaMdi!*

maXu: [...]

*gaddi gAdixalu wiMtAyi;*

*manuRyulu winaru.*

**Translation:**

Lubdha: Uncle is just pulling your leg. Do you think he will forsake you?

[...]

Rama: Teach her a lesson like that (Idiom with the literal meaning of 'feed her grass')

Madhu: [..]

Grass is eaten by donkeys, not people.

**Context:**

Rama is reading a letter written by Girisam where the latter refers to him as a donkey. In response to Rama's suggestion of teaching Madhu a lesson, she mocks him indirectly by referring to the letter when she says, "Grass is eaten by donkeys, not by people".

### 4.4.3  Banter (Ba)

If there is a continuous exchange of retorts and teasing in a multi-turn conversation, it is called banter (Dynel, 2008; Norrick, 1993: 29). This rapid exchange of repartees is observed in interactions such as a conversation between parents, coworkers at the office (example 2 in Holmes and Marra, 2002), etc. It is important to note that Banter cannot be a hierarchical category encompassing Retort and Teasing as they can also occur independently.

maXu: *wAkattuvaswuva wappiMcuku pAripoweno?*

    *kukkA, nakkA, kAxugaxA goVlusuluvesi kattadAniki?*

karata: *nI valallo paddaprANi mari wappiMcukupovadaM yalAga?*

    *vAtiki vunna patuwvaM yevukku goVlusulakU vuMdaxu.*

maXu: *valalo muwyapu cippalupadiwe lABaMgAni, nawwagullalupadiwe mowacetu.*

karata: *yaMwasepU dabbu, dabbenA?*

    *snehaM, valapU, anevi vuMtAyA?*

maXu: *snehaM mIlAtivAricota*

**Translation:**

Madhu: What if you run away after pawning it?

You aren't a dog or a fox to tie you with chains.

Karata: Can any living being be freed from your trap?

Its hold is stronger than that of any chain.

Madhu: Only if pearls are trapped, it is of any use. Getting a hold on rocks/shells will only increase my burden.

Karata: Why are you always concerned about money? What about friendship, justice, etc.?

Madhu: Friendship with people like you (with sarcasm)

**Context:**

Madhu is hesitant to depart from her necklace, which Karata is asking for. Karata teases her by flattery and hopes it will help in achieving his goal. However, Madhu retorts by indirectly comparing him to a weed/stone. Subsequently, in response to his reprimand that she always talks about money, she retorts using sarcasm once more.

### 4.4.4  Schadenfreude (S)

Schadenfreude is a German word that refers to the pleasure derived from another's misfortune (Dijk et al., 2009). It is the "malicious joy" evoked by the downfall of others, mostly high achievers (Feather and Sherman, 2002; Smith et al., 1996). This emotion is majorly associated with negative connotations, (Smith et al., 2009, Leach et al., 2003; cf. Kuipers, 2014) All instances of Schadenfreude in this study agree with the non-benign viewpoint. The intent of the utterance is to be truly abusive and denigrating to the person it is directed towards (butt). An important aspect of annotation to note here is that, when a segment is tagged as Schadenfreude, we need not laugh at the plight of the character whose utterance it is.

PUta: *AveVXavavuMte nAkeM kAvAli, vuMdakuMte nAkeM kAvAli.*

    *vAdu nIkiccina yiravayi rUpAyalU yicceVy.*

MaXu: *yavadi kiccAvo vANNe adagavammA.*

PUta: *veVXavakanabadiwe sigapAyixIsi cIpurugattawo moVwwuxunu, yeVkkadaxAcAvevizti?*

**Translation:**

Puta: I couldn't care less about that idiot's whereabouts. Just give me the 20 rupees that he gave you.

Madhu: Ask the person you gave it to.

Puta: I will cut his hair and thrash him with a broom if I find him, where did you hide him?

**Context:**

Puta comes to Madhu's house, searching for Girisam, who has run away with her money. On getting no help from Madhu in finding his whereabouts, Puta is immensely angered, and humor is found in Girisam's plight.

## 4.5 Techniques:

### 4.5.1 Dramatic Irony (DIrn)

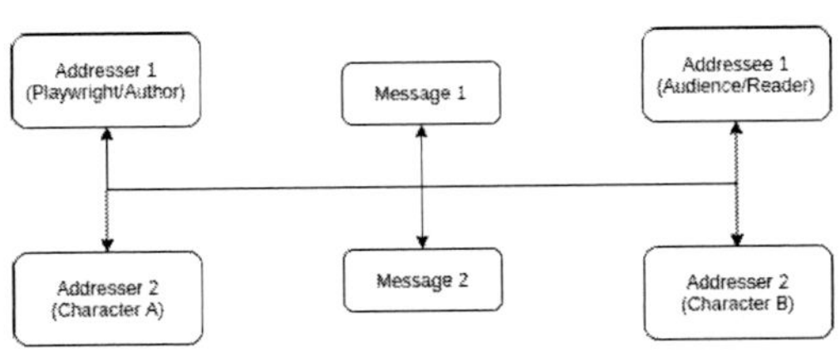


Figure 2: Levels of discourse

In a stage play setting, there exist two or more levels of discourse, the author-audience/reader, and the character-character level (Short and Mick, 1996). When the character is portraying pretense with one character, another character may or may not be in on it, but the readers necessarily are. Hence, other than the knowledge that exists between the characters, the audience is also privy to knowledge only they possess (Kreuz and Roberts, 1993).

girI: *AlrEt - gAni - nAkikkada cAlA vyavahAramulalo naRtaMvaswuMxe - munasabugAri pillalki Salavullo pATAlceVpiweV PiptI rupij yiswAvaznnAru; ayinA nI viRayavEz yaMwa lAs vaccinA nenu ker ceVyyanu.*

**Translation:**

Giri: It's alright. But I'll incur a lot of losses here. The village head has promised to give 50 rupees for tutoring his kids over the vacation. However, I do not care about any loss when it comes to you.

**Context:**

Girisam lies that he has been offered a valuable job opportunity but that he will reject it as he genuinely cares for his pupil Venka. The audience knows that this is untrue as, before this conversation, Girisam was plotting to take advantage of Venka's economic resources.

As mentioned above, a requisite component of teasing is that of pretense. Nevertheless, teasing is not mandatorily marked with dramatic irony as there is a difference in intent. In dramatic irony, the intent is to dupe the listener by pretending to have values, attributes, etc. that the speaker does not possess. Whereas, in teasing, the motivation is to reduce the social distance or to poke fun at the listener benignly.

### 4.5.2 Satire (Str)

Satire has been defined as the ridicule of a subject (a person, situation, or an institution) to point out its faults (Beckson and Ganz, 1989). It does not need to be present at the scene of action. Studies on Telugu literature have concluded satire to consist of 4 elements. Vyangyam, Chatuvulu, Prahasanams, and Adhikshepam (Rao, 2004). The main features of each are sarcasm, ridiculing, intention of social reform, and intention of teaching morals and ethics through severe criticism. The presence of these elements in satire is only culturally significant, and such a clear-cut difference may not be found in English.

SiRyudu: *ArneVllakomAtu poVswakaMpattukuMte koVwwaSlokAlu pAwaSlokAlu oVkkalA gkana-padawAyi.*

*mAguruvugAriki xoVMdakAya kUra yiRTaM lexu, guruvugAri peVlYlAM peVratlo xoVMda-pAxuMxani rojU AkUreV voVMduwuMxi.*

*bawikunnavAlYla yiRTaveVz yilA yeduswUMte caccinavAdi yiRTAyiRTAlwo yeMpani?*

*yIcaxuvikkadiwo cAliMci girISaMgAri xaggira nAlugiMgilIRu mukkalu nercukuMtAnu.*

**Translation:**

Student: If I open my books once in 6 months, then the poems I have already learned, and the new ones all look the same.

My teacher does not like ivy gourd curry. But his wife makes the same curry everyday owing to the ivy gourd plant in their house.

If the likes of a person who is very much alive are not cared about, how do the likes of someone dead matter?

I should stop these lessons here and learn a few English words from Mr. Girisam.

**Context:**

Karata's student is asked to learn a poem by heart where the poet talks about his likes and dislikes of flowers and nature. The student is fed up by this mode of learning and feels it is pointless to learn about a dead person's likes and dislikes when his own guru's likes are not cared about by the latter's wife. This example is a satire on the education being provided to the student by Karata. The element of satire being used here is Chatuvu (ridicule).

### 4.5.3  Sarcasm (Src)

The difference between irony and sarcasm is fuzzy and is often misunderstood, given that they are inevitably bound to each other. However, the relationship between them remains unclear to native speakers but is highlighted when a comparison is drawn between cultures or linguistic communities (Partington, 2006). Attardo, in his study, cites that sarcasm is an overly aggressive type of irony with more explicit markers or cues and a clear target (Attardo, 2000). Studies also cite the difference between irony and sarcasm as irony does not require the speaker's intention and can be directed towards situations. However, sarcasm must be deliberate and is a strictly verbal phenomenon (Haiman 1990,1998).

klArk: *iMtiperU, sAkInU yemitaMdI?*

BImA: *emitayyA?*

agni: *Ayanaperu girISaM, maraMwakaMta nAkuweVliyaxu.*

kaleV: *cAbAR;*

 *bAgAvuMxi!*

 *avaXAnlugAri koVmArweVni yeVvado wIsukupoyinAdu.*

 *kanaka vAdi vUrUperU yeVriginavAlYlu weVliyaceVyyavalasinaxani, xaMdorAkoVttiMci ge-*
*jatlo veyiMcaMdi.*

**Translation:**

Clerk: What is his surname and address?

Bhima: What is it, man?

Agni: His name is Girisam. I do not know anything else.

Kale: Great. Sounds good. Let's get it published in the newspaper that someone kidnapped Mr. Agni's daughter. And hence, anyone who knows his name and village should immediately inform us.

**Context:**

Agni goes to register a complaint against Girisam who runs away with the former's daughter. When Agni states that he knows only the first name and nothing else, the officer sarcastically praises him and suggests that it would be great to publish this news in the Gazette and ask the public's help to get to know Girisam's details.

### 4.5.4  Fallacious Reasoning (FR)

A fallacy is defined as an argument that has faulty reasoning (Gensler and Harry, 2010) either by intentional pretense by the speaker or by genuine ignorance. In a conversational setting, a fallacy need not be restricted to arguments presented by the speaker to reach a conclusion. However, the characteristics of a conversation can be taken advantage of. For instance, the topic is diverted by speaking about an unrelated topic, identifying a false cause and effect (Shewan and Edward, 1994), etc.

girISaM: *veVrigud!*

 *peVlYlanexi maMci paxArWavEzwe "aXikasya aXikaM PalaM" annAdu ganaka cinnapillani oVka musalAdiki peVlYlicesi, vAducaswe marodiki, maroducaswe marodiki, yilAga peVlYlimIxa peV-lYli, peVlYlimIxa peVlYliayi, vIdixaggiro veVyyi, vAdixaggiro veVyyi, marodixaggira maroveVyyi, roVt-teVmIxa neVyyi, newimIxa roVtteV lAga yekowravqxXigA kanyASulkaM lAgi, wuxaki nAlAMti buxXi-vazMwuNnicUsi peVlYlAdiwe ceVppAv majA?*

**Translation:**

Girisam: Very good. If marriage is a good thing, and since the more you do, the more you achieve, a young girl should be married to an old man and once he dies, another man and if he dies, then another one and so on while collecting a thousand from the first guy, then the next, then another, like butter on bread and bread on butter, collect all the *Kanyasulkam* (bride price) and finally if she gets married to a wise guy like me, isn't that enjoyable?

**Context:**

Girisam pretends to agree that selling young girls for marriage is good for society when widow re-marriage is allowed. He argues that for every man that dies naturally with old age over time if the child is married and re-married to other older men, the father of the child gets money until the girl can marry a sensible person like Girisam. It is evident that this is an example of "non sequitur" fallacy, where the premises are true, but the conclusion is false.

### 4.5.5 Utilizing a Foreign Language (FL)

Several studies have attempted to understand the motivations for using a foreign language to produce humor (Siegel, 1995; Kim, 2006). Grosjean (1982) states that situations, messages, attitudes, and emotions influence foreign language use. In *Kanyasulkam*, English is used sporadically only by one character, Girisam, to achieve his objective: to portray and distinguish himself among the characters as well-educated.

agni: *oVkkaxammidI yivvanu.*

    [. . . ]

    *ixaMwA topI vyavahAraMlA kanapaduwuMxi.*

karata: [...]

girISaM: *xisIj bArbaras, cUcAraMdI, jeVMtilmen anagA peVxxamaniRini yalA aMtunnAro!*

**Translation:**

Agni: I will not spare even one penny

[...]

Karata: [...]

Girisam: This is barbarous. Did you see how he is talking to a gentleman, meaning, learned person!

**Context:**

Upon being accused of cheating by Agni, Girisam is angered. Here, knowing fully well that the listeners do not understand English, Girisam still chooses to talk in English and then condescendingly explains what he means. He does this to establish superiority over others as people who knew English in those times were held in high regard.

### 4.5.6 Allusion (A)

(Norrick, 1989): Direct or indirect reference to an object or circumstance from a different context is defined as an allusion.

karata: *Ayanexo kurYrYavAdiwo yiMgillRu mAtaMte puccakAyalaxoVMgaMte bujAlwaduvuzkunnattu nImIxa peVttukuMtAveM?*

Karata: If he is talking to his student in English, why are you getting involved like the watermelon thief rubbing his shoulders (idiom) meaning, why are you letting yourself be caught red-handed by getting angry and proving that you do not understand a word of it?

### 4.5.7 Profanity (P)

(Beers Fägersten, 2012): Profanity is defined as language that is considered as strongly impolite, rude, or socially offensive.

girISaM: *rAskeVl vulakalexu palakalexu sarekaxA moVhaM pakkaki wippi kaduppagiletattu navvuwunnAdu.*

Girisam: Not only did that rascal fail to support me during my lecture, he turned to his side and laughed almost until his stomach burst.

### 4.5.8 Hyperbole/ Exaggeration (Ex)

(Norrick, 2004): It is the representation of an entity as more dramatic, better, or worse than it really is. Hyperbole is a figure of speech using exaggeration.

girISaM: *nene xAni hajbeVMdnEvuMte, nilabaddapAtuna nI waMdrini rivAlvarwo RUt ceSivuMxunu.*

Girisam: If I were her husband, I would have shot your father with a revolver from where I stood.

Although exaggeration necessarily has a pretense factor, any segment where exaggeration is identified, "dramatic irony" is not marked.

### 4.5.9 Other identified techniques (O)

(Dynel, 2009): Such as simile, metaphor, etc. are also marked during annotation.

maXu: *catlaki cAva nalupu, maniRiki cAva weVlupU.* (simile)

Madhu: A person's death is marked by white, like how a tree's death is marked by black.

## 5 Disagreement Analysis

The validity of the tag set and their definitions are measured using Cohen's Kappa ($\kappa$) (Cohen, 1960). Although the annotators were asked to mark all levels of the hierarchical scheme, the inter-annotator agreement (IAA) for level 2 (Monologue/Dialogue) was not measured as the definition for these categories provided no ambiguity. The annotation for level 1, Conversational vs. Non-Conversational Humor, gave a Kappa value of 0.48 (moderate agreement). The disagreement emerged could be attested to the variation in the perception of humor (Table 1). For instance, A2 could have found the character's trait (Non-conversational) humorous, whereas A1 identified a verbal technique in the speaker's utterance, causing disagreement. Annotation of level 3, Benign vs. Non-Benign Humor gave a Kappa value of 0.42 (moderate agreement). The disagreement exhibited can be due to the difference in perception of the benignity of the utterance (Table 2). A1 could be aware of a salient norm that can be violated (Section 4.3), whereas A2 is not producing disagreement.

Annotation of level 3 of the schema, types of Conversational Humor, resulted in a Kappa value of 0.49 (moderate agreement). Most of the disagreement shown in Table 2 (refer to Appendix), (Null, <some_type>) or (<some_type>, Null), is due to the failure or success of labelling the type by one annotator or a difference in perception of humor itself. A significant overlap of types can only be observed at (*Retort, Teasing*), which occurs at 11 segments. The dissimilarity of perception of the speaker's intent causes this overlap. Annotator A1 perceived that the speaker intends to outwit or challenge the listener, whereas A2 perceived that the speaker only intends to pull the listener's leg.

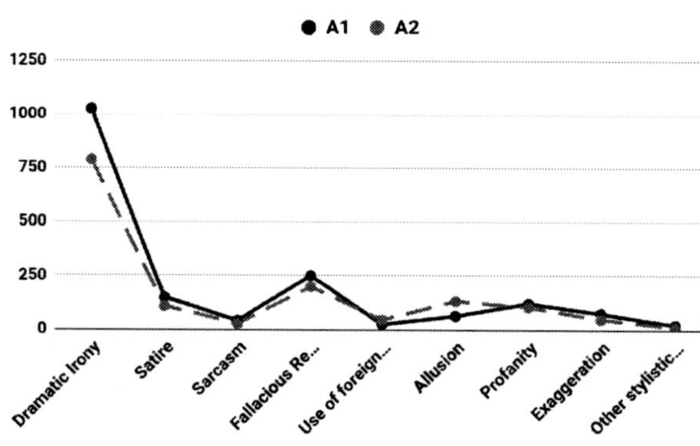


Figure 3: Distribution of Techniques by A1 and A2

For the final level of the schema, techniques of Conversational Humor (Figure 3), it is worthy to note that each segment can be marked with one or more techniques, but it is not mandatory. If level 1, 2, and 3 (Conversational/Non-conversational, Monologue/Dialogue, Benign/Non-Benign) are marked, then level 4 (Type, Technique) is to be tagged compulsorily. For this type of data, it was considered best to use Krippendorff's Alpha ($\alpha$) (Krippendorff, 2004) for measuring the agreement between both annotators, resulting in an alpha value of 0.691. According to Krippendorff (2004), tentative conclusions are acceptable where alpha $\leq$ 0.667. The low agreement value can be attested to the following observations. The role of the culture of the then period, and knowledge of the language itself to recognize allusion and wordplay respectively contribute majorly. Failure to understand the invalidity of the argument presented by the speaker leads to a Null tag in place of Fallacious Reasoning by the annotator. The common feature of dramatic irony with both exaggeration (Section 4.5.6) and Fallacious Reasoning is the presenting of a false statement to the listener, causing a grey area for annotation. Finally, the knowledge base possessed, culture exposed to, the emotion experienced at the time of annotation influences the individual's subjectivity of humor (Attardo, 2003; Jiang et al., 2019; Martin and Ford, 2018), contributing to the disagreement in the annotation of humor categories.

# 6 Conclusion and Future Work

The paper describes the work done on developing a fine-grained hierarchical annotation schema for Conversational Humor. The annotation was performed on a relevant dataset, a prominent Telugu play called *Kanyasulkam*. The inter-annotator disagreement highlighted the complexity of the task as well as the domain itself. As mentioned in the introduction, the schema can be utilised for persona identification, a use case especially beneficial for the literary field. For example, when analysing a Shakespearean character, analysing their sense of humor may help the researcher recognize their pertinent traits. This study also finds that inclusion of cultural nuances in the play has a significant effect on the perception of humor. Further, this annotation schema can be applied to other culturally significant works by utilizing the analysis provided in this work. However, when applying this schema to other works, it is to be noted that the types and techniques listed here are non-exhaustive and more can be added based on the language and cultural significance of the data being annotated. If a computer were to generate humor, the traditional meaning would mean that it could generate "jokes" (knock-knock jokes, etc.) but would fail to generate conversational humor. It is believed that this work will aid in automating this process.


## References

Richard Alexander. 1997. *Aspects of verbal humour in English*, volume 13. Gunter Narr Verlag.

Gordon W Allport. 1961. *Pattern and growth in personality*. New York: Holt, Rinehart and Winston.

Salvatore Attardo and Victor Raskin. 1991. Script theory revis (it) ed: Joke similarity and joke representation model. *Humor: International Journal of Humor Research*.

Salvatore Attardo. 2000. Irony as relevant inappropriateness. *Journal of pragmatics*, 32(6):793–826.

Salvatore Attardo. 2003. Introduction: the pragmatics of humor. *Journal of Pragmatics*, 35(9):1287–1294.

Karl E Beckson and Arthur Ganz. 1989. *Literary terms: A dictionary*. Macmillan.

Roy R Behrens. 1977. Beyond caricature: On types of humor in art. *Journal of Creative Behavior*, 11(3):165–75.

Kim Binsted, Anton Nijholt, Oliviero Stock, Carlo Strapparava, G Ritchie, R Manurung, H Pain, Annalu Waller, and D O'Mara. 2006. Computational humor. *IEEE Intelligent Systems*, 21(2):59–69.

Herbert H Clark. 1996. *Using language*. Cambridge university press.

Jacob Cohen. 1960. A coefficient of agreement for nominal scales. *Educational and psychological measurement*, 20(1):37–46.

Dirk Delabastita. 2005. Cross-language comedy in shakespeare. *Humor*, 18(2):161–184.

Marta Dynel. 2008. No aggression, only teasing: The pragmatics of teasing and banter. *Lodz papers in pragmatics*, 4(2):241–261.

Marta Dynel. 2009. Beyond a joke: Types of conversational humour. *Language and Linguistics Compass*, 3(5):1284–1299.

Marta Dynel. 2011. I'll be there for you: On participation-based sitcom humour. *The pragmatics of humour across discourse domains*, 311:333.

Marta Dynel. 2013. Humorous phenomena in dramatic discourse. *The European Journal of Humour Research*, 1(1):22–60.

Kristy Beers Fägersten. 2012. *Who's swearing now? The social aspects of conversational swearing*. Cambridge Scholars Publishing.

Norman T Feather and Rebecca Sherman. 2002. Envy, resentment, schadenfreude, and sympathy: Reactions to deserved and undeserved achievement and subsequent failure. *Personality and Social Psychology Bulletin*, 28(7):953–961.

Matthew Finch. 2010. Thrown voices: A series of dramatic monologues, with a discussion of the genre.

Harry J Gensler. 2010. *The A to Z of Logic*. Number 169. Rowman & Littlefield.

François Grosjean. 1982. *Life with two languages: An introduction to bilingualism*. Harvard University Press.

Christian Hempelmann, Victor Raskin, and Katrina E Triezenberg. 2006. Computer, tell me a joke... but please make it funny: Computational humor with ontological semantics. In *FLAIRS Conference*, volume 13, pages 746–751.

Janet Holmes and Meredith Marra. 2002. Having a laugh at work: How humour contributes to workplace culture. *Journal of pragmatics*, 34(12):1683–1710.

Tonglin Jiang, Hao Li, and Yubo Hou. 2019. Cultural differences in humor perception, usage, and implications. *Frontiers in psychology*, 10:123.

Leo Kant and Elisabeth Norman. 2019. You must be joking! benign violations, power asymmetry, and humor in a broader social context. *Frontiers in psychology*, 10:1380.

Eunhee Kim. 2006. Reasons and motivations for code-mixing and code-switching. *Issues in EFL*, 4(1):43–61.

Roger J Kreuz and Richard M Roberts. 1993. On satire and parody: The importance of being ironic. *Metaphor and Symbol*, 8(2):97–109.

Klaus Krippendorff. 2018. *Content analysis: An introduction to its methodology*. Sage publications.

Giselinde Kuipers et al. 2014. Schadenfreude and social life: a comparative perspective on the expression and regulation of mirth at the expense of others. *Schadenfreude. Understanding Pleasure at the Misfortune of Others. Cambridge University Press: Cambridge*, pages 259–294.

Colin Wayne Leach, Russell Spears, Nyla R Branscombe, and Bertjan Doosje. 2003. Malicious pleasure: Schadenfreude at the suffering of another group. *Journal of personality and social psychology*, 84(5):932.

Carsten Levisen. 2014. The story of "danish happiness": Global discourse and local semantics. *International Journal of Language and Culture*, 1(2):174–193.

Rod A Martin and Thomas Ford. 2018. *The psychology of humor: An integrative approach*. Academic press.

Abraham H Maslow. 1954. The instinctoid nature of basic needs. *Journal of personality*, 22(3):326–347.

Paul E McGhee. 1989. Introduction: Recent developments in humor research. *Journal of children in contemporary society*, 20(1-2):1–12.

A Peter McGraw and Caleb Warren. 2010. Benign violations: Making immoral behavior funny. *Psychological science*, 21(8):1141–1149.

John C Meyer. 2000. Humor as a double-edged sword: Four functions of humor in communication. *Communication theory*, 10(3):310–331.

Rada Mihalcea and Carlo Strapparava. 2006. Learning to laugh (automatically): Computational models for humor recognition. *Computational Intelligence*, 22(2):126–142.

Kerry Mullan and Christine Béal. 2018. Introduction: Conversational humor: Forms, functions and practices across cultures. *Intercultural Pragmatics*, 15(4):451–456.

Werner Neuse. 1934. " erlebte rede" und" innerer monolog" in den erzählenden schriften arthur schnitzlers. *Publications of the Modern Language Association of America*, pages 327–355.

Neal R Norrick. 1989. Intertextuality in humor. *Humor*, 2(2):117–140.

Neal R Norrick. 1993. *Conversational joking: Humor in everyday talk*. Indiana University Press.

Neal R Norrick. 2003. Issues in conversational joking. *Journal of pragmatics*, 35(9):1333–1359.

Neal R Norrick. 2004. Hyperbole, extreme case formulation. *Journal of Pragmatics*, 36(9):1727–1739.

Alan Partington. 2006. *The linguistics of laughter: A corpus-assisted study of laughter-talk*. Routledge.

Durga Srinivasa T Rao. 2004. Problems of translatiing satire from english to telugu and vice versa: an evaluation.

Victor Raskin. 1979. Semantic mechanisms of humor. In *Annual Meeting of the Berkeley Linguistics Society*, volume 5, pages 325–335.

Victor Raskin. 1985. Semantic theory of humor. In *Semantic Mechanisms of Humor*, pages 99–147. Springer.

Antonio Reyes, Paolo Rosso, and Davide Buscaldi. 2012. From humor recognition to irony detection: The figurative language of social media. *Data & Knowledge Engineering*, 74:1–12.

Harvey Sacks and Gail Jefferson. 1995. Lectures on conversation.

James M Shea. 1963. *Convention and invention: Soliloquy in Shakespearean tragedy*. University of Windsor.

Edward Shewan. 1994. *Applications of Grammar: Principles of Effective Communication, Book 4*. Christian Liberty Press.

Mick Short. 2018. *Exploring the language of poems, plays and prose*. Routledge.

Jeff Siegel. 1995. How to get a laugh in fijian: Code-switching and humor. *Language in Society*, pages 95–110.

Richard H Smith, Terence J Turner, Ron Garonzik, Colin W Leach, Vanessa Urch-Druskat, and Christine M Weston. 1996. Envy and schadenfreude. *Personality and Social Psychology Bulletin*, 22(2):158–168.

Richard H Smith, Caitlin AJ Powell, David JY Combs, and David Ryan Schurtz. 2009. Exploring the when and why of schadenfreude. *Social and Personality Psychology Compass*, 3(4):530–546.

Julia M Taylor. 2009. Computational detection of humor: A dream or a nightmare? the ontological semantics approach. In *2009 IEEE/WIC/ACM International Joint Conference on Web Intelligence and Intelligent Agent Technology*, volume 3, pages 429–432. IEEE.

Joanna Thornborrow and Shân Wareing. 1998. *Patterns in language: An introduction to language and literary style*. Psychology Press.

Wilco W Van Dijk, Jaap W Ouwerkerk, and Sjoerd Goslinga. 2009. The impact of deservingness on schadenfreude and sympathy: Further evidence. *The Journal of Social Psychology*, 149(3):390–392.

Bernard Weiner. 1993. On sin versus sickness: A theory of perceived responsibility and social motivation. *American psychologist*, 48(9):957.

Bernard Weiner. 2006. *Social motivation, justice, and the moral emotions: An attributional approach*. Psychology Press.

# Appendix

|  | **A2** | | | |
|---|---|---|---|---|
| **A1** | | Verbal | Situational | NULL | Total |
| | Verbal | 1559 | 120 | 566 | 2425 |
| | Situational | 191 | 354 | 284 | 829 |
| | Null | 290 | 208 | 2893 | 3391 |
| | Total | 2040 | 682 | 3923 | 6645 |

Table 1: Cohen's Kappa for Level-1

|  | **A2** | | | |
|---|---|---|---|---|
| **A1** | | Benign | Non-Benign | Null | Total |
| | Benign | 336 | 9 | 127 | 472 |
| | Non-benign | 412 | 802 | 739 | 1953 |
| | Null | 220 | 261 | 3739 | 4220 |
| | Total | 968 | 1072 | 4605 | 6645 |

Table 2: Cohen's Kappa for Level-3

|  | **A2** | | | | | |
|---|---|---|---|---|---|---|
| **A1** | | Teasing | Retort | Banter | Schadenfreude | Null | Total |
| | Teasing | 62 | 1 | 0 | 0 | 38 | 101 |
| | Retort | 11 | 10 | 0 | 0 | 13 | 33 |
| | Banter | 1 | 0 | 131 | 0 | 6 | 138 |
| | Schadenfreude | 3 | 5 | 0 | 93 | 185 | 286 |
| | Null | 123 | 10 | 12 | 107 | 5835 | 6087 |
| | Total | 200 | 26 | 143 | 200 | 6076 | 6645 |

Table 3: Cohen's Kappa for Level-4

| **Level-1** | **Level-2** | **Level-3** | **Level-4** | |
|---|---|---|---|---|
| Conversational | Monologue | Benign | **Types** | **Techniques** |
| Non-Conversational | Dialogue | Non-Benign | Teasing | Dramatic Irony |
| | | | Banter | Sarcasm |
| | | | Retort | Satire |
| | | | Schadenfreude | Fallacious Reasoning |
| | | | | Exaggeration |
| | | | | Use of Foreign Language |
| | | | | Allusion |
| | | | | Profanity |
| | | | | Other Stylistic Figures |

Table 4: Hierarchical Annotation Schema

| Tag | Description | Example |
|---|---|---|
| **C** | Conversational | *Conversation has one speaker and two listeners.* |
| **NC** | Non-Conversational | *The Three Stooges getting poked in the eye or thrown pies at their faces.* |
| **M** | Monologue | *Only one speaker present and no listeners.* |
| **D** | Dialogue | *Conversation has one speaker and three listeners.* |
| **B** | Benign | *[A short person can't reach a shelf by a wide margin] A friend says, "If only you were an inch taller."* |
| **NB** | Non-Benign | *"The woman who is yelling in the street is a rascal that bites men"* |
| **T** | Teasing | *[A woman spills her drink] Her boyfriend says, "Let me grab a sippy cup for you"* |
| **R** | Retort | *"I'm sorry but I don't speak bullshit."* |
| **Ba** | Banter | *A series of teases and retorts between speakers.* |
| **S** | Schadenfreude | *"Somebody stole my lunch out of the fridge at work today. The worst part about it... I'm working from home."* |
| **DIrn** | Dramatic Irony | *[A character is known to be promiscuous] He says, "None can be loyal to a woman as I am"* |
| **Sar** | Sarcasm | *[Torrential rain on an expected sunny day] "Oh what warm weather!"* |
| **Str** | Satire | *"People say jokes are dead. But one can be found alive and kicking in the White House."* |
| **FR** | Fallacious Reasoning | *"I never generalize because everyone who does is a hypocrite."* |
| **Ex** | Exaggeration | *"How are you still hungry? You have a bottomless pit for a stomach."* |
| **FL** | Use of Foreign language | *[A mother asks her son to come home] He replies, "Je ne comprends pas!"* |
| **A** | Allusion | *"Don't act like Romeo in front of her!"* |
| **P** | Profanity | *"The idiotic excuse of a brother I have has no sense of decency!"* |
| **O** | Other identified techniques | *"She was as tall as a six-foot-two-inch tree."* |

Table 5: Humor Tagset

# Modeling Ambiguity with Many Annotators and Self-Assessments of Annotator Certainty


**Melanie Andresen**
Institute for Natural Language Processing
University of Stuttgart
`melanie.andresen@ims.uni-stuttgart.de`

**Michael Vauth**
Institute of Linguistics and Literary Studies
TU Darmstadt
`vauth@linglit.tu-darmstadt.de`

**Heike Zinsmeister**
Institute for German Language and Literature
University of Hamburg
`heike.zinsmeister@uni-hamburg.de`


## Abstract


Most annotation efforts assume that annotators will agree on labels, if the annotation categories are well-defined and documented in annotation guidelines. However, this is not always true. For instance, content-related questions such as 'Is this sentence about topic X?' are unlikely to elicit the same answer from all annotators. Additional specifications in the guidelines are helpful to some extent, but can soon get overspecified by rules that cannot be justified by a research question. In this study, we model the semantic category 'illness' and its use in a gradual way. For this purpose, we (i) ask many annotators (30 votes per item, 960 items) for their opinion in a crowdsourcing experiment, (ii) ask annotators to indicate their certainty with respect to their annotation, and (iii) compare this across two different text types. We show that results of multiple annotations and average annotator certainty correlate, but many ambiguities can only be captured if several people contribute. The annotated data allow us to filter for sentences with high or low agreement and analyze causes of disagreement, thus getting a better understanding of people's perception of illness—as an example of a semantic category—as well as of the content of our annotated texts.


## 1 Introduction

Natural language is full of phenomena of ambiguity and uncertainty. However, we do not yet have a standard procedure for integrating ambiguities in formal models—or even for identifying ambiguities in the first place. Most supervised machine learning tasks assume that there is a ground truth—an inter-subjectively correct annotation. Algorithms rely on this as unambiguous training data. For the most part, annotation efforts assume that multiple annotators will agree on labels, if annotation categories are well-defined and the annotation guidelines are clear and comprehensive. Hence, low agreement scores are considered to indicate poor data quality. However, there is also an increasing awareness that this is not always the case (Poesio and Artstein, 2005; Beigman Klebanov et al., 2008; Morris, 2010; Rohde et al., 2016; Amidei et al., 2018; Pavlick and Kwiatkowski, 2019). This is backed up by findings in cognitive science and linguistics that suggest that language phenomena are predominantly gradual in nature instead of being discrete categories, for instance in prototype theory (Lakoff, 1987).






*The 14th Linguistic Annotation Workshop*, pages 48–59
Barcelona, Spain (Online), December 12, 2020.

Two common possible ways of capturing ambiguity in text are asking more than one annotator to annotate a category and/or asking annotators to explicitly mark ambiguities or uncertainties. In the study conducted for this paper, we combine both strategies to model the semantic category 'illness' and its use in a gradual way. Illness lends itself to this type of analysis, because it is a highly socially constructed concept that makes ambiguities and disagreements likely. Furthermore, this topic is of interest to linguists, humanists and social scientists alike and thus facilitated cooperation in our project *hermA* (Gaidys et al., 2017). We use crowdsourcing in order to get the input of many annotators and use their overall vote as a measure of how clearly a sentence belongs to the topic 'illness'. In addition, we ask annotators to indicate their certainty with respect to their annotation. Our aim is to investigate to what extent multiple annotations and self-assessments yield similar results, deriving recommendations for future research. Furthermore, we identify reasons for disagreement in a qualitative analysis contrasting controversial and non-controversial sentences. Our data comprise sentences from German literary texts and transcripts of political debates, thus allowing for a comparison of text types.

## 2 Related Work

In this section we present previous research dealing with ambiguity in annotation settings with multiple annotators. With regard to agreement and reliability, Potter and Levine-Donnerstein (1999) (in the context of content analysis) differentiate three types of content to be annotated: '*manifest content* (directly observable events), *pattern latent content* (events that need to be inferred indirectly from the observations), and *projective latent content* (loosely said, events that require a subjective interpretation from the annotator)' (Reidsma and op den Akker, 2008, 8, summarizing Potter and Levine-Donnerstein, 1999, 261). The type of question asked in this paper ('Is this sentence about topic X?') involves projective latent content and some disagreement is to be expected. When annotating something of which people have an everyday understanding, it can be more helpful to rely on the 'coders' existing schema' instead of defining more and more detailed annotation rules (Potter and Levine-Donnerstein, 1999, 260).

In our study, we combine multiple annotations and self-assessment of the annotators' certainty, as has been done before by Poesio and Artstein (2005). They study the annotation of anaphora in dialogue data, where many references are vague without leading to misunderstandings. (See also Versley (2006) for a detailed analysis of causes of ambiguities in coreference annotation.) The study attempts to capture ambiguities by, on the one hand, letting 18 students annotate the same text and, on the other hand, giving annotators the option of marking more than one antecedent if they perceive the reference as ambiguous. They conclude that it is important to consider cases of 'implicit ambiguity' which only emerge in the disagreements of multiple annotators and the individual annotator is not aware of. Nedoluzhko and Mírovský (2013) report on the annotation of coreference and bridging relations in the Prague Dependency Treebank. They let annotators explicitly mark how certain they were about each annotated item. The analysis shows a correlation between annotator certainty and agreement, but also reveals many cases of disagreement despite high certainty. They agree with Poesio and Artstein (2005) that ambiguity can be captured more fully by using multiple annotators instead of only letting annotators mark it explicitly.

Further studies consider disagreements between annotators as valuable information. Rohde et al. (2016) conduct a crowdsourcing experiment to study which discourse adverbials licence which conjunctions (e. g. a clause with *instead* can start with the conjunctions *but, so,* or *and*). 28 annotators were presented with sentences with one of 20 adverbials and a gap for a possible conjunction. The results show that all adverbials have one to three conjunctions that participants considered acceptable, depending on context as well as individual preference. This variability could only be captured by a high number of annotators per item (similar: Scholman and Demberg, 2017). Morris and Hirst (2004) investigate subjectivity in text interpretation. They let five annotators identify semantically related word groups in a text and specify the semantic relations between the words. While the annotators agree on some core words, individual differences are large. Morris (2010) extends this method and concludes that '40% of the lexical cohesion perceived in text is subjectively interpreted' (Morris, 2010, 141) and therefore argues for a more reader-oriented modeling of text in computational linguistics.

Annotation with multiple annotators has been explored in literary studies, as polyvalence is an important textual characteristic for the definition of literariness. Gius and Jacke (2017) pose the question of how the falsifiability of interpretations can be guaranteed. Their proposal is to use computer-aided narratological annotation to document interpretative decisions, which in turn can make conflicting interpretations visible. While some textual ambiguities do not have consequences for the overall interpretation, some ambiguities result in more than one possible interpretation of a literary text. Hammond et al. (2013) target ambiguity in *To the Lighthouse* by Virginia Woolf. The novel makes extensive use of free indirect speech that cannot be attributed unambiguously to one character or the narrator. To capture possible attributions, they let three to four student annotators analyze the same text span. They reach a raw agreement of slightly less than 70%, however, for many text spans more than one analysis is valid.

Multiple annotations have also been exploited for machine learning. Plank et al. (2014) use the information of annotator agreement to improve POS-tagging. In training their classification model, they sanction mistakes on tags with high inter-annotator agreement more heavily than on tags with low agreement. Their experiments result in annotation improvements in several evaluation settings. Reidsma and op den Akker (2008) optimize their classifiers for high precision by allowing the classifier to make no decision on low-agreement parts of the data. Pavlick and Kwiatkowski (2019) work on entailment, i. e. the question whether the proposition of a sentence $B$ can be inferred from the proposition of a sentence $A$. They ask 50 annotators for their judgment on several hundred sentence pairs and show that the disagreement in the annotations cannot be attributed to noise only, but indicates that different interpretations are possible for many sentence pairs. They argue that computational models for textual entailment should therefore produce a full distribution of possible human answers instead of just one aggregated score.

In a previous study of our own project, Adelmann et al. (2019) annotated illness and compared an approach based on semantic fields with manual annotations. The agreement between the two annotators was rather low. The attempt to rectify this problem by improving the annotation guidelines led to the inclusion of very detailed rules that for the most part could not be justified by the demands of the research questions. In truth, illness is simply not a discrete concept, but can be present in a sentence to varying degrees. For this reason, we decided to approach the annotation of illness in a different way. We conducted a crowdsourcing study on the decision task whether a sentence is about illness or not. Similar to Poesio and Artstein (2005) and Nedoluzhko and Mírovský (2013), we combine multiple annotators with a self-assessment of annotator certainty. Closer to Pavlick and Kwiatkowski (2019), we harvested a statistically relevant number of 30 judgements per sentence.

## 3   Annotation Experiment[1]

**Data.**   The sentences that were presented to the participants were extracted from two corpora that were compiled in the digital humanities project *hermA* (Gaidys et al., 2017):

- Fiction Corpus: 40 novels from the dystopian genre (2000–2019), 135,000 sentences
- Transcript Corpus: written versions of speeches from the German federal parliament ('Bundestag'), filtered for texts that cover an aspect of the topic of telemedicine, 990,000 sentences

We chose these two corpora because we wanted to cover different text types that we assume to differ with respect to ambiguity: Literary texts are said to be especially ambiguous and authors play with ambiguity to create artistic value. Political speeches aim more at a common understanding and should be as clear as possible, but can also be deliberately ambiguous. Both corpora were split into sentences.

**Sentence Selection.**   Sentences were sampled randomly. To ensure that the topic illness was present in a relatively large proportion of the sample, we filtered for sentences that contain a lexical item from the 'semantic field' (Lehrer, 1974; Vassilyev, 1974) of illness, which we realized as hyponyms of the term *illness* in GermaNet (Hamp and Feldweg, 1997; Henrich and Hinrichs, 2010).[2] For each corpus, we included 380 sentences with a lexical item related to illness and 100 without such a word, resulting in 960 items in total.

---

[1] We published the annotations as a Zenodo dataset. See `https://doi.org/10.5281/zenodo.4088446`.

[2] We extended the original list of 586 hyponyms with inflectional variants using the SMOR (Schmid et al., 2004) derivate Zmorge (Sennrich and Kunz, 2014), resulting in a list of 2,026 wordforms.

**Question Design.** The selected sentences were presented to the annotators with a context of five sentences before and after the target sentence. Less context was included if the text began or ended in this span. The target sentence was printed in bold. The annotators were presented with two or. three questions: The first one asked for a binary judgment in response to the question: Is the topic of illness discussed in the sentence printed in bold? ('Wird im fett gedruckten Satz das Thema Krankheit thematisiert?'). Given the condition that the answer to this question was 'yes', there was a follow-up question about topic centrality: Annotators were asked whether illness is the central or rather a marginal topic of the sentence. The final question asked for the annotators' certainty: How certain are you about the answer to question 1? ('Wie sicher bist Du Dir bei der Antwort zu Frage 1?'). Possible answers were very certain ('sehr sicher'), rather certain ('eher sicher'), rather uncertain ('eher unsicher'), and very uncertain ('sehr unsicher').

**Guidelines.** As already mentioned above, the goal of this study was not to review strictly formalized annotation guidelines nor the creation of a consensual gold standard. Since we want to depict ambiguities through annotations, we decided to use extremely minimalist guidelines. In the task description, we even pointed out that we are interested in the subjective assessments of the annotators. However, we gave three example sentences: In the first, illness is the central topic of the sentence (a), in the second, illness is a marginal topic (b), and in the third, illness is not discussed (c).

(a) *Frank liegt schon seit einer Woche mit Fieber im Bett.*
    'Frank has been in bed with a fever for a week.'
(b) *Ich freue mich sehr darauf, [...] meine Cousine zu treffen, die lange erkältet war.*
    'I am very much looking forward to meeting my cousin [...], who has had a cold for a long time-.'
(c) *Zum Frühstück esse ich am liebsten Müsli.*
    'For breakfast I prefer to eat cereal.'

The question whether a sentence deals with illness is an individual, conceptual decision. By using minimalist guidelines, we hope to cover disagreements caused by conceptual differences as to what the annotators consider to be illness as well as disagreements caused by grammar or style.

**Annotation Procedure.** We collected 30 judgments for each of the 960 items. For the annotation procedure, we used the crowdsourcing platform *Appen* The crowdworkers were paid $0.70 for each annotated page with ten sentences each. Based on a pretest, we assumed that this would result in more than a minimum wage of $10 for annotators working at average speed. During the annotation process it became apparent that the crowdsourcing platform could not supply us with a sufficient number of German speaking annotators. For this reason we additionally asked the students at our university to participate in the study. The students were paid €0.80 per page.

For purposes of quality control, a number of test questions were used to exclude annotators who either did not understand the task or did not intend to work seriously on the task. As test questions we selected sentences that we considered unambiguous with respect to the question whether they are about illness. However, some of the test sentences turned out to be more ambiguous than we expected. If the annotators gave arguments for their deviant answer, and thus showed that they were actively engaging with the task, we accepted their answers.

In total, 77 annotators participated in our study, 34 crowdworkers and 43 students. The extent of their work varies widely, ranging between 9 and 828 items. On average, participants annotated 374 items, with a huge standard deviation of 305 items. (See Figure 1 for the full distribution.) About half of our data set was annotated by crowdworkers, the other half by students. In order to identify a possible effect of annotator types, we compared the proportion of votes for illness per annotator from the two groups. There is a significant difference in the annotations of the sentences from the Fiction Corpus with semantic field words ($n = 380$, Mann-Whitney U test, $U = 259.0$, p$< 0.001$, students mean $0.64\pm0.14$, crowdworker mean $0.57\pm0.07$, rank-biserial correlation: $-0.55$). One possible reason for this difference is the fact that most of the students are studying language and literature and thus might approach the task differently than the crowdworkers. We do not consider this effect problematic and do not account for it in the analysis. There is no significant difference in the proportion of 'very sure' votes to the question on the annotators' certainty.

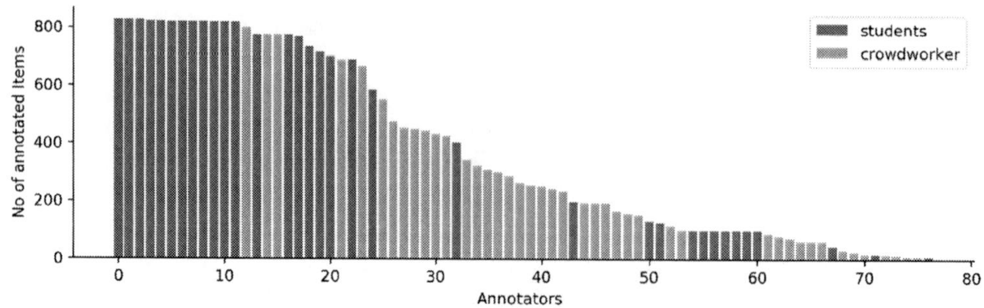

Figure 1: Our 77 annotators, sorted by the number of annotated items (crowdworkers in orange, students in blue)

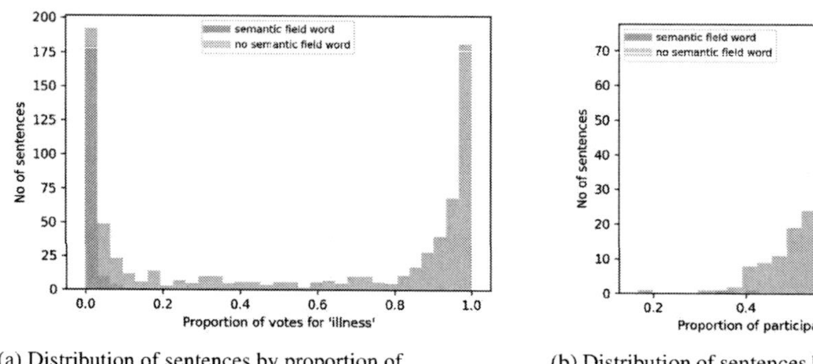

(a) Distribution of sentences by proportion of annotators that voted for 'illness' (n=980)

(b) Distribution of sentences by proportion of annotators that indicated to be 'very certain' (n=980)

Figure 2: Response distributions (blue bars: semantic field word, orange bars: not a semantic field word).

## 4   Results

**Distribution of Annotation Categories.**   Figure 2a shows the distribution of answers to the first question: 'Is this sentence about illness?'. A value of 0 on the x axis means that all 30 annotators said that this sentence is not about illness, a value of 1 means that all 30 annotators said that the sentence is about illness. We can see that for most of the sentences without a semantic field word (orange bars), all annotators agreed that this sentence is not about illness. Only 21 of 200 sentences got at least some votes for illness. On the other hand, responses for sentences with a semantic field word are distributed much more widely (blue bars). About one quarter of the sentences is unanimously considered to be about illness (181), another quarter is unanimously considered not to be about illness (192). About half of all sentences with a semantic field word caused some degree of disagreement between the annotators. We conclude that the absence of a semantic field word is a good indicator that the sentence is not about illness. However, the presence of a semantic field word still leaves us with about a 50:50 chance for the sentence to be about illness or not. This decision appears to be non-trivial for human annotators.

The second question ('How certain are you about your answer to question 1?') reveals that the annotators were, overall, rather confident about their answers: When looking at all 28,800 answers to this question, 81.9% of the time the annotators said they were 'very certain' about their assessment of the sentence, in 16.5% they were 'rather certain'. Only in very rare cases did the annotators indicate that they were 'rather uncertain' (1.5%) or even 'very uncertain' (0.2%). Aggregated to sentences this results in the distribution in Figure 2b. Despite the high number of 'very certain' votes overall, only 49 of 760 sentences with a semantic field word and 69 of 200 sentences without a semantic field word get 'very certain' votes only. This is because the annotators had very individual certainty profiles: The proportion of 'very sure' votes per annotator ranges between 0 (one annotator) and 1 (eight annotators), with a mean of $0.78 \pm 0.20$. In 362 cases an annotator (55 different annotators) asserted to be very sure about the topic annotation, but annotated against the majority vote. 17 different annotators declared at least once to be very sure while all other annotators were of the opposite opinion.

**Agreement.** For the calculation of inter-annotator agreement, we use the coefficient Krippendorff's $\alpha$ (Krippendorff, 1980; Krippendorff, 2013)[3]. This coefficient does not require all items to be annotated by the same annotators (see Artstein and Poesio, 2008, for an overview). Following the recommendations of Artstein (2017, 304), we additionally calculate the agreement scores for our two subcorpora and two conditions (semantic field word vs. non semantic field word) individually.

Regarding the first question ('Is this sentence about illness?'), the agreement for the full data set is 0.690. This value indicates substantial agreement (Landis and Koch, 1977). As Figure 2a suggests, the agreement varies depending on the presence of a semantic field word: The agreement on all sentences without a semantic field word is very high with 0.896. Sentences with a semantic field word achieve a much lower agreement of 0.658. This can be explained by the fact that most sentences without a semantic field word are totally unrelated to illness, making the question a trivial one. There is also a moderate difference in agreement between the two corpora: The agreement for the sentences of the Transcript Corpus is 0.756 and the agreement for the sentences of the Fiction Corpus is 0.637.

We did not calculate the agreement for the second question ('How certain are you about your answer to question 1?'), because in answering this question, the annotators do not judge the text shared by all annotators, but their individual annotation experience.

Overall, the agreement scores show a high annotation consistency, given the fact that the annotators did not get further instructions by annotation guidelines. There is a core idea of illness that is shared by most annotators. At the same time we see a considerable number of sentences where the annotators disagree. These sentences can be said to cover the peripheral understanding of illness that is only shared by subgroups of annotators. In the following section we will look more closely at how this relates to annotator certainty and possible causes of disagreement in the sentences themselves.

**Topic Centrality.** Annotators who said the sentence was about illness had to additionally specify whether illness is the central topic or only a marginal topic of the sentence. For this question, our annotators reach an agreement of 0.246, which is hardly above chance level. For this reason we will not analyze the data for this question in detail. The answers are correlated with the second question about annotator certainty: If the annotators considered illness the central topic, 83% were 'very certain' about their answer. If illness was only a marginal topic, only 58% were 'very certain'. We therefore assume that the (lacking) centrality of the topic is one of many possible reasons for uncertainty. The comprehensive assessment of causes of uncertainty would require a more complex question design.

**Disagreement and Uncertainty.** Our hypothesis was that if many annotators indicate a high uncertainty, the agreement for these items would be low. For the measurement of agreement per item we chose the highest proportion of participants that agree on one answer. As we have two categories, this is a value between 0.5 and 1 with 0.5 indicating that half of our annotators chose one answer and the other half the other answer, 1 indicating that all annotators agree (on either category).[4] Figure 3 shows the relationship between the agreement proportion on question 1 ('Is this sentence about illness?') on the y axis and the proportion of participants that were very certain about their answer on the x axis. Every data point is one possible value combination and the size corresponds to the number of sentences that match this value combination (between 1 and 129). We can see a clear correlation that is confirmed by a Pearson's correlation coefficient of 0.68 ($p < 0.001$):[5] If many participants were unsure about their answer, there is also much variation in their answers.

The correlation indicates that a considerable amount of variation can be captured by self-assessment of the annotators. However, there still remains a substantial amount of variation that is only captured

---

[3] As implemented in the R package 'irr' (https://cran.r-project.org/web/packages/irr/irr.pdf).

[4] This is similarly captured by the very common measure of entropy, however, we consider a linear measure more appropriate for our interpretation.

[5] This effect is robust even if all items with an agreement of 1 are excluded ($r = 0.57$).

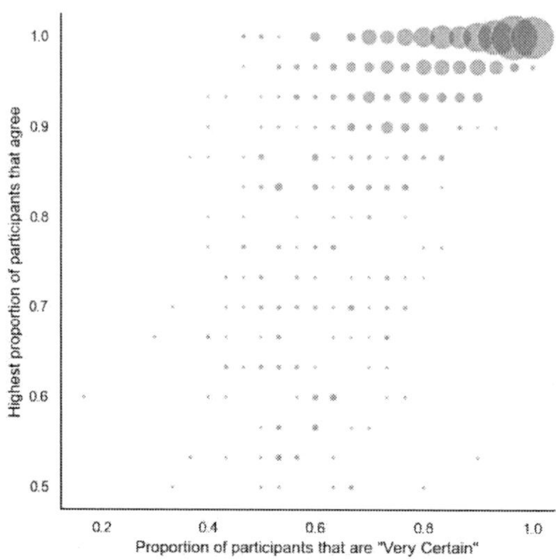

Figure 3: Relationship between the proportion of participants that agree on an answer and the proportion of participants indicating to be 'very certain' (n=960)

by the combination of multiple annotators. We also have to keep in mind that, while the proportion of annotators that are very certain correlates with the answers of the group, this must not be true for the individual annotators. If the annotation targets a phenomenon where ambiguity is expected and the research question makes it desirable to capture it, multiple annotators are highly beneficial.

**Reasons for Disagreement.** To explore the reasons for disagreement, we evaluate the semantic field words and the sentences on which the annotators disagreed most. We calculate the average agreement of all sentences in which the semantic field words occur, see Table 1. Among the semantic field words that occur in sentences with low average agreement is a group of words which refer to psychological states: *Paranoia* ('paranoia'), *Wahn* ('madness'), *Traumata* ('trauma'), *Sucht* ('addiction'), *Schock* ('shock') and *Anfall* ('seizure'). We assume that the low agreement values in sentences with these terms are caused by different opinions about whether these states have the status of a disease. Additionally, some of the terms describe only short-lived states that therefore have a debatable status: *Anfall* ('seizure'), *Schock* ('shock') and *Husten* ('cough'). We additionally inspected the ten words with the highest average agreement. For five of these words the annotators (almost) agreed that the sentences deal with illness. These words are specific names of diseases: *Tuberkulose* ('tuberculosis'), *Diabetes* ('diabetes'), *Malaria* ('malaria'), *Krebs* ('cancer'), *Leukämie* ('leukemia'). For the other five terms, the annotators agreed that they do not address any disease: *Flechten* ('lichens'), *Attacke(n)* ('attack(s)'), *Verdrängung* ('repression'), and *Abhängigkeiten* ('dependencies') are highly ambiguous, because they can describe a pathological state, but also have a completely separate semantic dimension.

In order to determine what causes disagreement above the lexical level, we manually inspected the 50 sentences with the lowest agreement scores and 50 random sentences with complete agreement. 38 of the sentences with low agreement belong to the Fiction Corpus. Some disagreements can be explained by the lexical phenomena described before: mental phenomena and short-lived states. In addition, some *grammatical* and *stylistic* phenomena prove to be important. One example are negations, which are either explicitly marked by a negator as in example (1), but can also be realized in a syntactically more complex way, as example (2) shows:

(1) *Kein Husten, kein Lebenszeichen.*
    'No cough, no sign of life.'
(2) *Das heißt jedoch auch, dass beispielsweise eine Frau, die vor vierunddreißig Jahren geboren wurde, keine persönlichen Erinnerungen an körperliches Leiden besitzt.*

| semantic field word | translation | frequency | agreement mean | proportion pos. annotations |
| --- | --- | --- | --- | --- |
| Flechten | lichens/eczemas | 5 | 1.00 | 0.00 |
| Tuberkulose | tuberculosis | 5 | 1.00 | 1.00 |
| Attacke | attack | 9 | 1.00 | 0.00 |
| Diabetes | diabetes | 8 | 1.00 | 1.00 |
| Attacken | attacks | 11 | 0.99 | 0.10 |
| Malaria | malaria | 5 | 0.99 | 0.99 |
| Verdrängung | displacement/repression | 11 | 0.99 | 0.01 |
| Krebs | cancer | 10 | 0.99 | 0.99 |
| Abhängigkeiten | addictions/dependencies | 6 | 0.99 | 0.01 |
| Leukämie | leukemia | 8 | 0.99 | 0.99 |
| ... | ... | ... | ... | ... |
| Pilz | mushroom/fungus | 5 | 0.91 | 0.09 |
| Anfall | seizure/fit | 11 | 0.86 | 0.45 |
| Leiden | suffering | 8 | 0.85 | 0.60 |
| Schock | shock | 29 | 0.80 | 0.24 |
| Pickel | pimples | 6 | 0.75 | 0.25 |
| Husten | cough | 15 | 0.73 | 0.68 |
| Sucht | addiction | 5 | 0.73 | 0.48 |
| Traumata | traumas | 9 | 0.73 | 0.71 |
| Wahn | delusion/madness | 6 | 0.72 | 0.34 |
| Paranoia | paranoia | 7 | 0.70 | 0.60 |

Table 1: Semantic field words with the lowest and highest agreement scores

> 'However, this also means that, for instance, a woman born forty-three years ago has no personal memories of physical suffering.'

Among the stylistic phenomena, metaphorical uses of disease symptoms in a non-medical context are the most frequent:

(3) *Diese Schizophrenie findet sich auch in der Öffentlichkeit.*
'This schizophrenia is also found in public.'

Finally, there are cases where the narrative representation of events may have led to low agreement values. In some sentences, the narrative instance makes speculative statements (example (4)) or presents the perspective of a narrated character (example (5)):

(4) *Das Ergebnis mochte dann am Ende ein Wahn sein, wie er Branagorn befallen hatte.*
'In the end, the result might have been a delusion, as it had infested Branagorn.'
(5) *Man erklärte es sich dann teils mit dem Schockzustand des Kindes und teils mit der erst her-aufziehenden Dämmerung [...].*
'This was explained partly by the child's state of shock and partly by the approaching dawn [...].'

The examples also show that several features which potentially cause disagreement among annotators can co-occur in a single sentence. Thus, in example (5) the behaviour of a character is attributed to a temporary state of shock and at the same time the narrator distances himself from this explanation.

**Influence of Text Type.** We have seen above that the inter-annotator agreement for the sentences from the Transcript Corpus (0.756) was higher than for those from the Fiction Corpus (0.637). In Figure 4 we compare the two corpora from two additional perspectives: Figure 4a shows one box plot per corpus for the agreement per sentence, measured as the highest proportion of participants that agree. Visual inspection gives an indication that the annotators disagreed more in the literary texts than in the debate transcripts on the question of whether illness was addressed in the sentences. The mean agreement is 0.91 ($\pm$0.13) for the Fiction Corpus sentences and 0.96 ($\pm$0.09) for the Transcript Corpus sentences. The Mann-Whitney rank test confirms that this is a significant difference ($U = 89024.0$, $p < 0.001$). With a rank-biserial correlation of 0.23, the effect size is rather small. As Figure 4b shows, there are also differences between the corpora in how confident the annotators are. The mean proportion of 'very

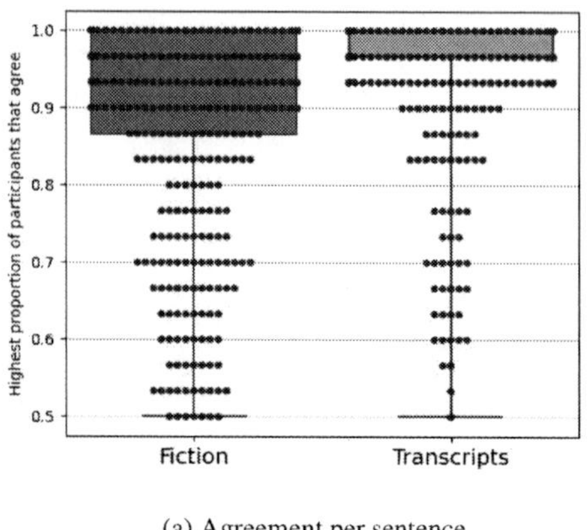

(a) Agreement per sentence

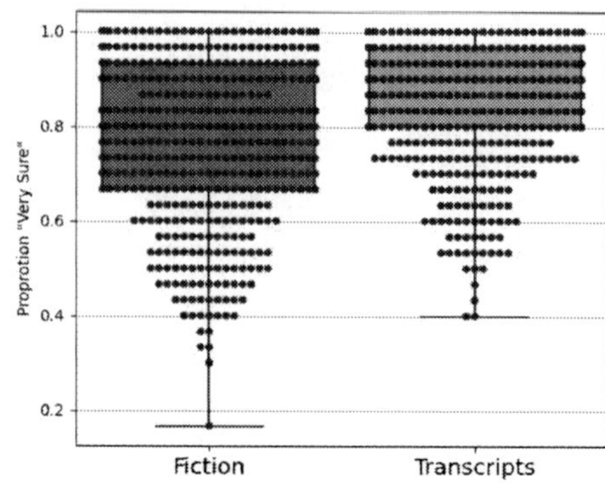

(b) Certainty per sentence

Figure 4: Distribution of agreement and annotation certainty for sentences from the Fiction Corpus (n=480) and the Transcript Corpus (n=480) in contrast

certain' annotators is 0.78($\pm$0.17) for the Fiction Corpus sentences and 0.86 ($\pm$0.13) for the Transcript Corpus sentences. This is a statistically significant difference ($U = 83232.5$, $p > 0.001$) and the effect size is slightly larger (rank-biserial correlation: 0.28).

The differences between the corpora can be explained by the vocabulary associated with the two text types. While the sentences for both corpora were selected by the same semantic field, the corpora largely cover different parts of the semantic field: Of 183 semantic field word types in our sentences, only 50 occur in sentences of both corpora. Table 2 presents the most common semantic field words for the two corpora. Only word forms of the general term *Krankheit* ('illness') are frequent in both corpora. Among the most frequent semantic field words in the transcripts are many abstract terms that have very general meanings: *Missbrauch* ('abuse/misuse'), *Abhängigkeit* ('addiction/dependence'), *Vermeidung* ('avoidance'), *Komplex* ('complex'). These are part of the more technical language that characterizes political discussions compared to literary texts. These words often occur in contexts that are not related to illness. This is also reflected in the overall annotation patterns: In the Transcript Corpus data, 59% of all sentences with full agreement were annotated as not being about illness while this is only true for 40% of sentences from the Fiction Corpus. Beyond that, the top ten include two very specific disease terms, *Aids* ('aids') and *Krebs* ('cancer') that will hardly cause disagreement.

The sentences from the Fiction Corpus, on the other hand, are more concrete. Novels tell the story of a character or a small group of characters, depicting the inner life of these characters. To this end, these texts tend to describe mental states that cannot be clearly classified as symptoms of illness. Furthermore, novels also include words that refer to (mostly) minor symptoms like *Husten* ('cough'), whose status as an illness is debatable and which would usually not be discussed in parliament.

## 5 Discussion and Future Work

In our study, we tested two ways of capturing and modeling ambiguity in texts: By asking many annotators for their judgment and by asking the annotators for a meta annotation about their annotation certainty. We found that low annotator certainty and high variation in judgments are highly correlated. However, many data points that individual annotators were certain about did display variation. In addition, the correlation need not be given for every annotator or even any annotator individually. We conclude that multiple annotations are a useful means to identify and document ambiguity in texts.

Disagreement between our annotators was caused by 1) different concepts of what qualifies as illness (mental phenomena and very short-lived states are controversial), 2) grammatical phenomena like negation, and 3) stylistic properties of the text such as metaphors. Especially in the Fiction Corpus, the information conveyed by the texts can also be ambiguous because the narrative is imprecise, vague or

| Fiction | | | Transcripts | | |
|---|---|---|---|---|---|
| word | translation | frequency | word | translation | frequency |
| Krankheit | disease | 34 | Missbrauch | abuse/misuse | 61 |
| Schock | shock | 28 | Krankheiten | diseases | 44 |
| Krankheiten | diseases | 18 | Abhängigkeit | addiction/dependence | 28 |
| Sommersprossen | freckles | 15 | Krankheit | disease | 26 |
| Husten | cough | 14 | Vermeidung | avoidance | 22 |
| Pilze | fungus/mushrooms | 13 | Komplex | complex | 14 |
| Anfall | seizure | 9 | Attacken | attacks | 9 |
| Tief | low/depression | 9 | Verdrängung | repression/displacement | 9 |
| Seuche | plague | 8 | Aids | aids | 7 |
| Attacke | attack | 7 | Krebs | cancer | 7 |

Table 2: Most common semantic field terms per corpus (ambiguous terms are marked in the translation)

character-driven, as is typical of literary narratives. In order to further differentiate the causes of disagreement and annotator uncertainty, a more comprehensive study would be necessary that gives the annotators more space to give reasons for why they think a sentence is (not) about illness.

Some of the causes of disagreement could easily be avoided by annotation guidelines. We decided against the use of guidelines because the aim of our study was to explore the whole range of possible views on illness in our data. This range could be used for inductively specifying categories for specific guidelines. In addition, if the research objective allowed for a clear position on whether mental phenomena are supposed to be annotated as illness or whether negated mentions of illness are supposed to be annotated, guidelines clarifying these points are highly recommended. However, beyond the definitions we can derive inductively or from a research question there will most likely be space for individual interpretation. We would like to encourage researchers to regard this variation not as a problem to be fixed but something that can be incorporated into our modeling of the world and in our analyses.

The semantic field as a tool to search for specific topics is ambivalent: While the absence of a semantic field word was a good indicator that the sentence is not about illness, the presence of a semantic field word only resulted in a 50% chance of the sentence being about illness. Based on our annotations we can derive a weighted semantic field that can, for instance, be filtered to get a core semantic field. This allows for a reduction of hits to only those sentences that most people consider to be about illness. However, this would systematically exclude phenomena from the data set, as especially psychological phenomena led to disagreements.

With respect to text types, our study revealed more ambiguous instances in the Fiction Corpus than in the Transcript Corpus. While one might consider metaphors to be the cause of ambiguity in literary text, this is not what the inspection of sentences with low agreement indicates. Instead, the transcripts are characterized by many abstract terms like *Abhängigkeiten* ('dependencies, addictions') which are mostly used in a way that is clearly unrelated to illness and do not cause any disagreement. The Fiction Corpus, on the other hand, names many minor symptoms (*Husten*, 'cough') as everyday situations are described and can also report the inner life of characters.

In the future, we plan to explore possibilities for training machine learning models on the data presented here. By showing how ambiguity levels can be represented by multiple annotations, we hope to prepare for the creation of a complex gold standard that incorporates conflicting evidence (Reidsma and op den Akker, 2008; Passonneau and Carpenter, 2014).

## Acknowledgements

The work on this paper was funded by the *Landesforschungsförderung Hamburg* (LFF-FV 35) in the context of the project *hermA* (Gaidys et al., 2017) at Universität Hamburg and Hamburg University of Technology. We thank Piklu Gupta and Carla Sökefeld for proofreading. All remaining errors are our own.

## References

Benedikt Adelmann, Melanie Andresen, Anke Begerow, Lina Franken, Evelyn Gius, and Michael Vauth. 2019. Evaluation of a Semantic Field-Based Approach to Identifying Text Sections about Specific Topics. In *DH 2019. Book of Abstracts.*

Jacopo Amidei, Paul Piwek, and Alistair Willis. 2018. Rethinking the agreement in human evaluation tasks. In *Proceedings of the 27th International Conference on Computational Linguistics*, pages 3318–3329, Santa Fe, New Mexico, USA, August. Association for Computational Linguistics.

Ron Artstein and Massimo Poesio. 2008. Inter-Coder Agreement for Computational Linguistics. *Computational Linguistics*, 34(4):555–596, September.

Ron Artstein. 2017. Inter-annotator agreement. In Nancy Ide and James Pustejovsky, editors, *Handbook of Linguistic Annotation*, pages 297–313. Springer.

Beata Beigman Klebanov, Eyal Beigman, and Daniel Diermeier. 2008. Analyzing Disagreements. In *Coling 2008: Proceedings of the Workshop on Human Judgements in Computational Linguistics*, pages 2–7, Manchester, UK, August. Coling 2008 Organizing Committee.

Uta Gaidys, Evelyn Gius, Margarete Jarchow, Gertraud Koch, Wolfgang Menzel, Dominik Orth, and Heike Zinsmeister. 2017. hermA: Automated modelling of hermeneutic processes. *Hamburger Journal für Kulturanthropologie*, (7):119–123.

Evelyn Gius and Janina Jacke. 2017. The Hermeneutic Profit of Annotation. On preventing and fostering disagreement in literary text analysis. *International Journal of Humanities and Arts Computing*, 11(2):233–254.

Adam Hammond, Julian Brooke, and Graeme Hirst. 2013. A Tale of Two Cultures: Bringing Literary Analysis and Computational Linguistics Together. In *Proceedings of the Workshop on Computational Linguistics for Literature*, pages 1–8. Association for Computational Linguistics.

Birgit Hamp and Helmut Feldweg. 1997. GermaNet – a Lexical-Semantic Net for German. In *Automatic Information Extraction and Building of Lexical Semantic Resources for NLP Applications*, pages 9–15.

Verena Henrich and Erhard Hinrichs. 2010. GernEdiT – The GermaNet Editing Tool. In *Proceedings of the Seventh Conference on International Language Resources and Evaluation (LREC 2010)*, pages 2228–2235, Valletta, Malta.

Klaus Krippendorff. 1980. *Content Analysis: An Introduction to Its Methodology.* Number 5 in The Sage Commtext Series. Sage, Beverly Hills, California.

Klaus Krippendorff. 2013. *Content Analysis: An Introduction to Its Methodology.* Sage, Los Angeles, third edition.

George Lakoff. 1987. *Women, Fire, and Dangerous Things. What Categories Reveal about the Mind.* The University of Chicago Press, Chicago, London.

J. Richard Landis and Gary G. Koch. 1977. The measurement of observer agreement for categorical data. *Biometrics*, 33(1):159–174.

Adrienne Lehrer. 1974. *Semantic fields and lexical structure.* North-Holland Publishing Company, Amsterdam.

Jane Morris and Graeme Hirst. 2004. The Subjectivity of Lexical Cohesion in Text. *AAAI Spring Symposium - Technical Report*, 20.

Jane Morris. 2010. Individual differences in the interpretation of text: Implications for information science. *Journal of the American Society for Information Science and Technology*, 61(1):141–149.

Anna Nedoluzhko and Jiří Mírovský. 2013. Annotators' Certainty and Disagreements in Coreference and Bridging Annotation in Prague Dependency Treebank. In *Proceedings of the Second International Conference on Dependency Linguistics (DepLing 2013)*, pages 236–243.

Rebecca J. Passonneau and Bob Carpenter. 2014. The Benefits of a Model of Annotation. *Transactions of the Association for Computational Linguistics*, 2:311–326, December.

Ellie Pavlick and Tom Kwiatkowski. 2019. Inherent disagreements in human textual inferences. *Transactions of the Association for Computational Linguistics*, 7:677–694.

Barbara Plank, Dirk Hovy, and Anders Søgaard. 2014. Learning part-of-speech taggers with inter-annotator agreement loss. In *Proceedings of the 14th Conference of the European Chapter of the Association for Computational Linguistics*, pages 742–751.

Massimo Poesio and Ron Artstein. 2005. The Reliability of Anaphoric Annotation, Reconsidered: Taking Ambiguity into Account. In *Proceedings of the Workshop on Frontiers in Corpus Annotations II: Pie in the Sky*, pages 76–83, Ann Arbor, Michigan, June.

W. James Potter and Deborah Levine-Donnerstein. 1999. Rethinking validity and reliability in content analysis. *Journal of Applied Communication Research*, 27(3):258–284, August.

Dennis Reidsma and Rieks op den Akker. 2008. Exploiting 'subjective' annotations. In *Coling 2008: Proceedings of the workshop on Human Judgements in Computational Linguistics*, pages 8–16, Manchester, UK, August. Coling 2008 Organizing Committee.

Hannah Rohde, Anna Dickinson, Nathan Schneider, Christopher N. L. Clark, Annie Louis, and Bonnie Webber. 2016. Filling in the Blanks in Understanding Discourse Adverbials: Consistency, Conflict, and Context-Dependence in a Crowdsourced Elicitation Task. In *Proceedings of the 10th Linguistic Annotation Workshop Held in Conjunction with ACL 2016 (LAW-X 2016)*, pages 49–58, Berlin, Germany, August.

Helmut Schmid, Arne Fitschen, and Ulrich Heid. 2004. SMOR: A German computational morphology covering derivation, composition and inflection. In *Proceedings of the Fourth International Conference on Language Resources and Evaluation (LREC'04)*, Lisbon, Portugal, May. European Language Resources Association (ELRA).

Merel Scholman and Vera Demberg. 2017. Crowdsourcing discourse interpretations: On the influence of context and the reliability of a connective insertion task. In *Proceedings of the 11th Linguistic Annotation Workshop*, pages 24–33, Valencia, Spain, April. Association for Computational Linguistics.

Rico Sennrich and Beat Kunz. 2014. Zmorge: A German morphological lexicon extracted from Wiktionary. In *Proceedings of the Ninth International Conference on Language Resources and Evaluation (LREC'14)*, pages 1063–1067, Reykjavik, Iceland, May. European Language Resources Association (ELRA).

Leonid M. Vassilyev. 1974. The theory of semantic fields: a survey. *Linguistics*, 12(137):79–94.

Yannick Versley. 2006. Disagreement Dissected: Vagueness as a Source of Ambiguity in Nominal (Co-)Reference. In *Proceedings of the Ambiguity in Anaphora Workshop (ESSLLI 2006)*, pages 83–89.

# Representation Problems in Linguistic Annotations:
## Ambiguity, Variation, Uncertainty, Error and Bias


**Christin Beck**[1], **Hannah Booth**[1,3], **Mennatallah El-Assady**[2], and **Miriam Butt**[1]

[1]Department of Linguistics
[2]Department of Computer Science
University of Konstanz, Germany

[3]Department of Linguistics
Ghent University, Belgium

`firstname.lastname@uni-konstanz.de`



## Abstract

The development of linguistic corpora is fraught with various problems of annotation and representation. These constitute a very real challenge for the development and use of annotated corpora, but as yet not much literature exists on how to address the underlying problems. In this paper, we identify and discuss five sources of representation problems, which are independent though interrelated: ambiguity, variation, uncertainty, error and bias. We outline and characterize these sources, discussing how their improper treatment can have stark consequences for research outcomes. Finally, we discuss how an adequate treatment can inform corpus-related linguistic research, both computational and theoretical, improving the reliability of research results and NLP models, as well as informing the more general reproducibility issue.


## 1 Introduction

Linguistically annotated corpora have for many decades occupied a firm place in the linguistics toolbox. They are of vital importance for theoretical and computational linguistic research in providing empirical evidence for language use, both from a qualitative and quantitative perspective. Moreover, machine learning algorithms typically applied in the context of Natural Language Processing (NLP) require annotated datasets for building language models. Annotated corpora now exist in many forms and much effort has been devoted to developing specific schemes for different levels of linguistic analysis (e.g., phonology, morphosyntax, semantics, pragmatics). For example, the Penn Treebank (Marcus et al., 1999) and the Universal Dependency Treebank (e.g., de Marneffe et al., 2014) are syntactically annotated corpora, while, e.g., discourse relations are annotated in the Penn Discourse Treebank (Webber et al., 2019). Although many levels of linguistic annotation can be performed via automated means, some manually annotated training data is typically required as a foundation. Moreover, there are certain types of corpora where manual annotation remains the best option in the face of complex linguistic phenomena (e.g., historical language stages or non-standard varieties).

Any manual annotation process represents a compromise between an accurate linguistic analysis and an annotation scheme which is generalizable enough to serve computational tools and the end user. Annotation schemes are typically designed with a specific purpose in mind, and this will bear heavily on the decisions made. The compromises tend to revolve around details of the annotation scheme and one possible result of hard-fought compromises is that the resulting representations may actually be inaccurate with respect to several factors. In this paper, we identify five major factors: (i) ambiguity, (ii) variation, (iii) uncertainty, (iv) error, and (v) bias (see also Figure 1). In particular, uncertainty has already been recognized as a problem in linguistic corpora (Jurgens, 2013; Cassidy et al., 2014), with a special focus on the interrelation between linguistic ambiguities and uncertainty in the annotation of historical linguistic data (Seemann et al., 2017; Merten and Seemann, 2018).

In this paper we extend the discussion beyond ambiguity and uncertainty to include variation, error and bias as sources of representation problems in linguistic annotations and argue for the importance of






*The 14th Linguistic Annotation Workshop*, pages 60–73
Barcelona, Spain (Online), December 12, 2020.

developing a robust framework which explicitly treats these problems. We focus primarily on representation problems in historical corpora, but the set of problems is transferable to other types of linguistically annotated resources (Chambers et al., 2014; Plank et al., 2014; Pavlick and Kwiatkowski, 2019). As part of future work, we intend to build a computational implementation that is based on the crucial foundations laid out in this paper.

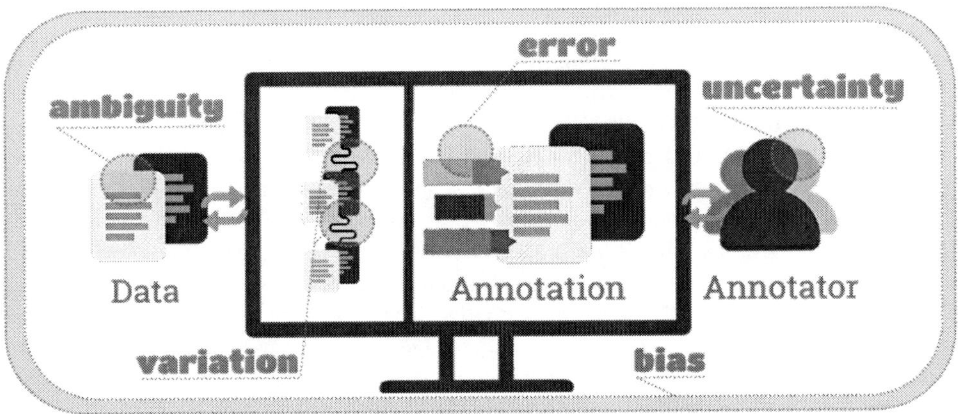


Figure 1: Representation problems in linguistic annotations come from five distinct sources: (i) **Ambiguities** are an inherent property of the *data*. (ii) **Variation** is also part of the *data* and can, e.g., occur across documents. (iii) **Uncertainty** is introduced by an *annotator*'s lack of knowledge or information. (iv) **Errors** can be found in the *annotations*. (v) **Biases** are a property of the *complete annotation system*.


## 2 Background and Related Work

Existing approaches typically treat representation problems in one of three ways in linguistic annotation processes: (i) stochastic treatment, (ii) assignment of an 'other/miscellaneous' category, (iii) left unannotated. In Part-of-Speech (POS) tagging and syntactic parsing, ambiguities are often treated in a stochastic manner, so that among the possibilities the option which is most likely is chosen (cf. Most Frequent Class Baseline; Jurafsky and Martin, 2009). In this way, each token receives a single tag and the ambiguity property is lost altogether. For example, Dipper et al. (2013) develop a POS tagging policy for historical German where ambiguous material receives the tag of the more frequent or of the historically older usage. Another approach is to mark entities about whose interpretation an annotator is uncertain with a specific tag ('other/miscellaneous' category), signaling that no adequate annotation is available. For example, in the Corpus of Historical Low German (Booth et al., 2020), clauses which are ambiguous between matrix (IP-MAT) and subordinate status (IP-SUB) are tagged as IP-X. A non-historical example comes from TimeBank-Dense (Chambers et al., 2014; Cassidy et al., 2014) where ambiguous temporal relations are tagged as 'vague'. Although this captures some level of ambiguity and uncertainty, it does not necessarily allow for an adequate representation of the underlying problem, information which is potentially of high interest to the end-user. A third option often employed is to leave uncertain material unannotated. In this case, the respective pieces of data are typically set aside and do not play a role in linguistic investigations or NLP downstream tasks.

Some efforts have been made towards more sophisticated schemes for explicitly marking representation problems. For instance, Merten and Seemann (2018) have developed a novel interface which enables an annotator to capture different sources of uncertainty while annotating POS and specific syntactic constructions in a historical corpus of Middle Low German (see also Seeman et al., 2017). Their scheme allows annotators to capture uncertainty via a tag indicating one of three types: (i) category A is more likely than B, (ii) A and B are equally likely, (iii) unsure. Lüdeling (2017) has proposed a corpus annotation model which captures variation, e.g., in word pronunciation, by explicitly labeling the type of variation and the variant involved in an additional annotation layer. Similarly, Dipper et al. (2013) capture spelling variation in their historical tagset by providing information on three levels: (i) the original token (diplomatic level), (ii) a modernized version of the token (tokenization level), and (iii) a tag for the type of variation (tag level). Likewise, Barteld et al. (2014) have proposed a multi-level annotation approach for incomplete language phenomena, i.e., ambiguity, underspecification or uncertainty.

In other contexts, uncertainty has been measured via various types of scale. For example, Jurgens (2013) employs a Likert-scale based approach for annotating ambiguous word senses, where the possible senses are rated on a numerical scale with respect to the likelihood of their occurrence in specific contexts. Vashishtha et al. (2019) use confidence ratings ranging from 'not at all confident' to 'absolutely confident' when annotating temporal relations between pairs of events. Zhang et al. (2017) let annotators specify whether an inference relation between sentences is 'very likely', 'likely', 'plausible', 'technically possible' or 'impossible' while annotating natural language inferences (NLI). Also in the context of NLI, Pavlick and Kwiatkowski (2019) make use of a sliding bar, which contains numerical values which range from indicating that an inference relation is 'definitely true' to indicating that it is 'definitely not true' to capture human judgements. Additionally, Pavlick and Kwiatkowski (2019) assess annotator disagreement as a measure of uncertainty by modeling these judgements as distributions instead of aggregated scores. Similarly, Chen et al. (2020) let annotators give judgements about the likelihood of inference relations via a sliding bar, and model 'uncertain natural language inferences' via scalar regression, predicting the probability at which a premise entails a hypothesis. Passonneau and Carpenter (2014), on the other hand, present a probabilistic model based on maximum likelihood estimation for annotating word senses, which gives a confidence estimate for each annotation label as a measure of certainty. Plank et al. (2014) capture uncertainty by measuring annotator disagreement on the basis of inter-annotator $F$1-scores and the confusion probability between annotators. In addition, Plank et al. (2014) show that by incorporating information about annotator disagreement into the training of an NLP-model for POS-tagging, relevant downstream tasks, i.e., Named Entity Recognition and Chunking, can be improved.

Although these approaches take up the problem of annotation and representation problems, they do not work out a generally applicable framework. Additionally, it is still unclear how the factors we identify as major problem sources interact throughout the various phases involved in corpus development and use. We see the important barrier to overcome here as a conceptual one, in the sense that concepts like 'uncertainty' and 'ambiguity' are often used interchangeably, despite there being inherent differences between the sources of these representation problems. Understanding these sources on their own terms, as this paper proposes, is a crucial prerequisite for developing more adequate treatments and in turn more reliably annotated corpora.

## 3  Phases of Corpus Development and Use

Developing an annotated corpus for linguistic research involves a number of work steps which are crucial for successful corpus design. The corpus development workflow consists of data selection and processing, typically including digitization, normalization and automatic pre-processing, and cycles of annotation. We see two major parts of a typical corpus development process: Data Selection and Processing (Phase I) and Annotation (Phase II). Following the corpus development, there is a third part, Interpretation (Phase III), which pertains to corpus use, addressing the issue of interpreting the annotated data.

### 3.1  Phase I: Data Selection and Processing

Prototypically, corpora consist of several machine-readable text files. Finding appropriate texts for a corpus is not a trivial task and data selection, i.e., text collection, is the first fundamental step in corpus construction. Ensuring a balanced corpus is a high desideratum, though often not achievable, particularly with respect to historical corpora, since often only a limited number of texts from particular domains are available. Data processing usually comprises digitization of any non-digitized textual material, spelling normalization and an automatic pre-processing (e.g., POS tagging, shallow syntactic parsing), and prepares the data for manual annotation by enriching the raw text with basic linguistic information.

### 3.2 Phase II: Annotation

Some corpus building stops after Phase I, because the amount of annotation is already sufficient for the intended task. Other corpora are enriched with further, often manual, annotations capturing more complex linguistic phenomena. The manual annotation process generally consists of iterative cycles of annotation, evaluation and error correction. At times, the manual annotation process is sped up by combining it with machine learning via successive cycles of manual annotation, training, automatic annotation and corrections. The annotation task itself can be broken down into two subtasks: identification and classification. First, the linguistic unit which is to be annotated has to be identified. The classification task then deals with assigning an annotation label to the previously identified linguistic unit. Manual annotation pipelines will also be guided to some extent by the specific tool which is used to conduct the annotation, of which a range exist, e.g., Annotald (Beck et al., 2015) and WebAnno (Eckart de Castilho et al., 2016).

### 3.3 Phase III: Interpretation

Annotations are usually informed by extensive theoretical analysis of linguistic structures. In turn, annotated corpora are essential for linguistic research, since they provide empirical evidence for a variety of linguistic phenomena, with end-users generating relevant insights for linguistic theory. In this way, the interpretation of the annotated values is crucial to future scientific developments. Moreover, corpora are a necessary prerequisite for the building of language models within NLP. Such models are based on interpretations (learning) of the annotated data. Thus, adequate representations of the linguistic data are vital for end-users of corpora. Without explicit treatment, representation problems often persist in post-hoc analyses of the annotations, rendering linguistic findings and computational models potentially unreliable or even misleading. In the next section, we characterise the various sources of representation problems, how they surface at the different phases, and show how they merit a more explicit treatment.

## 4 Sources of Representation Problems

We identify five sources of representation problems in linguistic resources, which we explain in this section: (i) ambiguity, (ii) variation, (iii) uncertainty, (iv) error and (v) bias. They are relevant at all three phases of corpus development and use, and interact with one another in a complex fashion.

### 4.1 Ambiguity

Ambiguity is an inherent property of natural language and therefore also of corpus data, see Figure 1. Ambiguity occurs whenever an entity in principle allows for multiple interpretations. Ambiguities between form and meaning appear frequently in natural language at all linguistic dimensions (e.g., phonological, morphosyntactic, lexical or pragmatic) and are a key source of representation problems. For our purposes, we define ambiguity as any instance where linguistic material in principle allows for more than one interpretation.

We propose to capture the extent to which an instance of linguistic ambiguity can be resolved (e.g., via contextual cues and/or world knowledge) via three broad categories: (i) ambiguity can be fully resolved; one interpretation, (ii) ambiguity cannot be entirely resolved, but a preference can be expressed for one interpretation; multiple interpretations, relatively ranked, and (iii) ambiguity cannot be resolved, and no preference can be expressed for any interpretation; multiple interpretations, equal ranking (see also Merten and Seemann (2018)). Ambiguity poses particular problems for representation at Phase II (annotation), leading to challenges in the identification and classification of linguistic units.

Many classic examples constitute *class ambiguity*, referring to cases where a linguistic unit allows for more than one classification. A well-known example from English concerns gerunds in *-ing*, which are often assumed to be a 'mixed category' between noun and verb (Hudson, 2003; Malouf, 1996).[1] However, not all *-ing* forms are equally unresolvable, see example (1), taken from Lowe (2016, 402). In (1-a), *missing* exhibits properties exclusively associated with nominals (adjectival premodification,

---

[1] This type of class ambiguity poses a problem to POS tagging, which we broadly described as a Phase I process. But POS tagging is at times part of the manual annotation (Phase II) and more generally feeds into the parsing of larger syntactic units.

PP complement), while in (1-b) the properties of *missing* are entirely verbal (adverbial modification, bare logical subject, bare object). In other words, a potentially ambiguous form can be resolved to one of the possible interpretations. The unresolvable ambiguity arises in contexts like (1-c), where *missing* exhibits both nominal properties (logical subject is a possessive phrase) and verbal properties (adverbial modification, bare object). This would be a case of two interpretations (N and V) with an equal ranking. Furthermore, the gerund example highlights a more general issue which feeds class ambiguity, i.e., that many of the categories widely recognized in linguistics and thus implemented in annotations are typically encoded through bundles of properties. As such, it is expected that there will be clear-cut cases, as (1-a)-(1-b), but also items whose properties indicate membership of more than one category, as (1-c).

(1)    a.    [His stupid **missing** of the penalty] lost us the game.    (unambiguously nominal)
        b.    [Him stupidly **missing** the penalty] lost us the game.    (unambiguously verbal)
        c.    [His stupidly **missing** the penalty] lost us the game.    (ambiguously nominal/verbal)

An example of ambiguity which is not fully resolvable, but where a preference *can* be expressed for one of the possible interpretations is shown in (2), where *crane* is ambiguous between the bird-type (animate) and the machine-type (inanimate). In (2), the preceding context does not point strongly towards a preference, but the subsequent context indicates the machine-type interpretation to be the most likely, based on the world knowledge that machine-type cranes are involved in apartment building.

(2)    On the river side, I saw a bunch of **cranes**. The new apartments are starting to look really nice.

For this example, the ambiguity does not concern POS tags but would be relevant in a resource where one is annotating for animacy, e.g., VerbNet (Kipper Schuler, 2005).

Moreover, class ambiguity can result from processes of historical language change, e.g., grammaticalization (Hopper and Traugott, 2003). A classic example is the development whereby a demonstrative becomes a complementizer via grammaticalization (Heine and Kuteva, 2002), as exhibited with English *that*, e.g. (3), where the demonstrative function remains ('persistence'; Hopper, 1991).

(3)    a.    I say **that**: there is a problem.    (demonstrative with cataphoric reference)
        b.    I say **that** there is a problem.    (complementizer)

Without punctuation and prosodic cues, the form *that* exhibits class ambiguity between demonstrative and complementizer. This is particularly relevant for historical language stages where one typically only has access to written texts, and thus to no prosodic information.

*Boundary ambiguity* refers to instances where a surface string can in principle be segmented into smaller units in more than one way, resulting in alternative boundary divisions. This is related to the identification part of the annotation task. An example from syntactic constituency is provided in (4), where *the man with the telescope* can be one larger nominal constituent with internal modification (embedded PP), see (4-a), or two separate constituents (NP PP), see (4-b).

(4)    Mary saw **the man with the telescope**
        a.    Mary saw [the man [with the telescope]]
        b.    Mary saw [the man] [with the telescope]

Moreover, such examples present a further type of ambiguity, *attachment ambiguity*, which is relevant for identifying relations between segments and arises when there is more than one possible interpretation of these relations. In (4), the PP *with the telescope* can in principle attach at more than one level in the phrase-structure: in (4-a), it attaches at NP-level; in (4-b), it attaches at VP-level. Just as grammaticalization can feed class ambiguity, reanalysis as a mechanism of change (de Smet, 2009) is related to boundary and attachment ambiguity, in the sense that a surface string is assigned a new bracketing interpretation, typically via ambiguous 'bridging contexts' (Heine, 2002).

Since ambiguity is inherent to the data, it can also occur as a representation problem at Phase I. For instance, word and sentence segmentation can be the locus of ambiguities, particularly in historical corpora. In many modern languages, word and sentence boundaries can be identified on the basis of white spaces and punctuation. In older handwritten manuscripts and early printed sources, however, the use of spaces and punctuation can differ quite substantially from the modern usage in terms of functionality (Dipper et al., 2013). For example, while in modern German words represent syntactically meaningful units, Old High German scribes often employed separation in the form of spaces or the absence thereof to group words into prosodic units (Fleischer, 2009). Thus white spaces can be ambiguous with respect to their linguistic function.

Although ambiguity is an omnipresent problem in the corpus development process, it is in most instances not captured by the annotations. Instead, the general practice is to stochastically determine and use the most probable annotation label, losing the ambiguity property altogether. If ambiguity does not receive adequate treatment, then this has consequences for the user at Phase III. If the ambiguity is not captured at all, then interpretations may be simply false, and indeed rich information will be lost which is often very relevant to linguistic investigations and likewise to computational language models.

## 4.2  Variation

Variation is when a particular variable is expressed via multiple variants. The variants are in principle interchangeable so that there are no (structural) conditions excluding one of the variants (Lüdeling, 2017). Variation may be conditioned by factors which are extra-linguistic, e.g., time period, dialect, genre, author/speaker of text, or linguistic factors such as language change or the linguistic environment a variable occurs in.

The dative alternation in English is an example of variation (Bresnan et al., 2007; Lüdeling, 2017). The dative alternation refers to the availability of two different (syntactic) dative constructions in English, which can be used interchangeably while expressing essentially the same meaning. The variants are illustrated in (5), with (5-a) showing the variant which contains a prepositional dative structure (NP PP) and (5-b) showing the double object variant (NP NP).

(5)    a.    Mary gave [an apple] [to John].
       b.    Mary gave [John] [an apple].

The variation here is determined by a conglomeration of different linguistic factors, including animacy, discourse accessibility (givenness/information structure) and weight (Bresnan et al., 2007).

Like ambiguity, variation is an inherent part of natural language and thus of the corpus data (see Figure 1). Therefore, variation constitutes a representation problem at all three phases of corpus development and use. In contrast to ambiguity, it is not an annotation issue in terms of identification and classification, but rather that a single interpretation (variable) manifests itself in two or more (variants). Sometimes, the variants are captured in an annotation scheme, but not necessarily linked to a single variable (e.g., Dipper et al., 2013; Lüdeling, 2017). Although such a treatment provides significant information about the variant, the variation as a whole cannot easily be harnessed without prior knowledge of the precise character of the variation, since crucial information about the other variant(s) is not easily accessible.

In other treatments, the variants are levelled out and expressed as a single interpretation (either as one of the variants or as a generalizing variable), in which case the variation property is lost overall. For example, normalization is a process at Phase I which leads to a levelling out of spelling variation, where one variant is favored over another. Spelling variation occurs across the board in historical texts, reflecting e.g., dialectal and/or temporal differences, as orthographic norms are a trait of modern times. For example, Bollmann et al. (2014) find the three dialect variants *chind, kínt, kynt* for 'child' in Early New High German, while *kind* is used in (late) New High German. In such cases, normalization is often a necessary means to an end. Normalization enables researchers to leverage existing algorithms and tools for text processing, facilitating, e.g., POS tagging (Bollmann et al., 2014). Furthermore, regularized spelling has the advantage of facilitating keyword and n-gram searches in corpora (Kytö, 2010). Yet, normalization can also lead to a crucial loss of information, since spelling variation may provide valuable linguistic insights relevant for annotation and interpretation.

A linguistically relevant instance of variation which could be levelled out by normalization is the variation between multi- and single-word spellings caused by univerbation (Dipper et al., 2013; Lüdeling, 2017). Univerbation is an instance of language change whereby multiple words which form a fixed expression are reanalyzed as one word, with an intermediate stage where both variants are used interchangeably. For instance, in the Penn Parsed Corpora of Historical English (Santorini, 2010) both *nevertheless* (single-word) and *never the less* (multi-word) occur. Keeping the spelling variation intact provides insights into where a particular text is situated on the trajectory of a change (Dipper et al., 2013) and potentially reveals the linguistic factors which led to the development of the fixed multi-word expression. Still, without a more explicit treatment of the variation, together with the relevant a priori knowledge, this is hard to explore.

Another reason why variation merits particularly nuanced treatment in historical corpora is because certain historical processes feed the issue, e.g., grammaticalization and competition. As mentioned, grammaticalization involves a change whereby a particular form takes on a new function. This in turn can result in variation, if a marker of this particular new function already exists in the language. Secondly, competition between variants of a single variable often results in decreased variation in a particular corner of the linguistic system, whereby one variant outcompetes another (Kroch, 1989; Pintzuk, 2003).

Overall, losing variation significantly impairs a language resource in terms of its accurate reflection of the linguistic characteristics of the data. As with ambiguity, this loss of information is not insignificant, since variation is another linguistically relevant property of language which is often of prime interest to the user (Labov, 1994; Tagliamonte, 2006; Chambers and Schilling, 2013).

### 4.3  Uncertainty

Uncertainty arises wherever multiple possible interpretations of data present themselves, but the relevant knowledge or information to unequivocally opt for one of the interpretations is not available (Bonneau et al., 2014). Uncertainties can be part of the process of data selection and processing. For instance, corpus developers might be uncertain about which texts fit best with the objective of the corpus and which parameters to choose for text processing. In addition, the NLP tools employed for pre-processing can introduce uncertainty (John et al., 2017). This is an issue particularly for historical corpora, since, e.g., POS taggers are often trained on data from more recent time periods, given that the necessary amount of annotated training data for the historical period is typically unavailable. This renders the tagging results on historical data potentially unreliable, which in turn leads to uncertainty.

Moreover, uncertainties occur frequently in the annotation phase, as depicted in Figure 1. An issue which arises with historical data is that the crucial knowledge for the annotation of a specific historical language structure may not yet have been generated. A further problem is that human annotators cannot function as native speakers of a historical language. Due to incomplete knowledge, annotators may not be able to readily identify and interpret a given structure, and may therefore be uncertain.

A further uncertainty is caused by the annotations themselves. Linguistic annotations instantiate theory to some degree, focusing on some phenomena over others, with many phenomena not yet studied in much depth. The corresponding code books or manuals for annotation therefore hardly ever tend to be comprehensive and complete before the begin of the annotation process and are necessarily extended and changed as part of a cyclical annotation process (Hovy and Lavid, 2010). This results in uncertainty as to how unanticipated phenomena should be annotated, new tags defined, and how phenomena not covered by established research should be treated (Hovy and Lavid, 2010). The uncertainties that are encountered at Phase I and II are marked as such and made transparently explicit to the end user only rarely, thus persisting into Phase III (interpretation).

### 4.4  Error

In addition to the sources already discussed (ambiguity, variation and uncertainty), errors may also occur in linguistic annotations as representation problems (see Figure 1). At Phase I, errors can already be present in the data sources themselves. For example, with respect to historical manuscripts, scribal errors are common, particularly in texts which have been copied multiple times by different scribes (Penzl, 1967; Neidorf, 2013). Moreover, the source texts are often not in good repair, with stains on the paper and damaged pages potentially producing digitization errors. Texts can be digitized by either hand-keying or scanning via OCR (optical character recognition) software. Handkeying has the advantage of generally being more accurate (though not error-free), but is time-consuming and might not be suitable when dealing with a large number of texts. OCR systems, on the other hand, generally work fast and are able to handle large quantities of data. Yet, the scripts, characters and diacritics of historical manuscripts and early printed texts are often challenging for OCR systems, requiring a non-trivial amount of post-processing, including error identification and correction (Boschetti et al., 2009; De Simone et al., 2018; Schulz and Kuhn, 2017). The process of identifying and correcting the erroneous text passages is laborious, produces a high cognitive workload and requires expert philological knowledge. The resulting corpus might therefore contain errors produced by the OCR system, but these will not necessarily be distinguishable from errors caused by human unsystematicity. These errors might have an impact on subsequent processes, e.g., POS tagging. Moreover, the automatic pre-processing steps are prone to errors themselves, which are often not transparent to annotators and users.

Manual annotation at Phase II is time-consuming and cognitively heavy. Human errors might therefore occur and not be detected, even in iterative rounds of annotation and correction. This is especially relevant for historical corpora, since human annotators lack native-speaker competence, as well as the cultural and pragmatic knowledge of the historical language stage, and may at times be unable to analyze certain linguistic structures accurately. Moreover, it is not always possible for the data to be annotated by several annotators, since the annotation of complex linguistic phenomena often requires expert knowledge. Again, this particularly applies to historical corpora, where only a few trained researchers with the relevant knowledge may exist. In this way, calculating inter-annotator agreement (e.g., via Cohen's kappa (Cohen, 1960), Krippendorf's alpha (Krippendorff, 2004) or inter-annotator $F1$-scores (Plank et al., 2014)) is not possible and significant errors may remain undetected.

Since revision and correction of annotations are costly procedures, it is often the case that a version of the corpus is already published after the first round of annotation, to provide the research community with the data as soon as possible. Errors are then usually reported by the community and the corpus developers can in principle react to this by re-annotating the data for the next release. However, in practice different sites often end up maintaining different versions of the corpus or researchers might 'curate' the data themselves, working with their own versions. This impedes reproducibility and may lead to imperfect research results.

## 4.5  Bias

Bias represents an influence which leads to a preference or tendency for one thing over another. Often, neither the end-user nor the annotator may be conscious of such biases, which can produce representation problems in every phase of corpus development and use.

In general, corpora should be representative and balanced (Leech, 1991; Gries and Berez, 2017). A corpus can be representative of a specific genre, register or variety, representing the targeted subgroup via the text samples contained in the corpus. A corpus is balanced (unbiased) when the size of the subsamples, i.e., the samples of different genres, registers, or varieties, is proportional to the size of the subgroups which the corpus aims to represent. With respect to diachronic corpora, genre imbalance is rather the norm than the exception, which in turn leads to a sampling or selection bias. While a large amount of textual data is usually available for more recent time stages of a language, the data for the longer standing past is generally scarce. The historically older and sparser data is generally less diverse, consisting of fewer genres, registers and text types (Gippert and Gehrke, 2015). It is often the case that all available historical texts for the relevant time periods are included in a corpus to be able to cover the diachrony of a language as much as possible (Reppen, 2010). Genre imbalances across time periods can hinder comparability over time, which is the core remit of diachronic investigations. Furthermore, text processing can be subject to a bias, since the parameters and tools chosen influence the shape of the resulting data. Søgaard et al. (2014) point out that language technology is generally biased towards English newswire (selection bias), with better overall performances of NLP tools on English newswire data than on any other text genre and other lower-resourced languages.

At Phase II, several more biases can occur. For one, the annotator might already have a theory in mind about the phenomenon to be annotated, which has not been empirically evidenced, imposing a theory bias on the data. Moreover, comparative fallacy (Merten and Seemann, 2018), e.g., misinterpretations arising through comparing the historical language with one's own native language, might lead to substantial biases. For another, a learning effect might occur during the course of annotation, biasing the resulting data, in the sense that the resource will not necessarily be internally consistent.

## 4.6 Interrelations between Sources

One type of representation problem rarely occurs on its own, with one type of problem often leading to another. *Ambiguity* interacts strongly with uncertainty, but it is crucial to differentiate between the two: while ambiguity is inherent to the data, a human annotator/user or an algorithm might be uncertain when multiple interpretations of the data present themselves, as sketched in Figure 1. Similarly, *variation* might produce uncertainty if the precise nature of the variants involved and/or their conditioning factors cannot be easily recovered (lack of knowledge/information). Moreover, the human might be uncertain about whether an annotation contains *errors* propagated through the corpus building and annotation process, or whether the resulting annotation is error-free. Likewise, *biases* can lead to uncertainty because one might be uncertain as to how representative the corpus is, and whether certain characteristics of the data are true properties of the language, or perhaps skewed due to a particular bias. As errors and biases are often found in the data independently of any annotation scheme (see Figure 1), each can result in further annotation challenges.

## 5 Research Opportunities and Open Challenges

The representation problems outlined above have real consequences in terms of the reproducibility, usability and trustworthiness of research results generated via annotated resources. It is thus important to treat the sources of these problems carefully, separating them out in corpus development and use. The aim is that outlining the different sources of representation problems, and how these surface in the various phases, will lead to a more nuanced understanding of the challenges involved. This in turn can inform future resources so that they are more faithful to the data they represent, increasing the end-user's confidence with respect to research results. As an initial step, we recommend that the various types of representation problems are properly identified in linguistic annotations and labelled explicitly. In this way, we hope to be able to capture and harness the full characteristics of corpus linguistic data in the future. Our hope is that this will further lead to more robust corpus-based findings in theoretical linguistics and more accurate NLP models. Specifically, we envisage new research opportunities in theoretical and computational linguistics, as well as novel responses in connection with the reproducibility crisis.

**Facilitating Theoretical Linguistic Research**  Modeling representation problems provides us with a clearer picture of the underlying data, furthering our understanding of the linguistic and extra-linguistic properties of the texts in a corpus. This could lead to novel research results which were previously hindered by these problems, advancing the respective state-of-the-art in theoretical linguistics. Furthermore, an explicit treatment of the problem sources could foster the emergence of new insights since, e.g., in historical linguistics, *variation* and *ambiguity* are seen as the key components of language change.

**Improving NLP Models**  In computational linguistics, propagating representation problems throughout NLP pipelines could inform computational models at each step, improving the accuracy of the respective algorithms and the resulting end-product. For example, it has been shown that the accuracy of NLP systems for event ordering can be improved by assigning specific tags in cases of ambiguity and uncertainty (Chambers et al., 2014). Similarly, Plank et al. (2014) have shown that providing information about annotator disagreements during training of an NLP model for POS tagging increases the performance of corresponding NLP downstream models. However, more recently, Pavlick and Kwiatkowski (2019) have shown that state-of-the-art NLP models for NLI are able to model some sort of uncertainty, but this is not the uncertainty that stems from human disagreement. Therefore, they advocate the need for a better understanding of the sources of linguistic uncertainty and the downstream propagation of such uncertainties in NLP models. Providing an NLP model with a more elaborate and explicit treatment of representation problems thus has the potential to immensely improve research results.

**Promoting Reproducibility**  A framework which models representation problems could be of great benefit for research into the reproducibility issue in computational linguistics. Cohen et al. (2018) define reproducibility in NLP as a property related to the outcomes of an experiment with the three reproducibility dimensions *conclusion* (an induction based on the results), *finding* (relationship between values), and *value* (a calculated or measured number). These dimensions also pertain to our described problem sources, since they have an impact on whether a conclusion, a finding or a value can be reproduced. Fokkens et al. (2013) moreover show that research into the reproducibility of experiments in NLP and in particular understanding the experimental *variation* can improve research results.

**Quantifying Representation Problems**  A future challenge will be the quantification of representation problems in linguistic annotations. For example, Likert-scales and other relational measurements have been proposed to measure the degree of uncertainty (see Section 2). We aim at experimenting with different measures in future work, exploring which measures work best for specific types of representation problems. Moreover, we intend to experiment with different kinds of probability measures in order to be able to provide a mathematical framework for propagating representation problems throughout the phases of corpus development and use.

**Guided Annotation Systems**  To support the annotation process throughout its different phases, systems can be designed based on guidelines for identifying, capturing, and treating representation problems (Sperrle et al., 2020). Best practices from current approaches can be taken into consideration to derive such guidelines. These will establish a systematic procedure for dealing with representation problems in a consistent manner. In addition, annotation systems that rely on such guidelines could detect annotation inconsistencies and irregularities to guide annotators to the presence of representation problems, enabling them to be captured and possibly avoided or treated. Based on the users' interaction with such a learning annotation system, it can adapt over time to the users' annotation preference (Sperrle et al., 2019), cementing best practices into instructions for future sessions. Such guided systems could facilitate the annotation process and ensure the correctness of the annotation results, enabling a more reliable interpretation of the annotated data.

## 6   Conclusion

In this paper, we presented five sources of representation problems in linguistic annotations: ambiguity, variation, uncertainty, error and bias. We characterized these sources, outlining their usual treatment in corpus linguistic processes. Moreover, we discussed the consequences which an insufficient or improper treatment of these problems may have in the three phases of corpus development and use: data selection and processing (Phase I), annotation (Phase II) and interpretation (Phase III). In this way, this paper highlights the importance of developing more adequate and explicit treatments of such representation problems in the future. Moreover, we argued that harnessing representation problems in the scientific process fosters research into the reproducibility crisis, in addition to providing more robust research results.

## Acknowledgements

This work was funded by the Deutsche Forschungsgemeinschaft (DFG, German Research Foundation) – Project-ID 251654672 – TRR 161. Many insights for the paper came from Hannah Booth's work developing the Corpus of Historical Low German ('CHLG'), with support from the Hercules Foundation/FWO, Grant number Hercules AUGE13/02 (July 2014–December 2015)/FWO G0F2614N (January 2016–present).

## References

Fabian Barteld, Sarah Ihden, Ingrid Schröder, and Heike Zinsmeister. 2014. Annotating descriptively incomplete language phenomena. In *Proceedings of LAW VIII - The 8th Linguistic Annotation Workshop*, pages 99–104, Dublin, Ireland, August. Association for Computational Linguistics and Dublin City University.

Jana Beck, Aaron Ecay, and Anton Karl Ingason. 2015. Annotald. version 1.3. 7.

Marcel Bollmann, Florian Petran, and Stefanie Dipper. 2014. Applying rule-based normalization to different types of historical texts — an evaluation. *Human Language Technology Challenges for Computer Science and Linguistics. 5th Language and Technology Conference, LTC 2011. Revised Selected Papers*, 8387:166–177.

Georges-Pierre Bonneau, Hans-Christian Hege, Chris R. Johnson, Manuel M. Oliveira, Kristin Potter, Penny Rheingans, and Thomas Schultz. 2014. Overview and state-of-the-art of uncertainty visualization. In Charles D. Hansen, Min Chen, Christopher R. Johnson, Arie E. Kaufman, and Hans Hagen, editors, *Scientific Visualization: Uncertainty, Multifield, Biomedical, and Scalable Visualization*, pages 3–27. Springer London, London.

Hannah Booth, Anne Breitbarth, Aaron Ecay, and Melissa Farasyn. 2020. A Penn-style Treebank of Middle Low German. In *Proceedings of The 12th Language Resources and Evaluation Conference*, pages 766–775, Marseille, France, May. European Language Resources Association.

Federico Boschetti, Matteo Romanello, Alison Babeu, and David Bamman. 2009. Improving OCR accuracy for classical critical editions. In *Proceedings of the 13th European Conference on Research and Advanced Technology for Digital Libraries*, pages 156–167, 09.

Joan Bresnan, Anna Cueni, Tatiana Nikitina, and Harald Baayen. 2007. Predicting the dative alternation. In Gerlof Bouma, Irene Kramer, and Joost Zwarts, editors, *Cognitive Foundations of Interpretation*, pages 69–94. Royal Netherlands Academy of Science, Amsterdam.

Taylor Cassidy, Bill McDowell, Nathanael Chambers, and Steven Bethard. 2014. An annotation framework for dense event ordering. In *Proceedings of the 52nd Annual Meeting of the Association for Computational Linguistics (Volume 2: Short Papers)*, pages 501–506, Baltimore, Maryland, June. Association for Computational Linguistics.

J. K. Chambers and Natalie Schilling. 2013. *The Handbook of Language Variation and Change*. Blackwell, Oxford, 2nd edition.

Nathanael Chambers, Taylor Cassidy, Bill McDowell, and Steven Bethard. 2014. Dense event ordering with a multi-pass architecture. *Transactions of the Association for Computational Linguistics*, 2:273–284.

Tongfei Chen, Zhengping Jiang, Adam Poliak, Keisuke Sakaguchi, and Benjamin Van Durme. 2020. Uncertain natural language inference. In *Proceedings of the 58th Annual Meeting of the Association for Computational Linguistics*, pages 8772–8779, Online, July. Association for Computational Linguistics.

K. Bretonnel Cohen, Jingbo Xia, Pierre Zweigenbaum, Tiffany Callahan, Orin Hargraves, Foster Goss, Nancy Ide, Aurélie Névéol, Cyril Grouin, and Lawrence E. Hunter. 2018. Three Dimensions of Reproducibility in Natural Language Processing. In Nicoletta Calzolari, Khalid Choukri, Christopher Cieri, Thierry Declerck, Sara Goggi, Koiti Hasida, Hitoshi Isahara, Bente Maegaard, Joseph Mariani, Hélène Mazo, Asuncion Moreno, Jan Odijk, Stelios Piperidis, and Takenobu Tokunaga, editors, *Proceedings of the Eleventh International Conference on Language Resources and Evaluation (LREC 2018)*, Miyazaki, Japan, May 7-12, 2018. European Language Resources Association (ELRA).

Jacob Cohen. 1960. A coefficient of agreement for nominal scales. *Educational and Psychological Measurement*, 20:37–46.

Marie-Catherine de Marneffe, Timothy Dozat, Natalia Silveira, Katri Haverinen, Filip Ginter, Joakim Nivre, and Christopher D. Manning. 2014. Universal Stanford dependencies: A cross-linguistic typology. In *Proceedings of International Conference on Language Resources and Evaluation (LREC)*, pages 4585–4592.

Flavia De Simone, Barbara Balbi, Vincenzo Broscritto, Simona Collina, Roberto Montanari, Federico Boschetti, and Anas Kahn. 2018. The impact of human factors on digitization: An eye-tracking study of OCR proofreading strategies. In *The Tenth International Conference on Advanced Cognitive Technologies and Applications (COGNITIVE 2018)*, pages 14–17, Barcelona, Spain.

Hendrik de Smet. 2009. Analysing reanalysis. *Lingua*, 119(11):1728–1755.

Stefanie Dipper, Karin Donhauser, Thomas Klein, Sonja Linde, Stefan Müller, and Klaus-Peter Wegera. 2013. HiTS: ein Tagset für historische Sprachstufen des Deutschen. *Journal for Language Technology and Computational Linguistics*, 28:85–137.

Richard Eckart de Castilho, Éva Mújdricza-Maydt, Seid Muhie Yimam, Silvana Hartmann, Iryna Gurevych, Anette Frank, and Chris Biemann. 2016. A web-based tool for the integrated annotation of semantic and syntactic structures. In *Proceedings of the Workshop on Language Technology Resources and Tools for Digital Humanities (LT4DH)*, pages 76–84, Osaka, Japan, December. The COLING 2016 Organizing Committee.

Jürg Fleischer. 2009. Paleographic clues to prosody? – Accents, word separation, and other phenomena in Old High German manuscripts. In Roland Hinterhölzl and Svetlana Petrova, editors, *Information structure and language change: new approaches to word order variation in Germanic*, volume 203 of *Trends in Linguistic Studies and Monographs*, pages 161–189. Mouton de Gruyter, Berlin/New York.

Antske Fokkens, Marieke van Erp, Marten Postma, Ted Pedersen, Piek Vossen, and Nuno Freire. 2013. Offspring from reproduction problems: What replication failure teaches us. In *Proceedings of the 51st Annual Meeting of the Association for Computational Linguistics (Volume 1: Long Papers)*, pages 1691–1701, Sofia, Bulgaria, August. Association for Computational Linguistics.

Jost Gippert and Ralf Gehrke. 2015. Historical corpora. Challenges and perspectives. In Jost Gippert and Ralf Gehrke, editors, *Historical Corpora. Challenges and Perspectives*, Korpuslinguistik und interdisziplinäre Perspektiven auf Sprache 5, pages 9–12. Narr, Tübingen.

Stefan Th. Gries and Andrea L. Berez. 2017. Linguistic annotation in/for corpus linguistics. In Nancy Ide and James Pustejovsky, editors, *Handbook of Linguistic Annotation*, pages 379–409. Springer, Dordrecht.

Bernd Heine and Tania Kuteva. 2002. *World lexicon of grammaticalization*. Cambridge University Press, Cambridge.

Bernd Heine. 2002. On the role of context in grammaticalization. In Ilse Wischer and Gabriele Diewald, editors, *New Reflections on Grammaticalization*, pages 83–101. John Benjamins, Amsterdam.

Paul J. Hopper and Elizabeth Closs Traugott. 2003. *Grammaticalization*. Cambridge University Press, Cambridge.

Paul J. Hopper. 1991. On some principles of grammaticalization. In Elizabeth Closs Traugott and Bernd Heine, editors, *Approaches to grammaticalization. Volume I. Theoretical and methodological issues*, pages 17–35. John Benjamins, Amsterdam/Philadelphia.

Eduard Hovy and Julia Lavid. 2010. Towards a 'science' of corpus annotation: A new methodological challenge for corpus linguistics. *International Journal of Translation*, 22(1).

Richard Hudson. 2003. Gerunds without phrase structure. *Natural Language & Linguistic Theory*, 21(3):579–615.

Markus John, Steffen Koch, and Thomas Ertl. 2017. Uncertainty in visual text analysis in the context of the digital humanities. In *Designing for Uncertainty in HCI: When does uncertainty help? (Workshop at CHI 2017)*.

Daniel Jurafsky and James H. Martin. 2009. *Speech and Language Processing: An Introduction to Natural Language Processing, Speech Recognition, and Computational Linguistics*. Prentice-Hall, 2nd edition.

David Jurgens. 2013. Embracing ambiguity: A comparison of annotation methodologies for crowdsourcing word sense labels. In *Proceedings of the 2013 Conference of the North American Chapter of the Association for Computational Linguistics: Human Language Technologies*, pages 556–562, Atlanta, Georgia, June. Association for Computational Linguistics.

Karin Kipper Schuler. 2005. *VerbNet: A Broad-Coverage, Comprehensive Verb Lexicon*. Ph.D. thesis, University of Pennsylvania.

Klaus Krippendorff. 2004. Reliability in content analysis: some common misconceptions and recommendations. *Human Communication Research*, 30(3):411–433.

Anthony Kroch. 1989. Reflexes of grammar in patterns of language change. *Language Variation and Change*, 1(3):199–244.

Merja Kytö. 2010. Corpora and historical linguistics. *Revista Brasileira de Linguística Aplicada*, 11:417–457, 12.

William Labov. 1994. *Principles of linguistic change. Volume I: Internal factors*. Blackwell, Oxford.

Geoffrey Leech. 1991. The state of the art of corpus linguistics. In *English Corpus Linguistics: Linguistic Studies in Honour of Jan Svartvik*, pages 8–29. Longman, London.

John Lowe. 2016. Participles, gerunds and syntactic categories. In Doug Arnold, Miriam Butt, Berthold Crysmann, Tracy Holloway King, and Stefan Müller, editors, *Proceedings of the Joint 2016 Conference on Head-driven Phrase Structure Grammar and Lexical Functional Grammar, Polish Academy of Sciences, Warsaw, Poland*, pages 401–421, Stanford, CA. CSLI Publications.

Anke Lüdeling. 2017. Variationistische Korpusstudien. In Marek Konopka and Angelika Wöllstein, editors, *Grammatische Variation. Empirische Zugänge und theoretische Modellierung. IDS Jahrbuch 2016*, pages 129–144. de Gruyter, Berlin.

Robert Malouf. 1996. A constructional approach to English verbal gerunds. *Annual Meeting of the Berkeley Linguistics Society*, 22(1):255–266.

Mitchell P. Marcus, Beatrice Santorini, Mary Ann Marcinkiewicz, and Ann Taylor. 1999. *Treebank-3*. Linguistic Data Consortium, Philadelphia.

Marie-Luis Merten and Nina Seemann. 2018. Analyzing constructional change: Linguistic annotation and sources of uncertainty. In *Proceedings of the Sixth International Conference on Technological Ecosystems for Enhancing Multiculturality*, TEEM'18, page 819–825, New York, NY, USA. Association for Computing Machinery.

Leonard Neidorf. 2013. Scribal errors of proper names in the Beowulf manuscript. *Anglo-Saxon England*, 42:249–269.

Rebecca J. Passonneau and Bob Carpenter. 2014. The benefits of a model of annotation. *Transactions of the Association for Computational Linguistics*, 2:311–326.

Ellie Pavlick and Tom Kwiatkowski. 2019. Inherent disagreements in human textual inferences. *Transactions of the Association for Computational Linguistics*, 7:677–694, March.

Herbert Penzl. 1967. The linguistic interpretation of scribal errors in Old High German texts. *Linguistics*, 5(32):79–82.

Susan Pintzuk. 2003. Variationist approaches to syntactic change. In Brian D. Joseph and Richard D. Janda, editors, *The Handbook of Historical Linguistics*, pages 509–528. Blackwell, Oxford.

Barbara Plank, Dirk Hovy, and Anders Søgaard. 2014. Learning part-of-speech taggers with inter-annotator agreement loss. In *Proceedings of the 14th Conference of the European Chapter of the Association for Computational Linguistics*, pages 742–751, Gothenburg, Sweden, April. Association for Computational Linguistics.

Randi Reppen. 2010. Building a corpus. In Anne O'Keeffe and Michael McCarthy, editors, *The Routledge Handbook of Corpus Linguistics*, pages 31–37. Routledge, London.

Beatrice Santorini. 2010. Annotation manual for the Penn Historical Corpora and the PCEEC. Department of Linguistics, University of Pennsylvania. https://www.ling.upenn.edu/hist-corpora/annotation/index.html.

Sarah Schulz and Jonas Kuhn. 2017. Multi-modular domain-tailored OCR post-correction. In *Proceedings of the 2017 Conference on Empirical Methods in Natural Language Processing*, pages 2716–2726, Copenhagen, Denmark, September. Association for Computational Linguistics.

Nina Seemann, Marie-Luis Merten, Michaela Geierhos, Doris Tophinke, and Eyke Hüllermeier. 2017. Annotation Challenges for Reconstructing the Structural Elaboration of Middle Low German. In *Proceedings of the Joint SIGHUM Workshop on Computational Linguistics for Cultural Heritage, Social Sciences, Humanities and Literature*, pages 40–45, Vancouver, Canada, August. Association for Computational Linguistics.

Anders Søgaard, Barbara Plank, and Dirk Hovy. 2014. Selection bias, label bias, and bias in ground truth. In *Proceedings of COLING 2014, the 25th International Conference on Computational Linguistics: Tutorial Abstracts*, pages 11–13, Dublin, Ireland, August. Dublin City University and Association for Computational Linguistics.

Fabian Sperrle, Rita Sevastjanova, Rebecca Kehlbeck, and Mennatallah El-Assady. 2019. VIANA: Visual interactive annotation of argumentation. In *2019 IEEE Conference on Visual Analytics Science and Technology (VAST)*, pages 11–22.

Fabian Sperrle, Mark-Matthias Zymla, Mennatallah El-Assady, Miriam Butt, and Daniel Keim. 2020. Guided linguistic annotation of argumentation through visual analytics. In *ArgVis 2020 — COMMA Workshop on Argument Visualization*.

Sali A. Tagliamonte. 2006. *Analysing sociolinguistic variation*. Cambridge University Press, Cambridge.

Siddharth Vashishtha, Benjamin Van Durme, and Aaron Steven White. 2019. Fine-grained temporal relation extraction. In *Proceedings of the 57th Annual Meeting of the Association for Computational Linguistics*, pages 2906–2919, Florence, Italy, July. Association for Computational Linguistics.

Bonnie Webber, Rashmi Prasad, Alan Lee, and Aravind Joshi. 2019. The Penn Discourse Treebank 3.0 annotation manual. https://catalog.ldc.upenn.edu/docs/LDC2019T05/PDTB3-Annotation-Manual.pdf.

Sheng Zhang, Rachel Rudinger, Kevin Duh, and Benjamin Van Durme. 2017. Ordinal common-sense inference. *Transactions of the Association for Computational Linguistics*, 5:379–395.

# Understanding the Tradeoff between Cost and Quality of Expert Annotations for Keyphrase Extraction


**Hung Chau**[*]
University of Pittsburgh
Pittsburgh, PA
hkc6@pitt.edu

**Saeid Balaneshin**
Zillow Group
Seattle, WA
saeidb@zillowgroup.com

**Kai Liu**
Zillow Group
Seattle, WA
kail@zillow.com

**Ondrej Linda**
Zillow Group
Seattle, WA
ondrejl@zillow.com


## Abstract


Generating expert ground truth annotations of documents can be a very expensive process. However, such annotations are essential for training domain-specific keyphrase extraction models, especially when utilizing data-intensive deep learning models in unique domains such as real-estate. Therefore, it is critical to optimize the manual annotation process to maximize the quality of the annotations while minimizing the cost of manual labor. To address this need, we explore multiple annotation strategies including self-review and peer-review as well as various methods of resolving annotator disagreements. We evaluate these annotation strategies with respect to their cost and on the task of learning keyphrase extraction models applied with an experimental dataset in the real-estate domain. The results demonstrate that different annotation strategies should be considered depending on specific metrics such as precision and recall.


## 1 Introduction

Automatic keyphrase extraction is an important technology on the crossroads of natural language processing and information access. Domain-specific keyphrase extraction models are widely used in many real-world applications such as document characterization and clustering (Hammouda et al., 2005), domain specific knowledge organization (Kosovac et al., 2002), topic-based access to document collections (Jones and Paynter, 1999), natural language question answering (Chaudhri et al., 2013), personalized recommendation of external content (Agrawal et al., 2014), and many other tasks (Papagiannopoulou and Tsoumakas, 2019).

One approach to such keyphrase extraction is to apply pre-trained or unsupervised models. However, such models might suffer from a lack of domain-specific knowledge. For example, while the terms "home" or "bedroom" alone can be called keyphrases in general, they carry very little information in the real-estate domain. Therefore, training domain-specific keyphrase extraction models based on expert knowledge is vital in such applications. In addition, for some easier tasks such as content linking or content recommendation, automatic processing could support sufficient levels of quality. For more challenging tasks, such as personalization, the use of expert annotation in some form is essential.

Annotations of domain-specific documents can be performed via crowd-sourcing, online workers and/or expert annotators (Su et al., 2007; Snow et al., 2008). This process can be done by each expert annotating a single document, doing self-review, multiple experts annotating the same document or doing peer-reviews. In the case of multi-annotator disagreement, a voting rule should be applied. In previous studies, a common practice to measure the quality of annotation labels is to compute inter-annotator agreement (Wilbur et al., 2006; Ogren et al., 2006; Kim et al., 2008; South et al., 2014; Augenstein et al., 2017). More annotation/review steps involved in this process often result in a better agreement between annotators.

---

[*] The author completed this work during an internship at Zillow Group.






*The 14th Linguistic Annotation Workshop*, pages 74–86
Barcelona, Spain (Online), December 12, 2020.

However, it is still unclear whether the training set extracted from annotations with multiple annotation/review steps would increase the performance of keyphrase extraction models significantly. In addition, multiple annotation/review steps inevitably increase the cost of the annotation process as multiple experts have to tag the same set of documents. Due to the cost of hiring domain experts, it is critical to select an annotation strategy that maximizes the quality while minimizing the cost. Despite this substantial higher cost, to the best of our knowledge, there is no study analyzing the tradeoff of using annotations by multiple experts and the performance improvements of the keyphrase extraction model.

To fill in this gap, this paper experimentally analyzes the tradeoff between the cost of annotation strategies and the impact these strategies have on the model performance. We measure the mean annotation time per document and compare the precision, recall and f1-score measures of classification and sequence labeling models over self-review, peer-review and different annotation aggregation methods. The experimental results demonstrate that different annotation strategies should be selected depending on whether the objective is to optimize for precision, recall or f1-score.

The rest of the paper is organized as follows. Section 2 reviews related work and Section 3 discusses annotation and keyphrase extraction methodology. The experimental results are presented in 4 and the paper is concluded in 5.

## 2  Related Work

### 2.1  Data Annotation

Annotation is the basis of any supervised natural language processing research. Annotation processes has been applied in various domains, including the scientific publication domain (Augenstein et al., 2017), biomedical literature (Wilbur et al., 2006; Kim et al., 2008), educational textbooks (Chau et al., 2020), and medical records  (Ogren et al., 2006; Xia and Yetisgen-Yildiz, 2012). These processes often start with recruiting domain experts and defining initial guidelines. Next, the guidelines are iteratively refined until the agreement reaches a pre-defined threshold. Each expert then annotates a larger scale document collection using the guideline. Eventually, ground truth data is selected based on the inter-annotator agreement. In the annotation process, organizing meetings with the annotators and involving them in reviewing and adjudication have shown positive impacts on the quality of annotations (Kim et al., 2008; Chau et al., 2020) but of course increase annotation efforts. Interestingly, Wilbur et al. (2006) found that the inter-annotator agreement could significantly increase among annotators who had gained experience working with the guidelines.

There are efforts in exploring the possibility of utilizing crowdsourcing for domain-specific text annotations. For instance, Uzuner et al. (2010) addressed the problem of annotating documents in the medical domain through experts to generate guidelines and a community of medical practitioners to perform annotations, which has a lower cost in comparison to employing experts for annotations. By utilizing guidelines generated by the experts and distributing them to the community annotators, they have achieved promising annotations. This indicates the value of including knowledge of the domain in generating high-quality annotation results in domain-specific tasks. Sabou et al. (2014) proposed a set of best practice guidelines for crowdsourced corpus acquisition and introduced an extension of the GATE NLP platform to facilitate the creation of crowdsourced tasks based on best practice. Liu et al. (2016) found that crowdsourced annotation can boost F1 score in relation extraction by Gated Instruction, which combines an interactive tutorial feedback to correct errors during training and improved screening, and they also claimed that with the high quality Gated Instruction annotations, a single annotation is more effective than majority vote over multiple annotators.

In contrast, researchers also explore the application of machine-assisted methods in expediting the text annotation process. A web survey conducted in 2009 (Tomanek and Olsson, 2009) shows that 20% of participants said they had used active learning as support in their annotation projects. There are also tools enabling semi-automatic annotation process, such as TURKSENT (Eryiğit et al., 2013), BRAT (Stenetorp et al., 2012), eHOST (South et al., 2012), and NER (Chen et al., 2017). They can generate annotations via experts correcting the output of a pre-trained linguistic system. Stenetorp et al. (2012) found a 15% decrease in total annotation time for a multicategory entity mention annotation task. However, South et al. (2014) claimed that manual annotation process produced higher quality data without taking more time in comparison with an annotation method that combines machine pre-annotations with an interactive annotation interface in the manual annotation process.

For labeling keyphrases in text documents, the process of gathering the annotators (usually weekly) to discuss, resolve conflicts and agree on the annotations is very expensive. Allowing annotators to review their own or others's annotation may help to improve annotation quality with lower cost. However, it is still not clear how those extra efforts could help to increase keyphrase extraction models overall. This study attempts to understand the tradeoff between those cost and quality of the keyphrase annotation.

## 2.2 Keyphrase Extraction

There is a wide range of automatic keyphrase extraction methods from using unsupervised learning to rule-based, supervised learning or deep neural network models. Typical keyphrase extraction systems firstly pre-process data, extract *candidate keyphrases* using predefined Lexico-Syntactic patterns (Florescu and Caragea, 2017; Le et al., 2016), Part-of-Speech (POS) tags (e.g., *nouns* or *noun-nouns*) (Mihalcea and Tarau, 2004; Bougouin et al., 2013; Liu et al., 2009a; Wan and Xiao, 2008) or $n$-grams with simple filtering rules (Witten et al., 1999; Medelyan et al., 2009); and then predict which of these candidates are correct keyphrases.

An example of *unsupervised* keyphrase extraction methods are *graph-based methods* explored by (Mihalcea and Tarau, 2004; Bougouin et al., 2013). They consider a candidate keyphrase as important if it is related to a large number of candidates and those candidates are also important in the document. Candidates and their relations form a graph for the given document and keyphrases are selected based on their *PageRank* score. In addition, *topic-based clustering methods* (Liu et al., 2009b; Liu et al., 2010; Grineva et al., 2009) attempt to group semantically similar candidates in a document as *topics*. Keyphrases are then selected based on the centroid of each cluster or the importance of each topic. Although unsupervised learning models can extract keyphrases without any need for labeled data, their performances are commonly insufficient.

*Supervised* keyphrase extraction models often frame this task as *binary classification* or *sequence labeling problems*. The classifiers use different kinds of features, including *statistics*-based features, *linguistics*-based features or *external resources* (Hammouda et al., 2005; Witten et al., 1999; Rose et al., 2010; Hulth, 2003; Wang et al., 2015; Yih et al., 2006; Nguyen and Kan, 2007; Chau et al., 2020) to train supervised models. Sequence labeling models for keyphrase extraction have shown promising results in a recent study (Gollapalli et al., 2017). The deep sequence labeling with Bi-LSTM-CRF models has shown to significantly outperform its unsupervised and supervised baseline models (Alzaidy et al., 2019). However, the deep learning models require a large amount of data to achieve their best performances compared with traditional machine learning approaches.

Due to the high cost of creating training data, advanced weak supervision approaches have recently been attractive to the NLP community; however, expert knowledge is still needed to define labeling functions (especially in specific domains) and extra steps are usually applied to create cleaner training data outputs for ML models (e.g., slice-based learning) (Ratner et al., 2017; Chen et al., 2019). In this study, we focus on understanding the cost and quality of expert annotation for keyphrase extraction when manual annotation is essential, and compare supervised models to unsupervised models which do not need extra efforts for the problem.

## 3 Methodology

### 3.1 Annotation Procedure

To evaluate the tradeoff between cost and quality of expert annotation labels, we analyze multiple methods and aggregation strategies (voting rules) for label generation. In this annotation process, three experts, who have at least six months experience of working in the real-estate domain, receive training and pass a test that focuses on the understanding of the task and the BRAT annotation interface[1]. They, then, develop guidelines (described in Section 3.1.1) through multiple weekly annotation discussions. In each iteration,

---

[1] https://brat.nlplab.org

| Guidelines |
| --- |
| Keyphrases should not contain multiple pieces of information. |
| Keyphrases should be the longest consecutive phrases. |
| Keyphrases should not have redundant words. |
| Keyphrases can have misspellings. |

Table 1: An example set of guidelines created by the experts.

the experts independently label keyphrases in 10 listing descriptions, followed up with a discussion to resolve disagreement and updating the guidelines. Next, the experts annotate a larger set of 50 listing descriptions and record the annotation time. The experts are not allowed to discuss their annotation/review before finishing all annotation tasks. All labels generated in the procedure are combined based on different strategies (described in Section 3.1.2) and used as ground truth data for training classification and sequence labeling models.

### 3.1.1 Guidelines

The annotation guidelines are created by experts through multiple annotation-discussion iterations. These iterations should continue until no guidelines are added or updated by the experts in a discussion session. An example set of these guidelines is shown in Table 1.

Some of the created guidelines can be used in the review process (presented in the next section) to reject an annotated keyphrase. For example, the guideline *"Keyphrases should not contain multiple pieces of information"* can be used to reject "4 bedrooms near Disneyland" which contains two pieces of information: "4 bedrooms" and "near Disneyland". On the other hand, a number of created guidelines such as *"Keyphrases can have misspellings"* can be used to guide the experts to accept keyphrases like "4 bedroom". For the guideline *"Keyphrases should be the longest consecutive phrases"*, *3 bedrooms* is the keyphrase in "This home has 3 bedrooms." but *3 bedrooms upstairs* is the keyphrase in "It has 3 bedrooms upstairs".

The experts may combine guidelines to select or reject a keyphrase. For example, an expert may consider the guideline *"Keyphrases should not contain multiple concepts"* in conjunction with the guideline *"Keyphrases should be the longest consecutive phrases"* and *"Keyphrases should not have redundant words"* to select/reject a keyphrase.

We use the annotation labels generated during the guideline development process as ground truth data for model evaluation during our experiments.

### 3.1.2 Coding Procedure for Training Set

Having experts resolve annotation conflicts via discussion can be very expensive and not scalable for a large number of listing descriptions. Instead, a review process can be adopted to ensure the keyphrases adhere to the guidelines. Performing review after annotation steps increases the cost of annotation, but it may help to improve the quality of the keyphrase labels by mitigating issues such as experts' fatigue and lack of attention. An additional factor influencing the tradeoff between annotation cost and quality is the number of experts required to annotate each listing.

The review process can be either a self-review or a peer-review process. In the case of a self-review process, the same expert reviews his/her keyphrase annotation to ensure that he/she has followed the provided guidelines. The self-review also provides a chance for the experts to adjust their annotations based on their interpretations of guidelines so far. For a peer-review, the experts are exposed to the interpretation of the guidelines by the other experts. This exposure may cause the experts to change their mind about some of their interpretations of guidelines. The final annotations are the results of the reviewers' edits.

By considering the mean annotation time per document including the review process, the lowest cost approach is to have each document annotated by a single expert with no review. On the other hand, the most costly approach is to annotate the same listing descriptions by all the experts and perform a peer-review. This process is schematically depicted in Figure 1.

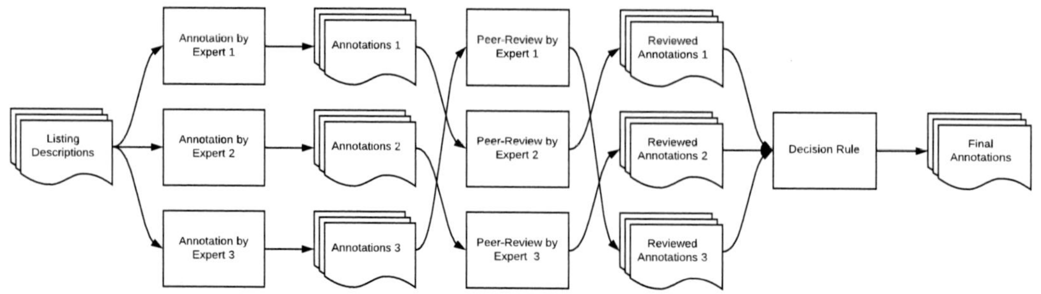

Figure 1: Process of generating training data based on peer-review.

## 3.2 Keyphrase Extraction Models

A domain-based keyphrase extraction task can be formulated as follows: *given a domain-specific text document, extract all phrases of interest to the users of that domain.* For this task, we investigate a shallow classification model and a deep sequence labeling model.

### 3.2.1 Classification Model (LogReg)

For the classification model, we recast the keyphrase extraction as a binary classification problem including three main steps:

**Pre-processing data**: We use spaCy[2], an open-source library for NLP, to tag part-of-speech (POS) and then apply pre-defined patterns with regular expressions to extract all possible candidates (i.e., mostly but not limited to nouns and noun phrases). We only extract keyphrase candidates which consist of a maximum of 4 words in accordance with our annotation guidelines.

**Feature Extraction**: we extract an extensive list of features for each of the candidates:

- *linguistic*-based features: length of $n$-grams, concatenated POS of all tokens (e.g., `["JJ", "NN"]` for "great location"), POS of each of the tokens, POS of two words before, POS of two words after, and whether the phrase contains any named entities (e.g., area names).
- *statistics*-based features: document term frequency, collection term frequency, tf-idf, okapi BM25 and c-value (i.e., calculated from a collection of five thousand listing descriptions).

We bin and discretize non-binary numerical features in our model. We also apply a one-hot encoding on all non-binary features.

**Model training and prediction**: A logistic regression model (LogReg) is trained on the labeled feature vectors of candidate keyphrases. For the prediction phase, an input document is also processed by the first two steps and then the trained model will predict keyphrase likelihood for all candidates.

### 3.2.2 Sequence Labeling Model (Bi-LSTM-CRF)

We also approach the keyphrase extraction problem as a sequence labeling task. This task can be formally stated as a named entity recognition (NER) problem. Given a sequence of $n$ words in a listing description $d = \{w_1, w_2, ..., w_n\}$, we want to infer their hidden class labels (i.e., belonging to a keyphrase class). In this model, we set 3 class labels $Y = \{k_B, k_I, k_O\}$, representing "beginning of a keyphrase", "inside of a keyphrase", and "not a part of a keyphrase".

In this study, we apply a Bi-LSTM-CRF architecture to perform this task, which has been shown to achieve the best performance across several public datasets (Alzaidy et al., 2019). The standard Bi-LSTM-CRF model consists of three main components (see Figure 2). We briefly present these components as below, for the detailed architecture refer to this work (Liu et al., 2018).

**Embedding Layer**: word and character-level embeddings are trained purely on un-annotated sequence data from a text corpus. While word embeddings capture syntactic and semantic regularities in language, character embeddings provide additional information about the underlying style and structure of words,

---
[2]`https://spacy.io/`

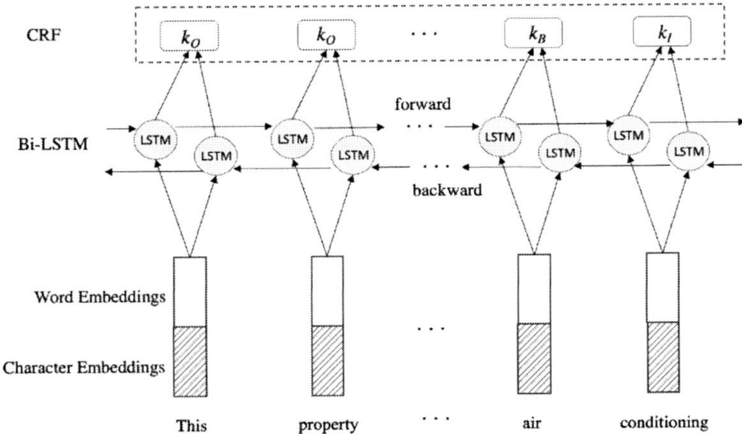


Figure 2: Bi-LSTM-CRF model for keyphrase extraction.

both improving many NLP tasks including NER. The one-hot vector of an input word $w_t$ is mapped to a fixed size dense vector in this layer.

**Bi-LSTM Layer**: the concatenation of character and word embeddings is the input for this layer. An LSTM unit has four components: *input gate, forget gate, memory cell* and *output gate*. The input vectors go through LSTM units in both directions, creating two hidden state vectors: $\overrightarrow{h_t}$ and $\overleftarrow{h_t}$ capturing information from words before and after $w_t$, respectively. The concatenation of these two vectors $\overleftrightarrow{h_t}$ represents the semantics and dependencies of $w_t$ in the context of the input text.

**CRF Layer**: Conditional Random Field (CRF) based models introduced by (Lafferty et al., 2001) have been successfully used in many sequence labeling tasks. $\overleftrightarrow{h_t}$ is the input for the CRF layer which produces a probability distribution over a tag sequence based on the mapping of the input vectors to the class space and the dependencies of adjacency class labels of the entire sequence. CRFs use the Viterbi algorithm to efficiently infer the optimal sequence of labels for an input sequence.

Our implementation of the model is based on the version presented in (Liu et al., 2018)[3]. We use the Glove pre-trained word embeddings of 100-dimensions[4]. Character embeddings are trained along with the main model with Bi-LSTM networks. The dimension of character embeddings is set to 30. We use a 300-dimension hidden layer for the character learning model as well as the main model. The models are trained using mini-batch stochastic gradient descent with momentum. The batch size is set to 5. The learning rate and decay ratio are set to 0.015 and 0.05, respectively. Dropout and gradient clipping of 5.0 are also applied to avoid over-fitting and increase stability.

## 4 Experiments and Results

### 4.1 Annotation Data Analysis

**Statistics**: We focus on the real-estate domain in English and create a dataset with 50 and 20 listing descriptions for training and evaluation. The average length of the sampled listing descriptions was 125 words, with some having as few as 50 and as many as 500. Table 2a lists the mean annotation time for each expert. It shows that, on average, experts conducted self- and peer-review in about half the time as the initial annotation.

**Count of Keyphrases**: Table 2b shows the average count of keyphrases per listing selected by experts in different steps of the annotation/review process. This table indicates that, on average, self- and peer-review steps slightly increase the number of selected keyphrases, indicating that experts more often added additional keyphrases than removed the already annotated ones.

---

[3]https://github.com/LiyuanLucasLiu/LM-LSTM-CRF
[4]https://nlp.stanford.edu/projects/glove/

| Step | Annotation | Self-Review | Peer-Review |
|------|------------|-------------|-------------|
| Time | 00:02:49 | 00:01:23 | 00:01:25 |

(a)

| Step/Expert | A | B | C |
|-------------|------|------|------|
| Annotation | 20.52 | 18.52 | 20.8 |
| Self-Review | 20.34 | 19.66 | 22.62 |
| Peer-Review | 20.74 | 20.24 | 21.98 |

(b)

Table 2: (a) Average time spent (in HH:MM:SS format) by each expert on each annotation/review step. (b) The average count of keyphrases selected by different experts from each listing description.

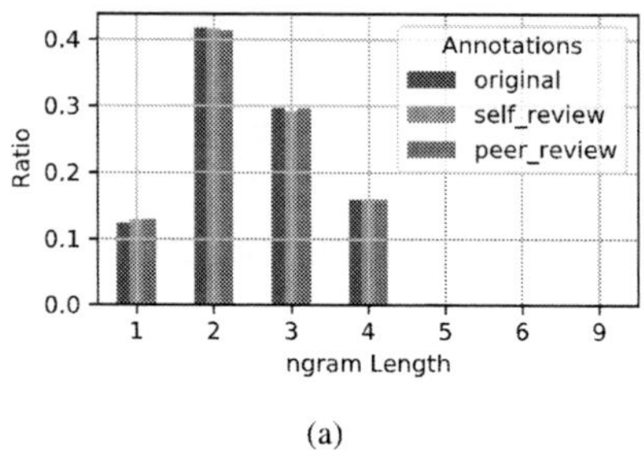

(a)

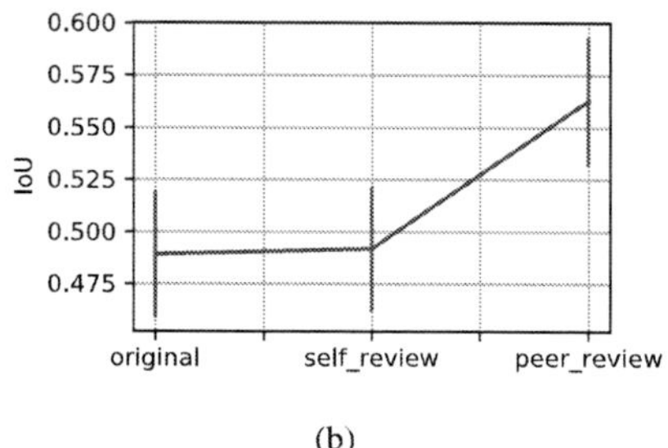

(b)

Figure 3: (a) The ratio of keyphrases with different lengths of $n$-grams. Bigrams are the most selected keyphrases. (b) Agreement (in terms of IoU) in selected keyphrases by different experts in different annotation/review steps. Peer-review is more effective than self-review in increasing the agreement.

$n$-**grams in Selected Keyphrases**: Figure 3a shows that the majority of selected keyphrases were bigrams (around 40%). Although per the guidelines, the experts were asked to limit the length of the annotated $n$-grams to 4, in less than 1% of cases, 5- and 6-grams were selected due to either a mistake or an incorrect interpretation of the guidelines (e.g., by selecting "14 x 14 covered dec" as a keyphrase). Figure 3a also shows that the length of the selected keyphrase did not change significantly after self- or peer-review processes.

**Self- and Peer-Review Processes**: In Figure 3b, we use the intersection-over-union (IoU) to measure the amount of agreement among experts, which is defined as # of keyphrases selected by all experts over # of keyphrases selected by any expert. The value of IoU ranges from 0 to 1, where 0 and 1 corresponds to no common keyphrases and all keyphrases being shared between experts, respectively.

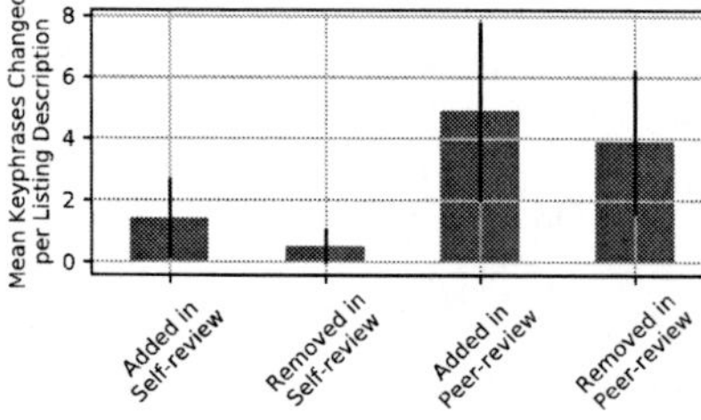

Figure 4: The average number of keyphrases added/removed per listing description during self and peer review steps.

| Method | Precision | Recall | F1-score |
|--------|-----------|--------|----------|
| TextRank | 0.32 | 0.46 | 0.35 |
| SingleRank | 0.36 | 0.46 | 0.39 |
| TopicRank | 0.28 | 0.47 | 0.33 |
| TopicalPageRank | 0.32 | 0.41 | 0.35 |
| PositionRank | 0.31 | 0.44 | 0.34 |
| MultipartiteRank | 0.28 | 0.51 | 0.34 |
| **LogReg** | **0.59** | **0.83** | **0.69** |
| **Bi-LSTM-CRF** | **0.60** | **0.66** | **0.63** |

Table 3: The performances of two supervised models (LogReg and Bi-LSTM-CRF) trained on *orig-one* dataset in comparison to multiple unsupervised baselines.

| Dataset | Average no. of keyphrases per Doc. | Time per Doc. (sec) | LogReg | | | Bi-LSTM-CRF | | |
| --- | --- | --- | --- | --- | --- | --- | --- | --- |
| | | | Precision | Recall | F1 | Precision | Recall | F1 |
| orig-one | 19.66 | 170 | 0.59 | 0.83 | 0.69 | 0.60 | 0.66 | 0.63 |
| orig-two-union | 24.3 | 340 | 0.54 | 0.86 | 0.66 | 0.59 | 0.68 | 0.63 |
| orig-two-unanimity | 15.34 | 340 | 0.60 | 0.83 | 0.69 | 0.70 | 0.58 | 0.64 |
| orig-three-union | 26.88 | 510 | 0.51 | 0.87 | 0.65 | 0.57 | 0.70 | 0.63 |
| orig-three-majority | 19 | 510 | 0.58 | 0.83 | 0.68 | 0.63 | 0.68 | 0.65 |
| orig-three-unanimity | 13.28 | 510 | **0.61** | 0.80 | 0.69 | **0.74** | 0.56 | 0.64 |
| self-one | 20.84 | 255 | 0.58 | 0.86 | 0.69 | 0.59 | 0.68 | 0.63 |
| self-two-union | 25.42 | 510 | 0.52 | 0.87 | 0.65 | 0.58 | 0.69 | 0.63 |
| self-two-unanimity | 15.98 | 510 | 0.60 | 0.84 | **0.70** | 0.68 | 0.62 | 0.65 |
| self-three-union | 28.1 | 765 | 0.49 | 0.87 | 0.63 | 0.52 | 0.72 | 0.60 |
| self-three-majority | 19.84 | 765 | 0.56 | 0.83 | 0.67 | 0.61 | 0.71 | 0.66 |
| self-three-unanimity | 13.94 | 765 | **0.61** | 0.82 | **0.70** | 0.71 | 0.59 | 0.64 |
| peer-one | 20.72 | 253 | 0.55 | 0.83 | 0.67 | 0.63 | 0.69 | 0.66 |
| peer-two-union | 24.86 | 506 | 0.51 | **0.89** | 0.65 | 0.56 | **0.74** | 0.64 |
| peer-two-unanimity | 16.7 | 506 | 0.60 | 0.85 | **0.70** | 0.66 | 0.66 | 0.66 |
| peer-three-union | 26.82 | 759 | 0.51 | **0.89** | 0.65 | 0.54 | **0.74** | 0.63 |
| peer-three-majority | 20.22 | 759 | 0.55 | 0.84 | 0.67 | 0.64 | 0.70 | **0.67** |
| peer-three-unanimity | 15.12 | 759 | 0.59 | 0.82 | 0.69 | 0.66 | 0.62 | 0.64 |

Table 4: The performance comparison of LogReg and Bi-LSTM-CRF models trained on different variations of our dataset.

Figure 3b shows that the ratio of common keyphrases between experts significantly increases during the peer-review process, while it remains unchanged during self-review. Therefore, in resolving the disagreements among experts, peer-review appears to be far more effective than self-review. The increase in agreements after the peer-review process can stem from the way that experts reconsidered their interpretation of guidelines when they were exposed to the annotations by other experts.

Top keyphrases that experts considered as acceptable after the peer-review process include "Dock", "Deck", and "Conveniently Located", and those removed after the peer-review process include "Stunning" and "Amenities".

When examining the average number of added and removed keyphrases across all listing descriptions, we found that the number of added/removed keyphrases in the peer-review process is around 5 times more than that in self-review process and that the number of added keyphrases is higher than removed in both self- and peer-review processes (see Figure 4). It suggests that experts more frequently tend to identify additional keyphrases that might have been missed previously in either self- or peer-review process.

## 4.2 Model Performance Comparison

As described in Section 3.1.2, we investigate the tradeoff between quality and cost of the annotations given the number of experts annotating each listing description and the type of review process. To do so, each listing description is firstly annotated by three experts separately and then it goes through the self- and peer-review processes. Therefore, the data we collected includes three annotations per each description. This allows us to create training sets with one or two expert annotations per listing description via uniformly sampling which one or two annotations out of the three available should be considered.

In this study, we also investigate three review types: (1) *orig*: original (no-review), (2) *self*: self-review, or (3) *peer*: peer-review. In the case of having more than one annotation per listing description, we investigate three voting rules: (1) *union*: a keyphrase is selected if it was annotated by at least one expert, (2) *majority*: a keyphrase is selected if it was annotated by two or more experts, or (3) *unanimity*: a keyphrase is selected if it was annotated by all three experts. By combining review types, number of annotators per listing description and the voting rules, we generated 18 different training data sets. The name of these data sets are described in Table 4 by the following format: review type (*orig, self*, or *peer*)-number of annotations per listing description (*one, two, three*)-voting rule (*union, majority*, or *unanimity*).

In Table 4, we show the performance of the classification (LogReg) and sequence labeling (Bi-LSTM-

| Output from LogReg | Output from Bi-LSTM-CRF |
| --- | --- |
| A ranch style home inside the Western Park community! Entering the home you step inside the large living room that basks in plenty of sunshine. The eat-in kitchen overlooks the living room, allowing you to chat while you cook dinner! The kitchen boasts countertop space, upper cabinetry, a large pantry, and sleek black appliances. | A ranch style home inside the Western Park community! Entering the home you step inside the large living room that basks in plenty of sunshine. The eat-in kitchen overlooks the living room, allowing you to chat while you cook dinner! The kitchen boasts countertop space, upper cabinetry, a large pantry, and sleek black appliances. |

Table 5: LogReg vs. Bi-LSTM-CRF: keyphrase extraction in real estate. The yellow keyphrases are true positives and the blue ones are false negatives.

CRF) keyphrase extraction models trained on all the 18 training data sets and evaluated on the common ground truth data, which as described in Section 3.1.1 includes 20 descriptions and has average of 14.8 keyphrases per document. As an example of the final output, Figure 5 depicts a listing description and the extracted phrases from LogReg and Bi-LSTM-CRF. In addition to comparing precision, recall and f1-scores, we also include the average number of keyphrases and the mean annotation time per listing description for each training set. The presented experimental results allow us to analyze the tradeoff between the cost and quality of the selected keyphrase annotation methods.

Observations from Table 4:

- **Precision vs. Time**: For both LogReg and Bi-LSTM-CRF models, using *orig-three-unanimity* data set results in the highest precision value.
- **Recall vs. Time**: the best recall was achieved by *peer-two-union* for both LogReg and Bi-LSTM-CRF models with regard to time.
- **F1-score vs. Time**: the best performance was achieved by *peer-two-unanimity* for LogReg and by *peer-three-majority* for Bi-LSTM-CRF models. However, in the case of LogReg model, *orig-one* only needs 170 seconds but its performance is very close to the best, which requires on average 506 seconds of annotation time.
- **Precision and Recall vs. Voting Rule**: From these results we can conclude that the more agreement is enforced among the annotators, the higher precision (e.g., Precision(*-three-unanimity*) > Precision(*-three-majority*) > Precision(*-three-union*)). The result consistently indicates that the larger the size of the training data, the higher the recall (e.g., Recall(*-three-union*) > Recall(*-three-majority*) > Recall(*-three-unanimity*)).
- **LogReg vs. Bi-LSTM-CRF**: the recall of LogReg model is higher than Bi-LSTM-CRF model; on the other hand, the precision of the latter is higher than the former. Overall, the F1-score of LogReg model is a bit better. The Bi-LSTM-CRF model typically requires much more labeled data to boost the performance or needs to fine tune on a pre-trained model. Nevertheless, with this small training set, the deep sequence labeling model is still able to obtain a good result that outperforms unsupervised models that will be presented shortly.
- *Original* vs. *self-review* vs. *peer-review*: the average performance as well as the mean annotation time of the *self-review* and *peer-review* data are very similar. The *original* data, which requires least effort, has the lowest recall but surprisingly the highest precision. For the average F1-scores, we do not see significant differences among these three.

In Table 3, we compare the performances of the two supervised models with state-of-the-art unsupervised models (Mihalcea and Tarau, 2004; Wan and Xiao, 2008; Bougouin et al., 2013; Sterckx et al., 2015; Florescu and Caragea, 2017; Boudin, 2018).[5] We choose *orig-one* dataset, which requires the least annotation effort, as the training data for the supervised models. Table 3 reveals that the supervised models substantially outperform all the unsupervised baselines in terms of *precision*, *recall* and *f1-score*. This performance again emphasizes the importance of exploiting domain-specific knowledge and expert annotations as labeled training data for training keyphrase extraction models.

## 5 Conclusions

In this paper, we presented multiple annotation strategies including self-review and peer-review processes as well as various ways of resolving annotator disagreement for keyphrase annotation problems. We trained a classification model with an extensive list of features in the domain of real-estate. In addition,

---

[5] https://github.com/boudinfl/pke

we applied a Bi-LSTM-CRF architecture for a sequence labeling approach to extract keyphrases. We evaluated the two models' performances with eighteen different training datasets generated from the aforementioned strategies to see the tradeoff between the cost and quality of expert annotations. The results showed that different annotation strategies can be considered depending on a specific metric. We observed the consistent improvement for precision or recall when applying different voting rules for all the three review types. With respect to average f1-scores, we do not see an improvement of self-review and peer-review over the original annotations. The comparison between the two supervised models with the state-of-the-art unsupervised models has shown the importance of exploiting domain-specific knowledge and expert annotations to keyphrase extraction problems. However, this work is limited to one small dataset. It could be extended and evaluated on multiple datasets from different domains (e.g., e-commerce, education or medical) to examine the general applicability of our proposed annotation strategies.

This work, to the best of our knowledge, is the first to understand the tradeoff between cost and quality of expert annotation for keyphrase extraction. There is still room to improve the models, for example by leveraging user search terms as a feature for LogReg or pre-trained language models and transfer learning for Bi-LSTM-CRF. Our priority is to investigate whether the approach is valid for other NLP tasks such as *relation extraction*. We also plan to investigate how useful the generated code book for weak supervision modeling, how to translate the rules in the guidelines to labeling functions in weak supervision.

## References


Rakesh Agrawal, Sreenivas Gollapudi, Anitha Kannan, and Krishnaram Kenthapadi. 2014. Study navigator: An algorithmically generated aid for learning from electronic textbooks. *Journal of Educational Data Mining*, 6(1):53–75.

Rabah Alzaidy, Cornelia Caragea, and C. Lee Giles. 2019. Bi-LSTM-CRF sequence labeling for keyphrase extraction from scholarly documents. In *The World Wide Web Conference*, WWW '19, page 2551–2557, New York, NY, USA. Association for Computing Machinery.

Isabelle Augenstein, Mrinal Das, Sebastian Riedel, Lakshmi Vikraman, and Andrew McCallum. 2017. Semeval 2017 task 10: ScienceIE-extracting keyphrases and relations from scientific publications. *arXiv preprint arXiv:1704.02853*.

Florian Boudin. 2018. Unsupervised keyphrase extraction with multipartite graphs. In *Proceedings of the 2018 Conference of the North American Chapter of the Association for Computational Linguistics: Human Language Technologies, Volume 2 (Short Papers)*, pages 667–672, New Orleans, Louisiana, June. Association for Computational Linguistics.

Adrien Bougouin, Florian Boudin, and Béatrice Daille. 2013. Topicrank: Graph-based topic ranking for keyphrase extraction. In *Proceedings of the Sixth International Joint Conference on Natural Language Processing*, pages 543–551, Nagoya, Japan. Asian Federation of Natural Language Processing.

Hung Chau, Igor Labutov, Khushboo Thaker, Daqing He, and Peter Brusilovsky. 2020. Automatic concept extraction for domain and student modeling in adaptive textbooks. *International Journal of Artificial Intelligence in Education*.

Vinay K. Chaudhri, Britte Cheng, Adam Overtholtzer, Jeremy Roschelle, Aaron Spaulding, Peter Clark, Mark Greaves, and Dave Gunning. 2013. Inquire biology: A textbook that answers questions. *AI Magazine*, 34(3):55–72.

Yukun Chen, Thomas A Lask, Qiaozhu Mei, Qingxia Chen, Sungrim Moon, Jingqi Wang, Ky Nguyen, Tolulola Dawodu, Trevor Cohen, Joshua C Denny, et al. 2017. An active learning-enabled annotation system for clinical named entity recognition. *BMC medical informatics and decision making*, 17(2):35–44.

Vincent Chen, Sen Wu, Alexander J Ratner, Jen Weng, and Christopher Ré. 2019. Slice-based learning: A programming model for residual learning in critical data slices. In H. Wallach, H. Larochelle, A. Beygelzimer, F. d Alché-Buc, E. Fox, and R. Garnett, editors, *Advances in Neural Information Processing Systems 32*, pages 9397–9407. Curran Associates, Inc.

Gülşen Eryiğit, Fatih Samet Cetin, Meltem Yanık, Tanel Temel, and Ilyas Ciçekli. 2013. Turksent: A sentiment annotation tool for social media. In *Proceedings of the 7th Linguistic Annotation Workshop and Interoperability with Discourse*, pages 131–134.

Corina Florescu and Cornelia Caragea. 2017. Positionrank: An unsupervised approach to keyphrase extraction from scholarly documents. In *Proceedings of the 55th Annual Meeting of the Association for Computational Linguistics (Volume 1: Long Papers)*, pages 1105–1115. Association for Computational Linguistics.

Sujatha Das Gollapalli, Xiao li Li, and Peng Yang. 2017. Incorporating expert knowledge into keyphrase extraction.

Maria Grineva, Maxim Grinev, and Dmitry Lizorkin. 2009. Extracting key terms from noisy and multitheme documents. In *Proceedings of the 18th International Conference on World Wide Web*, WWW '09, pages 661–670, New York, NY, USA. ACM.

Khaled M. Hammouda, Diego N. Matute, and Mohamed S. Kamel. 2005. Corephrase: Keyphrase extraction for document clustering. In Petra Perner and Atsushi Imiya, editors, *Machine Learning and Data Mining in Pattern Recognition*, pages 265–274, Berlin, Heidelberg. Springer Berlin Heidelberg.

Anette Hulth. 2003. Improved automatic keyword extraction given more linguistic knowledge. In *Proceedings of the 2003 Conference on Empirical Methods in Natural Language Processing*, EMNLP '03, pages 216–223, Stroudsburg, PA, USA. Association for Computational Linguistics.

Steve Jones and Gordon Paynter. 1999. Topic-based browsing within a digital library using keyphrases. In *Proceedings of the Fourth ACM Conference on Digital Libraries*, DL '99, page 114–121, New York, NY, USA. Association for Computing Machinery.

Jin-Dong Kim, Tomoko Ohta, and Jun'ichi Tsujii. 2008. Corpus annotation for mining biomedical events from literature. *BMC bioinformatics*, 9(1):10.

Branka Kosovac, Dana J. Vanier, and Thomas M. Froese. 2002. Use of keyphrase extraction software for creation of an aec/fm thesaurus. *Journal of Information Technology in Construction*, 5(2):25–36.

John D. Lafferty, Andrew McCallum, and Fernando C. N. Pereira. 2001. Conditional random fields: Probabilistic models for segmenting and labeling sequence data. In *Proceedings of the Eighteenth International Conference on Machine Learning*, ICML '01, page 282–289, San Francisco, CA, USA. Morgan Kaufmann Publishers Inc.

Tho Thi Ngoc Le, Minh Le Nguyen, and Akira Shimazu. 2016. Unsupervised keyphrase extraction: Introducing new kinds of words to keyphrases. In Byeong Ho Kang and Quan Bai, editors, *AI 2016: Advances in Artificial Intelligence*, pages 665–671, Cham. Springer International Publishing.

Feifan Liu, Deana Pennell, Fei Liu, and Yang Liu. 2009a. Unsupervised approaches for automatic keyword extraction using meeting transcripts. In *Proceedings of Human Language Technologies: The 2009 Annual Conference of the North American Chapter of the Association for Computational Linguistics*, NAACL '09, pages 620–628, Stroudsburg, PA, USA. Association for Computational Linguistics.

Zhiyuan Liu, Peng Li, Yabin Zheng, and Maosong Sun. 2009b. Clustering to find exemplar terms for keyphrase extraction. In *Proceedings of the 2009 Conference on Empirical Methods in Natural Language Processing: Volume 1 - Volume 1*, EMNLP '09, pages 257–266, Stroudsburg, PA, USA. Association for Computational Linguistics.

Zhiyuan Liu, Wenyi Huang, Yabin Zheng, and Maosong Sun. 2010. Automatic keyphrase extraction via topic decomposition. In *Proceedings of the 2010 Conference on Empirical Methods in Natural Language Processing*, EMNLP '10, pages 366–376, Stroudsburg, PA, USA. Association for Computational Linguistics.

Angli Liu, Stephen Soderland, Jonathan Bragg, Christopher H. Lin, Xiao Ling, and Daniel S. Weld. 2016. Effective crowd annotation for relation extraction. In *Proceedings of the 2016 Conference of the North American Chapter of the Association for Computational Linguistics: Human Language Technologies*, pages 897–906, San Diego, California, June. Association for Computational Linguistics.

Liyuan Liu, Jingbo Shang, Xiang Ren, Frank F. Xu, Huan Gui, Jian Peng, and Jiawei Han. 2018. Empower sequence labeling with task-aware neural language model. In *32nd AAAI Conference on Artificial Intelligence, AAAI 2018*, pages 5253–5260. AAAI Press.

Olena Medelyan, Eibe Frank, and Ian H. Witten. 2009. Human-competitive tagging using automatic keyphrase extraction. In *Proceedings of the 2009 Conference on Empirical Methods in Natural Language Processing: Volume 3 - Volume 3*, EMNLP '09, pages 1318–1327, Stroudsburg, PA, USA. Association for Computational Linguistics.

Rada. Mihalcea and Paul Tarau. 2004. TextRank: Bringing order into text. In *Proceedings of the 2004 Conference on Empirical Methods in Natural Language Processing*, Barcelona, Spain, July.

Thuy Dung Nguyen and Min-Yen Kan. 2007. Keyphrase extraction in scientific publications. In Dion Hoe-Lian Goh, Tru Hoang Cao, Ingeborg Torvik Sølvberg, and Edie Rasmussen, editors, *Asian Digital Libraries. Looking Back 10 Years and Forging New Frontiers*, pages 317–326, Berlin, Heidelberg. Springer Berlin Heidelberg.

Philip V Ogren, Guergana Savova, James D Buntrock, and Christopher G Chute. 2006. Building and evaluating annotated corpora for medical nlp systems. In *AMIA Annual Symposium proceedings. AMIA Symposium*, volume 2006, pages 1050–1050. American Medical Informatics Association.

Eirini Papagiannopoulou and Grigorios Tsoumakas. 2019. A review of keyphrase extraction. *Wiley Interdisciplinary Reviews: Data Mining and Knowledge Discovery (2019)*, e1339.

Alexander Ratner, Stephen H. Bach, Henry R. Ehrenberg, Jason Alan Fries, Sen Wu, and Christopher Ré. 2017. Snorkel: Rapid training data creation with weak supervision. *CoRR*, abs/1711.10160.

Stuart Rose, Dave Engel, Nick Cramer, and Wendy Cowley. 2010. Automatic keyword extraction from individual documents. In Michael W. Berry and Jacob Kogan, editors, *Text Mining: Applications and Theory*, pages 1–20. John Wiley and Sons, Ltd.

Marta Sabou, Kalina Bontcheva, Leon Derczynski, and Arno Scharl. 2014. Corpus annotation through crowdsourcing: Towards best practice guidelines. In *Proceedings of the Ninth International Conference on Language Resources and Evaluation (LREC'14)*, pages 859–866, Reykjavik, Iceland, May. European Language Resources Association (ELRA).

Rion Snow, Brendan O'connor, Dan Jurafsky, and Andrew Y Ng. 2008. Cheap and fast–but is it good? evaluating non-expert annotations for natural language tasks. In *Proceedings of the 2008 conference on empirical methods in natural language processing*, pages 254–263.

Brett South, Shuying Shen, Jianwei Leng, Tyler Forbush, Scott DuVall, and Wendy Chapman. 2012. A prototype tool set to support machine-assisted annotation. In *BioNLP: Proceedings of the 2012 Workshop on Biomedical Natural Language Processing*, pages 130–139, Montréal, Canada, June. Association for Computational Linguistics.

Brett R South, Danielle Mowery, Ying Suo, Jianwei Leng, Oscar Ferrández, Stephane M Meystre, and Wendy W Chapman. 2014. Evaluating the effects of machine pre-annotation and an interactive annotation interface on manual de-identification of clinical text. *Journal of biomedical informatics*, 50:162–172.

Pontus Stenetorp, Sampo Pyysalo, Goran Topić, Tomoko Ohta, Sophia Ananiadou, and Jun'ichi Tsujii. 2012. BRAT: a web-based tool for NLP-assisted text annotation. In *Proceedings of the Demonstrations at the 13th Conference of the European Chapter of the Association for Computational Linguistics*, pages 102–107, Avignon, France, April. Association for Computational Linguistics.

Lucas Sterckx, Thomas Demeester, Johannes Deleu, and Chris Develder. 2015. Topical word importance for fast keyphrase extraction. In *Proceedings of the 24th International Conference on World Wide Web*, WWW '15 Companion, page 121–122, New York, NY, USA. Association for Computing Machinery.

Qi Su, Dmitry Pavlov, Jyh-Herng Chow, and Wendell C Baker. 2007. Internet-scale collection of human-reviewed data. In *Proceedings of the 16th international conference on World Wide Web*, pages 231–240.

Katrin Tomanek and Fredrik Olsson. 2009. A web survey on the use of active learning to support annotation of text data. *Proceedings of Active Learning for Natural Language Processing (ALNLP-09)*, pages 45–48.

Özlem Uzuner, Imre Solti, Fei Xia, and Eithon Cadag. 2010. Community annotation experiment for ground truth generation for the i2b2 medication challenge. *Journal of the American Medical Informatics Association*, 17(5):519–523.

Xiaojun Wan and Jianguo Xiao. 2008. Collabrank: Towards a collaborative approach to single-document keyphrase extraction. In *Proceedings of the 22nd International Conference on Computational Linguistics (Coling 2008)*, pages 969–976. Coling 2008 Organizing Committee.

Shuting Wang, Chen Liang, Zhaohui Wu, Kyle Williams, Bart Pursel, Benjamin Brautigam, Sherwyn Saul, Hannah Williams, Kyle Bowen, and C. Lee Giles. 2015. Concept hierarchy extraction from textbooks. In *Proceedings of the 2015 ACM Symposium on Document Engineering*, DocEng '15, pages 147–156, New York, NY, USA. ACM.

W John Wilbur, Andrey Rzhetsky, and Hagit Shatkay. 2006. New directions in biomedical text annotation: definitions, guidelines and corpus construction. *BMC bioinformatics*, 7(1):1–10.

Ian H. Witten, Gordon W. Paynter, Eibe Frank, Carl Gutwin, and Craig G. Nevill-Manning. 1999. Kea: Practical automatic keyphrase extraction. In *Proceedings of the Fourth ACM Conference on Digital Libraries*, DL '99, pages 254–255, New York, NY, USA. ACM.

Fei Xia and Meliha Yetisgen-Yildiz. 2012. Clinical corpus annotation: challenges and strategies. In *Proceedings of the Third Workshop on Building and Evaluating Resources for Biomedical Text Mining (BioTxtM'2012) in conjunction with the International Conference on Language Resources and Evaluation (LREC), Istanbul, Turkey*.

Wen-tau Yih, Joshua Goodman, and Vitor R. Carvalho. 2006. Finding advertising keywords on web pages. In *Proceedings of the 15th International Conference on World Wide Web*, WWW '06, pages 213–222, New York, NY, USA. ACM.

# Cookpad Parsed Corpus: Linguistic Annotations of Japanese Recipes


**Jun Harashima** and **Makoto Hiramatsu**
Cookpad Inc.
`{jun-harashima, himkt}@cookpad.com`



## Abstract

It has become increasingly common for people to share cooking recipes on the Internet. Along with the increase in the number of shared recipes, there have been corresponding increases in recipe-related studies and datasets. However, there are still few datasets that provide linguistic annotations for the recipe-related studies even though such annotations should form the basis of the studies. This paper introduces a novel recipe-related dataset, named Cookpad Parsed Corpus, which contains linguistic annotations for Japanese recipes. We randomly extracted 500 recipes from the largest recipe-related dataset, the Cookpad Recipe Dataset, and annotated $4,738$ sentences in the recipes with morphemes, named entities, and dependency relations. This paper also reports benchmark results on our corpus for Japanese morphological analysis, named entity recognition, and dependency parsing. We show that there is still room for improvement in the analyses of recipes.


## 1 Introduction

Today, a great number of cooking recipes are available on the Internet. Many people upload their recipes to recipe-sharing services such as Cookpad and Yummly, with Cookpad having over six million recipes and Yummly over two million recipes, to date.

As the number of shared online recipes increases, many recipe-related datasets have been published (Salvador et al., 2017; Yagcioglu et al., 2018; Chandu et al., 2019; Lin et al., 2020). These datasets have successfully contributed their content to a variety of recipe-related studies about recipe understanding, recipe search, recipe generation, and so on.

Nevertheless, there are still few datasets that contain linguistic annotations for cooking recipes. Most of the recipe studies rely on linguistic analyses, like those focusing on other text such as newspaper articles. Since linguistic annotations play an important role in fundamental analyses, they are also deserving of more attention in this field.

In this paper, we introduce our Cookpad Parsed Corpus, which is a novel dataset of Japanese recipes. We extract 500 recipes randomly from the Cookpad Recipe Dataset (Harashima et al., 2016), currently the largest recipe dataset, and annotate $4,738$ sentences in the recipes with the most fundamental linguistic information: morphemes, named entities, and dependency relations.

We also report benchmark results of the corpus for morphological analysis (MA), named entity recognition (NER), and dependency parsing (DP) for Japanese, and investigate whether tools or methods which have been commonly used for these analyses perform sufficiently for cooking recipes.

## 2 Related Works

Table 1 summarizes existing recipe-related datasets and our corpus. As shown in the table, each resource has recipes with their own content, such as graph representations and cooking images of the recipes. This






*The 14th Linguistic Annotation Workshop*, pages 87–92
Barcelona, Spain (Online), December 12, 2020.

| Name | Main content (other than recipes) |
| --- | --- |
| Carnegie Mellon University Recipe Database (Tasse and Smith, 2008) | Machine-readable language representations |
| Flow Graph Corpus (Mori et al., 2014) | Graph representations and named entities |
| SIMMR Recipe Dataset (Jermsurawong and Habash, 2015) | Graph representations |
| Cookpad Recipe Dataset (Harashima et al., 2016) | Reviews and meals (combinations of recipes) |
| Cookpad Image Dataset (Harashima et al., 2017) | Food images and cooking images |
| Recipe1M (Salvador et al., 2017) | Food images |
| RecipeQA (Yagcioglu et al., 2018) | Question-answer pairs |
| Storyboarding Data (Chandu et al., 2019) | Cooking images |
| r-FG BB dataset (Nishimura et al., 2020) | Bounding boxes for cooking images |
| English Recipe Flow Graph Corpus (Yamakata et al., 2020) | Graph representations and named entities |
| Microsoft Research Multimodal Aligned Recipe Corpus (Lin et al., 2020) | URLs to YouTube videos |
| Multi-modal Recipe Structure dataset (Pan et al., 2020) | Graph representations and cooking images |
| **Cookpad Parsed Corpus** | **Linguistic annotations** |

Table 1: Existing recipe-related datasets and our corpus.

| Name | Target documents |
| --- | --- |
| Kyoto University Text Corpus (Kawahara et al., 2002) | Newspaper articles |
| GDA Corpus (Hashida, 2005) | Newspaper articles and dictionary entries |
| NAIST Text Corpus (Iida et al., 2007) | Newspaper articles |
| Kyoto University and NTT Blog Corpus (Hashimoto et al., 2011) | Blogs |
| Kyoto University Web Document Leads Corpus (Hangyo et al., 2012) | Web documents |
| Balanced Corpus of Contemporary Written Japanese (Maekawa et al., 2014) | Newspaper articles, books, magazines, etc |
| **Cookpad Parsed Corpus** | **Cooking recipes** |

Table 2: Existing Japanese parsed corpora and our corpus.

content has successfully promoted a variety of recipe-related studies about recipe understanding, recipe search, recipe generation, and so on.

Our corpus differs from these efforts in that it contains linguistic annotations of cooking recipes. In other words, the existing datasets have not taken account of the information, except for the Flow Graph Corpus (Mori et al., 2014) and English Recipe Flow Graph Corpus (Yamakata et al., 2020), which contain a few limited linguistic annotations such as named entities. By contrast, our corpus contains a variety of linguistic annotations such as morphemes, named entities, and dependency relations.

Table 2 summarizes existing Japanese parsed corpora and our corpus. There are several parsed corpora which have contributed their linguistic annotations to linguistic analyses such as MA, NER, and DP for Japanese. In particular, the Kyoto University Text Corpus (Kawahara et al., 2002) and NAIST Text Corpus (Iida et al., 2007) have been commonly used for such studies.

One of the biggest differences between these and our work is the target documents for annotations; that is, the other works focus on newspaper articles, dictionary entries, blogs, web documents, books, and magazines, whereas our corpus is the first to focus on cooking recipes.

## 3 Cookpad Parsed Corpus

In this study, we constructed a novel recipe-related dataset, named Cookpad Parsed Corpus, which contains linguistic annotations of Japanese recipes. We randomly selected 500 recipes from the largest recipe dataset, Cookpad Recipe Dataset (Harashima et al., 2016), which contains approximately 1.7 million Japanese recipes. We then annotated 4,738 sentences (hereafter called the target sentences) in the 500 recipes with morphemes, named entities, and dependency relations.

Figure 1 shows linguistic annotations for an example sentence in our corpus. The lines starting with # represent the IDs of the step in the recipe and the sentence in the step, respectively, while EOS represents the end of the sentence. The format of our corpus is based on the Kyoto University's corpora (Kawahara et al., 2002; Hashimoto et al., 2011; Hangyo et al., 2012) and output of CaboCha, which is one of the most popular dependency parsers for Japanese.

We first annotated the target sentences with morphemes. In Figure 1, the lines starting with a word such as 鮭 (salmon) give its morphological information such as part-of-speech (POS), fine-grained POS, base form, reading, pronunciation, and so on. We followed the IPA dictionary (Asahara and Matsumoto, 2003) to decide boundaries and POS for each morpheme because that resource is most commonly used

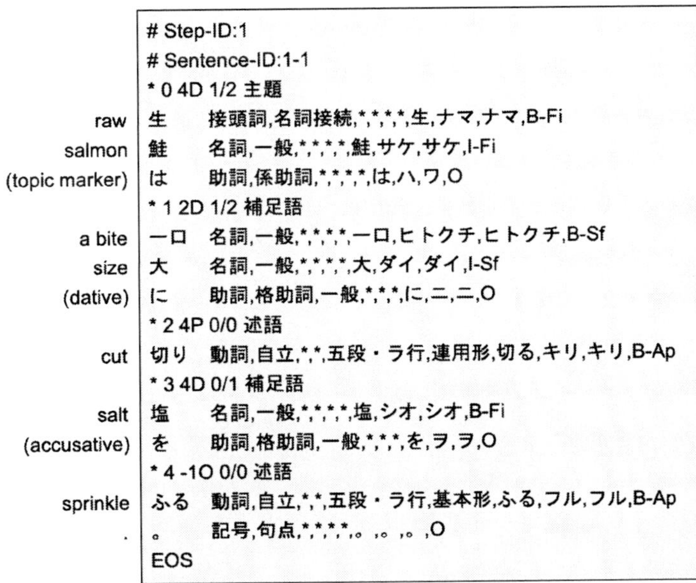

| Tag | Description |
| --- | --- |
| Fi | Food (ingredient) |
| Fe | Food (part to be eliminated) |
| Fd | Food (dish) |
| Fa | Food (attribute) |
| Tg | Tool (general) |
| Ta | Tool (attribute) |
| To | Tool (other) |
| Nd | Number (duration) |
| Nq | Number (quantity) |
| No | Number (other) |
| Af | Action (food) |
| At | Action (tool) |
| Ap | Action (person) |
| Sf | State (food) |
| St | State (tool) |
| Sap | State (person's action) |
| X | Unclassified named entity |

Table 3: Our named entity tags.

| Type | Description |
| --- | --- |
| 主題 | Topic |
| 補足語 | Complement |
| 連体修飾語 | Adnominal modifier |
| 連用修飾語 | Predicative modifier |
| 述語 | Predicate |
| 独立語 | Independent |
| その他 | Other |

Table 4: Our bunsetsu types.

Figure 1: Linguistic annotations for an example sentence, 生鮭は一口大に切り塩をふる。 (Cut the raw salmon into bite-size chunks and sprinkle them with salt.), in our corpus.

for Japanese MA. We also determined boundaries and POS for unknown words so that they fit the policies of the dictionary as much as possible. Consequently, $62,146$ morphemes were annotated in the target sentences.

We then annotated the $62,146$ morphemes with named entity tags. Table 3 shows our defined 17 tags, which are based on the 8 tags in the Flow Graph Corpus. In our corpus, the tags are located at the end of morphological information, as seen in Figure 1. Note that we used the common IOB2 format in NER to represent the inside (I), outside (O), and the beginning (B) of a named entity. For example, we can see from the figure that 生 (raw) is the beginning of the ingredient 生鮭 (raw salmon) because the morpheme is annotated with B-Fi. In this annotation, $22,359$ entities were finally obtained from the target sentences.

We annotated a further $26,501$ bunsetsus in the target sentences with dependency relations. A bunsetsu is a conventional unit of Japanese that consists of one or more content words (e.g., noun) and zero or more function words (e.g., particle). The example sentence in Figure 1 consists of five bunsetsus: 生鮭は, 一口大に, 切り, 塩を, and ふる。, and the lines starting with * give bunsetsu information. For example, the 0 in the first line starting with * denotes the index of the bunsetsu 生鮭は. The 4 in 4D denotes the index of the bunsetsu ふる。, which is the head of 生鮭は, while the D denotes the type of dependency relations, such as D (normal dependency), P (coordination dependency), and A (appositive dependency). Note that the index is set to -1 for the last bunsetsu in each sentence. This is because a dependency basically goes from left to right in Japanese, and thus the last bunsetsu has no head bunsetsu. Finally, we defined the 7 bunsetsu types in Table 4 and annotated all the bunsetsus with the types to clarify their roles in a sentence.

Our corpus enables researchers to use the above linguistic annotations for their studies. It was designed to link with two existing datasets: Cookpad Recipe Dataset and Cookpad Image Dataset (Harashima et al., 2017), which provide a variety of content such as reviews, meals, and images of the same 1.7 million recipes. As described, we extracted our 500 recipes from these recipes. This enables researchers to use not only the linguistic annotations of the 500 recipes in our corpus but also access the variety of content of the recipes in the two datasets for their studies.

|          | Precision | Recall | F1    |
|----------|-----------|--------|-------|
| MeCab    | 88.91     | 88.95  | 88.93 |
| MeCab w/ DA | 91.12  | 91.04  | 91.08 |

(a) MA.

|          | Accuracy |
|----------|----------|
| CaboCha  | 92.21    |
| CaboCha w/ DA | 94.68 |

(c) DP.

|                      | Accuracy | Precision | Recall | F1    |
|----------------------|----------|-----------|--------|-------|
| Sasada et al. (2015) | 88.30    | 74.65     | 82.77  | 78.50 |
| Lample et al. (2016) | 91.41    | 88.17     | 87.18  | 87.67 |

(b) NER.

Table 5: Benchmark results on our corpus.

## 4 Experiments

Finally, we present benchmark results of our corpus for fundamental linguistic analyses in Japanese. In our experiments, we randomly divided the corpus into 400 recipes ($3,783$ sentences) for a training set, 50 recipes (472 sentences) for a validation set, and 50 recipes (483 sentences) for a test set. Then, we trained, tuned, and tested popular tools or methods for Japanese MA, NER, and DP using these recipes.

Table 5(a) shows the results for MA. We measured the performance of MeCab, the de facto standard morphological analyzer for Japanese, with and without performing domain adaptation (DA) of the tool for cooking recipes using our training set. The precision, recall, and F1 in the table were calculated based on the correct morphemes which the analyzer could recognize in our test set. From the table, we can see that all the metrics were approximately 91% even if we performed DA. This indicates that MA for informal cooking recipes is still an unsolved problem, compared to that for formal newspaper articles on which the tool has already achieved metrics of over 98% in Kudo et al. (2004).

The results for NER are given in Table 5(b). As there is no existing named entity recognizer that uses our named entity tags, two recognizers proposed in Sasada et al. (2015) and Lample et al. (2016), which are popular in recipe and general domains, respectively, were trained and evaluated using our training and test sets. The metrics in the table were calculated in the same way in the CoNLL-2003 shared task (Sang and Meulder, 2003). From the table, it is clear that there is still room for improvement in NER for cooking recipes. Most of the errors in our experiment were caused by domain-specific unknown words. Thus, a domain-specific lexicon such as cooking ontology (Nanba et al., 2014) may play an important role in reducing such errors.

Table 5(c) shows the results for DP. For this experiment, we used CaboCha, also mentioned in the previous section. The accuracy in the table was the percentage of the correct dependencies which the parser could recognize in our test set. Interestingly, the accuracy of 92-94% of the parser on our corpus was higher than the 90% for the Kyoto University Text Corpus, reported in Kudo and Matsumoto (2002). In other words, DP for informal cooking recipes might be slightly easier than for formal newspaper articles. This is probably because sentences in cooking recipes are relatively short, compared to those in newspaper articles. Having said that, we found that over 20% of the sentences in our test set had at least one parsing error even when we performed DA with the parser. This suggests that DP for cooking recipes also remains an unsolved problem.

## 5 Conclusion

This paper introduced the Cookpad Parsed Corpus, which contains linguistic annotations of Japanese recipes. The corpus was composed of 500 recipes which were extracted from the Cookpad Recipe Dataset. A total of $4,738$ sentences in the recipes were annotated with morphemes, named entities, and dependency relations. Benchmark results on our corpus for Japanese MA, NER, and DP were reported, and showed that there is still room for improvement in these analyses of cooking recipes. We believe the linguistic annotations will form a basic infrastructure not only for the improvement of the fundamental analyses, but also for the variety of recipe-related studies based on the analyses. The dataset can be obtained by sending an e-mail request to the authors. In future work, we plan to enrich our corpus with further linguistic annotations such as predicate-argument structures and co-references.

## References

Masayuki Asahara and Yuji Matsumoto. 2003. ipadic version 2.7.0 User's Manual.

Khyathi Raghavi Chandu, Eric Nyberg, and Alan W Black. 2019. Storyboarding of recipes: Grounded contextual generation. In *Proceedings of the 57th Annual Meeting of the Association for Computational Linguistics (ACL 2019)*, pages 6040–6046.

Masatsugu Hangyo, Daisuke Kawahara, and Sadao Kurohashi. 2012. Building a Diverse Document Leads Corpus Annotated with Semantic Relations. In *Proceedings of the 26th Pacific Asia Conference on Language, Information, and Computation (PACLIC 2012)*, pages 535–544.

Jun Harashima, Michiaki Ariga, Kenta Murata, and Masayuki Ioki. 2016. A Large-scale Recipe and Meal Data Collection as Infrastructure for Food Research. In *Proceedings of the 10th International Conference on Language Resources and Evaluation (LREC 2016)*, pages 2455–2459.

Jun Harashima, Yuichiro Someya, and Yohei Kikuta. 2017. Cookpad Image Dataset: An Image Collection as Infrastructure for Food Research. In *Proceedings of the 40th International ACM SIGIR Conference on Research and Development in Information Retrieval (SIGIR 2017)*, pages 1229–1232.

Koichi Hashida. 2005. Global Document Annotation (GDA) Manual.

Chikara Hashimoto, Sadao Kurohashi, Daisuke Kawahara, Keiji Shinzato, and Masaaki Nagata. 2011. Construction of a Blog Corpus with Syntactic, Anaphoric, and Sentiment Annotations (in Japanese). *Natural Language Processing*, 18(2):175–201.

Ryu Iida, Mamoru Komachi, Kentaro Inui, and Yuji Matsumoto. 2007. Annotating a Japanese text corpus with predicate-argument and coreference relations. In *Proceedings of the Linguistic Annotation Workshop (LAW 2007)*, pages 132–139.

Jermsak Jermsurawong and Nizar Habash. 2015. Predicting the Structure of Cooking Recipes. In *Proceedings of the 2015 Conference on Empirical Methods in Natural Language Processing (EMNLP 2015)*, pages 781–786.

Daisuke Kawahara, Sadao Kurohashi, and Kôiti Hashida. 2002. Construction of a Japanese Relevance-tagged Corpus. In *Proceedings of the 3rd International Conference on Language Resources and Evaluation (LREC 2002)*, pages 2008–2013.

Taku Kudo and Yuji Matsumoto. 2002. Japanese dependency analysis using cascaded chunking. In *Proceedings of the 6th Conference on Natural Language Learning 2002 (CoNLL-2002)*.

Taku Kudo, Kaoru Yamamoto, and Yuji Matsumoto. 2004. Applying conditional random fields to japanese morphological analysis. In *Proceedings of the 2004 Conference on Empirical Methods in Natural Language Processing (EMNLP 2004)*, pages 230–237.

Guillaume Lample, Miguel Ballesteros, Sandeep Subramanian, Kazuya Kawakami, and Chris Dyer. 2016. Neural Architectures for Named Entity Recognition. In *Proceedings of the 2016 Conference of the North American Chapter of the Association for Computational Linguistics: Human Language Technologies (NAACL-HLT 2016)*, pages 260–270.

Angela S. Lin, Sudha Rao, Asli Celikyilmaz, Elnaz Nouri, Chris Brockett, Debadeepta Dey, and Bill Dolan. 2020. A recipe for creating multimodal aligned datasets for sequential tasks. In *Proceedings of the 58th Annual Meeting of the Association for Computational Linguistics (ACL 2020)*, pages 4871–4884.

Kikuo Maekawa, Makoto Yamazaki, Toshinobu Ogiso, Takehiko Maruyama, Hideki Ogura, Wakako Kashino, Hanae Koiso, Masaya Yamaguchi, Makiro Tanaka, and Yasuharu Den. 2014. Balanced Corpus of Contemporary Written Japanese. *Language Resources and Evaluation*, 48(2):345–371.

Shinsuke Mori, Hirokuni Maeta, Yoko Yamakata, and Tetsuro Sasada. 2014. Flow Graph Corpus from Recipe Texts. In *Proceedings of the 9th International Conference on Language Resources and Evaluation (LREC 2014)*, pages 2370–2377.

Hidetsugu Nanba, Yoko Doi, Miho Tsujita, Toshiyuki Takezawa, and Kazutoshi Sumiya. 2014. Construction of a Cooking Ontology from Cooking Recipes and Patents. In *Proceedings of the 6th Workshop on Multimedia for Cooking and Eating Activities (CEA 2014)*, pages 507–516.

Taichi Nishimura, Suzushi Tomori, Hayato Hashimoto, Atsushi Hashimoto, Yoko Yamakata, Jun Harashima, Yoshitaka Ushiku, and Shinsuke Mori. 2020. Visual grounding annotation of recipe flow graph. In *Proceedings of the 12th Language Resources and Evaluation Conference (LREC 2020)*, pages 4275–4284.

Liangming Pan, Jingjing Chen, Jianlong Wu, Shaoteng Liu, Chong-Wah Ngo, Min-Yen Kan, Yugang Jiang, and Tat-Seng Chua. 2020. Multi-modal cooking workflow construction for food recipes. In *Proceedings of the 27th ACM International Conference on Multimedia (ACM MM 2020)*.

Amaia Salvador, Nicholas Hynes, Yusuf Aytar, Javier Marin, Ferda Ofli, Ingmar Weber, and Antonio Torralba. 2017. Learning Cross-modal Embeddings for Cooking Recipes and Food Images. In *Proceedings of the 2017 IEEE Conference on Computer Vision and Pattern Recognition (CVPR 2017)*, pages 3020–3028.

Erik F. Tjong Kim Sang and Fien De Meulder. 2003. Introduction to the CoNLL-2003 Shared Task: Language-Independent Named Entity Recognition. In *Proceedings of the 7th Conference on Natural Language Learning (CoNLL 2003)*, pages 142–147.

Tetsuro Sasada, Shinsuke Mori, Tatsuya Kawahara, and Yoko Yamakata. 2015. Named Entity Recognizer Trainable from Partially Annotated Data. In *Proceedings of the 14th International Conference of the Pacific Association for Computational Linguistics (PACLING 2015)*, pages 148–160.

Dan Tasse and Noah A. Smith. 2008. SOUR CREAM: Toward Semantic Processing of Recipes. Technical report, Carnegie Mellon University.

Semih Yagcioglu, Aykut Erdem, Erkut Erdem, and Nazli Ikizler-Cinbis. 2018. RecipeQA: A Challenge Dataset for Multimodal Comprehension of Cooking Recipes. In *Proceedings of the 2018 Conference on Empirical Methods in Natural Language Processing (EMNLP 2018)*, pages 1358–1368.

Yoko Yamakata, Shinsuke Mori, and John Carroll. 2020. English recipe flow graph corpus. In *Proceedings of The 12th Language Resources and Evaluation Conference (LREC 2020)*, pages 5187–5194.

# Modelling and annotating interlinear glossed text from 280 different endangered languages as Linked Data with LIGT

Sebastian Nordhoff

Leibniz-Zentrum Allgemeine Sprachwissenschaft (ZAS)

nordhoff@leibniz-zas.de

## Abstract

This paper reports on the harvesting, analysis, and annotation of 20k documents from 4 different endangered language archives in 280 different low-resource languages. The documents are heterogeneous as to their provenance (holding archive, language, geographical area, creator) and internal structure (annotation types, metalanguages), but they have the ELAN-XML format in common. Typical annotations include sentence-level translations, morpheme-segmentation, morpheme-level translations, and parts-of-speech. The ELAN format gives a lot of freedom to document creators, and hence the data set is very heterogeneous. We use regularities in the ELAN format to arrive at a common internal representation of sentences, words, and morphemes, with translations into one or more additional languages. Building upon the paradigm of Linguistic Linked Open Data (LLOD, Chiarcos et al. (2012b)), the document elements receive unique identifiers and are linked to other resources such as Glottolog for languages, Wikidata for semantic concepts, and the Leipzig Glossing Rules list for category abbreviations. We provide an RDF export in the LIGT format (Chiarcos and Ionov (2019)), enabling uniform and interoperable access with some semantic enrichments to a formerly disparate resource type difficult to access. Two use cases (semantic search and colexification) are presented to show the viability of the approach.

## 1 Introduction

### 1.1 Understudied languages

A couple of major languages, most predominantly English, have been the mainstay of research and development in computational linguistics. Recently Joshi et al. (2020) have analysed the representation of different languages in the research world. They established 6 classes for 2 485 languages of the world. Table 1 gives their classification

We see that, next to English, there are only 6 further languages for which the resources can be considered satisfying (Class 5). As we relax requirements for labeled and unlabeled data, we arrive at



| | Class | example | # lgs | #spks | % | criteria | |
|---|---|---|---|---|---|---|---|
| | | | | | | unlabeled data | labeled data |
| 5 | winners | Spanish | 7 | 2.5B | 0.28 | good | good |
| 4 | underdogs | Russian | 18 | 2.2B | 1.07 | good | insufficient |
| 3 | rising stars | Indonesian | 28 | 1.8B | 4.42 | good | none |
| 2 | hopefuls | Zulu | 19 | 5.7M | 0.36 | ? | smallish sets |
| 1 | scraping-bys | Fijian | 222 | 30M | 5.49 | smallish | none |
| 0 | left-behinds | Warlpiri | 2 191 | 1.2B | 88.38 | none | none |

Table 1: Joshi et al's classes.



*The 14th Linguistic Annotation Workshop*, pages 93–104
Barcelona, Spain (Online), December 12, 2020.

classes 4, 3, and 2, with each one numbering languages in the low two-digit range. In class 1, only some unlabeled data are available, which Joshi et al find to be true for 222 languages. For 2 191, they find no noteworthy data whatsoever. Class 0 alone holds 7 times more languages than all of the other classes combined. Of course, there is more data available than Joshi et al include in their study. The Glottlog glottoscope[1] lists 7 794 languages, of which 2,088 have only a short word list or less, and 5 706 languages have better data available than "word list". This being said, virtually all those additional languages mentioned in Glottolog will be in Joshi et al's class 0: the resources listed are in the range of $10^2$ to $10^4$ tokens, whereas NLP applications typically require at least $10^6$ datapoints to work properly, possibly much more.

But the human language faculty is not restricted to the 7 languages where we have a good data situation. It is due to historical accidents that these languages are predominant today, and they are actually not very protoypical representatives of the class "natural language".[2] By focusing our attention, and our research, on these 7 larger languages, we are making a commercially sensible choice, but we might be missing important insights into the nature of the human mind.

But not all hope is lost, since for the last 25 years, data from many Class-0 languages have been collected, largely unnoticed by the NLP communities. These data reside tucked away in endangered language archives, waiting to be discovered.

### 1.1.1 Endangered language archives

Following upon a 1992 article by Hale et al. (1992) alerting to the danger of languages disappearing at an alarming rate, a number of endangered language documentation programs were set up (see Seifart et al. (2018) for an overview). Field linguists collected textual, audio, and video data from the speaker communities, annotated them and stored them in a number of archives. These archives set up the umbrella organisation Digital Endangered Languages and Musics Archives Network (DELAMAN) in 2003. There are currently 12 full members, of which the archives ELAR (UK), TLA (NL), AILLA (US), and PARADISEC (AU) host a very large number of documents, organised in over 1250 "collections" and are thus the most interesting to try computational approaches on large data sets of class 0 languages.[3] Schalley (2019) already points to the value of the data stored there: "If these data could be linked and integrated, current computational tools would allow for targeted searches across the body of knowledge", hinting at the same time at the major issue: integration and discoverability. This paper describes how data from the various archives can be programmatically accessed, integrated, and made searchable, thus establishing "endangered language archive scraping" as a novel collection method, an offshoot of conventional web scraping.

### 1.2 Novel types

While audio and video data also offer interesting use cases for automated approaches (Kisler et al. (2012), Paschen et al. (2020)), currently available technologies clearly focus on text. Endangered language archives typically contain interlinear glossed text (IGT, von Prince and Nordhoff (2020)), see Figure 1. Various formalisations for IGT have been proposed in the past (Nickles (2001), Drude (2002), Lewis (2006), Goodman et al. (2015), Chiarcos and Ionov (2019)). The different documentation projects contributing to the DELAMAN archives had different foci (phonetics vs. discourse; monologic data vs. dialogic data; etc.) but the great majority of projects build their textual data around the mappings of a vernacular utterance to a free translation, and a mapping of the component morphemes of that utterance to morphological glosses (Figure 1). For a given computational task, one has to model and

---

[1]https://glottolog.org/langdoc/status

[2]Cysouw (2011) concludes "The most fascinating [quantitative] result was that the northwestern European area, centred on Continental West Germanic, turned out to be one of the most linguistically unusual geographical areas word-wide. Many of the rare characteristics as attested in this area might have been considered the norm from a European perspective, though the typological data show that these characteristics are to be considered special structures of European languages, and not of human language in general."

[3]AILLA focuses on the Americas, PARADISEC has a focus on the Pacific. The other two archives have no particular regional focus. Together, they provide a very good coverage of work in the domain of language documentation of the last 25 years.

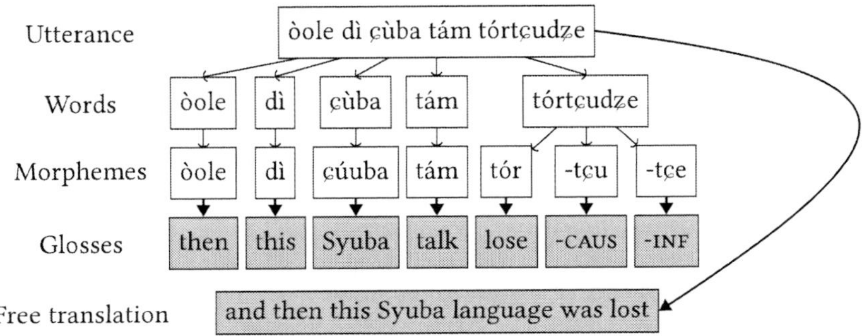


Figure 1: An example of interlinear text (Annotations-b-SUY1-140126-07, Gawne (2015)). Light arrows denote part-whole relations; thick arrows denote translational equivalents. Note that there is no translation for the word level, and that the citation form of the morphemes differs from their realization in a given word (çùba/çúuba; dʑe/tçe).

access the part-whole relations between utterances and morphemes in the documents; and the correspondence relations between vernacular language and translation. This then allows for querying and analysis.

## 2 Endangered language archives

### 2.1 State of the art in discovery, querying, and analysis of endangered language archive holdings.

In a recent overview, Cimiano et al. (2020) state:

> Language resources (dictionaries, terminologies, corpora, etc.) developed in the fields of corpus linguistics, computational linguistics and natural language processing (NLP) are often encoded in heterogeneous formats and developed in isolation from one another. This makes their discovery, reuse and integration for both the development of NLP tools and daily linguistic research a difficult and cumbersome task.

This could not be more true for endangered language archives. The value of cross-queryable IGT from distributed holdings was pointed out as early as 2006 by Lewis (2006), who setup the ODIN platform[4], which lists 2017 documents containing IGT from 1274 languages. The only querying possibility, however, is by language name. There is no possibility to find all IGT documents which mention 'boat', '2PL', or 'birth'. There used to be a download facility, but this is broken as of today.

All endangered language archives have some metadata search functionalities (title, language, keyword), but no content search. They all require users to register and sign a code-of-conduct in order to download documents. That code of conduct typically restricts the distribution of downloaded resources. See Seyfeddinipur et al. (2019) for context.

The EOPAS project (Schroeter and Thieberger. (2006))[5] provided a very nice web interface for searching across various annotated video files and display the content in the browser. This project was down for a while, but the technology is being integrated into the PARADISEC catalog (Nick Thieberger, personal communication 2020-08-20). It is possible to search for a string like "house", which yields 4 different documents mentioning the word "house". The corresponding media files can be played in the browser, and the XML can be displayed, but a download facility for the XML files seems to be missing for now.

The ELAN desktop software allows a search across multiple XML files in a local directory (thus not in a remote archive). It does not allow the specification of particular tiers or relations, however.[6]

---

[4]http://odin.linguistlist.org
[5]https://github.com/CoEDL/modpdsc
[6]https://www.mpi.nl/corpus/html/elan/ch07s02.html

Cimiano et al. (2020) state:

> [W]ith respect to the provision of access to data, most of the available repositories lack at least one of the following features: Provision of domain specific linguistic/language data, which is open for re-use and free of charge[;] Search functionality that facilitates finding specific resources[;] Possibility to narrow search to open data and to resources in linked data formats as well as to directly download the data.

The three aspects of free re-use, search functionalities, and bulk downloads mentioned by Cimiano et al are indeed also what we find in the domain of endangered language archives. We cannot address the legal issues here, but we show ways how to improve search and retrieval.

## 2.2  Provisos

The underlying data for this project come from four different endangered language archives (AILLA, ELAR, PARADISEC, TLA) and are collected opportunistically.[7] Everything which is listed, available, accessible, and parseable has been taken into account. No effort has been made to ensure a balanced representation of genealogical or geographical factors, but such aspects can easily be factored in based on available metadata (OLAC[8], Glottolog).

Different field linguists have different conventions (von Prince and Nordhoff (2020)), which do not always map neatly on each other. Furthermore, the archives also often contain files in a relatively incomplete state, with empty tiers, empty slots or placeholders like '???' or '***'. The data are thus relatively dirty, but they happen to be the best of what we have for the group-0 languages. It will probably not be possible to run very advanced statistical or stochastic methods on the data, but the following section will give a glimpse of what kinds of analyses the data do permit to be run.

## 2.3  Former results

Nordhoff (2020) performed analyses of the structure and the content of annotations. As for structure, he found that there is a wide variety of tier configurations in the surveyed files (see below for the concept of "tier"). While all files share the ELAN-XML Format, the configuration options are nearly never identical between two files.

As for content, Nordhoff was able to run meaningful analyses on the frequency of graphemes, grammatical categories, and semantic concepts found in the texts. He found for instance that the most frequent graphemes employed are ⟨a⟩, ⟨i⟩, ⟨n⟩, and ⟨e⟩, in that order. This makes some intuitive sense, but is different from the phonemic (type) frequencies reported in PHOIBLE[9] (Moran and McCloy (2019)), where we find /m/, /i/, /k/, /j/, /u/, in that order.[10]

The most frequent grammatical categories are "singular" and "plural", next to common verbal tense categories. This is also in line what would be expected, but the interesting question emerges which one of the two number categories should be more frequent than the other. Finally, Nordhoff found that the texts have a semantic bias towards agriculture.

Psychological (*What do people use?*), typological (*What do people use where and why?*), sociological (*What are Western research projects interested in and why?*), and text-genre based explanations (*What kinds of text do field workers collect and why?*) can be explored for these grammatical and semantic findings, but this paper will focus on technical refinements and representations rather than theoretical explanations.

---

[7]The Alaska Native Language Archive (ANLA) was included in a pilot but was later dropped due to the very low number of usable files.

[8]language-archives.org

[9]https://phoible.org/parameters

[10]Note that PHOIBLE is based on the phonology sections of grammatical descriptions, while Nordhoff is agnostic to phonological values and compares graphemes. It is reasonable to assume that ⟨m⟩ will represent /m/, but this approach has obvious limitations for other graphemes, like ⟨j⟩ or ⟨c⟩.

```xml
<?xml version="1.0" encoding="UTF-8"?>
<ANNOTATION_DOCUMENT>
    <TIME_ORDER>
        <TIME_SLOT TIME_SLOT_ID="ts1" TIME_VALUE="740"/>
        <TIME_SLOT TIME_SLOT_ID="ts2" TIME_VALUE="1360"/>
        <TIME_SLOT TIME_SLOT_ID="ts3" TIME_VALUE="3718"/>
        ...
    </TIME_ORDER>
    <TIER TIER_ID="ref@DAM" PARTICIPANT="Dambar Baram" ANNOTATOR="KP" LINGUISTIC_TYPE_REF="ref">
            <ANNOTATION>
                <ALIGNABLE_ANNOTATION ANNOTATION_ID="ann0" TIME_SLOT_REF1="ts1" TIME_SLOT_REF2="ts2">
                    <ANNOTATION_VALUE>. 001</ANNOTATION_VALUE>
                </ALIGNABLE_ANNOTATION>
            </ANNOTATION>
            <ANNOTATION>
                <ALIGNABLE_ANNOTATION ANNOTATION_ID="ann8" TIME_SLOT_REF1="ts3" TIME_SLOT_REF2="ts4">
                    <ANNOTATION_VALUE>. 002</ANNOTATION_VALUE>
                </ALIGNABLE_ANNOTATION>
            </ANNOTATION>
            ...
    </TIER>
    <TIER TIER_ID="ut@DAM" PARTICIPANT="Dambar Baram" ANNOTATOR="KP" LINGUISTIC_TYPE_REF="ut" PARENT_REF="ref@DAM">
            <ANNOTATION>
                <REF_ANNOTATION ANNOTATION_ID="ann1" ANNOTATION_REF="ann0">
                    <ANNOTATION_VALUE>əbə</ANNOTATION_VALUE>
                </REF_ANNOTATION>
            </ANNOTATION>
            <ANNOTATION>
                <REF_ANNOTATION ANNOTATION_ID="ann9" ANNOTATION_REF="ann8">
                    <ANNOTATION_VALUE>kunəi pudza tukle hon lə məlak</ANNOTATION_VALUE>
                </REF_ANNOTATION>
            </ANNOTATION>
            <ANNOTATION>
                <REF_ANNOTATION ANNOTATION_ID="ann36" ANNOTATION_REF="ann35">
                    <ANNOTATION_VALUE>hidi hudi pudza tukle alam alam wa lakle əbə</ANNOTATION_VALUE>
                </REF_ANNOTATION>
            </ANNOTATION>
            ...
    </TIER>
    <LINGUISTIC_TYPE LINGUISTIC_TYPE_ID="ref"/>
    <LINGUISTIC_TYPE LINGUISTIC_TYPE_ID="ut" CONSTRAINTS="Symbolic_Association"/>
    <LINGUISTIC_TYPE LINGUISTIC_TYPE_ID="txd" CONSTRAINTS="Symbolic_Association"/>
    <LINGUISTIC_TYPE LINGUISTIC_TYPE_ID="tx" CONSTRAINTS="Symbolic_Subdivision"/>
    <LINGUISTIC_TYPE LINGUISTIC_TYPE_ID="mb" CONSTRAINTS="Symbolic_Subdivision"/>
    <LINGUISTIC_TYPE LINGUISTIC_TYPE_ID="ge" CONSTRAINTS="Symbolic_Association"/>
    <LINGUISTIC_TYPE LINGUISTIC_TYPE_ID="ft" CONSTRAINTS="Symbolic_Association"/>
</ANNOTATION_DOCUMENT>
```

Figure 2: The ELAN-XML format with time slots, tiers, constraints, and the links between these elements. Didactically unnecessary markup removed. Parent relations are given in green. Tiers can be of a certain linguistic type (linked in purple), and they can be linked to specified time slots (orange).

## 3   Data

In the context of this study, we restrict ourselves to documents in the ELAN-XML format (*.eaf). The reason for this is that this is a well-structured format used for many documents. The competing Shoebox/Toolbox[11] format is idiosyncratic and undocumented, while the FLEx format[12] is not very well represented in the archives under discussion.

### 3.1   The ELAN-XML format

ELAN is an annotation software developed at the MPI for Psycholinguistics in Nijmegen[13] (Wittenburg et al. (2006)) and uses XML as a storage format. The central element type are tiers, time slots, and linguistic types defining constraints. Figure 2 gives a simplified sample document highlighting the relations between different elements.

There is no registry for tier names or tier types. Users are free to define the semantics and labels of linguistic types as they see fit. A linguistic type named "ut" as in Figure 2 could theoretically contain anything. In practice, however, a number of common naming patterns emerge, so "ut" is for instance commonly used for 'utterance', and never for 'free translation'. We have identified 99 common names for the transcription tier, 26 common names for the translation tier, and 8 common names for the gloss tier (cf. Figure 1, full lists are given in the appendix).

### 3.2   Data collection and preparation

We wrote a harvester to download all available ELAN files from the following four archives: ELAR, TLA, AILLA, PARADISEC. This yielded a total of roughly 20k ELAN files. We also wrote a parser which, for each file, identified the tiers containing transcription (=vernacular text), free translation, morpheme

---

[11]https://software.sil.org/toolbox/
[12]https://software.sil.org/fieldworks/
[13]https://archive.mpi.nl/tla/elan

segmentation, and morpheme translation, using information from the tier names, tier content, and the relation between tiers. The morpheme translation tier for instance has to be a daughter of the morpheme segmentation tier, the translation tier should pass a language identification test as "English" and so on. All code is freely available at https://github.com/ZAS-QUEST/eldpy.

### 3.3  Annotations

Representations of sentences, words,[14] and morphemes on the one hand, and their respective translations on the other was stored and cached as JSON. The result is an ordered list of sentences linked to their translations, and of the component morphemes of these sentences linked to their respective translations/glosses as well.

The list of morpheme translations is thus a list of 2-tuples (vernacular morpheme, English translation), which allows us to create a look-up function like "give me all words which are translated as 'moon'." Each tuple is in turn associated with a given language, so that words translated as 'moon' can be compared across languages (see §6).

## 4  Data enrichment

For the vernacular languages, there are no NLP tools available, as explained above, but an explanation on how to carve a canoe with an axe should yield the relevant concepts 'canoe' and 'axe' via the English translation just as well. In order to tackle the task of discoverability, we ran the grobid-ner named entity recognition service[15] on the English translation. For this, we collated all translations of all the sentences in a given document.

### 4.1  Wikidata concept lookup

Grobid-ner service outputs Wikidata IDs of the type 'Q12345'. A sample document in the Juǀ'hoansi language for instance yielded the following concepts via the English translation route: Q1029907: "stomach", Q25312: "flies", Q25439: "woodpecker", Q506131: "carrying pole", Q606886: "cardinal woodpecker", Q6842999: "midriff". Concepts like "cardinal woodpecker" and "carrying pole" show that a pretty granular analysis of semantic content can be achieved in this way. 8 457 different concepts could be identified and linked to Wikidata. It is of course true that only few people would actively search "cardinal woodpecker"; a search term like "bird" would be much more likely. But the document is not marked up for "bird". So we add this information via Wikidata.

### 4.2  Transitive closure on Wikidata concepts

Wikidata hosts over 95 million concepts. Of these, we only need the 8 457 found in the documents (like "woodpecker"), and their (transitive) parent concepts, like "bird" and "animal". Parent concepts can be either the instanceOf relation ("Woody Woodpecker" is an instance of "woodpecker") or the subclassOf relation ("woodpecker" is a subclass of "bird") and should form a directed acyclic graph.[16] We recursively retrieved all parent concepts of the 8457 initial concepts and stored the transitive closure in a lookup table. This lookup table allows us to retrieve all documents with information about "bird" or any of its transitive child concepts. The parent concept for "carrying pole" is "utensil". The following list gives a list of the most frequently found child concepts thereunder, with document frequencies in parentheses: Q18341850: "pestle" (20), Q381155: "sieve" (18), Q193358: "ladle" (18), Q207763: "rolling pin" (14), Q32489: "knives" (9), Q154038: "cooking pot" (8), Q127666: "frying pan" (8), Q208364: "wok" (6).

Anthropologists interested in material culture now have a very simple entry point into the data; the same is true for ethnozoologist/ornithologists and their kin. In the RDF output (see §5), we use the Dublin Core "subject" property to link the Wikidata concepts to the documents for the time being.

---

[14]The word level is needed as an intermediate helper category, but does not contribute to the analyses conducted here. While sentences and morphemes are typically accompanied by translations/glosses, word-level elements typically lack translations of their own. For more on the cognitive reality of "word" as a concept, see Schiering et al. (2010).

[15]https://github.com/kermitt2/grobid-ner

[16]Some loops in Wikidata were found during the course of the research.

### 4.3  Leipzig Glossing Rules

We have analysed morpheme translations as to their components, and linked glosses like "2SG.ACC" to the list provided by the Leipzig Glossing Rules (Comrie et al. (2008)), in this particular case, "2", "SG", and "ACC". While there are a variety of concept registries for grammatical categories, such as GOLD (Farrar and Langendoen (2003),Farrar and Langendoen (2010), ISOCAT (Kemps-Snijders et al. (2008)), and Clarin Concept Registry,[17] the original documents were not created with these registries in mind.[18] The Leipzig Glossing Rule provide a fairly short an simple list of common abbreviations, and linguist tend to adhere to them. Note that the LGR are a list of *abbreviations*, not a list of categories. For the present purposes, linking to LGR allows us to state that IMP is to be expanded as 'imperative', and not as 'imperfective'. The latter would be IPFV under the Leipzig Glossing Rules. This statement is a lot less powerful than linking IMP to something like gold:imperative. But cross-linguistic categories are fraught with conceptual difficulties, and there is an ongoing debate as to whether they can be defined in a meaningful way at all (see Haspelmath (2007) for discussion). For this reason, we prefer to err on the side of caution and only integrate with the list of abbreviations.

## 5  Models for IGT

Next to external links to the existing knowledge bases like Wikidata, and, in a less evolved fashion, LGR, we also provide a semantic model of the internal structure our IGT data based on the LIGT model (Chiarcos and Ionov (2019)). The LIGT model expands on existing ontologies and vocabularies, such as Dublin Core and NIF (Hellmann et al. (2013)). Figure 3 provides a visualization of this model. The model is based on a ligt:Document, a subclass of dc:Dataset. This document has a text, whose subcomponents are modelled recursively as substrings down to the layer of utterance. Within an utterance, LIGT distinguishes the elements of Word and Morph, which are ligt:Item's arranged in the respective tiers. The vernacular words and glosses are realized as labels, e.g. '"tám"@syw' and '"talk"@eng'. This maps neatly on the structure given in Figure 1.

For LGR glosses, we use a BCP47[19] private use subtag 'lgr' to specify the restricted variety of English we are using here. This yields '"ACC"@en-x-lgr' for the gloss ACC for 'accusative' for instance.

## 6  Integration

Our export as LIGT-RDF has, among other things, the advantage of an easy integration into the Linguistic Linked Open Data Cloud (LLODC, Chiarcos et al. (2012a; Cimiano et al. (2020)). Next to metadata about the languages from Glottolog, IGT data from endangered language archives can be integrated with various other resources with the Linked Data approach used here.

Chiarcos et al. (2017) used DBnary (Sérasset (2014)), based on Wiktionary, to provide glosses in 15 additional languages, beyond the glosses supplied in the original document.

Chiarcos and Ionov (2019) expanded on this and model IGT based on DublinCore, NIF (Hellmann et al. (2013)) and WebAnnotation (Sanderson et al. (2017)) vocabularies. This allows them to integrate IGT from Toolbox, FLEx, and the Xigt format into LIGT. To this set, we can now add the ELAN data from the endangered language archives.

Nordhoff (2020) enriched the documents with semantic concept annotations linked to Wikidata. He used this for an analysis of the most frequent semantic domains found in documents in endangered language archives (to wit, the Caucasus and agriculture). We have now added the transitive closure of the parent relations of these concepts.

Another integration is the generation of candidates for colexification (François (2008)). Concepts do not map alike on lexemes in the languages of the world. Some languages use different words for the concepts HAND and ARM for instance, while others use the same word. Those languages which use the same word are said to "colexify" the two concepts. The study of colexification is complicated by homonymous words which do not share any semantics, like $arm_{upper\ limb}$ and $arm_{weapon}$.

---

[17] https://www.clarin.eu/ccr

[18] For the checkered history of GOLD, ISOCAT, and CCR, see Cimiano et al. (2020).

[19] https://tools.ietf.org/html/bcp47

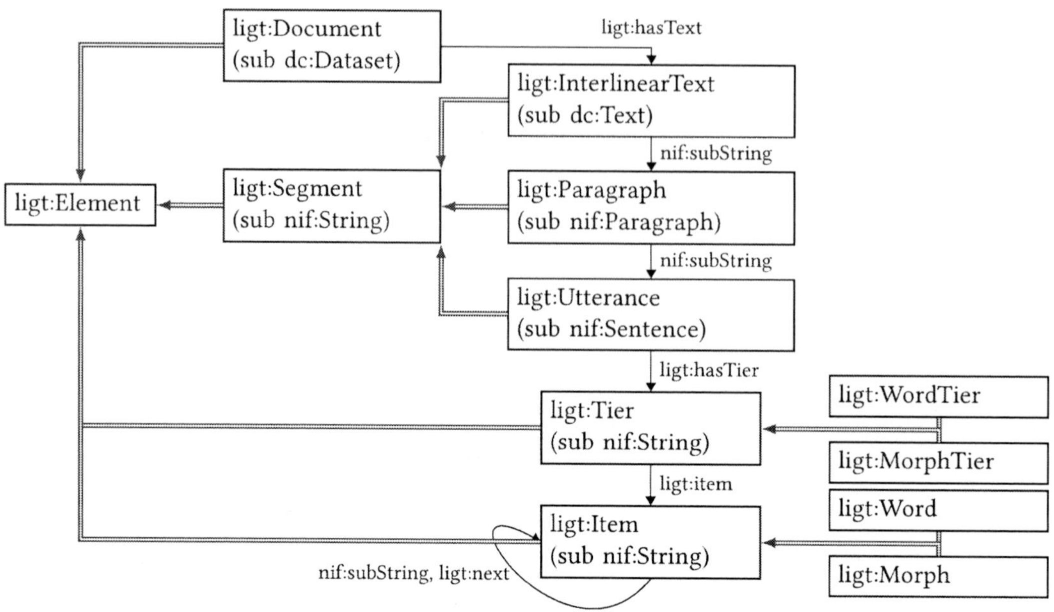

Figure 3: LIGT data model from Chiarcos and Ionov (2019) (adapted). Double arrows indicate subclass relations. Single arrows are labelled for the relations they express.

Figure 4: Retrieved colexifications (subset).

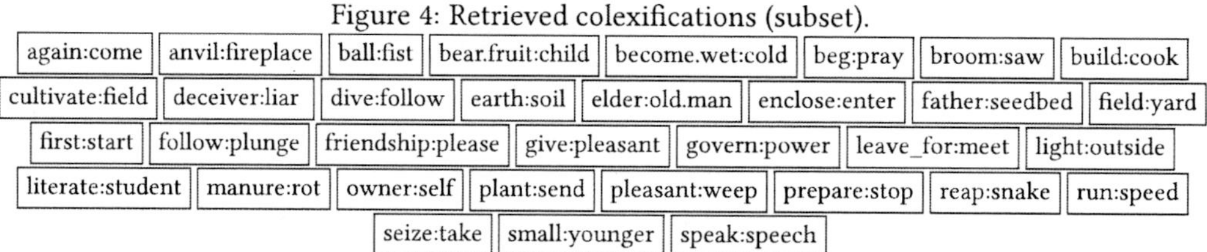

Studies of colexification have been undertaken with (modified) Swadesh lists and questionnaires as an input (List et al. (2018)), as these are available for many languages. The corpus of endangered language data allows us to go beyond these short lists and generate hypotheses about colexification. For this, we look for all words in a given collection which have two different English translations and list them as potential colexification candidates for the two concepts. If a given 2-tuple is found in more than one language, further investigation of the semantic of this is warranted to check whether we are dealing indeed with colexification. Figure 4 gives a list of pairs thus identified.

## 7 Sharing of resources

The legal status of the underlying documents is shaky. The legal domains concerned are privacy law on the one hand and intellectual property law on the other. Depending on where the data were collected, different legal frameworks might apply. Some data might not enjoy any protection, like someone counting from 1 to 10, while other documents have clearly copyrightable content, e.g. a narrative. The same holds true for translations of said content.

Things are different for linguistic analysis. The fact that in a given document, we find a word which has been glossed as "give-1PL.PRES" can probably be shared without too much of a legal risk. The same is true for lists of such annotations, i.e. morpheme-by-morpheme glosses of whole sentences. These

|           | collections | eaf files | transcribed | duration | words transcribed | export triples |
|-----------|------------|-----------|-------------|----------|-------------------|----------------|
| AILLA     | 10         | 1 674     | 1 447       | 532.7h   | 648 908           | 2.6M           |
| ELAR      | 201        | 13 758    | 10 139      | 2588.3h  | 2 498 122         | 24.2M          |
| PARADISEC | 78         | 2 619     | 1 776       | 302.0h   | 225 974           | 10.7M          |
| TLA       | (68)[20]   | 1 695     | 1 441       | 506.5h   | 677 959           | 1.6M           |
| total     | 289+       | 19 746    | 14 803      | 3929.5h  | 4 050 963         | 39.1M          |

Table 2: Holdings of the four investigated DELAMAN archives. Only collections with at least one accessible ELAN file are counted.

can be made available for further inspection.

Even less problematic are the semantic enrichments. The fact that a given document is a about a certain kind of woodpecker is unproblematic and can be shared. The Linked Data approach used here allows us to elegantly circumvent the problem: We use the landing page of a document in a given archive as our URI variable for linked data purposes. We can now predicate over this variable, and say things like that it contains 34 sentences, that it contains information about woodpeckers, and that the 2nd morpheme of the 4th word in the 3rd sentence is glossed as ACC. Interested users can look up the page on the archive and request access to the original document if they so wish. One remaining issue is that the semantic structuring of the archive web sites is slightly different. We have the logical levels of "collection", consisting of "bundles/sessions", in turn containing a number of "files", but not all of these have landing pages for each archive or are cross-linked in an obvious manner with a transparent URL. We are currently working on a resolver service which will allow the URIs used in RDF predicates to be resolved to the URLs in the endangered language archives.

## 8 Evaluation

Table 2 gives a breakdown of the holdings of the different archives as far as known.

Collections typically contain one language, but some projects working in multilingual settings have more than one language. On the other hand, some languages are found in more than one archive. Still, we can say that the number of collections is a good approximation of the number of different languages we know have structured and annotated data for.

For 4 100 files, at least one concept could be retrieved. In total, 34 336 concepts were retrieved from the texts, of which 8 457 are distinct.

As for LGR abbreviations, there are 438 874 instances of 80 distinct types (There are 84 abbreviations listed in the LGR).

## 9 Outlook

Rzymski et al. (2019) describe progress in the Database of Cross-Linguistic Colexifications (CLICS³). They set up a data format following Cross-Linguistic Data Formats (CLDF, Forkel et al. (2018)) and detail how other projects can add to their colexifcation data in a well-defined workflow. Colexification candidates generated from endangered language documentation archives would be a very good candidate for such a workflow.

## 10 Conclusion

Around 90% of all human languages fall into Joshi et al. (2020)'s 'group-0' languages with no noteworthy data capable of providing a starting point for NLP application development. In this paper, we have shown that structured data are indeed available from endangered language archives, a resource by and large ignored by the NLP community up to now. To the extent that legal and technical barriers can be overcome, analyzable and annotated data from almost 300 different languages could be downloaded,

---

[20]The current way of retrieving TLA metadata does not allow a grouping by collection, but grouping by sessions is possible.

parsed, processed, enriched, interlinked, and exported as RDF, making use of the LIGT model, so that we now have structurally interoperable data. The enriched data allow for semantic querying and provide a good starting point to connect pipelines such as the CLICS³ framework. The main issues to address in future work will be the precise legal conditions for sharing and reuse of the data as well as a good resolver service allowing a stable and precise dereferencing of the Linked Data URIs used.

## Appendix

**Tier names indicating translation tiers**  "eng", "english translation", "English translation", "fe", "fg", "fn", "fr", "free translation", "Free Translation", "Free-translation", "Free Translation (English)", "ft", "fte", "tf (free translation)", "Translation", "tl", "tn", "tn (translation in lingua franca)", "tf_eng (free english translation)", "trad1", "Traducción Español", "Tradución", "Traduccion", "Translate", "trad", "traduccion", "traducción", "traducción ", "Traducción", "Traducción español", "Traduction", "translation", "translations", "Translation", "xe".

**Tier names indicating transcription tiers**  "arta", "Arta", "conversación", "default-lt", "default-lt", "Dusun", "Fonética", "Frases", "Hablado", "Hakhun orthography", "Hija", "hija", "ilokano", "interlinear-text-item", "Ikaan sentences", "Khanty Speech", "main-tier", "Madre", "madre", "Matanvat text", "Matanvat Text", "Nese Utterances", "o", "or", "orth", "orthT", "orthografia", "orthografía", "orthography", "othography", "po", "po (practical orthography)", "phrase", "phrase-item", "Phrases", "Practical Orthography", "sentence", "sentences", "speech", "Standardised-phonology", "Sumi", "t", "Tamang", "texo ", "text", "Text", "Text ", "texto", "Texto", "texto ", "Texto principal", "Texto Principal", "tl", "time aligned", "timed chunk", "tl", "Transcribe", "Transcrição", "TRANSCRIÇÃO", "Transcript", "Transcripción chol", "transcripción chol", "Transcripción", "Transcripcion", "transcripción", "Transcripcion chol", "transcript", "Transcription", "transcription", "transcription_orthography", "trs", "trs@", "trs1", "tx", "tx2", "txt", "type_utterance", "unit", "ut", "utt", "Utterance", "utterance", "uterrances", "utterances", "utterrances", "Utterances", "utterance transcription", "UtteranceType", "vernacular", "Vernacular", "vilela", "Vilela", "word-txt", "word_orthography", "xv", "default transcript".

**Tier names indicating gloss tiers**  "ge", "morph-item", "gl", "Gloss", "gloss", "glosses", "word-gls", "gl (interlinear gloss)".


## References

Christian Chiarcos and Maxim Ionov. 2019. Ligt: An LLOD-Native Vocabulary for Representing Interlinear Glossed Text as RDF. In Maria Eskevich, Gerard de Melo, Christian Fäth, John P. McCrae, Paul Buitelaar, Christian Chiarcos, Bettina Klimek, and Milan Dojchinovski, editors, *2nd Conference on Language, Data and Knowledge (LDK 2019)*, number 70 in OpenAccess Series in Informatics (OASIcs), pages 3:1–3:15, Dagstuhl, Germany. Schloss Dagstuhl–Leibniz-Zentrum fuer Informatik.

Christian Chiarcos, Sebastian Hellmann, and Sebastian Nordhoff. 2012a. Linking linguistic resources: Examples from the Open Linguistics Working Group. In Chiarcos et al. (Chiarcos et al., 2012b), pages 201–216.

Christian Chiarcos, Sebastian Nordhoff, and Sebastian Hellmann, editors. 2012b. *Linked Data in Linguistics. Representing Language Data and Metadata.* Springer, Heidelberg.

Christian Chiarcos, Maxim Ionov, Monika Rind-Pawlowski, Christian Fäth, Jesse Wichers Schreur, and Irina Nevskaya. 2017. LLODifying linguistic glosses.

Philipp Cimiano, Christian Chiarcos, John P. McCrae, and Jorge Gracia. 2020. *Linguistic Linked Data: Representation, Generation and Applications.* Springer, Cham.

Bernard Comrie, Martin Haspelmath, and Balthasar Bickel. 2008. *The Leipzig Glossing Rules: Conventions for interlinear morpheme-by-morpheme glosses.* Max Planck Institute for Evolutionary Anthropology, Leipzig.

Michael Cysouw. 2011. Quantitative explorations of the worldwide distribution of rare characteristics, or: the exceptionality of northwestern European languages. In Horst J. Simon and Heike Wiese, editors, *Expecting the Unexpected: Exceptions in Grammar.* De Gruyter Mouton, Berlin, Boston.

Sebastian Drude. 2002. Advanced glossing: A language documentation format and its implementation with Shoebox. In Peter Austin, Helen Dry, and Peter Wittenburg, editors, *Proceedings of the International LREC workshop on Resources and Tools in Field Linguistics*.

Scott Farrar and D. Terence Langendoen. 2003. A linguistic ontology for the semantic web. *GLOT International*, 7(3):97–100.

Scott Farrar and D. Terence Langendoen. 2010. An OWL-DL implementation of GOLD: An ontology for the Semantic Web. In A. Witt and D. Metzing, editors, *Linguistic Modeling of Information and Markup Languages: Contributions to Language Technology*. Springer, Dordrecht.

Robert Forkel, Johann-Mattis List, Simon J. Greenhill, Christoph Rzymski, Sebastian Bank, Michael Cysouw, Harald Hammarström, Martin Haspelmath, Gereon A. Kaiping, and Russell D. Gray. 2018. Cross-linguistic data formats, advancing data sharing and re-use in comparative linguistics. *Scientific Data*, 5:180205.

Alex François. 2008. Semantic maps and the typology of colexification: Intertwining polysemous networks across languages. In Martine Vanhove, editor, *From Polysemy to Semantic Change*, number 106 in Studies in Language Companion Series, pages 163–216. John Benjamins, Amsterdam.

Lauren Gawne. 2015+. *Kagate (Syuba), an endangered Tibeto-Burman language of Nepal*. ELAR, London.

Michael Wayne Goodman, Joshua Crowgey, Fei Xia, and Emily M. Bender. 2015. Xigt: extensible interlinear glossed text for natural language processing. *LREC*, 49(2):455–485.

Kenneth Hale, Michael Krauss, Lucille J. Watahomigie, Akira Y. Yamamoto, Colette Craig, and LaVerne M. Jeanne. 1992. Endangered languages. *Language*, 68(1):1–42.

Martin Haspelmath. 2007. Pre-established categories don't exist: Consequences for language description and typology. *Linguistic Typology*, 11.1:119–132.

S. Hellmann, J. Lehmann, S. Auer, and M. Brümmer. 2013. Integrating NLP using linked data. In *Proceedings of the 12th International Semantic Web Conference, 21–25 October 2013, Sydney*.

Pratik Joshi, Sebastin Santy, Amar Budhiraja, Kalika Bali, and Monojit Choudhury. 2020. The state and fate of linguistic diversity and inclusion in the NLP world. In *Proceedings of the 58th Annual Meeting of the Association for Computational Linguistics*, page 6282–6293.

M. Kemps-Snijders, M. Windhouwer, P. Wittenburg, and S. E. Wright. 2008. ISOcat: Corralling data categories in the wild. In *Proceedings of the 6th International Conference on Language Resources and Evaluation (LREC)*, page 887–891.

T. Kisler, F. Schiel, and H. Sloetjes. 2012. Signal processing via web services: The use case WebMAUS. In *Proceedings Digital Humanities*, page 30–34. Hamburg.

William D. Lewis. 2006. *ODIN: A Model for Adapting and Enriching Legacy Infrastructure*. 2nd IEEE International Conference on E-Science and Grid Computing, Amsterdam.

Johann-Mattis List, Simon J. Greenhill, Cormac Anderson, Thomas Mayer, Tiago Tresoldi, and Robert Forkel. 2018. CLICS2: An improved database of cross-linguistic colexifications assembling lexical data with the help of cross-linguistic data formats. *Linguistic Typology*, 22(2):277–306.

Steven Moran and Daniel McCloy, editors. 2019. *PHOIBLE 2.0*. Max Planck Institute for the Science of Human History, Jena.

M. Nickles. 2001. *Systematics - Ein XML-basiertes Internet-Datenbanksystem für klassifikationsgestützte Sprachbeschreibungen*. Centrum für Informations- und Sprachverarbeitung, München.

Sebastian Nordhoff. 2020. From the attic to the cloud: mobilization of endangered language resources with linked data. In *Proceedings of the Workshop about Language Resources for the SSH Cloud*, pages 10–18, Marseille, France, May. European Language Resources Association.

Ludger Paschen, François Delafontaine, Christoph Draxler, Susanne Fuchs, Matthew Stave, and Frank Seifart. 2020. Building a time-aligned cross-linguistic reference corpus from language documentation data (DoReCo). In *Proceedings of the 12th Conference on Language Resources and Evaluation (LREC 2020)*, page 2657–2666.

Christoph Rzymski, Tiago Tresoldi, Simon J. Greenhill, Mei-Shin Wu, Nathanael E. Schweikhard, Maria Koptjevskaja-Tamm, Volker Gast, Timotheus A. Bodt, Abbie Hantgan, Gereon A. Kaiping, Sophie Chang, Yunfan Lai, Natalia Morozova, Heini Arjava, Nataliia Hübler, Ezequiel Koile, Steve Pepper, Mariann Proos, Briana Van Epps, Ingrid Blanco, Carolin Hundt, Sergei Monakhov, Kristina Pianykh, Sallona Ramesh, Russell D. Gray, Robert Forkel, and Johann-Mattis List. 2019. *The Database of Cross-Linguistic Colexifications, reproducible analysis of cross- linguistic polysemies*, volume 7.

Robert Sanderson, Paolo Ciccarese, and Benjamin Young. 2017. Web Annotation data model. Technical report, W3C Recommendation.

Andrea C. Schalley. 2019. Ontologies and ontological methods in linguistics. *Lang Linguist Compass*, 13(e12356).

R. Schiering, B. Bickel, and K. Hildebrandt. 2010. The prosodic word is not universal, but emergent. *Journal of Linguistics*, 46(3):657–709.

Ronald Schroeter and Nick Thieberger. 2006. Eopas, the ethnoer online representation of interlinear text. in sustainable data from digital fieldwork. In Linda Barwick and Nick Thieberger, editors, *Sustainable data from digital fieldwork*, pages 99–124. University of Sydney, Sydney.

Frank Seifart, Nicholas Evans, Harald Hammarström, and Stephen C. Levinson. 2018. Language documentation 25 years on. *Language*, 94(4):e324–e345.

G. Sérasset. 2014. DBnary: Wiktionary as a lemon-based multilingual lexical resource in RDF. *Semantic Web Journal*, 648.

Mandana Seyfeddinipur, Felix Ameka, Lissant Bolton, Jonathan Blumtritt, Brian Carpenter, Hilaria Cruz, Sebastian Drude, Patience L. Epps, Vera Ferreira, Ana Vilacy Galucio, Brigit Hellwig, Oliver Hinte, Gary Holton, Dagmar Jung, Irmgarda Kasinskaite Buddeberg, Manfred Krifka, Susan Kung, Miyuki Monroig, Ayu'nwi Ngwabe Neba, Sebastian Nordhoff, Brigitte Pakendorf, Kilu von Prince, Felix Rau, Keren Rice, Michael Rießler, Vera Szoelloesi Brenig, Nick Thieberger, Paul Trilsbeek, Hein van der Voort, and Tony Woodbury. 2019. Public access to research data in language documentation. *Language Documentation & Conservation*, 13:545–563, 10.

Kilu von Prince and Sebastian Nordhoff. 2020. An empirical evaluation of annotation practices in corpora from language documentation. In *Proceedings of LREC 2020*. LREC, Marseille.

P. Wittenburg, Brugman H., A. Russel, A. Klassmann, and H. Sloetjes. 2006. *ELAN: A Professional Framework for Multimodality Research*.

# PASTRIE: A Corpus of Prepositions Annotated with Supsersense Tags in Reddit International English

Michael Kranzlein    Emma Manning    Siyao Peng
Shira Wein    Aryaman Arora    Nathan Schneider
Georgetown University
{mmk119, esm76, sp1184, sw1158, aa2190, nathan.schneider}@georgetown.edu

## Abstract

We present the Prepositions Annotated with Supsersense Tags in Reddit International English ("PASTRIE") corpus, a new dataset containing manually annotated preposition supersenses of English data from presumed speakers of four L1s: English, French, German, and Spanish. The annotations are comprehensive, covering all preposition types and tokens in the sample. Along with the corpus, we provide analysis of distributional patterns across the included L1s and a discussion of the influence of L1s on L2 preposition choice.

## 1   Introduction

It is well-established that one's native language ("L1") leaves traces in second language ("L2") word choice and grammar, including subtle aspects of the use of function words such as prepositions—even for highly proficient L2 speakers (Lowie and Verspoor, 2004; Kujalowicz, 2005; Mueller, 2011; Nacey and Graedler, 2015). However, past corpus studies of L2 writing have had no way to control for the *meaning* of these grammatical items in context on a large scale. In this work, we describe a new corpus, PASTRIE,[1] consisting of English Reddit posts and comments (collectively "documents") that have been manually annotated with preposition supersenses.[2] Following Schneider et al. (2018), the annotations also cover possessives, prepositional multiword expressions ("MWEs"), and infinitives.[3] Examples of annotated sentences appear in (1) and (2).

(1)   I was just **on**/Locus it **to**/Purpose find the Copenhagen deal and couldn't find it **at_first**/Time .

(2)   Right **at**/Time the moment when that geyser **of**/Stuff light erupts **from**/Source the edge **of**/Whole the screen , we hear a massive rumble come from/Source the door , which was **in**/Locus that direction .

The annotations are comprehensive, covering all types and tokens of prepositional expressions, totaling 2400 tokens out of the 22.5k token corpus. The documents are drawn from the larger Reddit-L2 corpus (Rabinovich et al., 2018), which consists of English Reddit data of speakers of many different L1s. Our corpus includes English produced by presumed native speakers[4] of English, French, German, and Spanish.

Based on annotators' impressions, the English in the corpus produced by the nonnative speakers is highly fluent and unlike what might be found in learner corpora. This is understandable given that these users are taking it upon themselves to post in an online forum, something early learners are less likely to do. This corpus is not only a new resource for exploring preposition supersenses, but it also addresses an understudied niche of broad-coverage semantics for highly proficient non-native data. Using a large,

---



[1]PASTRIE is available at https://github.com/nert-nlp/pastrie

[2]Automatic lemmas and part-of-speech tags are also included.

[3]We may sometimes use the word "preposition" loosely to cover all of these categories. When specific analyses are being made, more precise terminology is used.

[4]Information on how L1s were identified is included in §3.1. Following Rabinovich et al. (2018), we simply say "native speakers" or "L1" with the understanding that this is an imperfect assumption.



*The 14th Linguistic Annotation Workshop*, pages 105–116
Barcelona, Spain (Online), December 12, 2020.

unannotated sample of the Reddit-L2 corpus as well as our semantically-annotated subcorpus, we conduct a preliminary investigation of preposition use among English speakers of different L1 backgrounds, extending Rabinovich et al.'s (2018) analysis of L2 lexical choice. We will release the corpus to facilitate further study of such phenomena.

## 2 Related Work

### 2.1 Preposition Supersenses

Supersenses are categories used to place both content and function words into unlexicalized semantic classes (Schneider and Smith, 2015), and have been applied to nouns, verbs, adjectives, and adpositions[5] (Miller, 1990; Fellbaum, 1990; Tsvetkov et al., 2015). Here, we focus on the latter. Though adpositions (which almost always occur as prepositions in English) are considered function words and often treated as less important in natural language processing contexts, Schneider et al. (2018) argue for the semantic value of adpositions and propose the Semantic Network of Adposition and Case Supersenses (SNACS) schema.

SNACS categorizes the use of adpositions and case markers, including English possessives, into 50 coarse-grained supersense classes. Each adposition token is annotated as a construal construction with two of these supersenses (Hwang et al., 2017). A construal includes a SCENE ROLE and a FUNCTION, where the former expresses the adposition's meaning in context and the latter denotes its lexical meaning. An example of construal is shown in (3), a sentence from our corpus.[6] In context, the possessive *my* expresses that the speaker is a member of an organization (the company that employs them), hence a scene role of ORGMEMBER; however, the lexical meaning of a grammatical possessive when not indicating possession expresses a looser relationship between entities, corresponding to the function GESTALT. Scene role and function are drawn from the same inventory of supersenses and are often identical. In the PASTRIE corpus, 72% of annotation targets have the same scene role and function.

(3)   This is why **my**/ORGMEMBER↝GESTALT employer has just finished updating 50 k users **from**/SOURCE XP **to**/GOAL Windows 7 .

### 2.2 Prepositions are Uniquely Challenging for Learners

Prepositions are notoriously difficult for language learners (Takahaski, 1969; Littlemore and Low, 2006; Mueller, 2012), which is one of the motivations for constructing this corpus. In studying English preposition usage patterns of high-proficiency learners with different L1 backgrounds, we aim to learn more about how these speakers' L1s might influence their English preposition usage, and how this information might be used to improve pedagogy. One of the problems with prepositions is that they often seem to convey less meaning than content words such as nouns or verbs, but at the same time can be nuanced and highly polysemous. Erarslan and Hol (2014) observed that "most L1 interference took place in the use of prepositions and vocabulary following it." Nacey and Graedler (2015) found rates of inappropriate preposition choice of 4–5% (out of all prepositions) in two corpora of advanced English speakers with a Norwegian L1. They found learners' oral production as challenging as written production and their analysis of the International Corpus of Learner English ("ICLE"; Granger et al., 2009) provided evidence of speakers' L1s influencing L2 lexical choice in both positive and negative ways.

Mahmoodzadeh (2012) conducted Persian-English translation task-based experiments focused on identifying preposition error types. He found that the intermediate Iranian learners of English made more errors of redundancy or inappropriate use than errors of omission and discussed several transfer-related causes of these errors. Gvarishvili (2013) explored negative L1 interference in English preposition usage and offered advice to language educators for mitigating it, but also suggested that educators take advantage of positive influence by pointing out to students L1 prepositions with similar use as their English counterparts.

---

[5]Adpositions include prepositions, postpositions, and circumpositions, but since we are concerned with English data, we often only mention "prepositions."

[6]Examples use the notation SCENEROLE↝FUNCTION. When Scene Role and Function have the same supersense label, we write it only once for conciseness.

The difficulty of acquiring prepositions when learning a new language is also addressed in cognitive studies. Lowie and Verspoor (2004) offered a cognitive discussion of the progression of preposition acquisition in Dutch learners of English; Hung et al. (2018) found a cognitive approach that focuses on both spatial and metaphorical meanings to be effective for teaching English prepositions; and Tyler (2012); Bratož (2014); Wong et al. (2018); Zhao et al. (2020) all advocate for a cognitively driven approach to teaching prepositions as well. Pedagogical approaches for teaching English prepositions are also compared in Mueller (2011, 2012). Given the particular difficulty of preposition acquisition, these cognitive pedagogical approaches and new insights from studying learner data should be put to use to help students.

Automatic grammatical error detection (and correction) is another tool that can aid students and has been widely studied, including for prepositions specifically. Models of native and non-native English have been used for this purpose (De Felice and Pulman, 2008; Tetreault and Chodorow, 2008; Hermet and Alain, 2009; Gamon, 2010), along with parse features (Tetreault et al., 2010) and rule-based features (Chodorow et al., 2007). Graën and Schneider (2017) took advantage of parallel corpora for identifying challenging prepositions for learners; Madnani et al. (2011) proposed a crowdsourcing-based approach for improving evaluation of grammatical error detection systems; and Huang et al. (2016) built a Chinese preposition selection model to aid in identifying errors and correcting them. Making explicit some notion of preposition *meaning*, as we do with the PASTRIE corpus, holds the potential to give more informative corrective feedback.

### 2.3   Reddit-L2: Our Source Corpus

The Reddit-L2 corpus was published in 2018 alongside an analysis of cognate effects in language produced by non-native speakers of English (Rabinovich et al., 2018). It contains 230M sentences and 3.5B tokens of English data from native and non-native speakers, whose L1s were heuristically identified. It was created by first selecting users with a self-specified country *flair* on a set of subreddits and then gathering additional content from those users on different subreddits. While knowing a user's country does not guarantee that their L1 is the majority language in that country, steps were taken to make this more likely, and the inherent noise in the data is acknowledged in the corpus description.[7] The corpus focuses on large languages (it includes authors with flairs from 31 countries representing the Germanic, Romance, and Balto-Slavic language families) and excludes multilingual countries like Switzerland.

Since being made available, the corpus has primarily been used for native language identification (Goldin et al., 2018; Kumar et al., 2019; Steinbakken, 2019; Sarwar et al., 2020). However, it has also been used in studies of bias in word embeddings and bias against non-native text (Manzini et al., 2019; Zhiltsova et al., 2019), as well as semantic infelicity detection (Rabinovich et al., 2019).

## 3   Corpus Description

### 3.1   The PASTRIE Corpus

The PASTRIE corpus consists of 1,155 sentences and 22,484 tokens from 255 Reddit documents sampled from the following languages and countries, with percentages of tokens in parentheses:

- English (24.07%): Australia, New Zealand, UK, US
- French (23.56%): France
- German (28.08%): Austria, Germany
- Spanish (24.29%): Argentina, Mexico, Spain

English was chosen as a baseline for comparisons, and French, German, and Spanish were chosen due to their relative similarity to English and wide availability in the Reddit-L2 corpus. While it's possible that some documents belong to the same Reddit thread, this was not a specific selection criterion.

In the corpus, there are 2,395 annotation targets. Of these targets, 2,193 are single tokens and 202 are prepositional MWEs. Sentence segmentation and tokenization were performed with StanfordNLP (Qi et al., 2018), and annotation targets, including prepositions, possessives, MWEs, and infinitives, were

---

[7]Further details on the construction of the Reddit-L2 corpus are available in section 3 of Rabinovich et al. (2018).

identified heuristically using the same script used for the STREUSLE corpus (Schneider et al., 2018) and then manually corrected during annotation.

## 3.2 Annotation

### 3.2.1 Annotation Process

We organized the annotation effort into smaller samples of data (annotation "tasks") that each included 15 documents, and we annotated a total of 17 tasks. All tasks were assigned documents randomly, and documents of each L1 appeared in each task. Tasks were independently annotated by two different annotators, then adjudicated in a meeting which included both annotators and at least one additional person who led the adjudication. Annotators and adjudicators were not shown the L1s of specific documents.

Four different annotators participated over the course of the project, all of whom were Linguistics graduate students and native English speakers; one additional person, a professor with expertise in the annotation scheme did not annotate, but participated in adjudication meetings, especially in the early stages of the project to ensure accuracy. Over all targets, the two annotators agreed on 59.2% of Scene roles (Cohen's $\kappa = 0.58$) and 68.2% of Function labels ($\kappa = 0.66$). This is lower than the SNACS IAA numbers found in Schneider et al. (2018) (74.4% agreement on Scene, 81.3% on Function); however, those were on a sample from a single text, The Little Prince; our data is likely more difficult due to the wide range of topics and authors on social media, and the use of informal and sometimes non-native language.

After initial annotation and adjudication was complete, we did an additional review to ensure annotations were consistent with version 2.5 of the guidelines (Schneider et al., 2020), since most annotation had been done with previous versions, and to resolve difficult cases that were initially left as open or marked as uncertain.

### 3.2.2 Challenging Cases

One challenge in annotating the data is that Reddit contains discussion of a wide range of topics, often using jargon that would be understood by members of a given subreddit but was not always familiar to annotators; in these cases, annotators looked up terminology or consulted with others to ensure they understood the sentences. The range of topics also meant that many interesting semantic relationships appeared in the data that had not been seen in the STREUSLE corpus. For example, (4) discusses the details of a video game, where a decision had to be made whether to treat *the game* as personified when annotating *by*.

(4)   Only Zin and Gore can be knocked **out_of**/SOURCE **their**/GESTALT charged modes , but those are n't considered **as**/CHARACTERISTIC↝IDENTITY enraged **by**/EXPERIENCER↝AGENT the game .

In some cases, adpositions represented ambiguous semantic relationships and adjudicators had to decide on the most likely interpretations. For example, in (5), we considered whether the recipe could be considered a personified ORIGINATOR of the suggestion, in which case the possessive would be annotated ORIGINATOR↝GESTALT. We decided that while this is a possible interpretation, it was more straightforward to consider the suggestion as part of the recipe, hence WHOLE↝GESTALT.

(5)   Never follow a recipe **'s**/WHOLE↝GESTALT suggestion **for**/TOPIC how much garlic you should put **in**/GOAL↝LOCUS .

Finally, as with most social media, Reddit text is largely written in an informal register with little or no editing. While this rarely posed a problem for annotation, there were some cases where it was difficult to discern the intended meaning of a sentence. For example, it is unclear whether (6) is referring to a hypothesis that leads to taking a measurement, or the hypothesis made based on a measurement. We decided that it was most likely either EXPLANATION or PURPOSE, and chose EXPLANATION because it is more general. In (7), the preposition *of* doesn't make sense; we annotated it as a typo for *off*, but it could conceivably be a typo for *on* instead.

(6) You can doubt the hypothesis **for**/EXPLANATION a measurement but you can not doubt the actual measurement .

(7) The easiest is getting a bunch of chickens , a rooster , and live **of**/INSTRUMENT↝SOURCE eggs .

## 4 Analysis

### 4.1 Preposition Usage

The PASTRIE corpus is an annotated subcorpus of a larger initial sample we drew from the Reddit-L2 corpus. This sample of roughly 2,500 documents is a more representative source for analysis of preposition usage and can serve as supplementary data for future annotation.

The statistics of the initial sample are described in table 1 and the statistics of the annotated PASTRIE corpus are described in table 2. We see no alarming deviations in PASTRIE compared to the initial sample. PASTRIE contains more English tokens generated by some L1s than others as a result of the random sampling involved in task generation.

| L1 | Documents | Tokens | Sentences | Prepositions | Prepositions/Token | Tokens/Doc | Sentences/Doc |
|---|---|---|---|---|---|---|---|
| English | 658 | 48.529 | 2,544 | 5038 | 10.28% | 73.75 | 3.87 |
| French | 677 | 52,093 | 2,689 | 5213 | 10.01% | 76.95 | 3.97 |
| German | 767 | 69,206 | 3,681 | 7380 | 10.66% | 90.23 | 4.80 |
| Spanish | 587 | 45,488 | 2,410 | 4588 | 10.09% | 77.49 | 4.11 |

Table 1: Characteristics of the initial sample of the Reddit-L2 corpus which tasks were created from.

| L1 | Documents | Tokens | Sentences | Prepositions | Prepositions/Token | Tokens/Doc | Sentences/Doc |
|---|---|---|---|---|---|---|---|
| English | 67 | 5,412 | 284 | 579 | 10.70% | 80.78 | 4.24 |
| French | 74 | 5,297 | 281 | 539 | 10.18% | 71.58 | 3.80 |
| German | 74 | 6,313 | 334 | 675 | 10.69% | 85.31 | 4.51 |
| Spanish | 65 | 5,462 | 256 | 602 | 11.00% | 84.03 | 3.94 |

Table 2: Characteristics of the PASTRIE corpus, the annotated subset of data.

As shown in table 1, prepositions tend to make up 10–11% of the data. The rate of preposition use is highest for German L1 speakers, followed by English and Spanish, with French being the lowest.[8] While German does have the highest rate of preposition use in the initial sample, the range is only 0.65%. This widens slightly to 0.82% for the annotated portion of the data, which has a slightly different ranking.

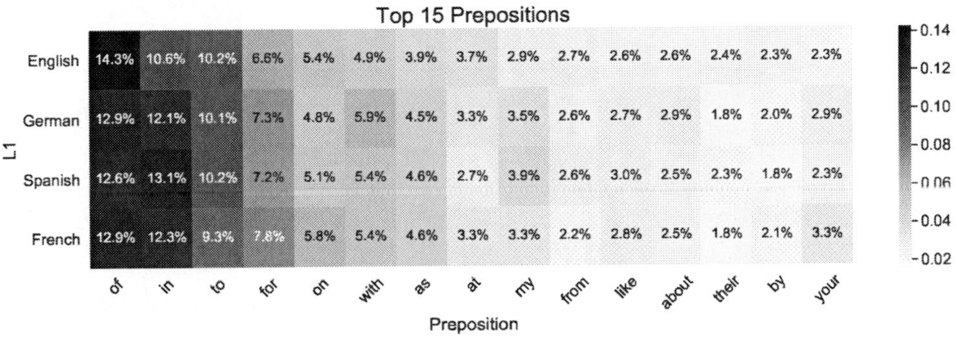


Figure 1: Relative frequencies (among all prepositions for the L1) of 15 most frequent prepositions in the larger unannotated sample of the Reddit-L2 corpus.

Figure 1 indicates that there are some differences in the usage of specific prepositions. Notably, *of* is generated more by native English speakers than by any other speaker, whereas words like *in* and *with* are

---

[8]The corpus only contains English data. When we mention other languages, we are referring to the L1 of the speaker.

generated more frequently by all other L1 speakers than by native English speakers in this corpus. This may suggest that multiple senses of *of* translate to distinct prepositions in other languages. This could also be due to the mechanics of possession in non-English languages.

Of the top 15 most frequently used prepositions, German L1 speakers collectively had lower relative frequency than at least one other category of L1 speaker for 13/15 prepositions, and a lower relative frequency than at least two other categories of L1 speakers for 11/15 prepositions. Broadly, this suggests that, as shown in Figure 1, German L1 speakers use the 15 most frequently used prepositions less frequently than other L1 speakers, indicating that L1 German learners of English may use a wider variety of prepositions. This could be due to prepositional transfer. The broader use of prepositions by German L1 speakers in this corpus is likely not exclusively due to increased proficiency or near-native English fluency, because German L1 preposition usage does not most closely match the preposition usage of L1 English speakers, as seen in figure 2a. These observations should be taken in context, with caveats of a small sample size and no control for topic and domain of the posts.

## 4.2 Supersense Usage

The distributions of preposition and supersense usage by L1, depicted in figure 2, are generally comparable in shape. In the preposition usage plot, values are normalized by total frequency of prepositions for each L1. In the supersense plot, values are normalized by the total frequency of the particular construals for each L1.

**L1 German Construal Usage**  Notably, German L1 speakers have the highest number of infrequent *construals*, and the lowest number of infrequent *prepositions*. German also has the longest tail when considering prepositions, while all languages have tails of similar length in the construals plot. The peaked head close to the y-axis indicates a high number of prepositions that are used infrequently and a small number of prepositions that occur frequently. The plot also shows that a few construals and prepositions dominate usage, while most construals and prepositions are infrequently used. The density plot of German L1 construal usage has a less peaked head (/smaller number of low-frequency prepositions) and a less steep decline, meaning German L1 speakers were more likely to use moderate- or high-frequency prepositions.

This supports our claim in Section 4.1, that the range of German L1 preposition usage is being impacted by prepositional transfer. The construal usage by L1 German speakers is not mirroring the construal usage of L1 English speakers, which would be an indication of near-native English fluency and usage, but instead presents differently than the construal usage by all three other L1 speakers.

The density values are normalized by the number of total prepositions generated by each L1, so the less peaked head is not caused by German L1 speakers having generated a larger number of prepositions.

| | | All | | English | | French | | German | | Spanish | |
|---|---|---|---|---|---|---|---|---|---|---|---|
| **Scene Role** | | Locus | 168 | `i | 45 | Topic | 35 | Topic | 49 | Locus | 51 |
| | | Topic | 155 | Locus | 41 | Theme | 35 | Locus | 41 | Time | 39 |
| | | Theme | 139 | Topic | 39 | Locus | 35 | CompRef. | 38 | Theme | 38 |
| | | `i | 137 | Gestalt | 38 | Gestalt | 30 | Gestalt | 37 | Goal | 36 |
| | | Gestalt | 127 | Theme | 37 | Circum. | 28 | Circum. | 35 | CompRef. | 35 |
| **Function** | | Gestalt | 325 | Gestalt | 88 | Gestalt | 74 | Gestalt | 87 | Gestalt | 76 |
| | | Locus | 242 | Locus | 55 | Locus | 55 | Locus | 60 | Locus | 72 |
| | | Topic | 154 | Goal | 49 | Topic | 33 | Topic | 51 | Topic | 36 |
| | | Goal | 153 | `i | 45 | CompRef. | 30 | Goal | 44 | Time | 35 |
| | | `i | 137 | Topic | 34 | Goal | 28 | CompRef. | 35 | Goal | 32 |
| **Construal** | | Locus | 146 | `i | 45 | Topic | 31 | Topic | 44 | Locus | 46 |
| | | Topic | 137 | Gestalt | 37 | Locus | 29 | Locus | 37 | Time | 35 |
| | | `i | 137 | Locus | 34 | Gestalt | 28 | `i | 35 | Topic | 31 |
| | | Gestalt | 121 | Topic | 31 | `i | 28 | Gestalt | 34 | `i | 29 |
| | | Time | 106 | Goal | 27 | `d | 22 | Circum. | 32 | Theme | 27 |
| | | **Total** | 2395 | **Total** | 579 | **Total** | 539 | **Total** | 675 | **Total** | 602 |

Table 3:  Top scene roles, functions, and construals by L1. In all of the most common construals, the scene role matches the function, so only one supersense is shown.

**Most frequent supersenses**    Table 3 shows that the top labels (for scene role, function, and construal as a whole) across all L1s draw from a limited set of supersenses. The top function supersense across all languages is GESTALT, which is a prototypical function of the English genitives: *of*, *'s*, and the various pronominal forms. Schneider et al. (2018) formulated the SNACS guidelines for these as they were very frequent in past annotated corpora and are highly polysemous; both of these attributes are evident in PASTRIE.

LOCUS is the second most common function in all of the languages. Another example of variation is English's relatively high use of `i, the infinitival uses of *to* and *for*, which are idiomatic to English and thus more difficult to acquire for L2 speakers (Heil and López, 2019).

**Supersense distribution comparison**    Table 4 is a pairwise quantitative comparison of the construals that were encountered between each L1. It shows slight variation in scene role and function and almost no variation in the distribution of construal usage between every pair of languages. This suggests that the general set of meanings that are filled by prepositions is not substantially affected by the L1 of the speaker. Rather, we find that differences manifest in preposition choice for specific construals. An instance of variation in preposition choice for LOCUS is examined below.

| L1        vs. **L1** | Scene | Fxn. | Cons. |
|---|---|---|---|
| English vs. German | 0.71 | 0.73 | 0.61 |
| English vs. French | 0.71 | 0.76 | 0.61 |
| French  vs. Spanish | 0.70 | 0.76 | 0.59 |
| English vs. Spanish | 0.70 | 0.73 | 0.61 |
| French  vs. German | 0.69 | 0.71 | 0.60 |
| German vs. Spanish | 0.67 | 0.72 | 0.61 |

Table 4: Jaccard similarity coefficients of the multisets of scene roles, functions, and construals between every language pair. Jaccard similarity is a metric of similarity between two sets $A$, $B$, defined as $\frac{|A \cap B|}{|A \cup B|}$.

**Variation in LOCUS prepositions**    When the data is examined more narrowly, we do find examples of L1 influence on preposition choice. The most common prepositions used to represent the scene role of LOCUS are *in* and *on*. In the British National Corpus (BNC, 2007), which draws from both formal and informal, written and spoken sources of English, for every instance of *in* there are only 0.35 instances of *on*. In the entire PASTRIE corpus, we find 0.44 instances of *on* for each *in* (disregarding supersense labels).

However, we find that the L1 of non-native speakers significantly skews this ratio when only considering spatial uses of these prepositions. Figure 3 shows that the rate of LOCUS use of *on* relative to *in* is much greater for French (0.91) and German (0.67) than for English (0.23) and Spanish (0.19).

Previous work has observed that spatial relations are categorized differently across languages (Bowerman and Choi, 2001; Feist, 2008) and have complex semantics (Feist, 2000). In English, *in* and *on*, both highly polysemous prepositions, further serve a variety of spatial and metaphoric non-spatial roles (Rice, 1992) which can be difficult for non-native speakers to learn. Language acquisition in regards to motion events between satellite-framed and verb-framed languages is known to be hindered by typological differences (Hickmann and Hendriks, 2010), and more generally due to differences in the semantic fields of spatial markers (Reshöft and Gralla, 2013).

The most likely explanation for these discrepancies across prepositions for LOCUS across L1s is that the semantic fields of spatial markers used in the L1 influences the use of those in the L2. Šeškauskienė and Juknevičienė (2020), from a pedagogical standpoint, do find this effect in Lithuanian L1 speakers' acquisition of English—*in* is learned more readily because it has a clear equivalent in Lithuanian's locative case, while *on* is more difficult because it lacks such an equivalent. Johannes et al. (2016) also examine spatial prepositions in the context of L1 English acquisition, finding that in children the semantic field of *on* is learned much later than that of *in*.

It is possible that the cross-L1 variation in this dataset is due at least in part to varying topics and domains (i.e. which subreddits the documents were sampled from); nevertheless, this example illustrates the utility of SNACS in examining and comparing adposition and case semantics.

## 5    Conclusion

With data drawn from the Reddit-L2 corpus (Rabinovich et al., 2018), we created PASTRIE, a new corpus of preposition supersense annotations that is publicly available. This corpus adds to existing resources with preposition supersenses and includes annotations of native English data and data produced by L1 speakers of French, German, and Spanish. We demonstrated the applicability of SNACS and the construal analysis to L2 English. We presented detailed discussion of the annotation process, general corpus statistics, and an analysis of usage phenomena across the L1s, including variations between speakers of different L1 backgrounds.

Future work may consider a wider variety of L1s than the typologically similar and closely genetically related languages examined in this work. Computational applications of PASTRIE in natural language understanding (NLU) of non-native English merit further investigation. Finally, corpus-based research such as in this paper can be used to empirically investigate theories of language acquisition.

## Acknowledgments

We thank Shuly Wintner, Ella Rabinovich, and Liat Nativ for their assistance in sampling data from the Reddit-L2 corpus. We are grateful to Tripp Maloney, Ryan Mannion, and Sasha Slone for their careful annotation work, and to anonymous reviewers for their feedback. This research was supported in part by NSF award IIS-1812778 and grant 2016375 from the United States–Israel Binational Science Foundation (BSF), Jerusalem, Israel.

## References

BNC. 2007. The British National Corpus, version 3 (BNC XML Edition).

Melissa Bowerman and Soonja Choi. 2001. Shaping meanings for language: universal and language-specific in the acquisition of spatial semantic categories. In Melissa Bowerman and Stephen Levinson, editors, *Language Acquisition and Conceptual Development*, number 3 in Language, Culture & Cognition, pages 475–511. Cambridge University Press, Cambridge, UK.

Silva Bratož. 2014. Teaching English locative prepositions: A cognitive perspective. *Linguistica*, 54(1):325–337.

Martin Chodorow, Joel R. Tetreault, and Na-Rae Han. 2007. Detection of grammatical errors involving prepositions. In *Proc. of the Fourth ACL-SIGSEM Workshop on Prepositions*, pages 25–30, Prague, Czech Republic.

Rachele De Felice and Stephen G. Pulman. 2008. A classifier-based approach to preposition and determiner error correction in L2 English. In *Proc. of Coling*, pages 169–176, Manchester, UK.

Ali Erarslan and Devrim Hol. 2014. Language interference on English: Transfer on the vocabulary, tense and preposition use of freshmen Turkish EFL learners. *ELTA Journal*, 2(2):4–22.

Michele I Feist. 2000. *On in and on: An investigation into the linguistic encoding of spatial scenes*. Ph.D. thesis, Northwestern University.

Michele I. Feist. 2008. Space between languages. *Cognitive Science*, 32(7):1177–1199.

Christiane Fellbaum. 1990. English verbs as a semantic net. *International Journal of Lexicography*, 3(4):278–301.

Michael Gamon. 2010. Using mostly native data to correct errors in learners' writing: a meta-classifier approach. In *Proc. of NAACL-HLT*, pages 163–171, Los Angeles, California.

Gili Goldin, Ella Rabinovich, and Shuly Wintner. 2018. Native language identification with user generated content. In *Proc. of EMNLP*, pages 3591–3601, Brussels, Belgium.

Johannes Graën and Gerold Schneider. 2017. Crossing the border twice: reimporting prepositions to alleviate L1-specific transfer errors. In *Proc. of the Joint 6th Workshop on NLP for Computer Assisted Language Learning and 2nd Workshop on NLP for Research on Language Acquisition at NoDaLiDa, Gothenburg, 22nd May 2017*, pages 18–26, Gothenburg, Sweden.

Sylviane Granger, Estelle Dagneaux, Fanny Meunier, and Magali Paquot. 2009. *International Corpus of Learner English*. Louvain-la-Neuve, Belgium: Presses universitaires de Louvain.

Zeinab Gvarishvili. 2013. Interference of L1 prepositional knowledge in acquiring of prepositional usage in English. *Procedia - Social and Behavioral Sciences*, 70:1565–1573.

Jeanne Heil and Luis López. 2019. Acquisition without evidence: English infinitives and poverty of stimulus in adult second language acquisition. *Second Language Research*.

Matthieu Hermet and Désilets Alain. 2009. Using first and second language models to correct preposition errors in second language authoring. In *Proc. of the Fourth Workshop on Innovative Use of NLP for Building Educational Applications*, pages 64–72, Boulder, Colorado.

Maya Hickmann and Henriëtte Hendriks. 2010. Typological constraints on the acquisition of spatial language in French and English. *Cognitive Linguistics*, 21(2):189–215.

Hen-Hsen Huang, Yen-Chi Shao, and Hsin-Hsi Chen. 2016. Chinese preposition selection for grammatical error diagnosis. In *Proc. of COLING*, pages 888–899, Osaka, Japan.

Bui Phu Hung, Truong Vien, and Nguyen Ngoc Vu. 2018. Applying cognitive linguistics to teaching English prepositions: A quasi-experimental study. *International Journal of Instruction*, 11(3):327–346.

Jena D. Hwang, Archna Bhatia, Na-Rae Han, Tim O'Gorman, Vivek Srikumar, and Nathan Schneider. 2017. Double trouble: the problem of construal in semantic annotation of adpositions. In *Proc. of *SEM*, pages 178–188, Vancouver, Canada.

Kristen Johannes, Colin Wilson, and Barbara Landau. 2016. The importance of lexical verbs in the acquisition of spatial prepositions: The case of in and on. *Cognition*, 157:174–189.

Agnieszka Kujalowicz. 2005. Cross-linguistic influence in the production of German prepositions by Polish learners of English and German. *Studia Anglica Posnaniensia: International Review of English Studies*, 41:187–198.

Sachin Kumar, Shuly Wintner, Noah A. Smith, and Yulia Tsvetkov. 2019. Topics to avoid: demoting latent confounds in text classification. In *Proc. of EMNLP-IJCNLP*, pages 4153–4163, Hong Kong, China.

Jeannette Littlemore and Graham D Low. 2006. *Figurative thinking and foreign language learning*. Springer.

Wander Lowie and Marjolijn Verspoor. 2004. Input versus transfer? - the role of frequency and similarity in the acquisition of L2 prepositions. In Peter Jordens, Michel Achard, and Susanne Niemeier, editors, *Cognitive Linguistics, Second Language Acquisition, and Foreign Language Teaching*, 2004 edition, volume 18, pages 77–94. Mouton de Gruyter, Berlin, New York.

Nitin Madnani, Martin Chodorow, Joel Tetreault, and Alla Rozovskaya. 2011. They can help: using crowdsourcing to improve the evaluation of grammatical error detection systems. In *Proc. of ACL-HLT*, pages 508–513, Portland, Oregon, USA.

Masoud Mahmoodzadeh. 2012. A cross-linguistic study of prepositions in Persian and English: The effect of transfer. *Theory and Practice in Language Studies*, 2(4):734–740.

Thomas Manzini, Lim Yao Chong, Alan W Black, and Yulia Tsvetkov. 2019. Black is to criminal as Caucasian is to police: detecting and removing multiclass bias in word embeddings. In *Proc. of NAACL-HLT*, pages 615–621, Minneapolis, Minnesota.

George A. Miller. 1990. Nouns in WordNet: A lexical inheritance system. *International Journal of Lexicography*, 3(4):245–264.

Charles M. Mueller. 2011. English learners' knowledge of prepositions: Collocational knowledge or knowledge based on meaning? *System*, 39(4):480–490.

Charles M Mueller. 2012. *Comparison of an Integrative Inductive Approach, Presentation-and-Practice Approach, and Two Hybrid Approaches to Instruction of English Prepositions*. Ph.D. thesis, University of Maryland.

Susan Nacey and Anne-Line Graedler. 2015. Preposition use in oral and written learner language. *Bergen Language and Linguistics Studies*, 6.

Peng Qi, Timothy Dozat, Yuhao Zhang, and Christopher D. Manning. 2018. Universal Dependency parsing from scratch. In *Proc. of CoNLL*, pages 160–170, Brussels, Belgium.

Ella Rabinovich, Yulia Tsvetkov, and Shuly Wintner. 2018. Native language cognate effects on second language lexical choice. *Transactions of the Association for Computational Linguistics*, 6:329–342.

Ella Rabinovich, Julia Watson, Barend Beekhuizen, and Suzanne Stevenson. 2019. Say anything: automatic semantic infelicity detection in L2 English indefinite pronouns. In *Proc. of CoNLL*, pages 77–86, Hong Kong, China.

Nina Reshöft and Linn Gralla. 2013. On the use of spatial prepositions: Differences in L1 and L2 English. *Twenty Years of Learner Corpus Research: Looking back, Moving ahead. Corpora and Language in Use–Proceedings*, 1:389–400.

Sally A Rice. 1992. Polysemy and lexical representation: The case of three English prepositions. In *Proceedings of the Fourteenth Annual Conference of the Cognitive Science Society*, pages 89–94.

Raheem Sarwar, Attapol T. Rutherford, Saeed-Ul Hassan, Thanawin Rakthanmanon, and Sarana Nutanong. 2020. Native language identification of fluent and advanced non-native writers. *ACM Transactions on Asian and Low-Resource Language Information Processing*, 19(4):1–19.

Nathan Schneider, Jena D. Hwang, Archna Bhatia, Vivek Srikumar, Na-Rae Han, Tim O'Gorman, Sarah R. Moeller, Omri Abend, Adi Shalev, Austin Blodgett, and Jakob Prange. 2020. Adposition and Case Supersenses v2.5: Guidelines for English. *arXiv:1704.02134v6 [cs]*.

Nathan Schneider, Jena D. Hwang, Vivek Srikumar, Jakob Prange, Austin Blodgett, Sarah R. Moeller, Aviram Stern, Adi Bitan, and Omri Abend. 2018. Comprehensive supersense disambiguation of English prepositions and possessives. In *Proc. of ACL*, pages 185–196, Melbourne, Australia.

Nathan Schneider and Noah A. Smith. 2015. A corpus and model integrating multiword expressions and supersenses. In *Proc. of NAACL-HLT*, pages 1537–1547, Denver, Colorado.

Inesa Šeškauskienė and Rita Juknevičienė. 2020. Prepositions in L2 written English, or why on poses more difficulties than in. *Nordic Journal of English Studies*, 19(1).

Stian Steinbakken. 2019. *Paying Attention to Native-Language Identification*. Ph.D. thesis, Norwegian University of Science and Technology.

George Takahaski. 1969. Perception of space and the function of certain English prepositions. *Language Learning*, 19(3-4):217–234.

Joel Tetreault, Jennifer Foster, and Martin Chodorow. 2010. Using parse features for preposition selection and error detection. In *Proc. of the ACL 2010 Conference Short Papers*, pages 353–358, Uppsala, Sweden.

Joel R. Tetreault and Martin Chodorow. 2008. The ups and downs of preposition error detection in ESL writing. In *Proc. of Coling*, pages 865–872, Manchester, UK.

Yulia Tsvetkov, Manaal Faruqui, Wang Ling, Guillaume Lample, and Chris Dyer. 2015. Evaluation of word vector representations by subspace alignment. In *Proc. of EMNLP*, pages 2049–2054, Lisbon, Portugal.

Andrea Tyler. 2012. *Cognitive Linguistics and Second Language Learning: Theoretical Basics and Experimental Evidence*. Routledge.

Man Ho Ivy Wong, Helen Zhao, and Brian MacWhinney. 2018. A cognitive linguistics application for second language pedagogy: The English preposition tutor. *Language Learning*, 68(2):438–468.

Helen Zhao, Shuting Huang, Yacong Zhou, and Ruiming Wang. 2020. Schematic diagrams in second language learning of English prepositions - a behavioral and event-related potential study. *Studies in Second Language Acquisition*, pages 1–28.

Alina Zhiltsova, Simon Caton, and Catherine Mulwa. 2019. Mitigation of unintended biases against non-native English texts in sentiment analysis. In *Proceedings for the 27th AIAI Irish Conference on Artificial Intelligence and Cognitive Science*, page 12.

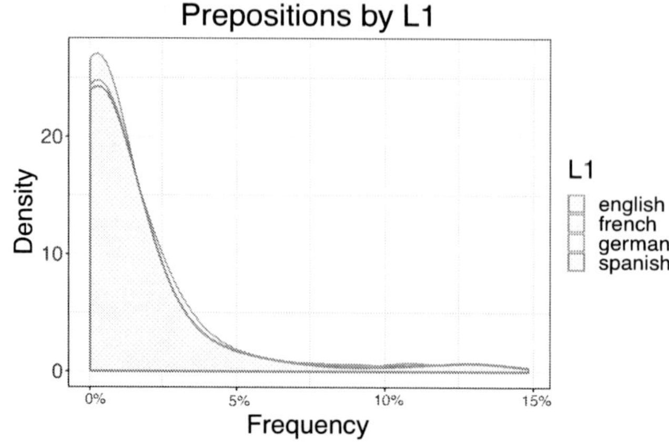

(a) Density plot for preposition usage by L1, demonstrating that German has the longest tail, while English and French have the shortest tails.

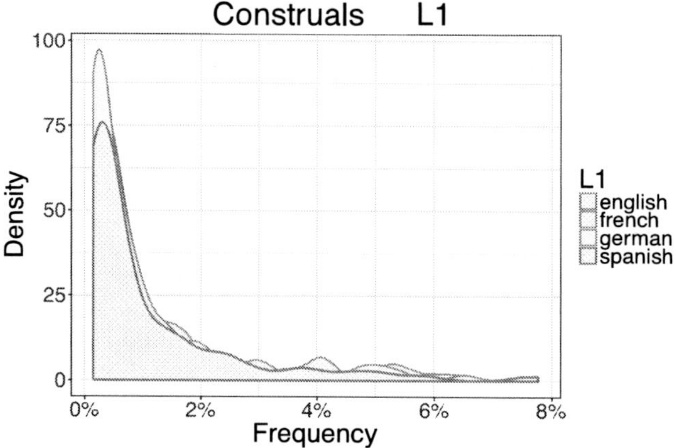

(b) Density plot of construals by L1. This depicts the number of construals (y-axis) that have a certain frequency (x-axis) in the annotated corpus. Most construals are used rarely, and there are only a few high-frequency construals.

Figure 2: Density plots for prepositions and construals, normalized by total number of prepositions per L1. Recall that a construal is a pair of supersenses—a SCENE ROLE and a FUNCTION.

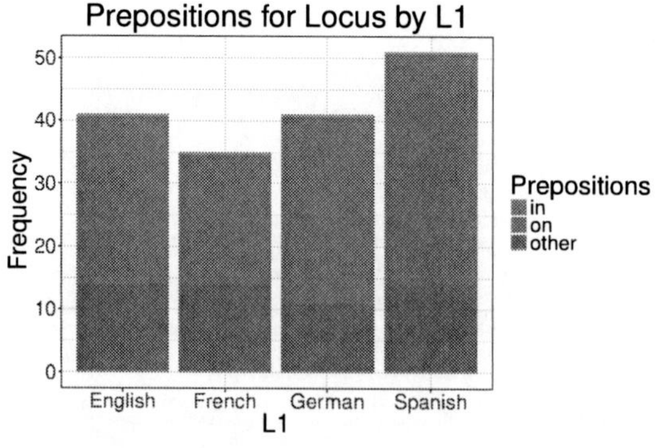

Figure 3: Frequency counts of tokens annotated with LOCUS as the scene role, broken down by native language and preposition type: *in*, *on*, and others.

# Supersense and Sensibility:
# Proxy Tasks for Semantic Annotation of Prepositions


**Luke Gessler    Shira Wein    Nathan Schneider**
Georgetown University
{lg876, sw1158, nathan.schneider}@georgetown.edu



## Abstract

Prepositional supersense annotation is time-consuming and requires expert training. Here, we present two sensible methods for obtaining prepositional supersense annotations *indirectly* by eliciting surface substitution and similarity judgments. Four pilot studies suggest that both methods have potential for producing prepositional supersense annotations that are comparable in quality to expert annotations.


## 1 Introduction

Prepositions are highly ambiguous function words which can express a wide variety of relationships (Litkowski and Hargraves, 2005; Tratz, 2011). Supersenses have been proposed as an analytic framework for studying their lexical semantics, but extant gold-annotated corpora (e.g. Schneider et al., 2018; Peng et al., 2020) are small because preposition supersense annotation is a relatively complex annotation task that requires substantial training and time.

We ask whether preposition supersense annotation could be made cheaper and quicker with crowdsourced labor. This will require "sensible" annotation tasks accessible to non-experts. In this work we present two possible designs for **proxy** tasks for crowdsourcing from which supersense labels can be recovered indirectly. These designs involve in-context *substitution* and *similarity* judgments. Based on four in-house pilot experiments, we conclude that both designs are promising as methods for building a large preposition supersense–annotated corpus, and that they differ in how difficult they are for the workers and for the researchers. However, the setup should be considered a proof of concept, as we work with an idealized pool of workers (in-house computational linguistics graduate students). Future research will be necessary to ascertain whether the paradigm is suited to naïve crowdworkers as well.

## 2 Preposition Supersenses

Prepositions[1] can express many different kinds of semantic relations. Schneider et al. (2018) present SNACS, a coarse-grained annotation framework for prepositions encoding these relations. The meanings of prepositions are expressed in terms of supersenses, of which there are 50 in SNACS v2.5.[2] For instance, the preposition *in* can be used to express time, place, and other relations: "I rented an apartment in$_{\text{LOCUS}}$ Boston", "I hope to see you in$_{\text{TIME}}$ the future".[3]

Compared to other tagging tasks, supersense annotation is relatively hard: the SNACS guidelines, which are only for prepositional supersenses, are around 100 pages in length, and a single preposition can often have multiple plausible annotations which must be carefully considered before a final decision.

---



[1]And adpositions, more generally—but since all data in the present work is from English, we will write *preposition* throughout.

[2]See: http://flat.nert.georgetown.edu/supersenses/

[3]In SNACS, prepositions are actually annotated with *two* supersenses: one for their *scene role*, which describes the "basic semantic relation between the preposition-linked elements", and one for their *function*, which captures the "semantic relation literally or metaphorically present in the scene [...] highlighted by the choice of adposition". Whenever the scene role does not match the function role, the two are notationally separated with a pipe, as in "You are meticulous in your work and it shows in$_{\text{MANNER|LOCUS}}$ my smile." For the purposes of the present work, we will simplify our discussion of the prepositional supersense tagging task and speak of it as if it consisted of assigning a single label (the scene role and function tags, concatenated).




*The 14th Linguistic Annotation Workshop*, pages 117–126
Barcelona, Spain (Online), December 12, 2020.

## 3 Two Task Designs

Our ultimate goal is to obtain supersense labels for prepositions in context from crowdsourced data. One possible technique would be to provide definitions and canonical examples of each label, or subsets of labels, and ask the crowdworker which label most closely applies to the annotation target (Munro et al., 2010). Another tactic would be to decompose our labels into more readily intuitive semantic *features* (Reisinger et al., 2015). But given the extensive semantic range of the many prepositions we seek to annotate, both of these approaches seem difficult to achieve with crowdworkers.

Instead, we explore what we term *proxy tasks*:[4] rather than teach and elicit supersenses (or semantic features associated with supersenses) directly, we elicit judgments of surface substitution/similarity, as has been done by previous work on word sense crowdsourcing (§5). This approach leverages current annotated data in combination with the proxy annotations to infer supersense labels via crowdsourcing. Here we outline two different approaches for framing a crowdsourcing task from which annotations can be derived. Details will be explained in more depth when we turn to discuss our pilot studies.

### 3.1 Preposition Substitution

This design consists of two crowdsourced tasks and requires an unlabeled corpus $\mathcal{U}$. First, in the *generation task*, we identify an unlabeled instance $\langle s,t \rangle \in \mathcal{U}$, where $s$ is a sentence and $t \in s$ is the *target preposition* to be disambiguated. The sentence $s$ is presented to a crowdworker, and the worker is asked to provide a substitute $t'$ for $t$ which approximately preserves the meaning of $s$ when substituted with $t$ and does not contain $t$. E.g., for the sentence "The book is **by** the lamp", "close to" and "near" would both be good substitutes because "The book is **close to** the lamp" and "The book is **near** the lamp" both have similar meanings. Substitutes can be anything: they do not have to be prepositions, and they do not have to be a single word. By the end of this task, several potential substitutes $t'_1,\ldots,t'_n$ will have been proposed by workers, but this data alone is not enough to infer a supersense label.

More information is collected in the second task, the *selection task*. The substitutes from the generation task $t'_1,\ldots,t'_n$ populate a multiple-choice list, and crowdworkers choose all items on the list which are acceptable substitutes for $t$ in $s$. Once enough crowdworkers have completed the selection task, we are left with a frequency distribution over the substitutes. (For an example of such a distribution, see figure 2.)

These distributions must somehow be turned into supersense labels. One way to do this is to source labeled instances $\langle s,t,\ell_{\text{gold}} \rangle$ for the tasks above from a gold-labeled corpus $\mathcal{L}$. This would allow a classifier to predict each instance's annotation from its substitution distribution, which could then be used to label unseen data. However, one concern is that a statistical classifier based on substitutes would be no more accurate for infrequent prepositions than training a supersense classifier directly; a set of heuristic rules for disambiguating supersenses that could use the selected substitutes may be effective here.

### 3.2 Neighbor Selection

This design consists of a single crowdsourced task and requires a labeled corpus $\mathcal{L}$, an unlabeled input corpus $\mathcal{U}$, and some similarity function $sim(x,y)$ that can compare two unlabeled instances $\langle s_1,t_1 \rangle$, $\langle s_2,t_2 \rangle$ and represent as a real number how similar the two usages of prepositions $t_1$ and $t_2$ are in their contexts.[5]

An unlabeled instance $\langle s,t \rangle \in \mathcal{U}$ is selected, which we call the *target* instance. *sim* is used to compare it to every instance in $\mathcal{L}$, and the top $k$ most similar inst/ances in $\mathcal{L}$ are retrieved with their labels, $\langle s_1,t_1,\ell_1 \rangle,\ldots,\langle s_k,t_k,\ell_k \rangle$. We call these retrieved instances the target's *neighbors*. Neighbors may optionally be filtered, e.g. to ensure that no label $\ell$ is represented more than once among $\ell_1,\ldots,\ell_k$.

The target sentence $s$ is presented to crowdworkers along with $s_1,\ldots,s_k$ from the neighbors, with the target preposition indicated in each, and crowdworkers are asked to select any neighbors for which the

---

[4]This is unrelated to the term "proxy task" as used by Mostafazadeh et al. (2016), where it is used to refer to intrinsic evaluations for word embeddings.

[5]We deliberately do not mention a specific metric or representation here, since there are many ways to implement this design. As we describe in §4.3, we use cosine distance between supersense membership softmax vectors from a supersense tagger for our pilots in this work, though one could imagine other implementations, such as Euclidean distance between raw or fine-tuned BERT embeddings.

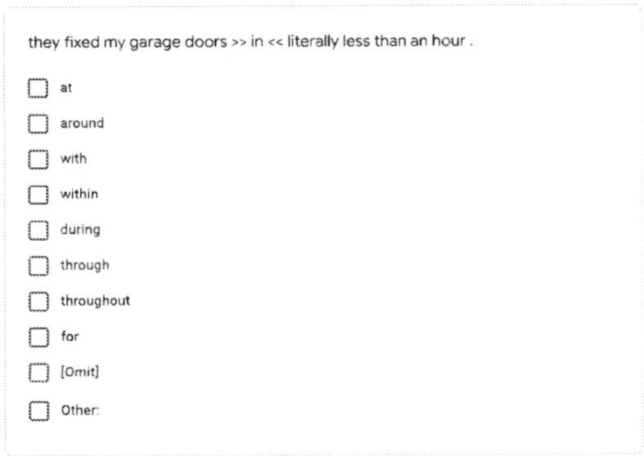

Figure 1a and 1b — prompt screenshots.



(a) A prompt from pilot 2, substitute selection, for a single instance: the target preposition is indicated with angle brackets, and workers are tasked with selecting substitutes which roughly preserve the sentence's meaning.

(b) A prompt from pilot 3. Although six retrieval strategies were used to contribute neighbors for this candidate sentence, only three unique neighbors were retrieved across them.

**Figure 1:** Prompts for pilots 2 and 3.

usage of the preposition $t_i$ in $s_i$ most resembles the usage of $t$ in $s$.[6] For example, if the target sentence were "I was booked **at** the hotel", "There was no cabbage **at** the store" would be a neighbor to choose, while "My technician arrived **at** 11 pm" would not be a good neighbor to choose. The predicted supersense tag is taken from the neighbor sentence that was selected most often by crowdworkers.

## 3.3 Comparison

We hypothesize that the substitution design, a two-task design with a non-trivial annotation inference step, would be more time- and resource-intensive than the one-task neighbor selection design. On the other hand, we expect the neighbor selection design to work well only as long as $\mathcal{L}$ is big enough to contain relevant neighbors, which may not be the case for rarer supersense tags. Moreover, the neighbor selection design relies on a similarity metric which may not always successfully find good neighbors. Thus it is worth exploring whether the two designs have complementary strengths.

## 4 Pilot Studies

In order to assess the quality and characteristics of these two designs before large-scale deployment, we conducted a series of pilot studies with a small number of participants. Participants in each study were drawn from a group of several graduate students, all of whom had at least some familiarity with SNACS. This is an unrealistic quality for crowdworkers to have, but our aim is to assess how well these designs can work in ideal conditions.

### 4.1 Pilot 1: Substitute Generation

First, we carry out the generation task of the substitution design. Five common prepositions are selected for annotation: *for, with, to, from, in*. For each preposition, 30 instances were retrieved from STREUSLE, with 10–20 supersenses represented across all of a given preposition's instances. Seven workers were shown the instances and asked to write a single substitution per instance according to the guidelines in §3.1.

We find that for any given instance, all workers tended to produce different substitutes. If workers had tended to converge on a single substitute, there might have been some hope of recovering a supersense label directly, but as there was almost never consensus, an additional task is needed to determine tags.

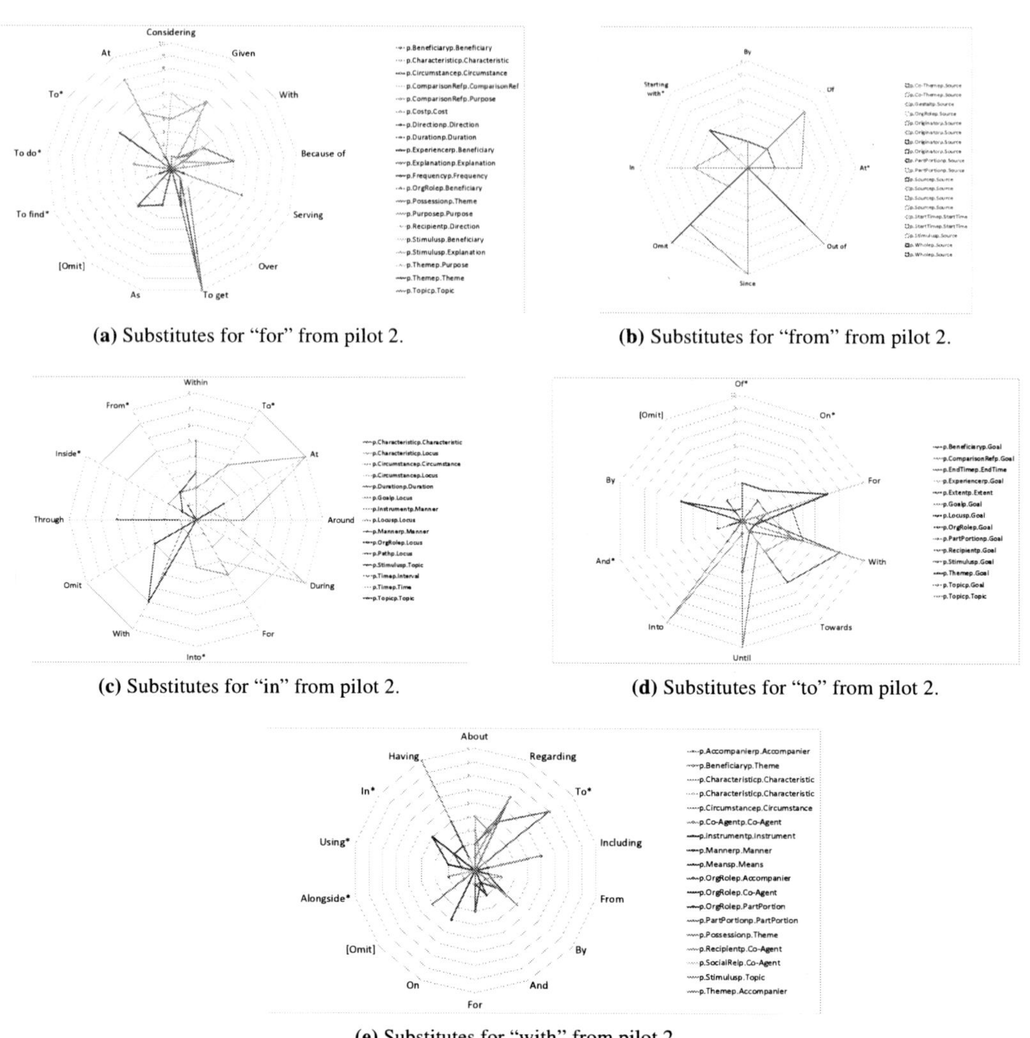

(a) Substitutes for "for" from pilot 2.

(b) Substitutes for "from" from pilot 2.

(c) Substitutes for "in" from pilot 2.

(d) Substitutes for "to" from pilot 2.

(e) Substitutes for "with" from pilot 2.

**Figure 2:** Substitutes from pilot 2. Each "spoke" represents a substitute, and every point on each colored line represents the frequency of a substitute used for an instance that was gold-labeled with a particular supersense tag. For instance, in (c), we can see that of all the instances of "in" that were gold-tagged with GOAL‖LOCUS, *with* was picked once, *into* three times, and *for* four times. Only substitutes that were picked three or more times across all 5 prepositions are shown. Asterisked paraphrases were written in by workers during the selection task and were not produced by the generation task.

## 4.2 Pilot 2: Substitute Selection

In pilot study 2, we carry out the second task of the substitution design, substitute selection. For each of the 5 prepositions investigated in pilot 1, we select 30 instances from STREUSLE, yielding a total of 150 instances for this pilot. The substitutes for each preposition are selected by taking the top 8 most commonly provided substitutes for all instances of that preposition in pilot 1. In addition to these substitutes, workers could also indicate that none of the 8 substitutes are appropriate, either by choosing "[Omit]", or providing an alternative substitute. (See figure 1a.) Seven workers participated in this pilot.

As described in §3.1, in a full implementation of this task, the next step would be to train classifiers to predict the tag for each instance from its substitute distribution. However, our dataset is too small to train a classifier, so we inspect our results qualitatively.

---

[6]Strictly speaking, this design could be implemented with or without any formal guidance given to workers on what should count as "similar enough" for this task, but for our pilot studies, we deliberately choose not to give workers any guidance. Our motivation for this was to see what kind of granularity we would get from worker judgments without any explicit instruction.

| Strategy | Votes | Majority |
|---|---|---|
| None | 21 | 6 |
| Random, same-word, same-supersense | 22 | 8 |
| Random, same-word | 10 | 2 |
| Cosine, same-word, same-supersense | 74 | 24 |
| Cosine, same-word | 79 | 27 |
| Cosine, same-supersense | 74 | 24 |
| Cosine, no constraints | 79 | 27 |
| Theoretical Maximum | 120 | 40 |

**(a)** A tabulation of the number of times a strategy's retrieved neighbor was selected by a worker in pilot 3. Three workers examined 40 instances, so the maximum possible tally is 120, shown in the "votes" column. The "Majority" column tallies the neighbors that received a majority among the workers (ties possible).

| Case | Tagger | Crowd | "None" |
|---|---|---|---|
| 1 (Tagger correct, gold present) | 17/17 | 17/17 | 0/17 |
| 2 (Tagger incorrect, gold present) | 0/12 | 6/12 | 5/12 |
| 3 (Tagger correct, gold absent) | 3/3 | 0/3 | 2/3 |
| 4 (Tagger incorrect, gold absent) | 0/8 | 0/8 | 5/8 |

**(b)** Tagger and crowd accuracy for pilot 4 grouped by whether the tagger correctly predicted the target's gold tag and whether the target's gold tag was present among the 5 neighbors. "None" column indicates how many times "None" was chosen by the crowd. (These results should not be taken to be indicative of real-world performance, since pilot 4's dataset was deliberately constructed to include correctly and incorrectly tagged instances in equal proportions, while in a real scenario we expect the tagger would be correct more often than not.)

**Table 1:** Data from pilots 3 and 4.

Recall that for a single instance $\langle s,t \rangle$, the substitute selection task leaves us with a frequency distribution over $t$'s substitutes $t'_1, \ldots, t'_k$. If we aggregate these distributions over every instance of $t$, and then group them by the supersense label $\ell$, we are left with distributions as shown in figure 2, each of which tells us the number of times a particular substitute was chosen across all instances of $t$ that had the tag $\ell$. While no firm conclusions can be drawn because of the limited size of the data, we see enough separation between regions to suggest that supersenses have distinguishable substitute distributions—and therefore, the distributions obtained from crowdworkers would be effective for classifying the supersense.

### 4.3  Pilot 3: Neighbor Selection Retrieval Strategy

The neighbor selection design retrieves similar sentences from a labeled corpus for a similarity judgment. This design critically relies on the quality of the top $k$ instances which are retrieved. In pilot 3 we compare several strategies for retrieving the top $k$ instances.

Our $sim(\langle s_1, t_1 \rangle, \langle s_2, t_2 \rangle)$ relies on Liu et al.'s (2020) supersense tagger, and is implemented as the cosine similarity between the tagger's vectors of supersense label probabilities for $t_1$ and $t_2$ as they are used in $s_1$ and $s_2$. In order to obtain high-quality vectors for the entire corpus, we use a strategy similar to jackknife resampling: we partition the corpus's documents so that they are approximately balanced by token count, yielding 5 splits $\mathcal{L}_1, \ldots, \mathcal{L}_5$. Now, for each $\mathcal{L}_i$, the vectors for instances contained within $\mathcal{L}_i$ are obtained by training the tagger on the other 4 splits and predicting on $\mathcal{L}_i$.

For each of the same 5 prepositions as above, we first identify from the STREUSLE test and development sets 8 instances: 4 of which the tagger correctly predicts, and 4 of which it incorrectly predicts. We focus on incorrect predictions especially because it is important to understand how well this method works when the tagger's predictions are wrong. (There would be little purpose to crowdsourcing if it were only accurate for instances that the tagger already classified correctly!)

Next, six retrieval strategies are identified. These strategies differ in three parameters: their ranking method (cosine ranking, versus random ranking as a baseline); whether neighbors are required to feature the same preposition as the target (the same-word constraint); and whether neighbors are required to be tagged with the same supersense as the target (the same-supersense constraint; this is an oracle of sorts to potentially reduce situations where none of the options are relevant). This yields 8 possibilities, but we exclude random ranking without the same-word constraint because it would obviously yield bad results.

For each of the 40 instances, each strategy contributes a single neighbor, and these neighbors are deduplicated before being presented to a worker so they could choose the best neighbors (possibly multiple if there is a tie), as shown in figure 1b. A "None" option is again provided in case no neighbor is close enough to the target. In order to determine the success of each strategy, we simply tally the number of times a neighbor that was contributed by that strategy was selected by a worker, of which there were three for this study. The results are given in table 1a. The results show that, on the whole, unconstrained cosine ranking successfully finds neighbors that workers deem relevant. Moreover, overall, strategies with the same-word and same-supersense constraints do not outperform cosine without constraints. That

**Target sentence:** One time we even left after sitting at the table for 20 minutes and not being greeted with$_{\text{MEANS,POSSESSION|ACCOMPANIER}}$ a drink order .

**Neighbor sentences:**
(1) I can not tell you how often I am complimented on$_{\text{TOPIC}}$ my hair ( style AND color ) !
(2) A simple follow - up phone call with$_{\text{CO-AGENT}}$ a woman quickly turned into a nightmare .
(3) wow , the representative went way above and beyond in helping me with$_{\text{THEME}}$ my account set up .
(**4, selected**) This store is proof that you can fool people with$_{\text{MEANS}}$ good advertising .
(5) She has taken care of my sweet girl for almost 4 years now and I would not let Gracee go with$_{\text{ACCOMPANIER|CO-AGENT}}$ anyone besides her !!!
(6) None

**Target sentence:** The atmosphere is your typical indie outfit with old movie posters and memorabilia from$_{\text{STARTTIME,ORIGINATOR|SOURCE}}$ the 70's and 80's .

**Neighbor sentences:**
(1) I just got back from$_{\text{SOURCE}}$ france yesterday and just missed the food already !
(2) prepared the road test with a driving ... prepared the road test with a driving school in edmonton , but my instructor only trained me in a narrow street , hence I took one 90 minute lesson from$_{\text{ORGROLE|SOURCE}}$ the Noble driving school to learn the skill of changing lane , and found them very friendly and professional .
(3) yet again it was a great stay from$_{\text{STARTTIME}}$ begiinning to end .
(4) We order take out from$_{\text{ORIGINATOR|SOURCE}}$ here all the time and we are never disappointed .
(5) # 2 the decor is tasteful and artistic , from$_{\text{PARTPORTION|SOURCE}}$ the comfortable chairs to the elegant light fixtures .... and ( most importantly ) # 3 the food is FANTASTIC .
(**6, selected**) None

(**a**) A case 2 instance from pilot 4 where workers identified the neighbor with the gold label.

(**b**) A case 2 instance from pilot 4, where workers chose "None" even though a gold-tagged neighbor was present.

**Figure 3:** Two instances from Pilot 4. Tags from the gold-annotated source corpus are given in blue, and the supersense tagger's predictions (which in these two examples are also incorrect) are given in red.

the same-supersense methods, which have access to the gold label for the target, do not outperform the unconstrained cosine strategy suggests that the latter is reasonably robust on its own. It remains possible that these strategies could have complementary strengths, though our data here is too limited to speculate.

## 4.4 Pilot 4: Neighbor Selection

In pilot 4, we carry out a small-scale version of the neighbor selection design, using the same 40 instances from pilot 3 and using cosine ranking to identify 5 neighbors for each instance. We do not use the same-word or same-supersense constraints from pilot 3, but we do introduce a diversity constraint, which requires that all neighbors have different supersense tags. This maximizes our odds that one of the 5 neighbors will have the correct tag for the target.

We analyze results from 5 workers, who were shown each target with its 5 neighbors and asked to choose the most relevant neighbors, or "None", similar to figure 1b. We use the workers' plurality vote to select a neighbor, and use the neighbor's gold tag as the target's predicted tag. Ideally, our participants will arrive on a plurality vote for the correct neighbor when the gold tag is present among them, and if the gold tag is not present, they will either select "None" or choose neighbors with gold tags that are similar, but not identical, to the target's gold tag.

Our results show that our participants performed fairly close to this ideal: broadly, whenever the crowd selects a neighbor it usually has the correct gold label, and when no neighbor is a good choice or there is something pathological about the instance, the crowd often selects "None". In our discussion we will partition this pilot's results according to two parameters: whether the tagger correctly predicted the target preposition's supersense tag, and whether a neighbor was retrieved whose gold tag matched the target preposition's tag (thereby affording workers the opportunity to correctly label the instance). A summary of results is given in table 1b.

**Case 1: tagger correct, gold-tagged neighbor present**   When the tagger produces the correct supersense label for the target preposition and also succeeds in finding a gold-tagged neighbor, the crowd always chooses the correct neighbor. This is an encouraging result for the question of whether crowdworkers can perform worse than the tagger: it seems that in cases where the tagger finds it easy to tag correctly and produce a gold-tagged neighbor, humans are also able to easily recognize the right answer.

**Case 2: tagger incorrect, gold-tagged neighbor present**   The case when the tagger was incorrect but still manages to retrieve a relevant neighbor is an important one, because it is where humans have the opportunity to *improve on* the tagger's performance, rather than keep up with it (case 1) or fall behind it (cases 3 and 4). In case 2, workers managed to retrieve the correct tag 6/12 times and in the remaining cases unambiguously choose "None" or tie vote for "None" 5/6 times. This result tells us that in case 2, workers are able to either choose the neighbor with the correct tag or refuse to choose a neighbor most of the time. A representative example is given in figure 3a: here, the gold label of "with" in the target sentence is MEANS, while the model gives the similar but mistaken tag POSSESSION|ACCOMPANIER.[7]

A more interesting instance is given in figure 3b. The tagger has mistagged the target instance, "from_STARTTIME the 70's and 80's", and although it still manages to find a gold neighbor "from_STARTTIME beginning to end", the crowd rejects it in favor of "None". Although SNACS assigns STARTTIME to both instances, this obscures a notable difference in meaning: the former use describes when an object was made, and the latter use the beginning of an event. The most likely explanation, then, is that the crowd perceived this difference in meaning and decided the latter instance was not similar enough in meaning to be acceptable. This instance therefore constitutes evidence that workers are capable of making some distinctions that are *more* nuanced than those made by SNACS.

The remaining instances from case 2 mostly either demonstrated the tagger's misunderstanding of subtle distinctions which humans were able to recover from (either by choosing "None" or the gold neighbor), although some other instances featured metaphor which posed a challenge for both the tagger and humans. The instance "Food is awful and the place caters to_BENEFICIARY|GOAL the yuppy crowd ." has the expression *caters to* which has a literal sense ('serving food to') that differs from its metaphorical sense ('pandering to'). Interpreting a metaphorical expression literally or metaphorically will almost always entail a difference in supersense and is an issue for SNACS in general.

**Case 3: tagger correct, no gold-tagged neighbor**  The 3 times where the tagger correctly predicted the target's gold tag but did not manage to retrieve any neighbors with this tag were all somehow exceptional. Looking into them, we determined that in one case, the target was not well treated by the SNACS guidelines and could plausibly have been annotated differently, and that the two other instances were metaphorical and similarly could have been annotated differently (cf. case 2). While it is difficult to generalize from so few instances, we see that the tagger's top predicted supersense is sometimes not represented in the cosine-retrieved neighbors, even though the cosine measure makes use of the tagging model. This suggests that it might be advantageous in future iterations of this design to consult the tagger's prediction and require at least one neighbor to have the same supersense.

**Case 4: tagger incorrect, no gold-tagged neighbor**  In the last case where the tagger was wrong and no neighbors with the correct tag were retrieved, we found similarly hard cases which were due to vagueness in the SNACS guidelines, well-formedness issues, or other relatively uncommon causes. In these cases, we felt that expert human annotators also would have struggled to choose the correct tag or could have defensibly argued for different analyses. One instance, for example, contains a crucial typo: "it was a little to high dollar for me". The "to" should have been a "too", and "too" is highly connected to the fact that this instance of "for" is involved in a comparison.

**Summary**  We have seen in pilot 4 that human crowdworkers, in aggregate, are generally cautious, good at being confident when they should be, and choosing "None" when no neighbors are appropriate.[8] It should be noted that the "None" result is not simply a dead end—if an instance receives a "None", additional steps can in principle be taken to attempt to elicit an answer, e.g. by fetching a new batch of neighbors and putting it back into the annotation pool. We also reiterate that the dataset in pilot 4 was deliberately constructed so that half of its instances would have incorrect tag predictions. Even still, if we take pilot 4 results as a measure of performance, our crowdsourcing method delivers higher-quality annotations than the tagger alone (which can already achieve $F_1$ in the low 80s on STREUSLE's test split), demonstrating the potential of this approach.

---

[7]This is because "with a drink order" is describing the manner of the greeting, not an item that was in someone's possession for the main event, as in "I arrived with_POSSESSION|ACCOMPANIER my box to ship."

[8]The extent to which this is also true of *individual* crowdworkers before their responses have been aggregated is unclear from the work we have discussed here.

## 5   Related Work

Crowdsourcing on Amazon Mechanical Turk has been a popular method for scaling up linguistic annotation. Early studies on its efficacy for semantic annotations like word sense disambiguation, textual entailment, and word similarity (Snow et al., 2008) and psycholinguistic studies and judgment elicitation (Munro et al., 2010) have shown that crowdsourced annotations can be as good as if not even better than annotations produced using traditional methods. Several studies have focused specifically on word sense annotations for content-words like nouns, adjectives, and verbs (Rumshisky, 2011; Jurgens, 2013; Biemann and Nygaard, 2010; Biemann, 2012; Tsvetkov et al., 2014), but function words have received less attention. To our knowledge, the only work carried out specifically on prepositional sense annotation using a non-traditional annotation methodology is due to Tratz (2011, §4.2), who describes a process by which existing prepositional sense annotations were refined by three annotators, two of which have unspecified levels of linguistic or other competencies. We conjecture that one reason why content-words have been favored over function-words for crowdsourced annotation is that their comparatively less abstract meanings make reasoning about their semantics more approachable to linguistically naïve crowdworkers, simplifying task design, while for function words, it can be difficult to tap into crowdworkers' intuitions without changing the task considerably.

Some work has investigated gamification with the hope that bringing gamelike elements would allow crowdworkers to produce good annotations without a traditional training process, in some cases achieving performance on par with or better than expert annotation (Fort et al., 2020; Hartshorne et al., 2014; Schneider et al., 2014). Independent from the matter of whether to crowdsource or gamify, some have modified their annotation schemes with an eye explicitly to annotation expense (in terms of time or money). In the QA-SRL annotation scheme proposed by He et al. (2015), plain-language questions are used to describe the predicate-argument structures of verbs instead of formalisms such as frames or predicates, rendering it theory- and formalism-neutral and easier to explain to non-expert workers.

Our work is different from the work we have reviewed here in that we have attempted to have participants solve a task that is *not* the same task we would have given to an expert annotator. Pursuing such a proxy task, as we have termed it, introduces the challenge of turning proxy data into gold data, but reduces the need for worker training. Proxy tasks have been successfully pursued in other domains, like in the ESP game designed by von Ahn and Dabbish (2004) for image labeling, where player data for a game played with an image—the proxy task—is used to infer image labels.

## 6   Conclusion

We have presented two designs for deriving prepositional supersense tags from crowdsourced tasks, and we have investigated their efficacy through four pilot studies, finding that both hold promise for producing high-quality prepositional supersense annotations. We have seen that the two designs differ in their complexity and performance characteristics: the neighbor selection design, while consisting of only one task instead of two, requires a gold-annotated corpus of sufficient size to give every tag sufficient coverage, while the substitution design could reveal, bottom-up, clusters of usages that may not be well-represented in the training data.

We have made several idealizations throughout this work: all data was drawn from STREUSLE, guaranteeing that it would be homogeneous with respect to genre, and crowdworkers had some knowledge of the SNACS guidelines which likely made them better at the tasks than real-world crowdworkers. Moreover, we studied only 5 common prepositions covering 20 or so supersenses out of SNACS's 50. In future work, we intend to implement these designs on platforms such as Amazon Mechanical Turk to further investigate these designs' efficacy and the extent to which these idealizations affect our results.

### Acknowledgements

This research was supported in part by NSF award IIS-1812778. We thank our pilot participants Shabnam Behzad, Michael Kranzlein, Yang Liu, Emma Manning, and Jakob Prange, and we also thank Yang (again) and Siyao Peng for their helpful comments on a draft of this paper. Finally, we thank our anonymous reviewers from LAW XIV and DMR 2020 for their detailed and thoughtful comments.

## References

Luis von Ahn and Laura Dabbish. 2004. Labeling images with a computer game. In *Proceedings of the SIGCHI Conference on Human Factors in Computing Systems*, CHI '04, pages 319–326, Vienna, Austria. Association for Computing Machinery.

Chris Biemann. 2012. Turk Bootstrap Word Sense Inventory 2.0: A large-scale resource for lexical substitution. In *Proceedings of the Eighth International Conference on Language Resources and Evaluation (LREC'12)*, pages 4038–4042, Istanbul, Turkey. European Language Resources Association (ELRA).

Chris Biemann and Valerie Nygaard. 2010. Crowdsourcing WordNet. In *Proceedings of the 5th Global WordNet Conference*, Mumbai, India.

Karën Fort, Bruno Guillaume, Yann-Alan Pilatte, Mathieu Constant, and Nicolas Lefèbvre. 2020. Rigor Mortis: Annotating MWEs with a gamified platform. In *Proceedings of The 12th Language Resources and Evaluation Conference*, pages 4395–4401, Marseille, France. European Language Resources Association.

Joshua K. Hartshorne, Claire Bonial, and Martha Palmer. 2014. The VerbCorner Project: Findings from Phase 1 of crowd-sourcing a semantic decomposition of verbs. In *Proceedings of the 52nd Annual Meeting of the Association for Computational Linguistics (Volume 2: Short Papers)*, pages 397–402, Baltimore, Maryland. Association for Computational Linguistics.

Luheng He, Mike Lewis, and Luke Zettlemoyer. 2015. Question-answer driven semantic role labeling: Using natural language to annotate natural language. In *Proceedings of the 2015 Conference on Empirical Methods in Natural Language Processing*, pages 643–653, Lisbon, Portugal. Association for Computational Linguistics.

David Jurgens. 2013. Embracing ambiguity: A comparison of annotation methodologies for crowdsourcing word sense labels. In *Proceedings of the 2013 Conference of the North American Chapter of the Association for Computational Linguistics: Human Language Technologies*, pages 556–562, Atlanta, Georgia. Association for Computational Linguistics.

Ken Litkowski and Orin Hargraves. 2005. The Preposition Project. In *Proceedings of the Second ACL-SIGSEM Workshop on the Linguistic Dimensions of Prepositions and their Use in Computational Linguistics Formalisms and Applications*, pages 171–179, Colchester, Essex, UK.

Nelson F. Liu, Daniel Hershcovich, Michael Kranzlein, and Nathan Schneider. 2020. Lexical semantic recognition. *arXiv:2004.15008 [cs]*.

Nasrin Mostafazadeh, Lucy Vanderwende, Wen-tau Yih, Pushmeet Kohli, and James Allen. 2016. Story Cloze Evaluator: Vector space representation evaluation by predicting what happens next. In *Proceedings of the 1st Workshop on Evaluating Vector-Space Representations for NLP*, pages 24–29, Berlin, Germany. Association for Computational Linguistics.

Robert Munro, Steven Bethard, Victor Kuperman, Vicky Tzuyin Lai, Robin Melnick, Christopher Potts, Tyler Schnoebelen, and Harry Tily. 2010. Crowdsourcing and language studies: the new generation of linguistic data. In *Proceedings of the NAACL HLT 2010 Workshop on Creating Speech and Language Data with Amazon's Mechanical Turk*, pages 122–130, Los Angeles. Association for Computational Linguistics.

Siyao Peng, Yang Liu, Yilun Zhu, Austin Blodgett, Yushi Zhao, and Nathan Schneider. 2020. A corpus of adpositional supersenses for Mandarin Chinese. In *Proceedings of The 12th Language Resources and Evaluation Conference*, pages 5986–5994, Marseille, France. European Language Resources Association.

Drew Reisinger, Rachel Rudinger, Francis Ferraro, Craig Harman, Kyle Rawlins, and Benjamin Van Durme. 2015. Semantic Proto-Roles. *Transactions of the Association for Computational Linguistics*, 3:475–488.

Anna Rumshisky. 2011. Crowdsourcing word sense definition. In *Proceedings of the 5th Linguistic Annotation Workshop*, pages 74–81, Portland, Oregon, USA. Association for Computational Linguistics.

Nathan Schneider, Jena D. Hwang, Vivek Srikumar, Jakob Prange, Austin Blodgett, Sarah R. Moeller, Aviram Stern, Adi Bitan, and Omri Abend. 2018. Comprehensive supersense disambiguation of English prepositions and possessives. In *Proceedings of the 56th Annual Meeting of the Association for Computational Linguistics (Volume 1: Long Papers)*, pages 185–196, Melbourne, Australia. Association for Computational Linguistics.

Nathan Schneider, Spencer Onuffer, Nora Kazour, Emily Danchik, Michael T. Mordowanec, Henrietta Conrad, and Noah A. Smith. 2014. Comprehensive annotation of multiword expressions in a social web corpus. In *Proceedings of the Ninth International Conference on Language Resources and Evaluation (LREC'14)*, pages 455–461, Reykjavik, Iceland. European Language Resources Association (ELRA).

Rion Snow, Brendan O'Connor, Daniel Jurafsky, and Andrew Ng. 2008. Cheap and fast — but is it good? Evaluating non-expert annotations for natural language tasks. In *Proceedings of the 2008 Conference on Empirical Methods in Natural Language Processing*, pages 254–263, Honolulu, Hawaii. Association for Computational Linguistics.

Stephen Tratz. 2011. *Semantically-enriched parsing for natural language understanding*. Ph.D. dissertation, University of Southern California, Los Angeles, California.

Yulia Tsvetkov, Nathan Schneider, Dirk Hovy, Archna Bhatia, Manaal Faruqui, and Chris Dyer. 2014. Augmenting English adjective senses with supersenses. In *Proceedings of the Ninth International Conference on Language Resources and Evaluation (LREC'14)*, pages 4359–4365, Reykjavík, Iceland. European Language Resources Association (ELRA).

# Sprucing up Supersenses: Untangling the Semantic Clusters of Accompaniment and Purpose


**Jena D. Hwang**
Allen Institute for AI
jenah@allenai.org

**Nathan Schneider**
Georgetown University
nathan.schneider@georgetown.edu

**Vivek Srikumar**
University of Utah
svivek@cs.utah.edu



## Abstract

We reevaluate an existing adpositional annotation scheme with respect to two thorny semantic domains: accompaniment and purpose. 'Accompaniment' broadly speaking includes two entities situated together or participating in the same event, while 'purpose' broadly speaking covers the desired outcome of an action, the intended use or evaluated use of an entity, and more. We argue the policy in the SNACS scheme for English should be recalibrated with respect to these clusters of interrelated meanings without adding complexity to the overall scheme. Our analysis highlights tradeoffs in lumping vs. splitting decisions as well as the flexibility afforded by the construal analysis.


## 1 Introduction

Creating a semantic annotation scheme is a delicate balancing act between two seemingly contradictory requirements. An annotation schemer must *specialize* their labels to segregate them in semantically meaningful ways, but whenever possible they must also *generalize* as to capture semantic similarities across varying labels. While this lumper-splitter problem pervades categorization efforts across disciplines, a linguistic annotation schemer faces an additional constraint: they must resolve the problem while making the schema accessible to annotators for the production of consistent annotations. Generally, semantic resources have maintained the balance in one of two ways: by creating many fine-grained labels that are systematically organized into hierarchies or ontologies, or by resorting to very small number of distinct labels and making them conditional on the relation they annotate. FrameNet (Ruppenhofer et al., 2016) and the TRIPS ontology (Allen et al., 2008) exemplify the former approach, while PropBank's numbered arguments (Palmer et al., 2005) illustrate the latter one.

This paper focuses on the SNACS framework of Schneider et al. (2018)—a hierarchy of 50 semantic labels that seeks to characterize the semantic space of prepositions. Like most resources, SNACS falls somewhere in between the two extremes described above. What is unique about this scheme is that it tries to be as economical as possible with regards to the number of semantic types of prepositions it accepts into the hierarchy. However, it does so while being lexically agnostic of the identity of its syntactic governor (e.g., the governing verb). As a balancing mechanism between specialization and generalization of categories, it employs *construals*, a two-level annotation scheme: at the *function* level, it recognizes the semantics of individual prepositions, then at *scene role* level, it generalizes to the overall semantics projected by the frame or scene set by the verb or the construction.

In this paper, we identify two areas within SNACS that require attention, centered around the notions of purpose and accompaniment. The abstract concepts of purpose and accompaniment both span broad semantic areas, and contain many clusters of meaning, with nuanced differences between them. We argue that SNACS treats both too simplistically, and by ignoring the nuances, makes annotation difficult.

Both accompaniment and purpose present an opportunity for lumping the various sub-categories of meaning into standalone labels, or splitting them into many finer ones. We ask whether the mechanism






*The 14th Linguistic Annotation Workshop*, pages 127–137
Barcelona, Spain (Online), December 12, 2020.

| Group | Examples | Old analysis (SNACS v2.3) | New analysis (SNACS v2.5) |
|---|---|---|---|
| co-location | the forks are **with** the knives; I'm over here **with** your sister | ACCOMPANIER | LOCUS↝ANCILLARY |
| compound entity | rice **with** beans; a polite smile **with** a nod is quite enough | ACCOMPANIER | ENSEMBLE↝ANCILLARY |
| property, part, or possession | kid **with** red hair/shorts/boundless energy; They arrived **with** a pie | {CHARACTERISTIC,PARTPORTION,POSSESSION}↝A. | |
| co-participant | Stop chatting/meeting/fighting **with** Jo; Combine butter **with** vanilla; the car collided **with** a mailbox | {CO-THEME,CO-AGENT}↝A. | {AGENT,THEME,...}↝A. |
| added participant | Walk **with** me to the park; Ron fought **with** Harry (against Voldemort); vacations **with** young children | ACCOMPANIER↝CO-AGENT | ANCILLARY |

**Table 1:** Notions of accompaniment. The proposed approach alters the hierarchy, removing ACCOMPANIER, CO-AGENT, and CO-THEME and adding ANCILLARY and ENSEMBLE. "A." is short for ACCOMPANIER in the old scheme and ANCILLARY in the new scheme.

of construal offers a balance. Our analysis suggests refinements to the existing SNACS guidelines to handle accompaniment and purpose. With the case of accompaniment, we propose a more specialized set of labels to better capture the nunaces in the semantics. With purpose, we take the opposing approach where the definitions are further generalized in such a way that it is more amenable for edge cases. With an eye towards annotation, in both cases, we present tests that an annotator can employ to ascertain the boundaries of the new categories.

## 2 Background: SNACS Framework

The Semantic Network of Adposition and Case Supersenses (SNACS) is a framework specifically created for the annotation of preposition semantics (Schneider et al., 2018). SNACS includes 50 broad-coverage semantic labels called *supersenses*, which is organized into three broad branches reflecting event participant roles (e.g., AGENT, THEME, RECIPIENT), roles relating to the circumstance of an event (e.g., TIME, LOCATION, GOAL) and relational roles between two entities (e.g., IDENTITY, POSSESSION). A supersense label, thus, indicates the semantic relationship between the constituent *object* or the *governing head* of the preposition. Unlike prior dictionary-based efforts in representing postpositional semantics (Litkowski, 2014; Litkowski and Hargraves, 2005), SNACS labels the prepositions within its context (e.g., "cat **on**/LOCUS the mat" vs. "found the cat in/LOCUS the box") irrespective of the lexical type the target represents.

SNACS also utilizes the *construal analysis*, a mechanism that allows annotators to assign a preposition with *two* labels instead of one in a systematic manner. All prepositions are labeled at both the **scene role** and the **function** levels, where the scene role specifies the preposition's role with respect to the scene set by the governing head (typically a verb) and function label indicates the semantic contribution the preposition makes. Construals are denoted by the convention SCENE ROLE↝FUNCTION.

(1)  a.  The cat is **on** the mat. LOCUS↝LOCUS (or simply LOCUS)
    b.  Put the cat **on** the mat. GOAL↝LOCUS
    c.  Banish the cat **to** the mat. GOAL↝GOAL

In examples (1a, 1b) above, the function label reflects the generalization that both of the examples indicate a location (as contributed by **on**). The scene role, however, recognizes the divergence in meanings triggered by the verb *put*. With (1c), the prepositional phrase represents the final GOAL much like (1b) but differs in its function label.

## 3 Accompaniment

One of the most capricious English prepositions is the word **with**. It can take on many semantic guises, including INSTRUMENT (*open the door **with** a key*) and MANNER (*play the piano **with** gusto*). Here we are concerned with the meanings in table 1, all associated with a loose notion of *accompaniment* or *togetherness* (also known as *comitative*): being in the same location, engaging in the same activity, etc.

The SNACS v2.3 guidelines analyze these usages as related by specifying ACCOMPANIER as the scene role and/or function. ACCOMPANIER is defined as "Entity that another entity is together with" (Schneider et al., 2019, p. 63). Effectively, the co-location and compound entity varieties are treated as the most basic examples of accompaniment and the others are treated as extended meanings, as can be seen in the third column of the table.

### 3.1 Problems

We point out several weaknesses of this analysis.

☞ Analyzing **co-location** examples as simply ACCOMPANIER misses the generalization that these can answer *Where?* questions, like locative PPs.

☞ The **compound entity** usage (as in the noun phrase *rice **with** beans is a delicious dish*) is semantically very similar to a coordinating conjunction (*rice **and** beans is a delicious dish*) in grouping two items together on roughly equal footing: neither item is a part of the other, in contrast to the "property, part, or possession" examples.

☞ The "**co-participant**" usages of **with** in table 1 involve a core participant in the situation engaged symetrically, reciprocally, or in a qualitatively different way with respect to another participant. With respect to the criteria for applying SNACS labels, the sole distinction between the two participants is morphosyntactic (one is marked by a preposition and the other is not).[1] As such, it seems wrong to distinguish AGENT and CO-AGENT (or THEME and CO-THEME) at the scene level; SNACS ordinarily reflects morphosyntactic choices in the *function* label.

☞ Another problem with the co-participant analysis is that specifying CO-AGENT and CO-THEME labels as part of the hierarchy (which was based on VerbNet) ties our hands when confronted with other participant roles marked with **with**. For example:

(2)  I agree **with** her. (scene: EXPERIENCER)

(3)  I share a house **with** my friend. (scene: POSSESSOR)

(4)  Let me check **with** my supervisor. (scene: RECIPIENT)

(5)  Don't compare baseball **with** basketball. (scene: COMPARISONREF)

In (2), *agree* is a cognitive situation in which two individuals share the same mindset on an issue; in SNACS, nonagentive cognizers normally receive the scene role of EXPERIENCER. Similarly, (3) describes joint possession of an item. (4) describes an event in which the speaker contacts someone else; as the target of communication the supervisor should be a RECIPIENT. (5) uses the verb to express a comparison relation where the thing being compared against is marked by **with**. Ideally the scene role for such co-participant usages wouldn't be constrained to CO-AGENT or CO-THEME.

☞ The difference between the last two rows of table 1 is that "**added participant**" usages reflect a freer (adjunct PP) addition of a participant that would not normally be assumed to play a distinct role in a scene. Typically the added participant is present when the main participant engages in the activity, and may engage in that activity in a similar manner or in cooperation.[2] Counterintuitively, SNACS v2.3 prescribes CO-AGENT as the function for such cases, leading to the bizarre situation where the same labels are swapped for the two kinds of agentive participants even though the preposition has not changed (again, usually the function reflects the choice of preposition):

(6)  a.  Ron fought **with** Harry because he was jealous of him. [They fought each other.]
      (co-participant: CO-AGENT⤳ACCOMPANIER [old approach])

---

[1]This is not to say they are fully interchangeable—*a car collided **with** a mailbox* ≠ *a mailbox collided **with** a car*. However the SNACS semantic role criteria are not sufficiently fine-grained to distinguish these; both meet the semantic criteria for THEME.

[2]Though in general SNACS avoids a core/non-core role distinction to avoid being tied to any particular predicate lexicon, it makes the distinction between co-participants and added participants in order to disambiguate cases like (6), where there is a crucial difference in how the event is interpreted.

   b.  Ron fought **with** Harry against Voldemort. [They fought on the same side.]
       (added participant: ACCOMPANIER⤳CO-AGENT [old approach])

While *fight* **with** presents a clear ambiguity, the current approach resolves it in a confusing way. Moreover, the v2.3 guidelines provide no test to determine whether the co-participant or added participant analysis is appropriate in borderline cases.

☞ We note that **with** as a marker seems to have less of an agentivity preference than many other morphosyntactic realizations of participants. In *vacations* **with** *young children*, for instance, it may be tough to decide whether children are AGENT-like (embarking on vacation with adults) or THEME-like (brought along at the mercy of adults). Thus, as far as the *function* is concerned, it may not be worthwhile to establish a CO-AGENT vs. CO-THEME contrast.[3]

## 3.2   Solution

Our solution is to dispense with the labels ACCOMPANIER, CO-AGENT, and CO-THEME, and add two new labels:

- ANCILLARY, defined as a **surplus participant** in relation to an event (or state/situation).
- ENSEMBLE, defined as an **entity that another entity is grouped with**.

ANCILLARY canonically applies to added participants, but also serves as the function label for all the usages in table 1: a broad notion of 'second thing' is taken to motivate the use of **with** for all these examples. We retire the name ACCOMPANIER to avoid confusion with the old scheme. Removing CO-AGENT and CO-THEME frees up the scene role slot for a wider range of supersenses in the co-participant usages: (2) becomes EXPERIENCER⤳ANCILLARY, (3) becomes POSSESSOR⤳ANCILLARY, etc.

ENSEMBLE applies to compound entity usages, as can be seen in table 1. In English, ENSEMBLE is used as scene role only, leaving the label open for more prototypical ENSEMBLE usages for conjunctive adpositions found in languages like Japanese and Korean.

**Co-participants vs. added participants.**   We still face the issue of distinguishing co-participants like (6a) from added participants like (6b). We propose to do this via a *together*-insertion test. Generally speaking, added participants (not licensed by the predicate) allow for the the insertion of the adverbial *together*, while co-participants do not. ANCILLARY also applies as the scene role only if *together* can be inserted:

(7)  a.  Please trade your paper (*together) **with** the person behind you. AGENT⤳ANCILLARY
    b.  Gina met (*together) **with** John. AGENT⤳ANCILLARY
    c.  The plane collided (*together) **with** a dirigible. THEME⤳ANCILLARY

(8)  Harry is travelling (together) **with** his family. ANCILLARY

Note that this policy of using plain ANCILLARY for adjunct-like participant accompaniers excuses us from having to determine whether the accompanier is agentive. This can be viewed as an advantage since agentivity of added participants may be difficult to judge (e.g., if they are small children being brought somewhere by adults). On the other hand, it means that the event-specific role that the added participant ultimately fills is left underspecified. Consider the minimal pair with the verb *arrest*, which normally licenses a single AGENT arrester and a single THEME arrestee (Bill Croft, p.c.):

(9)  a.  The officer$_i$ arrested her$_j$ (together) **with** his deputy. ANCILLARY$^{(i)}$
    b.  The officer$_i$ arrested her$_j$ (together) **with** her husband. ANCILLARY$^{(j)}$

Both are simply labeled ANCILLARY.[4] However this masks an important difference: In the preferred

---

[3] We considered merging these into a CO-PARTICIPANT label to serve only as a function, but in the end we settled on the broader label ANCILLARY as there was no additional disambiguation to be achieved by separating ANCILLARY and CO-PARTICIPANT.

[4] FrameNet's policy is similar: the analogue of ANCILLARY is CO-PARTICIPANT, defined generally as "an entity that participates in a coordinated way in the same event as the primary protagonist, regardless of whether the protagonist, and hence the CO-PARTICIPANT, is more agent- or more undergoer-like. ... In the **Arresting** frame, for instance, the extra-thematic frame

| Group | Examples | Old analysis (SNACS v2.3) | New analysis (SNACS v2.5) |
|---|---|---|---|
| motivation & desired outcome | Minerva rose **to** give a speech; Everyone cheered **for** an encore; education **for** self-management | PURPOSE | PURPOSE |
| intended use | a shoulder **to** cry on; tools **for** weeding | CHARACTERISTIC↝PURPOSE | PURPOSE |
| evaluated use | This cleaner is good **for** ∘ hardwood floors; a great place **for** Quidditch | PURPOSE | PURPOSE |
| valued services | It costs $10 **to** see the movie; $100 **for** ∘ wine is excessive; they paid **for** the meal | THEME↝PURPOSE | THEME↝PURPOSE |
| sufficiency & excess | That is too large a bag **for** ∘ groceries; scissors sharp enough **to** cut nails | COMPARISONREF↝PURPOSE | COMPARISONREF↝PURPOSE |
| modal construction | He needs **to** leave; We ready **to** help; They managed **to** exceed our expectations! | other-inf | other-inf |

**Table 2:** Semantic groupings associated with purposes. ∘ denotes an implicit event in the purpose.

reading of (9a), the officer and deputy are both doing the arresting; the deputy may be equally active or may be assisting the officer in the arrest, but in any case is a surplus with respect to the AGENT role. Whereas in the preferred reading of (9b), the husband is also being arrested (treated like a surplus THEME). This is generally true of predicates with more than 2 participants. An additional layer of representation could index the added participant as ANCILLARY to another primary role (subscripts/superscripts in (9)) to facilitate the appropriate inferences.[5]

**Configurational accompaniment.** In addition to accompaniers that signal participation in an event or a situation, there are those that mediate configurational information with respect to its governing head. In (10a), the accompaniment specifies the location where Harry is standing; with phrase in (10b), specifies Vernon's professional association with respect to a company; **together** signifies Lily and James' particular state of social relationship in (10c); and in (10d), the preposition describes the possessive arrangement of the cup of tea with respect to Albus. Each of these cases receive a scene role, which reflects the configurational relationship.

(10)  a.  Harry is standing **with** Hagrid. LOCUS↝ANCILLARY
      b.  Vernon is **with** Grunnings. ORG↝ANCILLARY
      c.  Lily and James are **together** (in a relationship). SOCIALREL↝ANCILLARY
      d.  Albus settled into his chair **with** a hot cup of tea. POSSESSION↝ANCILLARY

## 4  Purpose

Much like ACCOMPANIER, PURPOSE also demarcates a large semantic area and generally deals with motivation and intent of an action. In English, the preposition **for** is largely responsible for serving the role of purposive mediator in a given event. Additionally, SNACS annotation includes *infinitive* **to** that typically also marks PURPOSE clauses alongside **for**.

The SNACS v2.3 guidelines define PURPOSE as "Something that somebody wants to bring about, [which is] asserted to be why something was done, is the case, or exists". PURPOSE is often defined as expressing the 'why' of the event, indicating a desired outcome as the motive for an action.[6]

(11)  a.  Minerva rose **to** give a speech. *Q: Why did she rise? A: To give a speech.*
      b.  He plays **for** trophies. *Q: Why does he play? A: To (obtain) trophies.*

In practice, however, the semantic space associated with PURPOSE, especially as expressed with infinitives

---

element CO-PARTICIPANT should be used to label phrases denoting people that are arrested… along with the SUSPECT, or others that assist the AUTHORITIES" (Ruppenhofer et al., 2016, p. 107).

[5]It seems that the primary use of the role will always be overt: *She was arrested* **with** *the deputy* cannot have the reading of (9a) where an implicit party and the deputy are sharing in the arrest.

[6]In the SNACS hierarchy, PURPOSE is a subtype of EXPLANATION, which additionally covers reasons that something happened which were not grounded in somebody's intention (e.g. *We got wet* **due to** *the rain*).

and **for**-PPs, is far from homogeneous. **To** and **for** in (12a, 12b) do not express why the event happened or should happen; rather they specify a general purpose or use for the governing head: a shoulder is needed *for the use of* crying and the particular place is great *for the purpose of* playing Quidditch. In example (12c), the question of 'why' is out of place for the purpose clause, since **for** here supplies a product that can be obtained at the value specified by the governing head.

(12)  a.   He needed a shoulder **to** cry on. *Q: Why does he need a shoulder? A: ??To cry on*
　　  b.   a great place **for** playing Quidditch. *Q: Why is it a great place? A: ??To play Quidditch*
　　  c.   $100 **for** wine is excessive. *Q: ??*

## 4.1   Problems

We identify a number of problems with the definition.

☞ SNACS requires a better way of dealing with *affordance*-leaning subtypes. In practice, the PURPOSE category subdivides into two broad types of overlapping semantics. In line with the more common definition is the type of PURPOSE that expresses the motive behind an action like those seen in (11) (**motivation & desired outcome** in table 2). The second use covers a range of abstract goals to which an action or an entity can be applied to. The goal can signal an affordance or use an object can provide (i.e. **intended use, evaluated use, sufficiency & excess** in table 2), or a commercial product or service a certain capital or asset can afford (**valued services** in table 2). This latter type generally is amenable to the *for-the-purpose-of* test as shown in (13).

(13)  a.   He needed a shoulder **to** cry on. *He needed a shoulder for the purpose of crying on.*
　　  b.   a great place **for** playing Quidditch. *This is a great place for the purpose of playing Quidditch.*
　　  c.   $100 **for** wine is excessive. *$100 for the purpose of purchasing wine is excessive.*

In SNACS, each of the subtypes—**intended use**, **valued services** and **sufficency & excess**—are given distinct construals in recognition of their semantic divergence from the more prototypical PURPOSE. **Evaluated use**, however, does not.

☞ We also note that adding to the complexity of annotation is a syntactic behavior exhibited by the **for**-phrases: the object only specifies the entity affected by an event; the event itself is not made explicit. The ability to omit the purpose event cuts across the PURPOSE subtypes in table 2, where the ∘ symbol stands for the implicit purpose event. Other instances where the object is an entity rather than an event are seen in example (14):

(14)  a.   I went to the store **for** chocolates. *I went out for the purpose of (buying) chocolates*
　　  b.   I had a surgery **for** my knee. *a surgery for the purpose of (fixing) my knee*

Generally the implicit event that underlies the affected entity is inferred via our general world knowledge about how the governor and the object are related. If we go to the store for chocolates, we are likely looking to *buy* some, and if we receive surgery for a knee, we are likely getting our knee *fixed*.

☞ Clearer guidelines are needed to deal with infinitival complements participating in **modal construc-tions**. The governing verb conveys desirability, necessity, likelihood or capability (among others) of the action in the infinitival phrase, and they are assigned the non-semantic label other-inf to indicate they are not covered by SNACS supersenses.[7]

## 4.2   Solution

We propose a single, unified PURPOSE category a more generalized definition that includes
- a desired outcome that somebody tries to achieve by performing an action
- a designed or incidental affordance with regards to an entity

The possibility of introducing a new label called AFFORDANCE to capture the latter definition was considered but discarded. As it turns out, the semantics of purpose and affordance sits on a cline, making their boundary rather difficult to identify and annotate. Consider borderline case examples in (15).

---

[7]In the existing SNACS guidelines these are notated `i. We use other-inf for clarity.

(15)  a.  I bought some detergent **to** wash hardwood floors.
      b.  I bought detergent **for** (the purpose of) washing hardwood floors.

Rather than split hairs here, it seems preferable to lump the affordance or **intended use** category with canonical PURPOSEs, discarding the CHARACTERISTIC↝PURPOSE analysis.[8]

As a more precise main definition of PURPOSE we suggest: "A desired outcome presented as contingent on some event, situation, entity, or resource. The PURPOSE may be specific (e.g., an outcome that somebody tries to achieve by performing an action) or generic (e.g., an entity that was designed for or incidentally provides some affordance)."

Further, we propose the following subcases and tests; infinitives that fail all tests should be labeled other-inf:

**Paraphrase tests.**   First, if the relation can be phrased with *in order to*, *in order for (someone) to*, *for the purpose of*, or *that (someone) intends to*, it is sufficient grounds to label it as PURPOSE. Note for example that infinitival complements of modal verbs and BENEFICIARY uses of **for** fail this test:

(16)  a.  (i)   Minerva rose (in order) **to** give a speech.
          (ii)  It costs $10 (in order) **to** give a speech.
          (iii) Bring it to the store (in order) **to** get it repaired / for us **to** repair it / for it **to** be repaired
          (iv)  He needs (*in order) **to** leave soon. (modal verb complement; other-inf)
          (v)   It is fun (*in order) **to** see this movie. (expletive construction; other-inf)
      b.  (i)   I found a party (that I intend) **to** attend.
          (ii)  I have a plane (that I intend) **to** catch.
          (iii) I want a sandwich (*that I intend) **to** eat. (modal verb complement; other-inf)
      c.  (i)   a couch **for** (the purpose of) sleeping on
          (ii)  I went to the store **for** (the purpose of *buying*) chocolate.
          (iii) Allison built a house **for** (*the purpose of) her mum. (BENEFICIARY)

For implicit purposes the annotators are instructed to test for the inferred verb as exemplified in (16c-ii), taking care to be vigilant that the semantics of the preposition may be better captured by another label as seen in (17).

(17)  a.  I babysat **for** (the purpose of *helping*) my uncle.
          = I babysat as a favor to my uncle. (BENEFICIARY)
      b.  We eat seaweed soup **for** (the purpose of *celebrating*) birthdays.
          = We eat seaweed soup on the occasion of birthdays. (CIRCUMSTANCE)

**Evaluated use.**   As shown in table 2, *good for*, *bad for*, etc. are covered as a special case of PURPOSE in the 2.3 guidelines. This is fitting as a variant of intended use or non-use—*a couch for sleeping on* is presumably *a good couch for sleeping on*—so we retain the label PURPOSE, which we have extended to intended use infinitivals.

**Indefinite pronoun head.**   Consider cases where the infinitival modifies an indefinite pronoun or maximally vague noun like *stuff*:

---

[8]In FrameNet 1.7, some frames specify an INHERENT_PURPOSE role: e.g., "money **for** our daughter's college education" is an example in the Money frame. This parallels the CHARACTERISTIC↝PURPOSE analysis, where CHARACTERISTIC represents the purpose as a constitutive property of the entity itself. But we find there is a slippery slope with regard to entity-modifying purposes: for some it is difficult to ascertain the creator's intended use or whether that use is considered intrinsic to the entity. For example, should "couch **for** sleeping on" be considered plain PURPOSE because sleeping is not the prototypical design of a couch, or should intent take into consideration the couch possessor's objective in owning said couch? Is there really an inherent use of a body part like shoulder in (12a) outside its biological/structural use? Lumping avoids the need to vex annotators with such questions.

A related notion is the telic quale of qualia structure (Pustejovsky, 1998) which is taken to explain why a default activity involving an entity may be left unspecified or underspecified in a sentence ("use", etc.), as well as metonymies such as entity-for-user. A Generative Lexicon analysis of the head noun might therefore distinguish inherent and transient purposes, but this is a different level of representation than SNACS seeks to achieve.

(18)  a.  I found something/stuff **to** eat. Purpose
      b.  I found something/stuff **to** do. other-inf

Schneider et al. (2019, p. 32) specify "something **to** eat" as an example of the intended use cluster, which in our revised approach is labeled Purpose. While this seems sensible, the same analysis is problematic for (18b), where the noun referring to an activity (*something* or *stuff*) cannot really be semantically separated from the infinitive verb (*do*). Thus, we propose the criterion that the vague head noun must imply an **entity referent** involved in the infinitival event in order for it to be considered a Purpose; otherwise it is other-inf.

**Sufficiency and excess.**  We maintain the distinction that infinitival clauses licensed by *too, enough,* and similar should receive ComparisonRef as the scene role, because they provide a reference point against which sufficiency or excess is evaluated. Thus the examples in table 2 remain Comparison-Ref↝Purpose, along with the following passive examples:

(19)  a.  I'm old enough **to** be allowed into the movie. ComparisonRef↝Purpose
      b.  (i)   The chick is too young **to** be eaten. ComparisonRef↝Purpose
          (ii)  The chick is too young (for someone) **to** eat. ComparisonRef↝Purpose

It is immaterial that (19b) does not specify who intends to eat the chick: much like the intended use category, the presumption is that somebody *might* want to do so.

What the SNACS 2.3 guidelines fail to point out is that this construction may also license infinitivals that do not meet the definition of Purpose because they are not desired outcomes. We use Goal as the function because these are potential **results** of the sufficiency or excess, and Goal subsumes the notion of end state or result:

(20)  a.  The forest canopy is too dense **to** let light through. ComparisonRef↝Goal
      b.  I'm clumsy enough **to** trip and kill myself. ComparisonRef↝Goal
      c.  The boat is small enough **to** be blown off course. ComparisonRef↝Goal

This is somewhat related to the infinitival surprise-result sense, which the guidelines specify as Goal:

(21)  We arrived at the airport only **to** find that our flight had been canceled. (Schneider et al., 2019, p. 23)

**Valued services.**  The guidelines state that a service within a commercial event which is expressed as a **for**-PP or infinitival should be Theme↝Purpose in order to capture that it is an intended outcome but also something that incurs a cost. This distinguishes a potential adjunct purpose:

(22)  I paid **for**/Theme↝Purpose the surgery (in order) **to**/Purpose prevent my friend from going bankrupt.

We retain this policy in our approach.

## 5  Additional Related Work

In the literature, there is a broad spectrum of linguistic work about the concepts of purpose (Faraci, 1974; Jones, 1991; Green, 1992; Johnston, 1999, *inter alia*) and accompaniment (Haspelmath, 2003; Schlesinger, 2006; Stassen, 2008, *inter alia*). The literature spans grammatical and syntactic issues, and defining the boundaries between purpose and accompaniment with respect to other semantic categories. However, space limitations prohibit an extensive discussion here. Table 3 briefly summarizes the how the various dimensions of meaning discussed above are handled in the literature.

**Purpose.**  The left side of table 3 shows a short list of works in the linguistics and semantic resource literature that provide semantic definitions for purpose. As expected, there is a general consensus that the most prototypical purposive cases, i.e., clauses specifying motivation and desired outcome, fall under the purpose category. Some sources also include adjunct Beneficiary clauses under the purpose category,

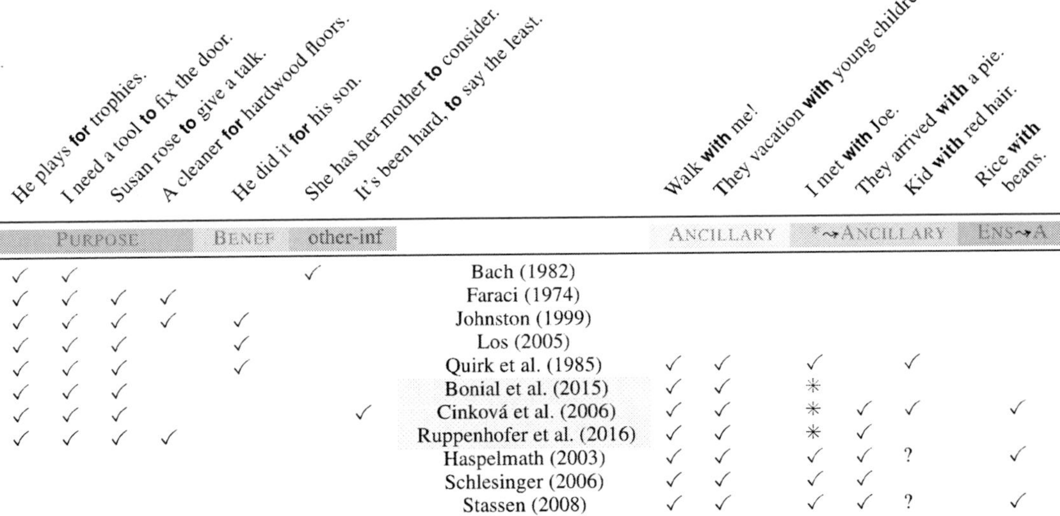

| PURPOSE | | | | BENEF | other-inf | | | ANCILLARY | | *↝ANCILLARY | | ENS↝A | |
|---|---|---|---|---|---|---|---|---|---|---|---|---|---|
| He plays for trophies. | I need a tool to fix the door. | Susan rose to give a talk. | A cleaner for hardwood floors. | He did it for his son. | She has her mother to consider. | It's been hard, to say the least. | Reference | Walk with me! | They vacation with young children. | I met with Joe. | They arrived with a pie. | Kid with red hair. | Rice with beans. |
| ✓ | ✓ | | | | ✓ | | Bach (1982) | | | | | | |
| ✓ | ✓ | ✓ | ✓ | | | | Faraci (1974) | | | | | | |
| ✓ | ✓ | ✓ | ✓ | ✓ | | | Johnston (1999) | | | | | | |
| ✓ | ✓ | ✓ | | ✓ | | | Los (2005) | | | | | | |
| ✓ | ✓ | ✓ | | ✓ | | | Quirk et al. (1985) | ✓ | ✓ | ✓ | | ✓ | |
| ✓ | ✓ | ✓ | | | | | Bonial et al. (2015) | ✓ | ✓ | * | | | |
| ✓ | ✓ | ✓ | | | | ✓ | Cinková et al. (2006) | ✓ | ✓ | * | ✓ | ✓ | ✓ |
| ✓ | ✓ | ✓ | ✓ | | | | Ruppenhofer et al. (2016) | ✓ | ✓ | * | ✓ | | |
| | | | | | | | Haspelmath (2003) | ✓ | ✓ | ✓ | ✓ | ? | ✓ |
| | | | | | | | Schlesinger (2006) | ✓ | ✓ | ✓ | ✓ | | |
| | | | | | | | Stassen (2008) | ✓ | ✓ | ✓ | ✓ | ? | ✓ |

**Table 3:** Coverage of purpose and accompaniment discussion in literature. On the left side are purpose and related examples, and on the right side are examples that relate to accompaniment. The middle three highlighted references (top-to-bottom) represent the annotation guidelines and manuals from PropBank, the tectogrammatical annotation layer of the Prague Czech-English Dependency Treebank, and FrameNet, respectively. Check marks show topics that are covered under each of the references. The asterisked cells (*) refer to co-participants that get separate treatment as verbal arguments. ENS and BENEF are short for ENSEMBLE and BENEFACTIVE, respectively.

and in a couple of cases we see non-SNACS other-inf usages included in the categorization. The discussion and categorization of purpose clauses with nominal heads has received less attention in the literature (fourth PURPOSE column in table 3).

**Accompaniment.** The right columns in table 3 show literature that deals with the semantics of accompaniment. It is a well-studied phenomenon as most languages retain grammatical strategies to mark accompaniment (Stassen, 2008). And as discussed earlier, its semantics is well-known to be be highly variable and can easily bleed into other semantic categories such as instrumental, possessive, and conjunctive uses (Schlesinger, 2006; Haspelmath, 2003). Each of the three semantic resources (highlighted in yellow in table 3) include a label that directly corresponds to ANCILLARY for added participants and the co-participants are distinguished via separate labels in each of these resources (e.g., PropBank assigns numbered labels and FrameNet uses the Co-Participant role). Much like purpose, discussion of clauses with nominal heads as accompaniers has, on the whole, received less attention that their verbal head counterparts.

## 6 Conclusion

We have detailed a revised approach to categorizing semantic relations associated with various flavors of accompaniment and purpose as marked by English prepositions and infinitive clauses. Our proposals involve restructuring the SNACS inventory in some cases and better circumscribing current categories in others. We suggest revised definitions and paraphrase tests to better delineate groups of usages for annotators. English annotation applying the revised guidelines is planned, and we also hope to investigate how well these criteria can be adapted to other languages.

Our improvements have been implemented in the SNACS v2.5 guidelines (Schneider et al., 2020) and the STREUSLE v4.3 dataset release.[9]

## Acknowledgments

We thank Bill Croft for helpful discussions as we were formulating the analysis.

---
[9] https://github.com/nert-nlp/streusle

**References**

James Allen, Mary Swift, and William de Beaumont. 2008. Deep semantic analysis of text. In *Semantics in Text Processing. STEP 2008 Conference Proceedings*, pages 343–354.

Emmon Bach. 1982. Purpose clauses and control. In *The nature of syntactic representation*, pages 35–57. Springer.

Claire Bonial, Julia Bonn, Kathryn Conger, Jena Hwang, Martha Palmer, and Nicholas Rease. 2015. English PropBank annotation guidelines. Technical report, University of Colorado at Boulder.

Silvie Cinková, Jan Hajič, Marie Mikulová, Lucie Mladová, Anja Nedolužko, Petr Pajas, Jarmila Panevová, Jiří Semecký, Jana Šindlerová, Josef Toman, Zdeňka Urešová, and Zdeněk Žabokrtský. 2006. Annotation of English on the tectogrammatical level: reference book. Technical report, Charles University, Prague. Version 1.0.1.

Robert A. Faraci. 1974. *Aspects of the grammar of infinitives and for-phrases*. Ph.D. dissertation, Massachusetts Institute of Technology.

Georgia M. Green. 1992. Purpose infinitives and their relatives. In Diane Brentari, Gary N. Larson, and Lynn A. MacLeod, editors, *The Joy of Grammar: A festschrift in honor of James D. McCawley*, pages 95–127. John Benjamins, Amsterdam.

Martin Haspelmath. 2003. The geometry of grammatical meaning: Semantic maps and cross-linguistic comparison. *The new psychology of language*, 2(1976):1–30.

Michael J. R. Johnston. 1999. A syntax and semantics for purposive adjuncts in HPSG. *Studies in Contemporary Phrase Structure Grammar*, pages 80–118.

Charles Jones. 1991. *Purpose clauses: Syntax, thematics, and semantics of English purpose constructions*, volume 47. Springer Science & Business Media.

Ken Litkowski. 2014. Pattern Dictionary of English Prepositions. In *Proc. of ACL*, pages 1274–1283, Baltimore, Maryland, USA.

Ken Litkowski and Orin Hargraves. 2005. The Preposition Project. In *Proc. of the Second ACL-SIGSEM Workshop on the Linguistic Dimensions of Prepositions and their Use in Computational Linguistics Formalisms and Applications*, pages 171–179, Colchester, Essex, UK.

Bettelou Los. 2005. *The rise of the* to-*infinitive*. Oxford University Press.

Martha Palmer, Daniel Gildea, and Paul Kingsbury. 2005. The Proposition Bank: An annotated corpus of semantic roles. *Computational Linguistics*, 31(1):71–106.

James Pustejovsky. 1998. *The Generative Lexicon*. MIT Press, Cambridge, MA.

Randolph Quirk, Sidney Greenbaum, Geoffrey Leech, Jan Svartvik, and David Crystal. 1985. *A comprehensive grammar of the English language*. Longman, London.

Josef Ruppenhofer, Michael Ellsworth, Miriam R. L. Petruck, Christopher R. Johnson, Collin F. Baker, and Jan Scheffczyk. 2016. FrameNet II: extended theory and practice.

Izchak M. Schlesinger. 2006. *Cognitive space and linguistic case: Semantic and syntactic categories in English*. Cambridge University Press.

Nathan Schneider, Jena D. Hwang, Archna Bhatia, Vivek Srikumar, Na-Rae Han, Tim O'Gorman, Sarah R. Moeller, Omri Abend, Adi Shalev, Austin Blodgett, and Jakob Prange. 2019. Adposition and Case Supersenses v2.3: Guidelines for English. *arXiv:1704.02134v4 [cs]*.

Nathan Schneider, Jena D. Hwang, Archna Bhatia, Vivek Srikumar, Na-Rae Han, Tim O'Gorman, Sarah R. Moeller, Omri Abend, Adi Shalev, Austin Blodgett, and Jakob Prange. 2020. Adposition and Case Supersenses v2.5: Guidelines for English. *arXiv:1704.02134v6 [cs]*.

Nathan Schneider, Jena D. Hwang, Vivek Srikumar, Jakob Prange, Austin Blodgett, Sarah R. Moeller, Aviram Stern, Adi Bitan, and Omri Abend. 2018. Comprehensive supersense disambiguation of English prepositions and possessives. In *Proc. of ACL*, pages 185–196, Melbourne, Australia.

Leon Stassen. 2008. Noun phrase conjunction: The coordinative and the comitative strategy. *Noun Phrase Structure in the Languages of Europe*.

# Querent Intent in Multi-Sentence Questions

**Laurie Burchell,* Jie Chi,* Tom Hosking,* Nina Markl,* Bonnie Webber**
Institute for Language, Cognition and Computation
University of Edinburgh
{laurie.burchell,jie.chi,tom.hosking,nina.markl}@ed.ac.uk

## Abstract

Multi-sentence questions (MSQs) are sequences of questions connected by relations which, unlike sequences of standalone questions, need to be answered as a unit. Following Rhetorical Structure Theory (RST), we recognise that different "question discourse relations" between the subparts of MSQs reflect different speaker intents, and consequently elicit different answering strategies. Correctly identifying these relations is therefore a crucial step in automatically answering MSQs. We identify five different types of MSQs in English, and define five novel relations to describe them. We extract over 162,000 MSQs from Stack Exchange to enable future research. Finally, we implement a high-precision baseline classifier based on surface features.

## 1 Introduction

A multi-sentence question (MSQ) is a dialogue turn that contains more than one question (cf. Ex. (1)). We refer to the speaker of such a turn as a *querent* (i.e., one who seeks).

(1)     Querent: How can I transport my cats if I am moving a long distance? (Q1)
            For example, flying them from NYC to London? (Q2)

A standard question answering system might consider these questions separately:

(2)     A1: You can take them in the car with you.
        A2: British Airways fly from NYC to London.

However, this naïve approach does not result in a good answer, since the querent intends that an answer take both questions into account: in (1), Q2 clarifies that taking pets by car is not a relevant option. The querent is likely looking for an answer like (3):

(3)     A:   British Airways will let you fly pets from NYC to London.

Whilst question answering (QA) has received significant research attention in recent years (Joshi et al., 2017; Agrawal et al., 2017), there is little research to date on answering MSQs, despite their prevalence in English. Furthermore, existing QA datasets are not appropriate for the study of MSQs as they tend to be sequences of standalone questions constructed in relation to a text by crowdworkers (e.g. SQuAD (Rajpurkar et al., 2016)). We are not aware of any work that has attempted to improve QA performance on MSQs, despite the potential for obvious errors as in the example above.

Our contribution towards the broader research goal of automatically answering MSQs is as follows:

- We create a new dataset of 162,745 English two-question MSQs from Stack Exchange.
- We define five types of MSQ according to how they are intended to be answered, inferring intent from relations between them.
- We design a baseline classifier based on surface features.

---

*Alphabetical order, equal contribution





*The 14th Linguistic Annotation Workshop*, pages 138–147
Barcelona, Spain (Online), December 12, 2020.

## 2 Prior work

Prior work on QA has focused on either single questions contained within dialogue (Choi et al., 2018; Reddy et al., 2019; Saeidi et al., 2018; Clark et al., 2018), or questions composed of two or more sentences crowd-sourced by community QA (cQA) services (John and Kurian, 2011; Tamura et al., 2005). Our definition of MSQs is similar to the latter, but it should be noted that sentences in existing cQA datasets can be declarative or standalone, while in our case they must be a sequence of questions that jointly imply some user intent. Popular tasks on cQA have only considered the semantics of individual questions and answers, while we are more focused on interactions between questions.

Huang et al. (2008) and Krishnan et al. (2005) classify questions to improve QA performance, but their work is limited to standalone questions. Ciurca (2019) was the first to identify MSQs as a distinct phenomenon, and curated a small dataset consisting of 300 MSQs extracted from Yahoo Answers. However, this dataset is too small to enable significant progress on automatic classification of MSQ intent.

## 3 Large-scale MSQ dataset

Stack Exchange is a network of question-answering sites, where each site covers a particular topic. Questions on Stack Exchange are formatted to have a short title and then a longer body describing the question, meaning that it is far more likely to contain MSQs than other question answering sites, which tend to focus attention on the title with only a short amount of description after the title. There is a voting system which allows us to proxy well-formedness, since badly-formed questions are likely to be rated poorly. It covers a variety of topics, meaning that we can obtain questions from a variety of domains.

To obtain the data, we used the Stack Exchange Data Explorer[1], an open source tool for running arbitrary queries against public data from the Stack Exchange network. We chose 93 sites within the network, and queried each site for entries with at least two question marks in the body of the question. We removed any questions with TeX and mark-up tags, then replaced any text matching a RegEx pattern for a website with '`[website]`'. From this cleaned text, we extracted pairs of MSQs by splitting the cleaned body of the question into sentences, then finding two adjacent sentences ending in '?'. We removed questions under 5 or over 300 characters in length. Finally, we removed any question identified as non-English using `langid.py` (Lui and Baldwin, 2012). Many of the questions labelled as 'non-English' were in fact badly formed English, making language identification a useful pre-processing step.

After cleaning and processing, we extracted 162,745 questions from 93 topics[2]. A full list of topics and the number of questions extracted from each is given in Appendix A. We restrict the dataset to pairs of questions, leaving longer sequences of MSQs for future work.

## 4 MSQ type as a proxy for speaker intent

MSQs are distinct from sequences of standalone questions in that their subparts need to be considered as a unit (see (1) in Section 1). This is because they form a **discourse**: a coherent sequence of utterances (Hobbs, 1979). In declarative sentences, the relationship between their different parts is specified by "discourse relations" (Stede, 2011; Kehler, 2006), which may be signalled with discourse markers (e.g. *if*, *because*) or discourse adverbials (e.g. *as a result*, see Rohde et al. (2015)). We propose adapting the notion of discourse relations to interrogatives.

A particularly useful approach to discourse relations in the context of MSQs is Rhetorical Structure Theory (RST) (Mann and Thompson, 1988), which understands them to be an expression of the speaker's communicative intent. Listeners can infer this intent under the assumptions that speakers are "cooperative" and keep their contributions as brief and relevant as possible (Grice, 1975). Transposing this theory to interrogatives, we can conceptualise the querent's communicative intent as a specific kind of answer. Reflecting this intent, the relation suggests an answering strategy.

We introduce five types of "question discourse relations" with a prototypical example from our data set, highlighting the inferred intent and the proposed answering strategy in Table 1.

---

[1] https://data.stackexchange.com/

[2] Our dataset is available at `https://github.com/laurieburchell/multi-sentence-questions`

SEPARABLE

| | |
|---|---|
| **Example** | *What's the recommended kitten food?* |
| | *How often should I feed it?* |
| **Intent** | Two questions on the same topic (the querent's kitten). |
| **Strategy** | Resolve coreference and answer both questions separately. |

REFORMULATED

| | |
|---|---|
| **Example** | *Is Himalayan pink salt okay to use in fish tanks?* |
| | *I read that aquarium salt is good but would pink salt work?* |
| **Intent** | Speaker wants to paraphrase Q1 (perhaps for clarity). |
| **Strategy** | Answer one of the two questions. |

DISJUNCTIVE

| | |
|---|---|
| **Example** | *Is it normal for my puppy to eat so quickly?* |
| | *Or should I take him to the vet?* |
| **Intent** | Querent offers two potential answers in the form of polar questions. |
| **Strategy** | Select one of the answers offered (e.g. "Yes, it is normal") or reject both (e.g. "Neither – try feeding it less but more often"). |

CONDITIONAL

| | |
|---|---|
| **Example** | *Has something changed that is making cats harder to buy?* |
| | *If so, what changed?* |
| **Intent** | Q2 only matters if the answer to Q1 is "yes". |
| **Strategy** | First consider what the answer to Q1 is and then answer Q2. |

ELABORATIVE

| | |
|---|---|
| **Example** | *How can I transport my cats if I am moving a long distance?* |
| | *For example, flying them from NYC to London?* |
| **Intent** | Querent wants a more specific answer. |
| **Strategy** | Combine context and answer the second question only. |

Table 1: The five types of MSQ we describe, an example of each, the querent's intent, and the resulting answering strategy. Mann and Thompson (1988)'s ELABORATION, CONDITION and RESTATEMENT relations correspond roughly to three of the relations we recognise.


## 5 Classification using contrastive features

Since Ciurca (2019) found that using conventional discourse parsers created for declaratives is not suitable for extracting discourse relations from MSQs, we design our own annotation scheme and use it to implement a baseline classifier. Following previous work on extracting discourse relations (Rohde et al., 2015), we use discourse markers and discourse adverbials alongside other markers indicative of the structure of the question (listed in appendix C) to identify explicitly signalled relations.[3]

We construct a high-precision, low-recall set of rules to distinguish the most prototypical forms of the five types using combinations of binary contrastive features. To derive the relevant features, we consider the minimal edits to examples of MSQs required to break or change the type of discourse relation between their parts. We then define a feature mask for each MSQ type which denotes whether each feature is required, disallowed or ignored by that type. Each mask is mutually exclusive by design.

Given a pair of questions, the system enumerates the values of each feature, and compares to the definitions in Appendix B. If a match is found, the pair is assigned the corresponding MSQ label, otherwise

---

[3]Since implicit discourse relations are pervasive and challenging to automatic systems (Sporleder and Lascarides, 2008), we make no attempt to extract them here.

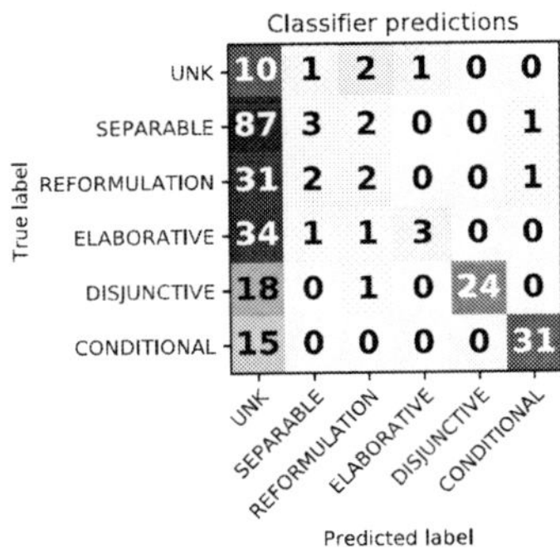

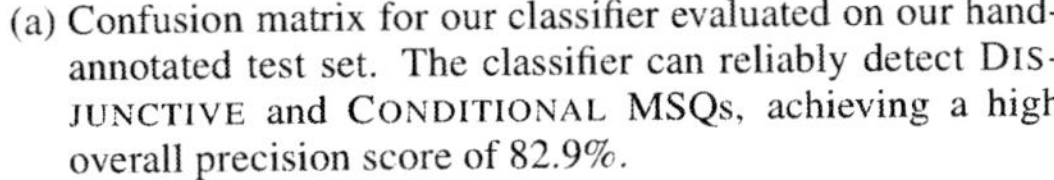

(a) Confusion matrix for our classifier evaluated on our hand-annotated test set. The classifier can reliably detect DIS-JUNCTIVE and CONDITIONAL MSQs, achieving a high overall precision score of 82.9%.

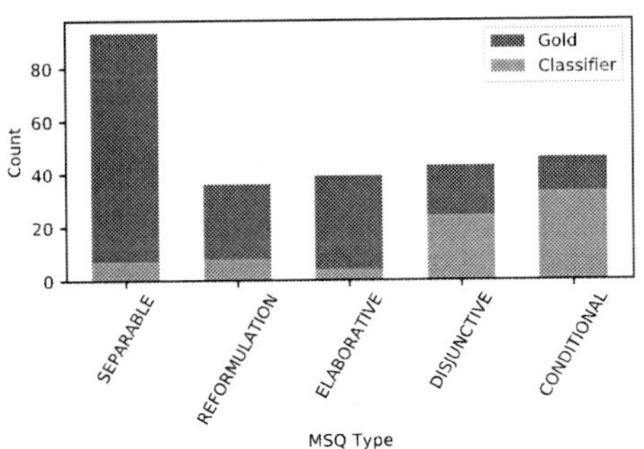

(b) Counts of each MSQ type in our test set, according to our annotation and our classifier. While SEPARABLE MSQs appear to be the most prevalent, the classifier identifies only a small fraction of them, implying that they are likely to be implicitly signalled. DISJUNCTIVE and CONDI-TIONAL are the most likely to be explicitly signalled.

Figure 1

it is assigned UNKNOWN. This process is illustrated in Appendix D.

To evaluate our classifier, 420 MSQs from our test set were annotated by two native speakers. We then evaluate the classifier on the subset of 271 samples for which both annotators agreed on the MSQ type. The resultant confusion matrix is shown in Figure 1a, with the classifier achieving 82.9% precision and 26.5% recall.

Overall, we find that our classifier performs well for a heuristic approach, but that real world data contains many subtleties that can break our assumptions. During the annotation process, we found many instances of single questions followed by a question which fulfils a purely social function, such as *"Is it just me or this a problem?"* (a *phatic* question, see Robinson et al. (1992)). MSQs can also exhibit more than one intent, presenting a challenge for both our classifier and the expert annotators (see Appendix E).

A limitation of our classifier is the focus on explicit MSQs, which can be identified with well-defined features. The low recall of our classifier indicates that MSQs are often implicit, missing certain markers or not completely fulfilling the distinguishing requirements. Figure 1b shows that while DISJUNCTIVE and CONDITIONAL MSQs are often explicitly signalled, the other types are likely to be implicit.

## 6   Conclusion

Inspired by the role of discourse relations in MSQ answering strategies, we propose a novel definition of five different categories of MSQs based on their corresponding speaker intents. We introduce a rich and diversified multi-sentence questions dataset, which contains 162,000 MSQs extracted from Stack Exchange. This achieves our goal of providing a resource for further study of MSQs. Additionally, we implement a baseline classifier based on surface features as a prelimininary step towards successful answering strategies for MSQs.

Future work could improve on our classifier by considering implicit MSQs, with one potential approach being to transform explicit MSQs into implicit examples by removing some markers while ensuring the relation is still valid. Other areas for further work include implementing appropriate answering strategies for different types of MSQs, and investigating whether and how longer chains of MSQs differ compared to pairs of connected questions.

## Acknowledgments

This work was supported in part by the UKRI Centre for Doctoral Training in Natural Language Processing, funded by the UKRI (grant EP/S022481/1) and the University of Edinburgh. We would like to thank Bonnie Webber for her supervision, and Ivan Titov and Adam Lopez for their useful advice.

# References

Aishwarya Agrawal, Jiasen Lu, Stanislaw Antol, Margaret Mitchell, C. Lawrence Zitnick, Devi Parikh, and Dhruv Batra. 2017. VQA: Visual question answering. *International Journal of Computer Vision*, 123(1):4–31, May.

Eunsol Choi, He He, Mohit Iyyer, Mark Yatskar, Wen-tau Yih, Yejin Choi, Percy Liang, and Luke Zettlemoyer. 2018. Quac: Question answering in context. *arXiv preprint arXiv:1808.07036*.

Tudor Ciurca. 2019. Sense classification of multi-sentence questions. Master's thesis, School of Informatics, University of Edinburgh.

Peter Clark, Isaac Cowhey, Oren Etzioni, Tushar Khot, Ashish Sabharwal, Carissa Schoenick, and Oyvind Tafjord. 2018. Think you have solved question answering? Try ARC, the AI2 reasoning challenge. *arXiv preprint arXiv:1803.05457*.

H. P. Grice. 1975. Logic and conversation. In P Cole and J Morgan, editors, *Syntax and Semantics 3*, pages 41–58. Academic Press.

Jerry R Hobbs. 1979. Coherence and coreference. *Cognitive Science*, 3(1):67–90.

Zhiheng Huang, Marcus Thint, and Zengchang Qin. 2008. Question classification using head words and their hypernyms. In *Proceedings of the 2008 Conference on Empirical Methods in Natural Language Processing*, pages 927–936, Honolulu, Hawaii, October. Association for Computational Linguistics.

Blooma John and Jayan Kurian. 2011. Research issues in community based question answering. In *PACIS 2011 - 15th Pacific Asia Conference on Information Systems: Quality Research in Pacific*, page 29, 01.

Mandar Joshi, Eunsol Choi, Daniel S. Weld, and Luke Zettlemoyer. 2017. Triviaqa: A large scale distantly supervised challenge dataset for reading comprehension. *CoRR*, abs/1705.03551.

Andrew Kehler. 2006. Discourse coherence. In Laurence Horn and Gregory Ward, editors, *The Handbook of Pragmatics*, pages 241–265. Blackwell Publishing Ltd.

Vijay Krishnan, Sujatha Das, and Soumen Chakrabarti. 2005. Enhanced answer type inference from questions using sequential models. In *Proceedings of Human Language Technology Conference and Conference on Empirical Methods in Natural Language Processing*, pages 315–322, Vancouver, British Columbia, Canada, October. Association for Computational Linguistics.

Marco Lui and Timothy Baldwin. 2012. langid.py: An off-the-shelf language identification tool. In *Proceedings of the ACL 2012 System Demonstrations*, pages 25–30, Jeju Island, Korea, July. Association for Computational Linguistics.

William C Mann and Sandra A Thompson. 1988. Rhetorical structure theory: Toward a functional theory of text organization. *Text: Interdisciplinary Journal for the Study of Discourse*, 8(3):243–281.

Pranav Rajpurkar, Jian Zhang, Konstantin Lopyrev, and Percy Liang. 2016. SQuAD: 100,000+ questions for machine comprehension of text. In *Proceedings of the 2016 Conference on Empirical Methods in Natural Language Processing*, pages 2383–2392. Association for Computational Linguistics.

Siva Reddy, Danqi Chen, and Christopher D. Manning. 2019. CoQA: A conversational question answering challenge. *Transactions of the Association for Computational Linguistics*, 7:249–266, March.

Jeffrey D Robinson, Nikolas Coupland, and Justine Coupland. 1992. "How Are You?": Negotiating Phatic Communion. *Language in Society*, 21(2):207–230.

Hannah Rohde, Anna Dickinson, Chris Clark, Annie Louis, and Bonnie Webber. 2015. Recovering discourse relations: Varying influence of discourse adverbials. In *Proceedings of the First Workshop on Linking Computational Models of Lexical, Sentential and Discourse-level Semantics*, pages 22–31.

Marzieh Saeidi, Max Bartolo, Patrick Lewis, Sameer Singh, Tim Rocktäschel, Mike Sheldon, Guillaume Bouchard, and Sebastian Riedel. 2018. Interpretation of natural language rules in conversational machine reading. *CoRR*, abs/1809.01494.

Caroline Sporleder and Alex Lascarides. 2008. Using automatically labelled examples to classify rhetorical relations: an assessment. *Natural Language Engineering*, 14(3):369–416.

Manfred Stede. 2011. Discourse processing. *Synthesis Lectures on Human Language Technologies*, 4(3):1–165, nov.

Akihiro Tamura, Hiroya Takamura, and Manabu Okumura. 2005. Classification of multiple-sentence questions. In *Second International Joint Conference on Natural Language Processing: Full Papers*.

Bonnie Webber, Rashmi Prasad, Alan Lee, and Aravind Joshi. 2019. The Penn discourse treebank 3.0 annotation manual.

# A  Number of questions by topic

| Topic | Number of questions | Topic | Number of questions |
|---|---|---|---|
| SuperUser | 17197 | Philosophy | 799 |
| ServerFault | 14780 | Hinduism | 760 |
| ElectricalEngineering | 9847 | PhysicalFitness | 760 |
| Arquade | 9704 | Homebrewing | 671 |
| Physics | 8192 | QuantFinance | 667 |
| English | 7851 | Outdoors | 599 |
| EnglishLearners | 5922 | Sports | 576 |
| SciFiFantasy | 4920 | Islam | 524 |
| InformationSecurity | 4652 | BiblicalHermeneutics | 507 |
| RPG | 4259 | Buddhism | 492 |
| DIY | 3017 | Engineering | 492 |
| Travel | 2985 | Linguistics | 484 |
| Academia | 2488 | TheorecticalCompSci | 484 |
| PersonalFinance | 2312 | Chess | 483 |
| StackOverflowMeta | 2265 | SoundDesign | 482 |
| SeasonedAdvice | 2234 | Pets | 473 |
| UX | 2219 | Economics | 472 |
| Workplace | 2189 | Parenting | 472 |
| Photography | 2111 | CognitiveSciences | 444 |
| Aviation | 1949 | Monero | 425 |
| Biology | 1832 | Health | 420 |
| Bitcoin | 1806 | ComputationalScience | 398 |
| Worldbuilding | 1801 | ReverseEngineering | 392 |
| MiYodeya | 1769 | EarthScience | 386 |
| Chemistry | 1652 | ProjectManagement | 383 |
| Music | 1589 | ArtificialIntelligence | 360 |
| ComputerScience | 1500 | Expatriates | 310 |
| Cryptography | 1487 | Robotics | 295 |
| GraphicDesign | 1450 | AmateurRadio | 285 |
| Ethereum | 1415 | Woodworking | 283 |
| BoardGames | 1402 | Literature | 234 |
| SpaceExploration | 1354 | HistoryScienceMathematics | 229 |
| Motors | 1285 | Tor | 219 |
| Bicycles | 1241 | Lego | 213 |
| Anime | 1208 | MartialArts | 202 |
| Law | 1188 | Mythology | 174 |
| NetworkEngineering | 1160 | InterpersonalSkills | 156 |
| Christianity | 1084 | Freelancing | 148 |
| Politics | 1074 | Poker | 145 |
| History | 1066 | Genealogy | 137 |
| Gardening | 1007 | MusicFans | 129 |
| DataScience | 955 | ArtsAndCrafts | 118 |
| SignalProcessing | 912 | Movies | 118 |
| Puzzling | 888 | SustainableLiving | 109 |
| Astronomy | 816 | OpenData | 105 |
| Skeptics | 807 | LifeHacks | 83 |
| Writers | 805 | | |

Table 2: Number of questions extracted by site topic in StackOverflow dataset, sorted by descending number of questions

## B  Contrastive features

Note that these requirements do not apply in all cases: if all conditions are met then we assert that a pair of questions *must* be of that type, but the absence of a feature does not *forbid* that relation from being present. A list of the lexical markers used to define features is given in Appendix C. Like discourse relations in declaratives, question discourse relations may be *implicit*, i.e. not marked with a connective or other marker but inferable to the listener. These implicit relations continue to be very challenging for automatic systems (Sporleder and Lascarides, 2008) and we do not attempt to handle them.

| Feature | Surface | Separable | Reformulated | Disjunctive | Conditional | Elaborative | Elab. Statement |
|---|---|---|---|---|---|---|---|
| Anaphora | Pronoun in Q2 | + | - | | | + | |
| | VP ellipsis in Q2 | - | | | | | |
| Polarity | Polar Q1 | - | | + | + | | |
| | Polar Q2 | | | + | | | - |
| | Wh Q1 | | | - | - | | |
| | Wh Q2 | | | - | | - | - |
| | Q2 = Statement | - | - | - | | - | + |
| Disc. Marker | "if" marker | - | - | - | + | - | - |
| | "or" | - | - | + | - | - | - |
| | "elab." marker | - | - | - | - | + | |
| | "sep." marker | - | - | - | - | - | - |
| Semantics | Word vector | | + | | | | + |

Table 3: Definitions for each MSQ type. '+' indicates that a feature is *required*, while '-' means the feature is *disallowed*. Types can be ignored for some features, meaning that the features are neither disallowed nor required.

We include the case where Q2 is a statement, as in *"How can I transport my cats if I am moving a long distance? For example, to London."*. Although these forms of MSQ do not appear in our dataset due to the filtering method used, they are in general valid, and we include them for completeness.

To evaluate semantic similarity between Q1 and Q2, we calculated the cosine similarity between the mean of the words vectors, and compared to a threshold of 0.8.

## C  Lexical Markers

Some of the discourse markers are drawn from the Penn Discourse Tree Bank (PDTB) annotation scheme (Webber et al., 2019).

### C.1  Anaphora Markers

To identify cases of anaphora, we searched for the following pronoun strings (and *it's*) in the second question:

she, he, it, they, her, his, its, their, them, it's

### C.2  Verb Ellipsis Markers

To identify cases of verb ellipsis, we searched for the following pro-forms of full verb phrases in the second question:

do so, did so, does so, do it, do too, does too, did too, did it too, do it too, does it too

## C.3 Polar Question Markers

do, does, did, didn't, will, won't, would, is, are, were, weren't, wasn't, can, can't, could, must, have, has, had, hasn't, haven't, should, shouldn't, may, might, shall, ought

## C.4 Wh- words

who, what, where, when, why, how, which

## C.5 Conditional *("if")* Markers

if so, accordingly, then, as a result, it follows, subsequently, consequently, if yes, if not, if the answer is yes, if the answer is no

## C.6 Elaborative Markers

for instance, for example, e.g., specifically, particularly, in particular, more specifically, more precisely, therefore

## C.7 Separable Markers

also, secondly, next, related, relatedly, similarly, furthermore

## D Classifier visualisation

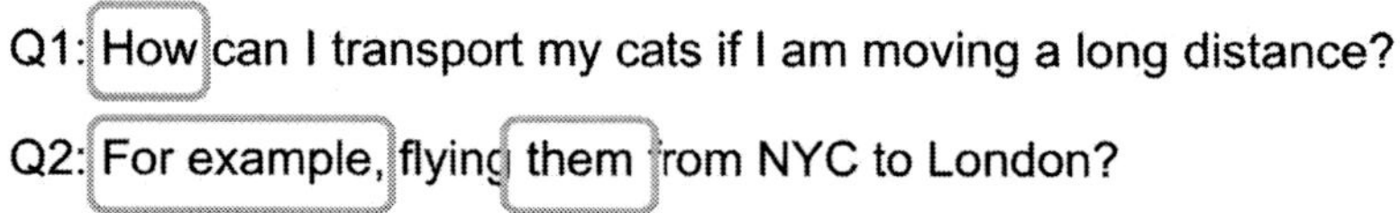


| Feature | Pronoun in Q2 | Q2 is statement | Wh- Q1 | Wh- Q2 | 'Or' marker | 'If' marker | 'Separable' marker | 'Elaboration' marker |
|---|---|---|---|---|---|---|---|---|
| Value | ✓ | ✗ | ✓ | ✗ | ✗ | ✗ | ✗ | ✓ |

**Compare to definitions:**

| | Pronoun in Q2 | Q2 is statement | Wh- Q1 | Wh- Q2 | 'Or' marker | 'If' marker | 'Separable' marker | 'Elaboration' marker |
|---|---|---|---|---|---|---|---|---|
| Elaborative | ✓ | ✗ | ✓ | ✗ | ✗ | ✗ | ✗ | ✓ |
| Disjunctive | | ✗ | ✗ | ✗ | ✓ | ✗ | ✗ | ✗ |

...

Figure 2: A visualisation of the labelling process. The system checks for the presence of each feature in the input text (circled in blue) and constructs a feature vector for the pair of questions. This feature vector is compared to the definitions, and if a match is found the questions are assigned the corresponding label. Note that not all features are shown.

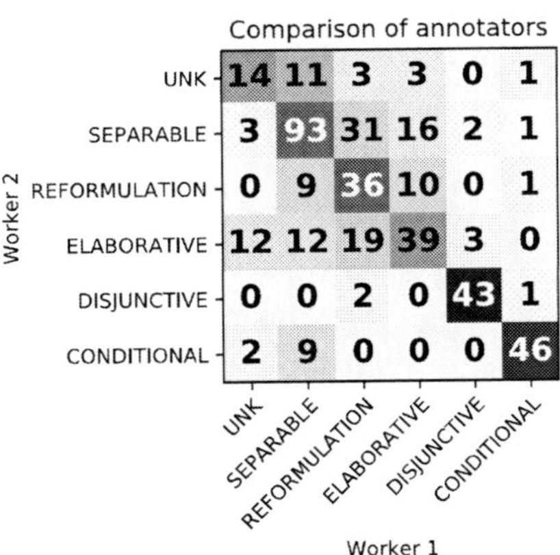


Figure 3: Confusion matrix between the two annotators who labelled our test set. While there is good agreement on the MSQ types that are often explicitly signalled (DISJUNCTIVE and CONDITIONAL), the other types are often more subtle, and examples may involve multiple intents.

# Annotating Errors and Emotions
# in Human-Chatbot Interactions in Italian


**Manuela Sanguinetti**[♡◇]    **Alessandro Mazzei**[♡]    **Viviana Patti**[♡]
**Marco Scalerandi**[♡]    **Dario Mana**[♣]    **Rossana Simeoni**[♣]

[♡]Dipartimento di Informatica, Università degli Studi di Torino, Italy
[◇]Dipartimento di Matematica e Informatica, Università degli Studi di Cagliari, Italy
[♣]TIM, Torino, Italy

[♡]`{first.last}@unito.it`, [◇]`{first.last}@unica.it`
[♣]`{first.last}@telecomitalia.it`


## Abstract


This paper describes a novel annotation scheme specifically designed for a customer-service context where written interactions take place between a given user and the chatbot of an Italian telecommunication company. More specifically, the scheme aims to detect and highlight two aspects: the presence of errors in the conversation on both sides (i.e. customer and chatbot) and the "emotional load" of the conversation. This can be inferred from the presence of emotions of some kind (especially negative ones) in the customer messages, and from the possible empathic responses provided by the agent. The dataset annotated according to this scheme is currently used to develop the prototype of a rule-based Natural Language Generation system aimed at improving the chatbot responses and the customer experience overall.


## 1 Introduction

Conversational agents, or chatbots, have become a widespread technology used by an ever increasing number of companies. Most often they are used to automate tasks such as customer support inquiries, providing a 24/7 livechat service via web-based interfaces or standalone mobile apps and enabling natural language interactions with the users. Chatbot systems typically include Natural Language Understanding (NLU) modules aimed at identifying users' intents and extracting the relevant information; these systems either resort to a set of predefined response templates or use Natural Language Generation (NLG) techniques to reply to the user.

Despite the ever increasing chatbot abilities to recognize user requests and provide appropriate answers, miscommunication is still a common issue in human-chatbot interactions (Sheehan et al., 2020). Such shortcomings go hand-in-hand with the need to strengthen, also and especially in customer support contexts, the ability of chatbots to interact in a human-like fashion, so as to encourage the users to engage more in the conversation and to comply with the agent's requests. An improved interaction quality also passes through the creation of emotion-aware chatbots able to recognize the emotional state of the customer and to respond appropriately, showing some form of empathy (Ma et al., 2020).

The work presented here forms part of a wider project consisting in the development of the prototype of a rule-based *genuine* NLG module (Van Deemter et al., 2005). The aim of this module is to improve the answers provided by the template-based chatbot of an Italian online customer service. Its main feature is that it takes as input a set of annotated dialogues between the chatbot and the customers, and it substitutes the template responses provided by the chatbot system, taking into account also various dimensions in the generation process, such as possible errors in the conversations and the presence of emotions (especially negative ones) in the user messages. The intended purposes in building this module are the enhancement of the chatbot responses on multiple levels. From a strict content viewpoint, a selection procedure inspired by narrative roles in explanation (Biran and McKeown, 2017) has been developed in order to generate more relevant and *ah hoc* responses to individual customers' requests as described in Di Lascio et al. (2020). In addition, an emotional layer has been added in the module design to generate empathic responses, more in line with customers' feelings and expectations.






*The 14th Linguistic Annotation Workshop*, pages 148–159
Barcelona, Spain (Online), December 12, 2020.

The development of task-oriented dialogue systems for Italian has raised great interest (especially from private companies) and there are high expectations for a new generation of dialogue systems that can naturally interact and assist humans in real scenarios. However, work on Italian language systems remains limited. Some related task with a focus on evaluation has been recently proposed in the context of EVALITA, the periodic evaluation campaign of NLP and speech tools for Italian (Cutugno et al., 2018). As this highlights, developing synergies between public institutions and private companies is extremely important to improve existing solutions for the Italian language, in particular with regard to effectiveness of the dialogue, user satisfaction and societal consequences and risks of dealing with conversational agents. Our aim with this contribution is also to partially fill this gap, presenting the result of a corpus-based study of a set of real human-chatbot conversations carried out in the context of a virtous example of collaboration between academia and private companies.

In this paper, we describe a multi-layer annotation scheme developed to annotate the aforementioned dialogues in the Italian language. The main novelty of this scheme is that it focuses on two dimensions: conversation errors and emotions. The design of the scheme has been driven by two main objectives: 1) to provide a qualitative analysis of these interactions, using a sample dataset to explore the possible interrelations between errors and emotions in conversation, thus providing the company with the opportunity to establish adequate error handling strategies, 2) to feed the NLG module with this additional information so as to improve the newly-generated responses. The distinguishing feature of the proposed scheme is that, in order to make sense of the complexity of the tagset relating to the possible errors, the error types have been clustered in a coarse-grained taxonomy whose classes are partially inspired by the popular Gricean maxims upon which the cooperative principle is built (Grice, 1989).

After outlining past related work, we hereby introduce the dataset used to apply the scheme. We then provide an overview of the scheme itself with some basic statistics and examples. Finally, we provide a qualitative analysis of the annotated data, discussing the main issues arisen during the annotation process.

## 2   Related Work

Error analysis and classification in both spoken and written human-machine interactions has been a matter of study for decades and its goal is mainly to define an improved set of error recovery strategies or to predict eventual conversation breakdowns. In Skantze (2005), a scheme was developed to establish the degree of comprehension of a task-oriented spoken dialogue system, along with the effects on the user experience. User utterances were thus annotated according to how well they were understood by the system, using the following set of tags: *Non-understanding, Misunderstanding, Partial Understanding, Full Understanding*. More recently, an improved taxonomy of errors was proposed in Higashinaka et al. (2018), based on the revision and comparison of two previous taxonomies (Higashinaka et al., 2015a; Higashinaka et al., 2015b) built according to a theory-driven, top-down approach the former, and with a data-driven, bottom-up approach the latter. In this revision process, both taxonomies were applied to the datasets used for the shared tasks on automatic breakdown detection (Higashinaka et al., 2016); these datasets consist of dialogues between humans and chat-oriented systems. The schemes were meant to identify systems' errors within conversations. The revision process and eventual comparison of the schemes showed a higher reliability, in terms of inter-annotator agreement results, of the bottom-up taxonomy. While the above-mentioned contributions focused on system's errors, a past work by Bernsen et al. (1996) aimed specifically at studying user errors, i.e., those cases where the user fails to comply with the normative model of the dialogue (e.g., not following the system's explicit instructions or deliberately refusing to be cooperative). Finally, in Möller et al. (2007), both parties are taken into account while designing an error annotation scheme within the context of a task-based spoken interaction. In fact, a set of errors on different levels (goal, task, command, concept) was defined for user utterances, but also a recognition-level error was introduced to capture system's mistyping and automatic speech-recognition errors. Interestingly, each user-system exchange was also annotated with a label aimed at capturing the consequences of such errors, which may be *stagnation, repetition* (as a special case of stagnation), *regression*, or rather *partial* or *complete progress*.

Parallel to error analysis is the annotation of human emotions in dialogues. While a large number of contributions on open-domain, human-human interactions can be found in literature (see Poria et al. (2019) for an overview), relatively fewer works are available on the annotation of human-machine dialogues, and more specifically in task-based domains, such as customer service. In addition, the distinguishing purpose of such systems – namely to complete a given task, be it booking a flight of providing assistance of any kind – often makes traditional schemes, such as those based on Ekman o Plutchik theories (Ekman, 1992; Plutchik, 1982), partially inadequate to provide a proper emotion representation within such contexts. As a result, work on this subject mostly focuses on negative emotions that may result from partial or complete failure in completing the given task. Typically, the range of negative emotions include *anger* (Liscombe et al., 2005; Herzig et al., 2016; Schmitt et al., 2012), *frustration* (Ang et al., 2002; Liscombe et al., 2005; Herzig et al., 2016) – even providing fine-grained distinctions between different degrees of emotions (Liscombe et al., 2005; Schmitt et al., 2012) – but also *confusion*, *disappointment* and *sadness* (Herzig et al., 2016). While such schemes usually apply to user emotions only, recent works also include agent's behavior, proposing annotation labels, as well as computational approaches that aim at identifying empathy on agent's responses (Alam et al., 2018; Herzig et al., 2016).

The annotation scheme described in this paper draws inspiration from the works briefly outlined in this section, and its main contribution lies in the attempt to encompass within a single framework all these different, though in a sense complementary, dimensions.

## 3   Dataset Description

The scheme has been applied to a corpus of interactions between humans and a task-oriented dialogue system[1]. More specifically, it contains dialogues between customers and a chatbot from the customer care unit of an Italian telecommunication service provider. The dialogues, which take place by means of a text chat, mainly deal with requests for commercial assistance, both on landline and mobile phones.

As briefly introduced in Section 1, the corpus development and its annotation have been designed so as to improve the NLG module of the chatbot, with a particular focus on explanations. Therefore, the dataset was created by selecting, from a sample of dialogues held over 24 hours, a reduced subset that included requests for explanations from customers. The resulting corpus consists of 142 dialogues, including 1540 turns – an average of about 11 turns per dialogue – and an average length of 9 tokens in customer turns and 38 tokens in the agent turns. Similar to Herzig et al. (2016), consecutive messages of the same party (customer or agent), if not interrupted by another message of the other party, were considered as a single turn. This explains the difference in the average turn lengths, as, especially in the case of the chatbot, a single turn may actually consist of more than one message. This difference is also due to the way the agent's responses are currently structured; agents' responses usually include detailed information (for example, on invoice items or available options), while customers' messages are generally more concise. In some cases, the latter are basic yes/no answers, or digits (1,2,...) corresponding to the options provided by the agent in its previous message, as in the example below:

| | |
|---|---|
| **Chatbot** | *Mi risultano 2 linee a te intestate: 1.* phoneNumber *2.* phoneNumber*.* |
| | *A quale linea devo fare riferimento?* |
| | *Scegli una delle linee indicate, selezionando la posizione nell'elenco (1,2,3...).* |
| | (I've found two numbers on your name: 1.phoneNumber 2. phoneNumber |
| | Which one should I refer to? |
| | Choose one by selecting the position in the list (1, 2, 3, ...)) |
| **Customer** | 1 |

The types of requests for explanations collected in this corpus basically reflect the different kinds of problems typically encountered with a telecom service provider, such as undue or unfamiliar charges in the bill or in the phone credit (these cases represent about 52% of the overall number of requests in this dataset). An issue emerged from the data in the corpus is the occurrence of breakdowns in conversation, i.e., whenever the interaction is interrupted because one or both parties give up the conversation without completing the task (Martinovsky and Traum, 2003). In fact, out of the 142 conversations in this

---

[1] Due to privacy reasons, the corpus cannot yet be publicly released, but we are currently working on its anonymization.

collection, 53 have been interrupted by the customer, who did not get to a proper answer or solution to the problem posed. As for the remaining conversations, only in 10 cases the conversation had a positive outcome (the chatbot provided a satisfactory explanation or proper help), while the other 79 ended with the handover to a human agent, which was often explicitly asked for by the customer.

Besides providing a rough indicator of the interaction quality, this prompted further analysis in order to explore, under different perspectives, the causes of such breakdowns and the dynamics behind these interactions. The analysis led to the development of a richer and fine-grained annotation scheme aiming to capture these aspects, as described in the next section.

## 4 Annotation Scheme

This section provides an overview of the tagset adopted for the annotation of both dimensions included in the scheme, i.e. errors and emotions. Detailed guidelines with examples can also be found in the following document (in both Italian and English): `https://cutt.ly/cdMcnyM`

### 4.1 Errors

The main motivation behind the design of this annotation scheme was to provide a detailed account of the possible errors that could be encountered in human-chatbot interactions, especially within a customer service domain. By error, in this context we mean any event that might have a negative impact on the flow of the interaction, and more in general on its quality, potentially resulting in conversation breakdowns. Such events usually represent a deviation from an expectation, both by the customer and the agent, or more simply a deviation from standard linguistic norms, which may also result in misinterpretations of any kind.

The tagset was conceived so as to include a wide range of phenomena on different levels and, unlike other taxonomies of errors specifically defined for just one party in the interaction (either user or system, as described in Section 2), it includes error categories that may apply to either only customer's or only chatbot's messages, or to messages from both. While certain errors can be attributed to only one party, others can be considered as transverse phenomena, and we are interested in providing a comprehensive view capturing all of them. This motivates the high variety of tags defined in the scheme. Despite this variety, however, we clustered the error types in a coarse-grained taxonomy whose classes are partially inspired by the popular Gricean maxims upon which the cooperative principle is built (Grice, 1989), more specifically to the maxim of Quantity, Relation and Manner[2]. We then define a more generic class of errors. The terminology used to define the error tags is partially borrowed from Higashinaka et al. (2018) and Bernsen et al. (1996), whose contributions focused only on system errors (the former) and on user errors (the latter).

Below we describe the general characteristics of the error classes. Table 1 reports the complete list of the error tags according to their corresponding class and it indicates whether they are specific to messages from one party (customer or agent) or if they can be applied to both.

**Quantity** This class includes all those messages that violate the maxim of Quantity, according to which contributions should be as informative as required, but not more informative than required. Therefore, with this class we define those messages in which insufficient information is provided to obtain a relevant response ("Lack of Information"), or, conversely, in which the text is unnecessarily verbose and redundant ("Excess of Information"). The error tags in this class are meant to be used for both parties.

**Relation** This class includes a large number of error types that signal the violation of the maxim of Relation (i.e. *"Be relevant"*) in various ways. The messages annotated with these tags do not have a relation to the previous message to various degrees: they might state something that only implicitly

---

[2]The first maxim, that of Quality (*"Try to make your contribution one that is true"*, (Grice, 1989), p.26) has not been considered here, as we assume that it is in the interest of both parties to be truthful and always provide the correct information.

| | Customer | Chatbot |
|---|---|---|
| **Quantity** | Lack of information | |
| | Excess of information | |
| **Relation** | Indirect response | |
| | Ignoring question/feedback | |
| | Repetition | |
| | Straight wrong response | |
| | | Topic change |
| | Answering with question | |
| **Manner** | Ill-formed | |
| | Indirect question | |
| | Non-understandable | |
| | | Grammatical error |
| **Generic** | Non-cooperativity | |
| | Other | |

Table 1: List of the error tags according to their corresponding class. Errors are displayed on the left, right or center column depending on whether they pertain messages from customer, chatbot or both.

answers the previous question ("Indirect response") or just provide an answer that seems not to take into account what was stated in the previous message ("Ignoring question/feedback"), also re-proposing the same content of past messages ("Repetition")[3], or giving an answer that is completely irrelevant with respect to the previous message ("Straight wrong response"). In case of misunderstandings, the chatbot could propose to switch to another topic ("Topic change"). It is also possible that the customer replies to a request by the chatbot with another question ("Answering with question").

**Manner**   The third class includes messages that violate the maxim of Manner ("*Be perspicuous*") and, in line with Grice's definition, it does not aim to draw attention to what is said but to *how* it is said. Therefore the error tags falling under this class mainly highlight flaws in the message form, rather than in its content. In this case, most of the errors are defined only for customer messages. In fact, the chatbot is a typical template-based dialogue system, and it uses a set of manually created responses, formulated so that they are as clear as possible, unambiguous and grammatically correct (except for some rare cases that we decided to report with the addition of the tag "Grammatical error"). On the customer side, it is more likely to find cases in which the message, although potentially relevant at that stage of the conversation, does not correspond to the form expected by the system (see the "Ill-formed" tag, which mostly applies to cases where the user fails to select the provided options in the expected way), it contains statements that may ambiguously sound like implicit requests ("Indirect question"), or it is nearly or completely obscure ("Non-understandable"). It is worth pointing out that while customers' messages may also contain grammatical errors, the corresponding tag was not used for such cases due to the fact that the user's text, as it appears in the dataset, is usually revised at run-time by a built-in module of the dialogue system that automatically corrects several typos and other basic grammatical errors. The NLU module of the system thus receives as input a potentially revised version of the message that we are not able to see, therefore we cannot determine whether the user's message still contains errors or not.

**Generic**   The last class includes two final tags: one is defined for those messages where the customer deliberately acts in a non-cooperative manner, refusing to provide the system with the information it requests ("Non-cooperativity"); the "Other" tag is finally used for messages presenting errors that do not fit in any of the other categories in this taxonomy.

---

[3]In this sense, "Repetition" can be considered as a specification of the "Ignoring question/feedback" tag.

|            | % **Customers** | % **Chatbot** |
|------------|-----------------|---------------|
| Quantity   | 3,43            | 1,07          |
| Relevance  | 13,57           | 14,05         |
| Manner     | 7,43            | 0,36          |
| Generic    | 2,86            | 0,60          |
| None       | 72,71           | 83,93         |

Table 2: Distribution of customers' and chatbot errors (%) by class over the total number of customers' and chatbot turns.

| **Customers Errors**      | **%**  |
|---------------------------|--------|
| Ignoring question/feedback | 20.94 |
| Ill-formed                | 13.09  |
| Repetition                | 12.04  |
| Excess of information     | 11.52  |
| Indirect response         | 8.90   |
| Non-cooperativity         | 8.90   |
| Answering with question   | 8.90   |
| Non-understandable        | 5.24   |
| Straight wrong response   | 4.71   |
| Indirect question         | 3.14   |
| Other                     | 1.57   |
| Lack of information       | 1.05   |

Table 3: Distribution of error types among customers errors only.

| **Chatbot Errors**         | **%**  |
|----------------------------|--------|
| Topic change               | 30.37  |
| Repetition                 | 23.70  |
| Straight wrong response    | 20.74  |
| Ignoring question/feedback | 6.67   |
| Indirect response          | 5.93   |
| Lack of information        | 4.44   |
| Other                      | 3.70   |
| Excess of information      | 2.22   |
| Grammatical error          | 2.22   |

Table 4: Distribution of error types among chatbot errors only.

Table 2 shows the error distribution in the customers' and chatbot messages, organized by main classes, while Tables 3 and 4 summarize the distribution of the specific error types computed over the total number of customers' and chatbot errors respectively (thus ignoring the largest portion of turns where no error occurs).

## 4.2 Emotions and Empathy

The annotation of the emotional dimension is meant to identify for each turn in the conversation both the customer's emotion and the possible signals of empathic response in the chatbot message.

**Customer's emotions** Due to the context where the interactions take place, i.e. a customer service, we selected a limited set of the possible range of emotions that can be typically applied to a corpus of conversations (such as in IEMOCAP (Busso et al., 2008), DailyDialog (Li et al., 2017) or EmoContext (Chatterjee et al., 2019), to name a few). We thus followed a similar scheme as the one adopted in Liscombe et al. (2005), including a generic "Positive" emotion that simply expresses a positive attitude towards the conversational agent and a "Neutral" tag to indicate whether no particular emotion is perceived in the message. We then introduced two negative emotions, *frustration* and *anger*, providing for both a fine-grained distinction with the tags "Somewhat/Very frustrated" and "Somewhat/Very angry". Frustration is defined as a *"key negative emotion that roots in disappointment, [...] an irritable distress after a wish collided with an unyielding reality"* (Jeronimus and Laceulle, 2017). In this context, frustration can derive from a sense of disappointment for not receiving the answers sought or a solution to the problem posed, and more generally, from an experience with the chatbot that is unsatisfactory and does not correspond to the expectations. The user can experience frustration whenever s/he feels that the interaction with the virtual agent is not leading anywhere. In this sense, the feeling of frustration can

| Emotion | % |
|---|---|
| Somewhat angry | 35.35 |
| Somewhat frustrated | 32.32 |
| Very frustrated | 9.09 |
| Other negative | 9.09 |
| Positive | 8.08 |
| Very angry | 6.06 |
| Empathy | 0,95 |

Table 5: Distribution of emotions detected in customers' turns and of empathic responses by the chatbot (%). The relative frequency of customers' emotions is computed discarding the share of neutral instances.

then be associated to signs of annoyance and dissatisfaction from the customer.

Anger, on the other hand, is intended as a negative emotion that impels aggressive behavior (Novaco, 2017), and it can be triggered, among other factors, by the perception of an unfair treatment. It is especially the idea of being treated unfairly that motivated the definition of the corresponding tag in our scheme. We thus labeled as "anger" any covert or overt hostility (e.g., when the customer threatens to end the use of the service) namely derived from this perception.

The two degrees of anger and frustration are distinguished on the basis of lexical and pragmatic cues (e.g., in the use of specific words or interjections) identified in the customer's message or other cues inferred from the context of the exchange. We finally added the "Other negative" tag for negative emotions that are neither anger nor frustration. The choice of including only two main negative emotions (excluding others used in previous works, as mentioned in Section 2) is motivated by an exploratory analysis of the data in the pre-annotation phase in which anger and frustration were found to be the two prevailing emotions. To avoid further sparseness on an already reduced dataset, we focused on these two emotions and added a third label to conflate any other negative emotions.

**Agent's Empathy**   The operational definition of empathy is borrowed from the work by Alam et al. (2018), who define empathy as "*a situation where an agent anticipates or views solutions and clarifications, based on the understanding of a customer's problem or issue, that can relieve or prevent the customer's unpleasant feelings*" (p.40). We found this definition suitable for this work as it applies to a fairly similar context, that is a collection of dyadic Italian task-oriented dialogues[4].

The inclusion of this tag was motivated by our interest in studying the agent's behavior and its ability to properly recognize and respond to customers' signs of dissatisfaction. The very low distribution of empathic responses as reported from the dataset, shows that there is much room for improvement in this respect, and the NLG module that is currently under development within this project should address this issue as well. Table 5 shows the distribution of emotions and empathy in the dataset. In the next section we describe the scheme usage while commenting on a few annotated examples.

### 4.3   Annotation Examples

Below, we report two dialogue excerpts[5] in which some of the tags in the scheme were used. The turn number in the actual conversation is written in subscript on the left.

---

[4]In Alam et al. (2018), however, the data at issue consists of human-human interactions.

[5]For privacy reasons, customers' personal information such as invoice or phone number are replaced with a placeholder.

**Example 1**

**Chatbot$_6$**    *Ecco il dettaglio delle voci di spesa presenti nella fattura* `InvoiceNumber`
*del mese di gennaio per la linea* `PhoneNumber`: [...]
*Vuoi avere il dettaglio di una specifica voce di spesa presente in fattura?*
(Here is the detail of the `InvoiceNumber` of January for the `PhoneNumber`: [...]
Do you want the detail of a specific item in the invoice?)

**Customer$_7$**    *Son rimasta senza internet 16 giorni a dicembre..non devo pagare questi giorni*
(I was left without internet for 16 days..I don't have to pay for those days)
**Error: Ignoring question/feedback -Emotion: Somewhat angry**

**Chatbot$_8$**    *Vuoi cambiare argomento?*
(Do you want to change topic?)
**Error: Topic change**

**Customer$_9$**    *Voglio una fattura giusta per il servizio che ho avuto*
(I want a fair invoice for the service I had)
**Emotion: Somewhat angry**

**Chatbot$_{10}$**    *Scusami, non ho capito bene la tua richiesta...*
*Puoi ripeterla in modo più semplice?*
(I'm sorry, I haven't understood your question very well...
Could you please rephrase it in a simpler way?)

**Customer$_{11}$**    *Voglio restituiti i soldi del servizio che non ho avuto per 16 gg*
(I want the money back for the service I haven't had for 16 days)
**Error: Repetition - Emotion: Somewhat angry**

**Chatbot$_{12}$**    *Verifico quali addebiti ci sono stati sul tuo* `PhoneNumber`
(I check which charges have been made on your `PhoneNumber`)
**Error: Straight wrong response**

---

**Breakdown**


**Example 2**

**Chatbot$_3$**    *Scusami, non ho capito bene la tua richiesta...*
*Puoi ripeterla in modo più semplice?*
(I'm sorry, I haven't understood your question very well...
Could you please rephrase it in a simpler way?)

**Customer$_4$**    *No non hai capito niente*
(No, you've got it all wrong)
**Error: Non-cooperativity - Emotion: Somewhat frustrated**

**Chatbot$_5$**    *Mi spiace non aver compreso correttamente.*
*Ho la possibilità di farti chattare con un operatore umano più esperto. Vuoi?*
(I'm sorry I haven't understood that correctly.
I can let you chat with an expert human representative. Do you want me to?)
**Empathy**


In Example 1, the customer contacts the service to ask for explanations regarding a charge in the bill. The chatbot reports the details of the invoice and it offers to provide additional information for each amount, but the customer responds in an irrelevant way, ignoring the agent's question and insisting on the problem, showing signs of anger, due to the feeling of being treated unfairly. This "sense of injustice" also persists in the customer's subsequent messages, with the message in turn 11 repeating what already said in turn 7. When the customer explicitly requests for a refund and the agent texts back with an incorrect response related to a charge check, the customer eventually leaves the conversation.

Example 2 shows a case of customer non-cooperativity, with the customer refusing to repeat the question (not reported in the excerpt) in a way that is more understandable to the system. In this context, we interpreted the customer's non-cooperative attitude as a sign of frustration for an interaction that did not bring the expected results. The chatbot response in turn 5, instead, was evaluated as sufficiently empathic, for it offers an apology and proactively suggests the possibility to switch to a human agent (who is expected to provide a higher-quality assistance).

### 4.4 Qualitative Analysis

Although the dataset used for the annotation experiments is quite small to draw ultimate conclusions, we were still able to get valuable insights on the main dynamics underlying these customer-chatbot interactions. First, the error distributions reported in Tables 2–4 shows that both customers and chatbot mostly tend to produce messages that violate the maxim of Relevance, i.e. they produce messages that are irrelevant to the context of the conversation. In the case of customers, the most frequent errors within this class are those in which the customer does not take into account the previous message posted by the chatbot ("Ignoring question/feedback"), and the one in which the same content appears in multiple messages ("Repetition"). On the chatbot side, the most representative error of this class is the one where the chatbot asks the user to switch to another topic ("Topic change"). This is a typical expedient used by the system when it does not properly recognize the user's intent, and it is relevant in this context as, in turn, in 53% of cases this is the result of an error in the preceding message by the user (mostly "Ignoring question/feedback" and "Indirect response" errors).

With a further analysis, we also observed the co-occurrence of customers' errors and negative emotions in an attempt to provide an explanation of the errors produced by the customers and, conversely, to find an empirical basis of the emotion definitions we eventually elaborated in our guidelines. We found that the type of customers' errors that mostly co-occur with negative emotions are "Non-cooperativity" (83.3% of cases), "Excess of information" (50%) and "Repetition" (43.5%). Due to the higher sparsity, we discarded the other types. For such errors, frustration is the prevailing negative emotion in "Non-cooperativity" and "Repetition", while anger is the one that mostly occurs in the remaining one. Unlike the relation between "Non-cooperativity" and "Repetition" on one side, and frustration on the other, the association between anger and "Excess of information" seemed less intuitive and required a manual inspection of concrete examples from the dataset. What emerged is that the longer messages that typically occur in this error type are often due to the fact that the customer is experiencing several problems and on different levels (e.g., undue charges, poor service quality, inefficiencies, etc.). This contributes to increase customers' perception of unfair treatment and anger.

## 5  Agreement Results and Discussion

The first round of the annotation process was carried out by two independent annotators, following the guidelines. The Inter-Annotator Agreement (IAA) statistics, measured using the Cohen's $k$ coefficient (Cohen, 1960), were then computed after this step, and, as expected, they reported from moderate to low results. More specifically, we obtained a $k=0.46$ for error categories, $k=0.43$ for the agent's empathy and $k=0.28$ for customers' emotions. The resulting annotation was then reviewed to solve the cases of disagreement, which were discussed by an extended team including two other partners of the project.

The goal of this annotation work was to have the broader coverage possible of the problems encountered in a conversational context such as that of a customer service chat. Hence, the need to create a large and varied tagset. However, this variety has been at the expense of annotation consistency, as the IAA results show. Despite the presence of detailed guidelines, the subjectivity of the individual annotators proved to be crucial, and not only - as one would have expected - with respect to the choices regarding emotions and empathy, but also in the error annotation. In the latter, in fact, the highest disagreement was reported where, for the same turn, one annotator identified an error while the other did not, thus showing different perceptions of the dialogue state and its deviation from a regular path. With a similar trend, most of the disagreement in the annotation of emotions was detected when an annotator identified an emotion of some kind in the customer's message, whereas the other one perceived the message as completely neutral. The second main cause of disagreement for this dimension was the different perception of anger and frustration between the two annotators. Despite an agreed-upon definition of both emotions, in practice, different interpretations were often given to the users' messages and to the conversational contexts in this respect. By contrast, the fine-grained distinction between somewhat/very angry or frustrated did not cause substantial disagreement between the annotators and the conflation of the two labels into a single one, both for anger and frustration, did not significantly improve IAA results, while conflating Frustration and Anger into a single label increased the agreement rate to $k=0.40$. These findings brought to a revision of the definition of both emotions in the guidelines.

It is worth pointing out that when designing the scheme for this dimension, we took into account the fact that customers' interventions could be affected by the awareness of the medium used. For example, customers may consider that politeness is not required or that their messages should be as simple as possible for the machine to understand them and, accordingly, their interventions may result quite straightforward and could be wrongly believed to carry some kind of anger. Instead, what we actually observed in the sample set is that most often – maybe due to little familiarity with such tools – customers are not fully aware of this. They keep posing questions or answering to the chatbot's questions as if they were interacting with a real person. We hypothesize that frustration and anger may arise even due to this factor. An in-depth study will be carried out to verify if there is enough evidence to confirm it.

Agreement results on empathy are also moderate, even more so if compared to the ones obtained in Alam et al. (2018), who reported a Cohen's $k=0.74$, and whose definition of empathy has been used in this work. We attribute such divergence to the differences in the type of data collected, as Alam et al. (2018) focus on human-human spoken interactions, while in this work we deal with conversations between humans and a chatbot system with a relatively limited set of predefined responses. Whether the same response, in different conversational contexts, could be considered as sufficiently empathic was thus left at the annotator's discretion. All these issues prove once again the complexity of this task, especially considering that it deals with interactions on a text chat, rather than via spoken conversations, in which other factors such as acoustic and prosodic features can help discriminate. This is also the reason why the reviewing phase to solve these cases was extended to two other group members who had not participated in the first step, so as to reach a final version as widely shared as possible.

## 6  Conclusions

In this paper, we described the main features of an annotation scheme designed to label a sample set of interactions between customers and the chatbot of an Italian telecom customer service unit. The ultimate goal of this scheme and its applications on the sample data is to develop a rule-based NLG module to be integrated within the template-based chatbot system and intended to substitute template responses with more context-dependent responses, with an eye in particular on the improvement of explanations. With this purpose in mind, a set of dialogues was selected, where the customer requests for an explanation of some kind. The specific characteristics of these conversational contexts - errors of various nature from both parties, potential customer dissatisfaction as perceived within the dialogues, etc. - as well as the expected output of the NLG module under development motivated the way the scheme was devised.

The annotation experiments carried out to validate the scheme highlighted the significant role played by subjectivity of individual annotators, which is reflected by a moderate IAA, but also the need to further analyze the inherent meaning of some of the labels that proved to be more controversial (as, for example, the ones introduced to define anger and frustration in customers' messages), and to revise their usage accordingly. The annotation layer devoted to make the presence of negative emotions in the customer's message explicit was designed with the aim of improving the chatbot's awareness of the user's emotional state. Indeed, this information is essential as a basis for generating an emotion-aware and empathic response, which is the subject of future work. On this line, we also aim at investigating how to manage the cases of frustrated or angry users who insult the chatbot, in order to avoid escalation or responses where the chatbot shows himself unaware of the insult (Cercas Curry and Rieser, 2019).

## Acknowledgements

The work of Alessandro Mazzei, Manuela Sanguinetti and Viviana Patti has been partially funded by TIM s.p.a. (*Studi e Ricerche su Sistemi Conversazionali Intelligenti*, CENF_CT_RIC_19_01).

# References


Firoj Alam, Morena Danieli, and Giuseppe Riccardi. 2018. Annotating and modeling empathy in spoken conversations. *Computer Speech and Language*, 50:40 – 61.

Jeremy Ang, Rajdip Dhillon, Ashley Krupski, Elizabeth Shriberg, and Andreas Stolcke. 2002. Prosody-based automatic detection of annoyance and frustration in human-computer dialog. In *7th International Conference on Spoken Language Processing, ICSLP2002 - INTERSPEECH 2002, Denver, Colorado, USA, September 16-20, 2002*. ISCA.

Niels Ole Bernsen, Laila Dybkjær, and Hans Dybkjær. 1996. User errors in spoken human-machine dialogue. In *Proceedings of the ECAI '96 Workshop on Dialogue Processing in Spoken Language Systems*, ECAI '96, Berlin, Heidelberg. Springer-Verlag.

Or Biran and Kathleen McKeown. 2017. Human-centric justification of machine learning predictions. In *Proceedings of the Twenty-Sixth International Joint Conference on Artificial Intelligence, IJCAI-17*, pages 1461–1467. International Joint Conferences on Artificial Intelligence Organization.

Carlos Busso, Murtaza Bulut, Chi-Chun Lee, Abe Kazemzadeh, Emily Mower, Samuel Kim, Jeannette N. Chang, Sungbok Lee, and Shrikanth S. Narayanan. 2008. IEMOCAP: interactive emotional dyadic motion capture database. *Language Resources and Evaluation*, 42(4):335–359.

Amanda Cercas Curry and Verena Rieser. 2019. A crowd-based evaluation of abuse response strategies in conversational agents. In *Proceedings of the 20th Annual SIGdial Meeting on Discourse and Dialogue*, pages 361–366, Stockholm, Sweden, September. Association for Computational Linguistics.

Ankush Chatterjee, Kedhar Nath Narahari, Meghana Joshi, and Puneet Agrawal. 2019. SemEval-2019 task 3: EmoContext contextual emotion detection in text. In *Proceedings of the 13th International Workshop on Semantic Evaluation*, pages 39–48, Minneapolis, Minnesota, USA, June. Association for Computational Linguistics.

Jacob Cohen. 1960. A Coefficient of Agreement for Nominal Scales. *Educational and Psychological Measurement*, 20(1):37–46.

Francesco Cutugno, Maria Di Maro, Sara Falcone, Marco Guerini, Bernardo Magnini, and Antonio Origlia. 2018. Overview of the EVALITA 2018 evaluation of italian dialogue systems (IDIAL) task. In Tommaso Caselli, Nicole Novielli, Viviana Patti, and Paolo Rosso, editors, *Proceedings of the Sixth Evaluation Campaign of Natural Language Processing and Speech Tools for Italian. Final Workshop (EVALITA 2018) co-located with the Fifth Italian Conference on Computational Linguistics (CLiC-it 2018), Turin, Italy, December 12-13, 2018*, volume 2263 of *CEUR Workshop Proceedings*. CEUR-WS.org.

Mirko Di Lascio, Manuela Sanguinetti, Luca Anselma, Dario Mana, Alessandro Mazzei, Rossana Simeoni, and Viviana Patti. 2020. Natural language generation in dialogue systems for customer care. In *Proceedings of the 7th Italian Conference on Computational Linguistics (CLiC-It 2020)*. CEUR-ws.org.

Paul Ekman. 1992. An argument for basic emotions. *Cognition and Emotion*, 6(3-4):169–200.

Paul Grice. 1989. *Studies in the Way of Words*. Harvard University Press, Cambridge, Massachussets.

Jonathan Herzig, Guy Feigenblat, Michal Shmueli-Scheuer, David Konopnicki, Anat Rafaeli, Daniel Altman, and David Spivak. 2016. Classifying emotions in customer support dialogues in social media. In *Proceedings of the 17th Annual Meeting of the Special Interest Group on Discourse and Dialogue*, pages 64–73, Los Angeles, September. Association for Computational Linguistics.

Ryuichiro Higashinaka, Kotaro Funakoshi, Masahiro Araki, Hiroshi Tsukahara, Yuka Kobayashi, and Masahiro Mizukami. 2015a. Towards taxonomy of errors in chat-oriented dialogue systems. In *Proceedings of the 16th Annual Meeting of the Special Interest Group on Discourse and Dialogue*, pages 87–95, Prague, Czech Republic, September. Association for Computational Linguistics.

Ryuichiro Higashinaka, Masahiro Mizukami, Kotaro Funakoshi, Masahiro Araki, Hiroshi Tsukahara, and Yuka Kobayashi. 2015b. Fatal or not? finding errors that lead to dialogue breakdowns in chat-oriented dialogue systems. In *Proceedings of the 2015 Conference on Empirical Methods in Natural Language Processing*, pages 2243–2248, Lisbon, Portugal. Association for Computational Linguistics.

Ryuichiro Higashinaka, Kotaro Funakoshi, Yuka Kobayashi, and Michimasa Inaba. 2016. The dialogue breakdown detection challenge: Task description, datasets, and evaluation metrics. In Nicoletta Calzolari (Conference Chair), Khalid Choukri, Thierry Declerck, Sara Goggi, Marko Grobelnik, Bente Maegaard, Joseph Mariani, Helene Mazo, Asuncion Moreno, Jan Odijk, and Stelios Piperidis, editors, *Proceedings of the Tenth International Conference on Language Resources and Evaluation (LREC 2016)*, Paris, France. European Language Resources Association (ELRA).

Ryuichiro Higashinaka, Masahiro Araki, Hiroshi Tsukahara, and Masahiro Mizukami. 2018. Improving taxonomy of errors in chat-oriented dialogue systems. In *Proceedings of the Ninth International Workshop on Spoken Dialogue Systems Technology (IWSDS 2018)*.

Bertus F. Jeronimus and Odilia M. Laceulle. 2017. Frustration. In Virgil Zeigler-Hill and Todd K. Shackelford, editors, *Encyclopedia of Personality and Individual Differences*, pages 1–5. Springer International Publishing, Cham.

Yanran Li, Hui Su, Xiaoyu Shen, Wenjie Li, Ziqiang Cao, and Shuzi Niu. 2017. DailyDialog: A manually labelled multi-turn dialogue dataset. In *Proceedings of the Eighth International Joint Conference on Natural Language Processing (Volume 1: Long Papers)*, pages 986–995, Taipei, Taiwan, November. Asian Federation of Natural Language Processing.

Jackson Liscombe, Giuseppe Riccardi, and Dilek Hakkani-Tür. 2005. Using context to improve emotion detection in spoken dialog systems. In *INTERSPEECH 2005 - Eurospeech, 9th European Conference on Speech Communication and Technology*, pages 1845–1848. ISCA.

Yukun Ma, Khanh Linh Nguyen, Frank Z. Xing, and Erik Cambria. 2020. A survey on empathetic dialogue systems. *Information Fusion*, 64:50 – 70.

Bilyana Martinovsky and David Traum. 2003. The error is the clue: Breakdown in human-machine interaction. In *Proceedings of the ISCA Workshop on Error Handling in Dialogue Systems*.

Sebastian Möller, Klaus-Peter Engelbrecht, and Antti Oulasvirta. 2007. Analysis of communication failures for spoken dialogue systems. In *INTERSPEECH 2007, 8th Annual Conference of the International Speech Communication Association, Antwerp, Belgium, August 27-31, 2007*, pages 134–137. ISCA.

Raymond W. Novaco. 2017. Anger. In Virgil Zeigler-Hill and Todd K. Shackelford, editors, *Encyclopedia of Personality and Individual Differences*, pages 1–5. Springer International Publishing, Cham.

R. Plutchik. 1982. A psychoevolutionary theory of emotions. *Social Science Information*, 21:529 – 553.

S. Poria, N. Majumder, R. Mihalcea, and E. Hovy. 2019. Emotion recognition in conversation: Research challenges, datasets, and recent advances. *IEEE Access*, 7:100943–100953.

Alexander Schmitt, Stefan Ultes, and Wolfgang Minker. 2012. A parameterized and annotated spoken dialog corpus of the CMU let's go bus information system. In *Proceedings of the Eighth International Conference on Language Resources and Evaluation, LREC 2012, Istanbul, Turkey, May 23-25, 2012*, pages 3369–3373. European Language Resources Association (ELRA).

Ben Sheehan, Hyun Seung Jin, and Udo Gottlieb. 2020. Customer service chatbots: Anthropomorphism and adoption. *Journal of Business Research*, 115:14 – 24.

Gabriel Skantze. 2005. Exploring human error recovery strategies: Implications for spoken dialogue systems. *Speech Communication*, 45(3):325 – 341.

Kees Van Deemter, Emiel Krahmer, and Mariët Theune. 2005. Real versus template-based natural language generation: A false opposition? *Comput. Linguist.*, 31(1):15–24, March.

# Towards a standardized, fine-grained manual annotation protocol for verbal fluency data

Gabriel Frazer-McKee[1,2], Joël Macoir[1,2], Lydia Gagnon[1] & Pascale Tremblay[1,2]

[1]CERVO Brain Research Center, Quebec City, Canada
[2]Faculty of Medicine, Department of Rehabilitation, University Laval, Canada

## Abstract

We propose a new method for annotating verbal fluency data, which allows the reliable detection of the age-related decline of lexical access capacity. The main innovation is that annotators should inferentially assess the intention of the speaker when producing a word form during a verbal fluency test. Our method correlates probable speaker intentions such as "intended as a valid answer" or "intended as a meta-comment" with linguistic features such as word intensity (e.g. reduced intensity suggests private speech) and syntactic integration. The annotation scheme can be implemented with high reliability, and minimal linguistic training. When fluency data are annotated using this scheme, a relation between fluency and age emerges; this is in contrast to a strict implementation of the traditional method of annotating verbal fluency data, which has no way of dealing with score-confounding phenomena because it force-groups all verbal fluency productions –regardless of speaker intention— into one of three taxonomic groups (i.e. valid answers, perseverations, and intrusions). The traditional lack of fine-grained annotation units is especially problematic when analyzing the qualitatively distinct fluency data of older participants and may cause studies to miss the relation between lexical access capacity and age.

## 1  Introduction

Verbal fluency tasks (also known as verbal fluency tests; VFTs) are hybrid neuropsychological tasks (Shao et al., 2014) that assess both lexical access capacity –the capacity to retrieve lexical units from the mental lexicon (Indefrey & Levelt, 2004)— and executive function. In VFTs, participants are required to provide as many (non-repeated) words as possible that correspond to the experimental criteria within a time-limit (typically, 60 seconds). These criteria are either semantic (e.g. name as many animals as possible) or phonemic (e.g. list words that begin with the letter *P*). VFTs are amongst the most widely used language tasks in both research and clinical settings owing to their sensitivity to a wide variety of psycho-neurobiological phenomena –dementia (e.g. Troyer et al., 1997), bilingualism (e.g. Sandoval et al., 2010), and aging (e.g. Gordon et al., 2017), to name but these. Performance on these tasks has been used to characterize the fluency capacity of various groups, the classic performance measures being the number of correct answers, the number of intrusions (words that do not meet the experimental criteria), and the number of perseverations (correct answers that have been repeated) (e.g. Strauss et al., 2006).

While the traditional three-way taxonomy (i.e. correct answers, perseverations, intrusions) is easy to use and is widespread in the fluency literature (e.g. Ledoux et al., 2014; Strauss et al., 2006; Troyer et al., 1997), it has a serious shortcoming: it can only handle clean data. Consider, for instance, the following illustrative example of a series of verbal productions drawn from the T fluency condition. Font size is used to suggest speech intensity (volume), ellipsis is used to represent pauses, colons denote an





*The 14th Linguistic Annotation Workshop*, pages 160–166
Barcelona, Spain (Online), December 12, 2020.

elongated speech sound, dashes are used to denote temporal proximity, and forward slashes represent truncation; the data of interest is underlined:

1. Participant F027: *Tama/—tamarin!*
   [Tama (type of drum) tamarind! → **false start**]

2. Participant F038: *tro/* Euh *trottoir je l'ai dit*
   [side—! uhm, I already said *sidewalk* → **intentional repetition found in a comment**]

3. Participant F037: *trois! ta ... : ta: ... tapis!*
   [three! your ... your ... rug → **syllable play**]

The above illustrates some of the interesting, but potentially score-confounding phenomena found in fluency data: presumably attempts to connect contextually meaningless syllables (e.g. *ta: ta:*) with words stored in the mental lexicon (example 3 above), very much intentional repetitions (example 2 above), and unintentional false starts that happen to correspond to actual words (example 1 above).

Existing fluency protocols completely gloss over these types of phenomena (e.g. Strauss et al., 2006), but in our own fluency corpus we have observed that such phenomena are not unusual amongst cognitively healthy participants, especially older ones (see subsection 3 for some descriptive statistics). Importantly, it is well-documented that older adults experience not only a decline in lexical access but also have different narrative styles compared to younger adults, particularly when the task is difficult (Mortensen et al., 2006). It is therefore possible that older adults' verbal fluency data differs qualitatively compared to that of younger adults; to our knowledge, no verbal fluency study has investigated this issue to date. The open question is whether there are sufficient instances of these score-confounding phenomena in the fluency data to impact performance scores (and thus study findings) in one or more fluency conditions, and more specifically whether the performance measures in these conditions vary with age when score-confounding phenomena are controlled for. What is needed to investigate this research question is to separate the data of interest from score-confounding phenomena using a standardized, fine-grained taxonomy that allows fluency annotators to make replicable, theoretically-justified categorization choices based on linguistic features that correlate with specific, contextually-plausible communicative intentions. In this paper, we briefly describe such a taxonomy and report promising preliminary findings bearing on a) the reliability of our protocol's transcription-annotation process, and b) the effect this taxonomy has on two classic measures of fluency performance in younger and older adults compared to a strict implementation of the traditional annotation scheme.

## 2 Creation of the fluency corpus

To date, 38 depression-free (GDS-15≥5; Sheikh & Yesavage, 1986), cognitively-normal (MoCA≥26; Nasreddine et al., 2005), right-handed (Oldfield≥14; Oldfield, 1971) native speakers of French (age=62.3 years; SD=17.08; range=28-88; females=21; schooling=14.65 years; SD=2.17) have been audio-recorded during the execution of 4 verbal fluency tasks (letters: T-N-P; category: animals). Participants are classified into one of two age groups: younger (n=14; M=40.48 years; SD=8.76; range=22-54) and older (n=24; M=73.44 years; SD=6.71; range=65-88). Participants were recorded in a double-walled soundproof room (Génie Audio. Inc, Canada) using a Shure headset microphone (Microflex Beta 53) connected to a Quartet USB audio interface (Apogee Electronics, Santa Monica, CA 90404, USA) that fed into an iMac computer. This permitted the capture of very low-intensity phenomena (e.g. whispering). The recordings were made using Sound Studio 4 (Felt Tip Inc., NYC, USA) at a sampling rate of 48 kHz with 24 bits of quantization. Per traditional procedure (e.g. Strauss et al., 2006), participants were instructed to produce as many words as possible that corresponded to the experimenter-provided criteria within 60 seconds, avoiding repetitions, proper names, and words that merely have different suffixes (e.g. *pitch/pitched* or *cat/cats*). The fluency tasks were administered as a part of a battery of tests within a large on-going project that was approved (#1733-2018) by the neurosciences and health ethics review board of the *Centre intégré universitaire de la santé et des services sociaux de la Capitale Nationale* (translation: Integrated Health and Social Services Centre of the National Capital) in Quebec City, Canada. The raw fluency audio recordings were transcribed and annotated in Praat

(Boersma & van Heuven, 2001) using the extended version of the transcription-annotation scheme described below (see Appendix B).

## 3   Towards a finer-grained annotation scheme: The linguistic correlates of intent

Our expanded fluency taxonomy rests on two fundamental assumptions. Firstly, a fluency taxonomy should be comprised of categories that reflect speaker communicative intentions. Simply put, the issue is not whether the *fluency annotators* can associate –using all knowledge at their disposal— a given phonetic sequence within the data with conceptual content and thereby categorize the sequence using some rule-scheme. The issue, fundamentally, is whether one can reasonably infer that the *speaker* associated the sequence with conceptual content at the moment of verbalization, and, what is more, whether they produced the sequence to *satisfy* the experimental criteria (intentionality).

Our second fundamental assumption is that speaker intent has linguistic correlates (cf. Sperber & Wilson, 2002). Using a corpus-driven approach (Biber, 2009), we associated probable pragmatic intentions (e.g. intent to satisfy the experimental criteria, etc.) with syntactic and phonetic features. The taxonomy's key categories are briefly described below; a full list can be found in Appendix B. Percentage frequency of occurrence of each of the annotation units is featured in parentheses in the manner that follows: relative frequency in the whole corpus, relative frequency in the fluency data of adults aged 28-54, and relative frequency in the fluency data of adults aged 65+. Features that served to make annotation decisions are also included in each description.

1. **Correct answers** (56.10% / 28-54: 59.06% / 65+: 54.51%): verbal productions that a) meet the category-criteria, and b) were <u>intended</u> by the speaker to satisfy the experimental criteria (i.e. to be answers); they are fully pronounced words that are typically the loudest verbal productions in the data (per visual inspection of the spectrograms of 100 randomly selected datapoints from our fluency corpus); they tend to cluster with other correct answers and/or vocalics.

2. **Perseverations** (2.21% / 28-54: 1.19% / 65+: 2.82%): repetition of a previous answer (often with intervening linguistic material between the two instances); participants are sometimes aware of these mistakes (cf. Day, 1979). *Conscious* perseverations are typically followed by a) a vocalic that indicates error awareness or b) a meta-comment such as *"said it"*. Conscious perseverations can also be truncated (e.g. *side—uhm [sidewalk]*). Otherwise, perseverations usually have the phonetic/syntactic characteristics of correct answers.

3. **Vocalics** (23.43% / 28-54: 27.22% / 65+: 20.80%): paralinguistic verbal productions, such as sighs, hesitations, frustration noises, etc. (Burgoon et al., 2016); they often occur between (clusters of) answers (where they indicate active search) or follow truncated phonemic sequences (where they serve to evaluate the verbal production).

4. **Self-talk** (2.31% / 28-54: 1.26% / 65+: 2.93%): (repeated) (correct) answers that are instances of "thinking-out-loud" during a cognitive task (cf. Duncan & Cheyne, 2001) rather than perseverations per se, as evidenced by a) (dramatically) lowered voice intensity –a feature associated with the notion of privacy (Cirillo, 2004)— or b) syntactic integration with a temporally proximate meta-comment (e.g. *uhm, I said sidewalk*);

5. **Meta-comments** (6.89% / 28-54: 5.97% / 65+: 7.42%): comments on the participant's own performance or on something the participant just said (e.g. *aunt –person; ant –insect*) or a remark/question on the experimental task itself (McDowd et al., 2011; Roberts & Le Dorze, 1997); often delivered at a comparatively rapid rate of speech and considerably lower intensity than correct answers, per visual inspection of the spectrograms of 50 randomly selected meta-comments from our fluency corpus.

6. **Syllable play** (5.02% / 28-54: 1.46% / 65+: 7.02%): a syllable in the participant's language that could be considered as a word (i.e. conventional form-meaning pairing) but that is either a) a false start (e.g. *tama—tamarind*) or that b) the participant has likely failed to associate with lexical content, as evidenced by following meta-comments or acoustic characteristics such as vowel elongation and reduced speech intensity (e.g. *pa: pa: Ah, come on!*). Instances of syllable play tend to be clustered together or to occur shortly before a correct answer/perseveration.

## 4   Testing the new annotation scheme

In the following, we assess our fluency annotation scheme's reliability as well as its effect on two classic measures of fluency performance. We also show that our fluency protocol is sensitive to age-related decline of lexical access, and that this decline emerges largely because of the way in which syllable play and self-talk are handled by our inferential annotation scheme.

## 4.1 Measures of agreement

17.5% of the transcriptions (n=7 participants; 823 unique datapoints) and 47.5% of the annotations (n=19 participants; 2062 datapoints) have been independently analyzed by two annotators. Raw agreement for both the transcriptions and annotations is excellent, averaging respectively 95.26% and 99.38% between the 4 fluency conditions (see Tables 3 and 4 in Appendix A for condition-specific details). The overall intra-class correlation coefficient (ICC) for the annotations of the fluency corpus is also excellent (0,987; see Table 4 in Appendix A for condition-specific details), per well-known magnitude interpretations of ICCs (e.g. Koo & Mae, 2016). Our annotation protocol's ICC is very comparable to the ICCs of the traditional taxonomy (e.g. ≈0.98 in Passos et al., 2011). Thus, taking considerably more phenomena into consideration does not adversely affect the accuracy or the reliability of the transcription-annotation process.

## 4.2 Comparison of the two annotation protocols

The true test of our taxonomy is whether it offers concrete empirical advantages –for instance, whether it reveals different associations between age groups and performance measures compared to an annotation scheme that has no way of handling score-confounding phenomena.

A linear mixed model with participants as random intercepts was used to evaluate the interaction between age (inter-subject categorical variable), annotation system (intra-subject variable), and number of correct answers (dependent variable) in each of the fluency conditions (N, P, T and Animals). The traditional system was found to yield more correct answers than our protocol in the T ($p < 0.001$) and N ($p > 0.01$) fluency conditions (Table 1A).

|  | A. Number of correct answers | B. Number of perseverations |
|---|---|---|
|  | (Linear Mixed Model) | (Mann-Whitney U test) |
| N | $p < 0.000$ | $p < 0.048$ |
| P | assumption violation | $p < 0.033$ |
| T | $p < 0.01$ | $p < 0.018$ |
| Animals | assumption violation | $p < 0.043$ |

Table 1. Comparison of two fluency protocols along two classic performance parameters: number of correct answers and number of perseverations ($\alpha$=0.05)

What is more, a statistically significant interaction was found between age and type of protocol in the T ($p < 0.05$) and N ($p < 0.010$) conditions: while the traditional taxonomy suggests that fluency performance is stable in these conditions with age, our inferential system suggests that phonemic fluency performance declines slightly with age.

Since a) the perseveration data were not distributed normally and b) were relatively infrequent to begin with, it was not possible to use a linear mixed model to assess their relationship with taxonomy-type and participant age. We therefore performed a Mann-Whitney U test to determine whether the two protocols (independent variable) yield significantly different perseveration scores (dependent variable) in each of the fluency conditions. The traditional taxonomy was found to produce significantly higher perseveration scores in all of the fluency conditions (see Table 1B).

As was predicted, the protocol-x-age interaction effect was found to largely be due to the prevalence of self-talk and syllable play in the two age groups and how these data are respectively handled by the two protocols. Significant differences were found between younger and older participants' use of syllable play and self-talk, per Table 2 below:

|  | Syllable play | | Self-talk | |
|---|---|---|---|---|
|  | 28-54 (n=14) | 65+ (n=24) | 28-54 (n=14) | 65+ (n=24) |
| N | 14.29% | 62.50% | 14.29% | 50.00% |
| P | 21.42% | 50.00% | 21.42% | 16.67% |
| T | 35.71% | 75.00% | 21.42% | 58.33% |
| Animals | 0.00% | 0.00% | 14.29% | 48.00% |

Table 2. Percentage of participants who produced at least one instance of syllable play/self-talk according to age-group (28-54 vs. 65+)

These two categories account for only just over 7% of the corpus (see subsection 3 of this article), but are not evenly distributed according to age-group. Compared to the younger participants, older participants were between 1.9x to over 4x more likely to produce at least one instance of self-talk or syllable play in all but one fluency condition (i.e. self-talk in the P fluency condition).

## 5 Discussion and future work

The traditional fluency taxonomy has been used for decades but it offers no formally codified means to avoid the force-grouping of data that have fundamentally different cognitive causes (e.g. correct answers and syllable play), and whose use may, crucially, differ across the adult lifespan. Given that fluency scores are typically based on a mere 60 seconds of verbal production and that differences in fluency performance between groups are often modest to begin with (e.g. Macoir et al., 2019), the non-systematic treatment of score-confounding phenomena has the potential to alter individual performance scores (and thereby study results). The accuracy of the annotation process is thus not a trivial matter, particularly for studies with small effect sizes and/or studies with small sample sizes (where annotation choices carry comparatively greater statistical weight). If fluency studies are to be maximally consistent and their results maximally comparable, the handling of fluency data cannot fall under the scope of "researcher degrees of freedom" –undeclared "flexibility in data collection, analysis, and reporting" (Simmons et al., 2011, p. 1359). A detailed, publicly accessible annotation protocol –one that weighs the linguistic evidence that bears upon the participant-speaker's communicative intentions— is required to separate the fluency data into finer-grained categories in a non-arbitrary manner so that cognitively similar phenomena of interest may be identified and isolated for the purpose of statistical analysis. The extended fluency taxonomy briefly described and tested here constitutes a promising first step towards such a standardized transcription-annotation fluency protocol. Preliminary results suggest that a) the protocol is highly implementable, as evidenced by excellent agreement and reliability scores; b) it requires minimal linguistic training (as evidenced by its successful use by LG, a first year undergraduate Linguistics student); and c) most importantly, it yields non-inflated fluency performance scores compared to a purely mechanistic implementation of the traditional fluency taxonomy. Preliminary findings suggest that the adoption of such a protocol is particularly germane for the comparative analysis of the verbal fluency data of adult participants of different ages. Based on our corpus here, we suggest that older adults tend to produce qualitatively distinct fluency data compared to younger adults (likely as a compensatory strategy for declining lexical access ability), hence why the two annotation schemes produce significantly dissimilar performance measures for this group).

With a new, finer-grained annotation scheme to structure the data also come new, exciting research questions. Does the use of fillers and self-talk in fluency data vary along sociodemographic and/or cognitive parameters? What proportion of fluency errors are cognitively normal participants aware of? How effective is syllable play as a word identification strategy and is its effectiveness moderated by age? Do older participants who use lexical access strategies such as self-talk and syllable play achieve lesser or greater performance scores according to our fluency protocol? Perhaps most importantly of all, might the controversy regarding the maintenance or decline of phonemic fluency performance over the lifespan (cf. Gordon et al., 2017) be partly attributable to inconsistent annotation procedures between fluency studies? We intend to soon investigate these and other questions using a considerably expanded fluency corpus (120-150 participants).

## Acknowledgements

Authors' contributions: Gabriel Frazer-McKee (data collection and analysis, study conceptualization, article drafting and revision); Joël Macoir (study conceptualization, article revision); Lydia Gagnon (data collection and analysis, article revision); Pascale Tremblay (funding acquisition, project supervision, study conceptualization, article revision).

The authors thank the following for their contributions: Valérie Brisson (statistical advice), Elisabeth Maillard (data collection), Alison Arseneault (data collection), Sophie Simard (data collection), Catherine Savard (data collection), Julia Picard (data collection), and all of the study's participants. The authors would also like to sincerely thank the two anonymous evaluators for their insightful and encouraging comments on the submitted version of this article.

This work was supported by a grant to Pascale Tremblay from the Fonds de recherche Nature et Technologies du Québec (2019-PR-254714), and a Globalink research internship from MITACS. Pascale Tremblay holds a Career award from the *Fonds de la Recherche en Santé du Québec* (FRQ-S, #35016).

## References

Biber, D. (2009). Corpus-based and corpus-driven analyses of language variation and use. In B. Heine & H. Narrog (Eds.), *The Oxford handbook of linguistic analysis* (pp. 193–224). Oxford University Press.

Boersma, P., & van Heuven, V. (2001). Speak and unSpeak with PRAAT. *Glot International, 5*(9–10), 341–347.

Burgoon, J. K., Guerrero, L. K., & Manusov, V. (2016). *Nonverbal Communication*. Routledge.

Cirillo, J. (2004). Communication by unvoiced speech: The role of whispering. *Anais Da Academia Brasileira de Ciências, 76*(2), 413–423.

Day, R. S. (1979). Verbal fluency and the language-bound effect. In C. J. Fillmore, D. Kempler, & W. S.-Y. Wang (Eds.), *Individual differences in language ability and language behavior* (pp. 57–84). Academic Press.

Duncan, R. M., & Cheyne, J. A. (2001). Private speech in young adults: Task difficulty, self-regulation, and psychological predication. *Cognitive Development, 16*(4), 889–906.

Gordon, J. K., Young, M., & Garcia, C. (2017). Why do older adults have difficulty with semantic fluency? *Aging, Neuropsychology, and Cognition, 25*(6), 1–26.

Indefrey, P., & Levelt, W. J. M. (2004). The spatial and temporal signatures of word production components. *Cognition, 92*, 101–144.

Koo, T. K., & Mae, Y. L. (2016). A guideline of selecting and reporting Intraclass Correlation Coefficients for reliability research. *Journal of Chiropractic Medicine, 15*(2), 155–163.

Ledoux, K., Vannorsdall, T. D., Pickett, E. J., Bosley, L. V., Gordon, B., & Schretlen, D. J. (2014). Capturing additional information about the organization of entries in the lexicon from verbal fluency productions. *Journal of Clinical and Experimental Neuropsychology, 36*(2), 205–220.

Macoir, J., Lafay, A., & Hudon, C. (2019). Reduced lexical access to verbs in individuals with Subjective Cognitive Decline. *American Journal of Alzheimer's Disease & Other Dementias, 34*(1), 1–15.

McDowd, J., Hoffman, L., Rozek, E., Lyons, K. E., Pahwa, R., Burns, J., & Kemper, S. (2011). Understanding verbal fluency in healthy aging, Alzheimer's disease, and Parkinson's disease. *Neuropsychology, 25*(2), 210–225.

Mortensen, L., Meyer, A. S., & Humphreys, G. W. (2006). Age-related effects on speech production: A review. *Language and Cognitive Processes, 21*(1–3), 238–290.

Nasreddine, Z. S., Phillips, N. A., Bédirian, V., Charbonneau, S., Whitehead, V., Collin, I., Cummings, J. L., & Chertkow, H. (2005). The Montreal Cognitive Assessment, MoCA: A brief screening tool for mild cognitive impairment. *Journal of the American Geriatrics Society, 53*(4), 695–699.

Oldfield, R. C. (1971). The assessment and analysis of handedness: The Edinburgh Inventory. *Neuropsychologia, 9*, 97–113.

Passos, V. M. de A., Giatti, L., Barreto, S. M., Figuereido, R. C., Caramelli, P., Benseñor, I., & Trinidade, A. A. M. da. (2011). Passos, V. M. de A., Giatti, L., Barreto, S. M., Figueiredo, R. C., Caramelli, P., Benseñor, I., … Trindade, A. A. M. da. (2011). Verbal fluency tests reliability in a Brazilian multicentric study, ELSA-Brasil. , 69(5), 814–816. Doi:10.1590/s0004-282x2011000600017. *Arquivos de Neuro-Psiquiatria, 69*(5), 814–816.

Roberts, P. M., & Le Dorze, G. (1997). Semantic organization, strategy use, and productivity in bilingual semantic verbal fluency. *Brain & Language, 59*(3), 412–449.

Sandoval, T. C., Gollan, T. H., Ferreira, V. S., & Salmon, D. P. (2010). What causes the bilingual disadvantage in verbal fluency? The dual-task analogy. *Bilingualism: Language and Cognition, 13*(2), 231–252.

Shao, Z., Janse, E., Visser, K., & Meyer, A. S. (2014). What do verbal fluency tasks measure? Predictors of verbal fluency performance in older adults. *Frontiers in Psychology*, *5*(772), 1–10.

Sheikh, J. I., & Yesavage, J. A. (1986). Geriatric Depression Scale (GDS): Recent evidence and development of a shorter version. *Clinical Gerontologist: The Journal of Aging and Mental Health*, *5*(1–2), 165–173.

Simmons, J. P., Nelson, L. D., & Simonsohn, U. (2011). False-positive psychology: Undisclosed flexibility in data collection and analysis allows presenting anything as significant. *Psychological Science*, *22*(11).

Sperber, D., & Wilson, D. (2002). Pragmatics, Modularity and Mind-reading. *Mind & Language*, *17*(1), 3–33.

Strauss, E., Sherman, E. S., & Spreen, O. (2006). Verbal fluency. In *A compendium of neuropsychological tests: Administration, norms, and commentary* (pp. 499–526). Oxford University Press.

Troyer, A. K., Moscovitch, M., & Winocur, G. (1997). Clustering and switching as two components of verbal fluency: Evidence from younger and older healthy adults. *Neuropsychology*, *11*(1), 138–146.

## Appendix A. Detailed agreement measure tables.

|  | Agreements | Disagreements | Raw agreement |
|---|---|---|---|
| **N** | 164 | 14 | 92.13% |
| **P** | 184 | 4 | 97.87% |
| **T** | 175 | 11 | 94.09% |
| **Animals** | 261 | 14 | 94.91% |
| Total | 784 | 39 | 95.26% |

Table 3. Inter-rater agreement for transcription decisions based on a subsample of the fluency corpus' participants (n=7)

|  | Agreements | Disagreements | Raw agreement | *ICC |
|---|---|---|---|---|
| **N** | 424 | 4 | 99.07% | 0.974 |
| **P** | 472 | 4 | 99.15% | 0.991 |
| **T** | 506 | 2 | 99.61% | 0.997 |
| **Animals** | 647 | 3 | 99.56% | 0.983 |
| Total | 2049 | 13 | 99.37% | 0.987 |

Table 4. Inter-rater agreement and reliability for annotation decisions based on a subsample of the fluency corpus' participants (n=19)

*ICC=Intra-class Correlation Coefficient (average measure)

## Appendix B. The current annotation scheme (in alphabetic order).

* diacritic appended to errors to indicate participant error awareness (e.g. *INTRU); **CONTINU** Continuous perseveration (e.g. *Bee! ...Bee*). **CORR** Correction (e.g. repetition of a word with clearer or with more prestigious pronunciation). **F** false start  (e.g. *p— pr—*). **HMPHN** Homophone (a type of correct answer). **INTRU** Intrusion. **META** Meta-comment. **NONCE** Nonce word. **PHON** Phonological error (e.g. cat + dog → *cog!*). **PRP** Proper name (type of intrusion). **RECUR** Recurrent perseveration (e.g. *cow, ox, cow*). **SELF** Self-talk. **SYLLAB** Syllable (play). **VAL** Correct answer; **VOC** Vocalic.

# pyMMAX2: Deep Access to MMAX2 Projects from Python

**Mark-Christoph Müller**
Heidelberg Institute for Theoretical Studies gGmbH
Heidelberg, Germany
mark-christoph.mueller@h-its.org

## Abstract

pyMMAX2 is an API for processing MMAX2 stand-off annotation data in Python. It provides a lightweight basis for the development of code which opens up the Java- and XML-based ecosystem of MMAX2 for more recent, Python-based NLP and data science methods. While pyMMAX2 is pure Python, and most functionality is implemented from scratch, the API re-uses the complex implementation of the essential business logic for MMAX2 annotation schemes by interfacing with the original MMAX2 Java libraries. pyMMAX2 is available for download at http://github.com/nlpAThits/pyMMAX2.

## 1 Introduction

MMAX2[1] (Müller and Strube, 2006) is a multi-level annotation tool implemented in Java, with a focus on rich, discourse-level features in small to mid-sized corpora. MMAX2 has been used in many different annotation projects (e.g. Desmet and Hoste (2010), Dipper et al. (2011), Liu (2011), Hendrickx et al. (2012), Schäfer et al. (2012), Martínez et al. (2016), Lapshinova-Koltunski et al. (2019), Faessler et al. (2020), and Uryupina et al. (2020)), and a considerable number of richly annotated data sets are available in the MMAX2 stand-off annotation format.

This short paper introduces pyMMAX2[2], an API for processing MMAX2 stand-off annotation data in Python (3.6 or higher). pyMMAX2 provides a lightweight basis for the development of code which opens up the Java- and XML-based ecosystem of MMAX2 for more recent, Python-based NLP and data science methods. This way, existing MMAX2 data sets are easily made available for processing in Python. At the same time, the creation of *new* MMAX2 annotation projects (either from raw or pre-annotated data) is facilitated, thus potentially lowering the entry barriers for using the tool for manual annotation. pyMMAX2 is written in pure Python, and most functionality is implemented from scratch, taking advantage of powerful libraries from the Python ecosystem. However, for the *annotation scheme* business logic, which constitutes an essential component of MMAX2, the API re-uses the complex original Java implementation, by transparently interfacing with the MMAX2 Java libraries at run time (cf. Section 2.2 below). It is in this sense that pyMMAX2 provides 'deep' access to MMAX2 projects.

pyMMAX2 is intended as a general-purpose API to support and encourage the development of modern, lightweight, and flexible Python code for accessing MMAX2 projects. As such, it replaces the built-in MMAX2 Project Wizard with its only rudimentary functionality, and the MMAX2 Discourse API (Müller and Strube, 2002) with its dependence on Java. Another way of creating MMAX2 data sets from pre-annotated data is by using one of the well-established annotation converters which support MMAX2 both as source and target format. These include e.g. PAULA (Chiarcos et al., 2008), the PEPPER framework (Zipser and Romary, 2010), or discoursegraphs (Neumann, 2015). For conversion among common, supported data formats, these tools are clearly the best choice. However, when it comes to processing pre-annotated data in a less common or entirely idiosyncratic format, more flexible

---



[1]https://github.com/nlpAThits/MMAX2

[2]Available for download at https://github.com/nlpAThits/pyMMAX2



*The 14th Linguistic Annotation Workshop*, pages 167–173
Barcelona, Spain (Online), December 12, 2020.

solutions are required, because adding support for a new format to e.g. PEPPER can quickly bring about development overhead which is unjustified for a one-off data conversion requirement.

When compared to newer tools like e.g. brat (Stenetorp et al., 2012), WebAnno (Yimam et al., 2013), and INCEpTION (Klie et al., 2018).[3], MMAX2 is quite different. These tools are all web-based, supporting distributed annotation, role-based annotation project management, and other advanced features. While there are clearly settings that can benefit from the infrastructure and control offered by these tools, including annotation projects with a large number of annotators, there is also a considerable overhead involved here. MMAX2, in contrast, is completely self-contained, light-weight, and requires no installation.

## 2 The pyMMAX2 API in a Nutshell

In MMAX2 parlance, the term *basedata* is used for tokenized text, which is the basis of every annotation project. Annotations for (potentially non-contiguous) sequences of basedata elements exist in the form of *markable* objects, which refer to the IDs of their underlying basedata elements by means of their `span` attribute, and which contain the actual annotations in the form of attribute-value pairs. Markables are organized in named *markable levels*, each of which can be dedicated to representing a particular (linguistic or other) phenomenon. For each markable level, there is a so-called *annotation scheme* which defines the attributes and permissible values resp. value combinations that can be assigned to markables on that level.

MMAX2 basedata, markables, and annotation schemes are all stored as XML files. For each MMAX2 project, references to these files are stored in a `.mmax` file and a `common_paths.xml`[4] file. Access to a MMAX2 project is established through a single *discourse* object, which serves as the single entry point from which all related data can be accessed.

With the exception of the annotation schemes (cf. Section 2.2), pyMMAX2 implements all of the above-mentioned objects (and several more) straightforwardly in pure Python, making use of tried and tested libraries like Beautiful Soup. This approach results in compact, fast, and easily extensible code. In general, the philosophy of pyMMAX2 is to offer lightweight Python objects with transparent functionality as a foundation for the development of more advanced annotation processing functionality.

### 2.1 Basedata Creation, Rendering, and Matching

Basedata elements are the smallest units that annotations can be associated with. They are individual tokens (mostly words and punctuation) in a simple XML format which assigns, as the only *required* attribute, an ID to each token, which is then used in markables' `span` attributes. In addition, basedata elements can have an arbitrary number of user-defined, XML-compliant attributes. These basedata-level attributes are expressly *not* intended for storing annotations (which are supposed to be on the level of markables), but they are used by the pyMMAX2 BASEDATA class for storing tokenization meta-information. This class contains the method `add_elements_from_string()` for creating basedata elements from raw Unicode strings. The method includes a basedata tokenizer which uses Unicode character categories[5] for determining token boundaries in the input string in a universal, language-independent way. This procedure is rather aggressive, creating considerably more and shorter tokens than 'standard' tokenizers, which are often only sensitive to white space and punctuation. Most notably, the basedata tokenizer will also split the input string at word-internal non-word characters, including hyphens. As a result, hyphenated words (e.g. noun compounds and other hyphenated multi-word expressions) will be spread across several contiguous basedata elements, allowing for more fine-grained annotation.[6] At the same time, the tokenizer keeps track of the original input string composition, including white space, and stores, for

---

[3]See also Neves and Ševa (2019) for an extensive overview.

[4]As the name implies, the latter file collects information that is used by more than one MMAX2 project. By default, each MMAX2 project expects a `common_paths.xml` file in the same folder as the `.mmax` file, but this can be overridden by supplying a different file at startup (cf. the example in Section 2.2 below).

[5]`http://www.unicode.org/reports/tr44/#General_Category_Values`

[6]This is particularly useful for expressions appearing in both *open* and *hyphenated* spellings. It prevents the arbitrary spelling difference from introducing two separate and one hyphenated basedata elements, which would be completely unrelated due to the atomic nature of basedata elements, while they actually represent the same lexemes.

every basedata element, the number of leading white space characters $<> 1$ (default) in the element's `spc` attribute. This tokenization meta-data can be utilized in the following ways: First, it is available to the XSL style sheets which are used to build the MMAX2 GUI for annotation. Second, and more importantly, it is used by the `render_string()` method of the BASEDATA class, which accepts a list of basedata element IDs and returns the reconstructed original input string, a list containing the basedata elements' text, and a dictionary which maps string positions (as keys) to basedata IDs (as values). The following code snippet demonstrates this functionality.

```
from pymmax2 import pyMMAX2 as pmx
bd = pmx.Basedata('sample_basedata.xml', encoding='utf-8')
bd_ids = bd.add_elements_from_string('Self-isolation for 14 days is required!')
s,w,m = bd.render_string(for_ids=[bd_ids], mapping=True)
print ("%s\n%s\n%s"%(s,w,m))

>> Self-isolation for 14 days is required!
>> ['Self', '-', 'isolation', 'for', '14', 'days', 'is', 'required', '!']
>> {0: 'word_0', 1: 'word_0', 2: 'word_0', 3: 'word_0', 4: 'word_1', ...
   34: 'word_7', 35: 'word_7', 36: 'word_7', 37: 'word_7', 38: 'word_8'}
```

The `spc` attribute default value of 1 makes sure that the method also works with older MMAX2 basedata. The BASEDATA class also supports tokenization-agnostic regular expression (RegEx) matching, which uses the above method to render the original string for all or selected basedata IDs, applies a list of one or more RegExs, and returns, for each RegEx, the IDs of the matched basedata elements. RegExs are required to have a named capturing group m (see example below), which is used to determine the relevant part of the match. Optionally, a descriptive label can be assigned to each RegEx, which is returned alongside all of its matches. The following code snippet demonstrates the matching functionality, where each RegEx yields exactly one match.

```
# This uses the previously defined bd and bd_ids objects
for m,p,l in bd.match_string([(r'(?P<m>\S-\S)','hyphen'),(r'(?P<m>\d)','numeric')], for_ids=[bd_ids]):
    print ("%s\t%s"%(m,l))

>> [[['word_0', 'word_1', 'word_2']]] hyphen
>> [[['word_4']], [['word_4']]] numeric
```

## 2.2 Annotation Schemes & Validation

For each markable level in a MMAX2 project, there can be one *annotation scheme* which defines the attributes and permissible values resp. value combinations that can be assigned to markables on that level. Annotation schemes can be very complex and expressive, which makes them a central component of MMAX2. They can include dependencies between attributes, such that some attribute will only be valid (and available for manual annotation in the MMAX2 GUI) if some other attribute has a particular value. From the viewpoint of user ergonomics in an actual manual MMAX2 annotation setting, a well-designed annotation scheme can support annotators by prompting them to provide values for only those attributes that are permissible in the current situation, based on previous annotations of the same markable, and by doing so *one attribute at a time*. And, even more importantly, from the viewpoint of annotation data management, annotation schemes are essential for enforcing correctness and consistency of annotations by means of validation. Due to their essential role and complex annotation business logic, the handling of annotation schemes is not re-implemented in the pyMMAX2 API. Instead, a *hybrid* approach is used which accesses functionality from the original MMAX2 Java code base in the background. Technically, this is realized at Python execution time by instantiating and accessing MMAX2 Java classes by means of JPype[7]. JPype allows Python programs full access to Java class libraries, interfacing both the Python and Java virtual machines at the native level. The following code snippet demonstrates the functionality by opening a file from the ACL Anthology Corpus (Schäfer et al., 2012) which consists of ACL papers annotated for coreference. The original annotation was done with MMAX2 and the dataset is freely available[8].

---

[7]https://github.com/jpype-project/jpype/
[8]http://dfki.de/~uschaefer/C12-2103-dataset/C12-2103-dataset.zip

```
from pymmax2 import pyMMAX2 as pmx
import jpype
MMAX2_CP = PATH_TO_MMAX2_LIBS # path to all MMAX2-related jar files
jpype.startJVM(jpype.getDefaultJVMPath(), '-Djava.class.path='+MMAX2_CP)

pd = pmx.MMAX2Discourse('./C12-2103/annotation/C/C02-1001/C02-1001.mmax',
                        common_paths='./C12-2103/common/common_paths.xml',
                        mmax2_java_binding=jpype)
try:
    pd.load_markables()
except pmx.MultipleInvalidMMAX2AttributeExceptions as mive:
    print('%s exceptions, e.g.\n%s'%(str(mive.get_exception_count()),
                                str(mive.get_exception_at(0)).strip())))
pd.info()

>> MMAX2 Project Info:
>> --------------------
>> .mmax file         : ./C12-2103/annotation/C/C02-1001/C02-1001.mmax
>> Basedata elements  : 2471
>> Markable levels    :
>>    coref            : 216 markables [default: <>NP_Form:none, Sure:yes]
>>    sentence         : 126 markables [default: imported_tag_type:]
```

The existing MMAX2 project is accessed through a MMAX2DISCOURSE object, which is created by
providing the `.mmax` file name and (optionally) a `common_paths` parameter which allows to use an
alternative `common_paths.xml` file.[9] After the creation of the MMAX2DISCOURSE object, markables are loaded via an explicit call to its `load_markables()` method. The subsequent call to the
`info()` method prints some project info to the console. It includes the default attribute-value pairs
for each markable level, which are obtained by querying the MMAX2 Java code for annotation scheme
handling in the background.[10]

When calling `load_markables()`, all markables on all markable levels will be loaded *and validated*
against their respective annotation schemes. In line with the general pyMMAX2 philosophy mentioned
in Section 2 above, the role of validation is to detect and inform about annotation inconsistencies, but it
does not include fixing or consolidating them. This is mainly because, at least for a significant subset
of possible annotation inconsistencies, there is no simple, *default* way of dealing with them. Validation is implemented on the level of the individual markable, because it is here that annotation inconsistencies occur. Markable attributes are set via the `set_attributes()` method, which will raise
an INVALIDMMAX2ATTRIBUTEEXCEPTION if inconsistencies are detected. The provided attributes,
however, will be set nonetheless. The raised exception provides details about the validation problem,
making it the user's responsibility to decide how to handle it. In order to allow bulk loading and validation of markables (as in the `load_markables()` method), all exceptions raised while validating
individual markables are collected, and if at least one exception was raised, a MULTIPLEINVALID-
MMAX2ATTRIBUTEEXCEPTIONS exception will be raised in turn, which provides access to detailed
information on the contained exceptions. The effect of validation can be observed when temporarily
removing the possible value `ne` from the `np_form` attribute in the annotation scheme for the coref level.
Running the above code again will produce the output below.

```
58 exceptions, e.g.
Level: coref, ID: markable_825
Supplied: {'coref_class': 'set_114', 'sure': 'yes', 'np_form': 'ne'}
Valid:    {'sure': 'yes'}
Extra:    {'coref_class': 'set_114', 'np_form': 'ne'}
```

Note how the `coref_class` attribute is not recognized as valid because it depends on the `np_form`
attribute having a valid value itself.

### 2.3 Creating a New MMAX2 Project from Pre-Annotated Data

The LitCovid dataset[11] (Chen et al., 2020) contains almost 45,000 Covid-19-related documents. It has
annotations in the BioC XML format (Comeau et al., 2013) for six different biomedical entity types. In

---

[9]For collections consisting of many homogeneous MMAX2 projects (like the ACL Anthology Corpus), providing a *global*
`common_paths.xml` file in this way is strongly recommended, because it allows to maintain properties shared by all projects
(e.g. adding and removing of markable levels, styles, customizations, etc.) in a single place.

[10]If no `mmax2_java_binding` parameter is provided, this information is not available.

[11]https://ftp.ncbi.nlm.nih.gov/pub/lu/LitCovid/

a nut shell, each document comes as a sequence of `<passage>` elements, each containing a `<text>` element and one or more `<annotation>` elements, which associate annotations with the passage text by means of character offsets and lengths. The following two code fragments demonstrate the creation of a new MMAX2 project from a single LitCovid document (ID 32393453). Two simple annotation schemes for the passages and the entities level, covering all defined values plus a `none` value as default, were created manually. The first code snippet creates some helper objects and a rudimentary MMAX2DISCOURSE object with two initially empty markable levels. In this case, no value is provided for `mmax2_java_binding`, so that no validation will be performed during project creation.

```
dirname = './litcovid-mmax2/'
mmax2project = pmx.MMAX2Project(dirname+'project', {'words':'words.xml'})
mmax2project.write()
cp_path = 'common_paths.xml'
cp = pmx.MMAX2CommonPaths(dirname+cp_path)
cp.write(overwrite=True)
pmx_disc = pmx.MMAX2Discourse(mmax2project.get_mmax2_path(full=True), common_paths=dirname+cp_path)
passages_level=pmx_disc.add_markable_level('passages',
            namespace='xmlns="www.pymmax2.org/NameSpaces/passages"', create_if_missing=True)
entities_level=pmx_disc.add_markable_level('entities',
            namespace='xmlns="www.pymmax2.org/NameSpaces/entities"', create_if_missing=True)
```

The second code snippet creates basedata and markables and assigns attributes to the latter. Markables on the passages level are directly created along with the basedata chunks they cover. The `add_markable` method creates a new markable and returns the tuple (True, new markable) *only* if no other markable with an identical span exists on the level, in which case it returns (False, existing markable).

```
with open('samplelitcovid.xml', 'r') as f:
    contents = f.read()
    soup = bs(contents, 'lxml')
    neg_offset=0
    for p in soup.find_all('passage'):
        p_text = p.find('text').text
        p_type = p.find('infon',{'key':'type'}).text.lower()
        new_m, pm = passages_level.add_markable([pd.add_basedata_elements_from_string(p_text)])
        if new_m:   pm.set_attributes({'type':p_type})
        mt,_,pos2id = pd.get_basedata().render_string(pm.get_spanlists(), mapping=True)
        for anno in p.find_all('annotation'):
            offset = int(anno.find('location')['offset'])
            length = int(anno.find('location')['length'])
            e_type = anno.find('infon',{'key':'type'}).text.lower()
            anno_span=[]
            for f in range(length):
                try:
                    if pos2id[f+offset-neg_offset] not in anno_span:
                        anno_span.append(pos2id[f+offset-neg_offset])
                except KeyError:
                    pass
            new_m, pm = entities_level.add_markable([anno_span])
            if new_m:    pm.set_attributes({'entity_type':e_type})
        neg_offset=neg_offset+(len(mt))
pd.get_basedata().write(to_path=dirname, dtd_base_path='"', overwrite=True)
passages_level.write(to_path=dirname, overwrite=True)
entities_level.write(to_path=dirname, overwrite=True)
pd.get_commonpaths().write(overwrite=True)
```

Finally, the newly created MMAX2 project can be re-loaded from scratch like the previous example in Section 2.1, including 'deep' access to the related annotation schemes. Calling the `info()` method will produce the following output, including correct default values for both markable levels.

```
MMAX2 Project Info:
-------------------
.mmax file       : ./litcovid-mmax2/project.mmax
Basedata elements : 179
Markable levels  :
  passages        : 2 markables [default: type:none]
  entities        : 4 markables [default: entity_type:none]
```

## Acknowledgements

The work described in this paper was done as part of the project DeepCurate, which is funded by the German Federal Ministry of Education and Research (BMBF) (No. 031L0204) and the Klaus Tschira Foundation, Heidelberg, Germany. We thank the anonymous reviewers for their helpful suggestions.

## References

Q. Chen, A. Allot, and Z. Lu. 2020. Keep up with the latest coronavirus research. *Nature*, 579(7798):193.

Christian Chiarcos, Stefanie Dipper, Michael Götze, Ulf Leser, Anke Lüdeling, Julia Ritz, and Manfred Stede. 2008. A flexible framework for integrating annotations from different tools and tag sets. *Trait. Autom. des Langues*, 49(2):217–246.

Donald C. Comeau, Rezarta Islamaj Dogan, Paolo Ciccarese, Kevin Bretonnel Cohen, Martin Krallinger, Florian Leitner, Zhiyong Lu, Yifan Peng, Fabio Rinaldi, Manabu Torii, Alfonso Valencia, Karin Verspoor, Thomas C. Wiegers, Cathy H. Wu, and W. John Wilbur. 2013. Bioc: a minimalist approach to interoperability for biomedical text processing. *Database J. Biol. Databases Curation*, 2013.

Bart Desmet and Véronique Hoste. 2010. Towards a balanced named entity corpus for dutch. In *LREC*. European Language Resources Association.

Stefanie Dipper, Christine Rieger, Melanie Seiss, and Heike Zinsmeister. 2011. Abstract anaphors in german and english. In *DAARC*, volume 7099 of *Lecture Notes in Computer Science*, pages 96–107. Springer.

Erik Faessler, Luise Modersohn, Christina Lohr, and Udo Hahn. 2020. Progene - A large-scale, high-quality protein-gene annotated benchmark corpus. In *LREC*, pages 4585–4596. European Language Resources Association.

Iris Hendrickx, Amália Mendes, and Silvia Mencarelli. 2012. Modality in text: a proposal for corpus annotation. In *LREC*, pages 1805–1812. European Language Resources Association (ELRA).

Jan-Christoph Klie, Michael Bugert, Beto Boullosa, Richard Eckart de Castilho, and Iryna Gurevych. 2018. The INCEpTION platform: Machine-assisted and knowledge-oriented interactive annotation. In *Proceedings of the 27th International Conference on Computational Linguistics: System Demonstrations*, pages 5–9. Association for Computational Linguistics, Juni.

Ekaterina Lapshinova-Koltunski, Cristina España-Bonet, and Josef van Genabith. 2019. Analysing coreference in transformer outputs. In *DiscoMT@EMNLP*, pages 1–12. Association for Computational Linguistics.

Chaopeng Liu. 2011. Application of MMAX2 tool in chinese-english parallel corpus building. In *CSISE (3)*, volume 106 of *Advances in Intelligent and Soft Computing*, pages 697–700. Springer.

José Manuel Martínez Martínez, Ekaterina Lapshinova-Koltunski, and Kerstin Kunz. 2016. Annotation of lexical cohesion in english and german: Automatic and manual procedures. In *KONVENS*, volume 16 of *Bochumer Linguistische Arbeitsberichte*.

Christoph Müller and Michael Strube. 2002. An API for discourse-level access to xml-encoded corpora. In *LREC*. European Language Resources Association.

Christoph Müller and Michael Strube. 2006. Multi-level annotation of linguistic data with MMAX2. In Sabine Braun, Kurt Kohn, and Joybrato Mukherjee, editors, *Corpus Technology and Language Pedagogy: New Resources, New Tools, New Methods*, pages 197–214. Peter Lang, Frankfurt a.M., Germany.

Arne Neumann. 2015. discoursegraphs: A graph-based merging tool and converter for multilayer annotated corpora. In *NODALIDA*, volume 109 of *Linköping Electronic Conference Proceedings*, pages 309–312. Linköping University Electronic Press / Association for Computational Linguistics.

Mariana Neves and Jurica Ševa. 2019. An extensive review of tools for manual annotation of documents. *Briefings in Bioinformatics*, 12. bbz130.

Ulrich Schäfer, Christian Spurk, and Jörg Steffen. 2012. A fully coreference-annotated corpus of scholarly papers from the ACL anthology. In *Proceedings of COLING 2012: Posters*, pages 1059–1070, Mumbai, India, December. The COLING 2012 Organizing Committee.

Pontus Stenetorp, Sampo Pyysalo, Goran Topic, Tomoko Ohta, Sophia Ananiadou, and Jun'ichi Tsujii. 2012. brat: a web-based tool for nlp-assisted text annotation. In *EACL*, pages 102–107. Association for Computational Linguistics.

Olga Uryupina, Ron Artstein, Antonella Bristot, Federica Cavicchio, Francesca Delogu, Kepa J. Rodriguez, and Massimo Poesio. 2020. Annotating a broad range of anaphoric phenomena, in a variety of genres: the arrau corpus. *Natural Language Engineering*, 26(1):95–128.

Seid Muhie Yimam, Iryna Gurevych, Richard Eckart de Castilho, and Chris Biemann. 2013. WebAnno: A flexible, web-based and visually supported system for distributed annotations. In *Proceedings of the 51st Annual Meeting of the Association for Computational Linguistics: System Demonstrations*, pages 1–6, Sofia, Bulgaria, August. Association for Computational Linguistics.

Florian Zipser and Laurent Romary. 2010. A model oriented approach to the mapping of annotation formats using standards. In *Workshop on Language Resource and Language Technology Standards, LREC 2010*, La Valette, Malta, May.

# Annotating Coherence Relations
# for Studying Topic Transitions in Social Talk


**Alex Lưu**
Brandeis University
alexluu@brandeis.edu

**Sophia A. Malamud**
Brandeis University
smalamud@brandeis.edu



## Abstract

This study develops the strand of research on topic transitions in social talk which aims to gain a better understanding of interlocutors' conversational goals. Lưu and Malamud (2020) proposed that one way to identify such transitions is to annotate coherence relations, and then to identify utterances potentially expressing new topics as those that fail to participate in these relations. This work validates and refines their suggested annotation methodology, focusing on annotating most prominent coherence relations in face-to-face social dialogue. The result is a publicly accessible gold standard corpus with efficient and reliable annotation, whose broad coverage provides a foundation for future steps of identifying and classifying new topic utterances.[1]


## 1 Introduction

In natural language interactions, speakers' conversational goals determine the course of conversation. Conversational goals are therefore an essential component of any dialogue model that possesses a genuine capability of natural language understanding and reasoning. While this component is predefined or able to be inferred from visible linguistic content in the dialogue systems for task-oriented conversation, it is inadequately represented or missing in the current dialogue systems implemented for social talk. For instance, open-domain dialog systems that evolve from task-oriented dialog systems usually extend the space of information to be exchanged, e.g. in terms of intents and topics, and treat social talk as multi-domain task-oriented talk; while end-to-end trained neural chatbots focus more on the utterance generation task, and do not have any explicit representation of conversational goals.

To gain better insight into conversational goals of the interlocutors in social talk, Lưu and Malamud (2020) conducted a pilot annotation study of new-topic utterances (NTUs), which begin a new topic not related to the content of prior discourse. While such utterances are legitimate in social talk, current models of dialogue would treat them as incoherent conversational moves because these models only focus on utterances within a topically coherent discourse segment. By identifying NTUs and studying patterns of the disjunctive topic changes (DTCs) which are signaled by these utterances, Lưu and Malamud (2020) was able to introduce new sequence-based social intents that are absent in traditional taxonomies of speech acts but clearly reflect the goal-directed aspect of social talk, and therefore advocate the enrichment of dialogue models for social talk.

We build on (Lưu and Malamud, 2020) to evaluate and refine their annotation methodology for identifying NTU candidates. Here, we report on a full annotation project which features a publicly accessible dataset of face-to-face casual dialogues in American English, refined annotation guidelines, detailed analyses of the annotation process, and fully adjudicated annotation results which can serve as a test set for computational evaluation.

This paper is organized as follows. Section 2 provides an overview of related prior research. Section 3 presents our work constructing a gold standard corpus of discourse relation annotation for the purpose of identifying NTUs. Section 4 reports quantitative and qualitative analyses of our annotation process and methodology, while Section 5 concludes and presents a plan for future work.

---

[1]The live version of this publication is located at https://osf.io/7t4rf/.






*The 14th Linguistic Annotation Workshop*, pages 174–179
Barcelona, Spain (Online), December 12, 2020.

## 2   Related Work

Riou (2015b) uses a mixed-methods approach to identify topic transitions in conversational interaction, including (1) the preliminary segmentation of conversation into turn-constructional units (TCUs), widely used in the Conversation Analysis framework as minimal interactional moves, and (2) the actual classification of each TCU into different categories such as topic continuity, stepwise topic transition, and disjunctive topic transition (i.e. DTC) (Riou, 2015a). The latter relies on the annotators' internal analysis rather than any explicit guidelines. Focusing on identifying DTCs, Lưu and Malamud (2020) propose a more formal approach which relies on well-tested coherence relation annotation to single out the NTU candidates as those utterances which do not bear any coherence relation to the content of prior discourse.

The annotation of coherence relations in (Lưu and Malamud, 2020) is different from previous attempts in two main aspects. First, as its ultimate goal is to identify NTUs, which do not participate in any coherence relations with prior discourse, the annotation aims at annotating coherence relations that cover as many utterances in the discourse as possible, rather than exhaustively annotating all available coherence relations of interest as in (Tonelli et al., 2010; Rehbein et al., 2016). Second, it relies on the superset of all well-known and tested coherence relations, rather than a specific taxonomy which may require ad hoc additions along the annotation process, as in (Xue et al., 2016; Yung et al., 2019).

It is noted that the pilot annotation in (Lưu and Malamud, 2020) does not fully comply with their proposed methodology. Instead of annotating targeted coherence relations from the ground up, they start with the Disco-SPICE corpus's *1,273* annotated coherence relations defined in the early version of the Penn Discourse Treebank (PDTB) 3.0 scheme (Webber et al., 2016). That optimizes the workload but does not provide an accurate view of the proposed annotation process because the goals of two annotation projects are different (as mentioned above).

This work seeks to elaborate and enrich Lưu and Malamud (2020)'s methodology for marking coherence relations as a way to identify NTU candidates in social talk, making the following contributions:

- a full development cycle of a high-quality gold standard corpus, which is publicly accessible,
- quantitative and qualitative assessments of the reliability and validity of the annotation process,
- carefully refined annotation guidelines, which are appropriate for large-scale annotation projects.

## 3   Gold Standard Corpus Creation

### 3.1   Data, Data Format, and Annotation Platform

The annotation data includes the initial *15*-minute extracts of *7* casual dialogues from the Santa Barbara Corpus of Spoken American English (SBCSAE) (Du Bois et al., 2000), segmented into TCUs by Riou (2015a) (see detail in Table 1) and accompanied by audio files that can be conveniently browsed at TalkBank.org. These face-to-face conversations are a perfect complement to the telephone dialogues annotated by Lưu and Malamud (2020). Working on the version segmented by Riou (2015a), we adopt her assumption that TCU-based utterances are the smallest units for topics in the conversational discourse, and will be able to use our annotation results to assess the reliability of her methodology.

The data is converted into the FoLiA format and annotated in the FoLiA Annotation Tool (FLAT), as in (Lưu and Malamud, 2020). Being a rich XML-based format for multiple linguistic annotation types, FoLiA stands out for its human-readability and portability by allowing both in-line and stand-off annotation layers and including all of these layers in a single file (van Gompel and Reynaert, 2013). It is especially suitable for discourse-level annotations which are likely to be enriched with the annotation of more form-constrained linguistic layers to facilitate the research on the form-function interface. The well developed and maintained FoLiA libraries such as FoLiApy for Python also allow us to easily manipulate the data at any point of the corpus development cycle, making the workflow flexible and interactive. An example of this is our use of various Python scripts described at the end of Subsection 3.2.

### 3.2   Corpus Development Cycle

We use the Model-Annotate-Model-Annotate (MAMA) cycle, introduced in (Pustejovsky and Stubbs, 2012). Specifically, one pilot annotation round and two MAMA iterations (Table 1) were performed by a team of three annotators,who are rising junior Linguistics majors and native American English speakers.

- Pilot round: Each team member annotates 'SBC034Time' to acclimate to the task and estimate annotation rate (TCUs per hour). Each person then adjudicates the others' annotations.
- MAMA iterations: each of the remaining six dialogues is annotated by two team members and adjudicated by the third.

| Dialogue name | Number of TCUs | Average hours to annotate | Hours to adjudicate |
|---|---|---|---|
| *Pilot:* | *379* | *6.00 ± 0.67* | *4.08 ± 1.22 (average)* |
| – SBC034Time | 379 | 6.00 ± 0.67 | 4.08 ± 1.22 (average) |
| *MAMA 1:* | *391 (average)* | *5.33 ± 0.67* | *3.00* |
| – SBC007Tree | 344 | 4.38 ± 0.63 | 4.00 |
| – SBC005Book | 393 | 5.38 ± 1.13 | 2.50 |
| – SBC017Notions | 437 | 6.25 ± 0.25 | 2.50 |
| *MAMA 2:* | *567 (average)* | *6.67 ± 0.33* | *4.75* |
| – SBC047Lot | 491 | 6.00 ± 0.00 | 4.75 |
| – SBC043Spoonfuls | 561 | 6.50 ± 0.50 | 3.00 |
| – SBC006Cuz | 648 | 7.50 ± 0.50 | 6.50 |
| **Total** | **3253** | **42.00 ± 3.67** | **27.33 ± 1.22 (average)** |

Table 1: Annotation and adjudication time

The accelerated annotation task yielded an average annotation rate of *77.45* TCU/hr, with natural improvement from the pilot (*63.17* TCUs/hr) to MAMA 1 (*73.38* TCU/hr) to MAMA 2 stage (*85* TCU/hr).

The annotators are asked to put themselves in the interlocutors' shoes and label the most easily recognizable coherence relation between each TCU, or a discourse segment containing this TCU, and its prior discourse, which can also consist of one or more TCUs (example in Table 2), using labels based on:

- the latest PDTB 3.0 taxonomy of discourse relations (Webber et al., 2019),
- semantic relations from (ISO, 2016) and (ISO, 2012), which model the interactive nature of dialogue in a finer-grained manner than those of PDTB 3.0, e.g. *feedback* or *prop Q-A* in Table 2b.

| Utterance | Simplified transcript |
|---|---|
| 1728-JIM | *And, so much of today's technology is soulless.* |
| 1729-JIM | *And has nothing to do with peace, it has to do with, just generally, chewing up, you know, consumerism basically and,* |
| 1730-MIC | *Mhm.* |
| 1731-JIM | *chewing up chewing up new uh, chewing up the human experience, and turning it into, some kind of consumer need.* |
| 1732-MIC | *Did you ever get into Tesla?* |
| 1733-JIM | *Uh, just, ever so peripherally.* |
| 1734-MIC | *He had a lot of real wacky ideas on big levels.* |
| 1735-MIC | *He wanted a world power system, that you could um, tap into the air basically, and get power anywhere on earth.* |

(a) Excerpt from 'SBC017Notions'

| Relation | Arg 1 | Arg 2 |
|---|---|---|
| *conjunction* | 1728 | 1729 |
| *feedback* | 1729 | 1730 |
| *entity-based* | 1729 | 1731 |
| *prop Q-A* | 1732 | 1733 |
| *entity-based* | 1732 | 1734 |
| *instantiation* | 1734 | 1735 |

(b) Annotated relations in (a)

Table 2: Annotation example

The annotators will skip less salient coherence relations which:

- are available between the TCU under consideration and other parts of prior discourse, or
- concurrently exist between the TCU under consideration and its counterpart in the annotated relations (as discussed in (Moore and Pollack, 1992; Rohde et al., 2018; Webber et al., 2019)).

This is because our goal is to identify NTUs - utterances that do not participate in any identifiable relation to their prior linguistic context, and therefore once we annotate even a single relation between two given discourse segments, we know that the utterances in them are not NTUs. Focusing on existence of relations rather than identity of these relations allows us to pursue this goal, and has additional methodological benefits. First, this reduces the annotators' cognitive load, enhances their concentration, and fosters their natural interpretation of the dialogues. Second, it provides valuable insight into the annotators' ranking of the coherence relations based on their salience. A possible trade-off are inter-annotator inconsistencies with respect to the identity of annotated relations, but this does not affect annotation consistency with respect to existence of relations between given utterances.

We never encountered a case when an annotator could not find a label for a coherence relation, which is evidence for the breadth of coverage of our predefined label set. We accelerated the annotation process with the following decisions:

- The annotators do not mark the actual discourse connectives or equivalent linguistic materials which lexicalize the annotated coherence relations.
- The label set is selected so that the two arguments of each coherence relation can be indexed chronologically, i.e. the second argument always appears after the first argument in the conversational flow, in an automatic manner, specifically:
    - we only use Level-2 discourse relations of PDTB 3.0 sense hierarchy, which are indirectional (symmetric)
    - we rely on the the chronological nature of the arguments of ISO-based semantic relations (e.g. answers always follow questions)

The refined annotation guidelines are publicly accessible at `https://alexluu.flowlu.com/hc/6/223--annotation-guidelines`.

Each input file for pair-wise adjudication is created as a spreadsheet using a Python script. Identical relations annotated by two different annotators are automatically accepted. For discrepancies, the adjudicator can agree or disagree on the relation labels or the argument spans or both. Finally, the adjudication results are reconstructed into the gold standard version of a FoLiA file by another Python script. The final gold standard corpus is publicly accessible at `https://alexluu.flowlu.com/hc/6/250--annotated-corpus`.

## 4 Annotation Analyses

### 4.1 Quantitative Analysis

Based on (Artstein and Poesio, 2008), we identify each utterance as an item (markable) for inter-annotator agreement (IAA) calculation wherein the categories which can be assigned to each item are:

- there is no coherence relation between the item and prior discourse.
- there is a coherence relation between the item and prior discourse which consists of two attributes: the first argument of the relation, and the label of the relation.

The pair-wise IAA statistics are presented in Table 3. The column '**Agree on arg 1**' shows the ratio of the number of relations agreeing on their first arguments to the total number of utterances, while the column '**Agree on arg 1** & **label**' shows the ratio of the number of identical relations to the total number of utterances. The final column displays the number of coherence relations accepted to the final gold standard corpus. It is worth noting that the IAA significantly improves between two MAMA cycles, which will become clearer in light of the qualitative analysis.

### 4.2 Qualitative Analysis

We conducted interviews and a post-project survey with the annotators. Based on these qualitative measures, the most confused pair of relations are *agreement* and *feedback* (audio helps, but not always). In general, *agreement* relates to a directive or the truth of a statement in the previous utterance, while *feedback* signals the success/failure of processing the message in the previous utterance, without signaling agreement. TCUs are generally good units for our annotation, but there are 'too short' cases which require the creation of multi-TCU arguments and therefore slow down the annotation process.

| Dialogue name | Agree on arg 1 | Agree on arg 1 & label | # of accepted relations |
|---|---|---|---|
| *Pilot:* | *0.527 ± 0.041 (avg)* | *0.365 ± 0.021 (avg)* | *279 ± 10 (avg)* |
| – SBC034Time | 0.527 ± 0.041 (avg) | 0.365 ± 0.021 (avg) | 279 ± 10 (avg) |
| *MAMA 1:* | *0.527* | *0.334* | *911 (total)* |
| – SBC007Tree | 0.753 | 0.491 | 303 |
| – SBC005Book | 0.354 | 0.204 | 266 |
| – SBC017Notions | 0.506 | 0.327 | 342 |
| *MAMA 2:* | *0.624* | *0.400* | *1330 (total)* |
| – SBC047Lot | 0.617 | 0.436 | 411 |
| – SBC043Spoonfuls | 0.652 | 0.387 | 461 |
| – SBC006Cuz | 0.603 | 0.384 | 458 |
| | | **Total** | **2520** |

Table 3: Pair-wise IAA statistics.

The annotators rate their independence as very high, slightly decreasing throughout the corpus development cycle due to our weekly meetings and the fact that annotators of some files are adjudicators of others. The trade-off is that the annotators become more confident, performing less pure but higher quality annotation. They also feel more competent at adjudication, and notice more convergence in their teammates' annotations. The annotators report having a very positive experience and are willing to participate in future projects on dialogic discourse.

## 5 Conclusion and Future Work

In summary, we have constructed a gold-standard corpus of most salient discourse relations as a way to identify NTU candidates in conversation. Our accelerated annotation methodology and the use of established relation taxonomies allowed for efficient and reliable annotation process with broad coverage.

Our next steps are, first, to compare the topic transitions inferred from our annotation and Riou (2015a)'s work to evaluate her methodology; and second, to identify NTUs and patterns of DTCs to enrich the classification of NTUs in (Lưu and Malamud, 2020). We plan to use this new classification as a step towards developing a dialogue agent capable of true understanding of the flow of social talk.

## Acknowledgements

We are extremely grateful to Marine Riou and John W Du Bois who gave us their full support for making our annotation publicly accessible. Our deepest gratitude goes to our well-rounded annotation team: Julia Kenneally, Tali Tukachinsky and Cole Peterson. Finally, we would like to thank our anonymous reviewers for their crystal clear and thoughtful feedback that made our revision process very efficient.

## References

Ron Artstein and Massimo Poesio. 2008. Inter-coder agreement for computational linguistics. *Computational Linguistics*, 34(4):555–596.

John W Du Bois, Wallace L Chafe, Charles Meyer, Sandra A Thompson, and Nii Martey. 2000. Santa Barbara corpus of spoken American English. *CD-ROM. Philadelphia: Linguistic Data Consortium.*

2012. Language resource management – semantic annotation framework (SemAF) – part 2: Dialogue acts. Technical report, International Organization for Standardization.

2016. Language resource management – semantic annotation framework (SemAF) – part 8: Semantic relations in discourse, core annotation schema (DR-core). Technical report, International Organization for Standardization.

Alex Lưu and Sophia A. Malamud. 2020. Non-topical coherence in social talk: A call for dialogue model enrichment. In *Proceedings of the 58th Annual Meeting of the Association for Computational Linguistics: Student Research Workshop*, pages 118–133, Online, July. Association for Computational Linguistics.

Johanna D. Moore and Martha E. Pollack. 1992. A problem for RST: The need for multi-level discourse analysis. *Computational Linguistics*, 18(4):537–544.

James Pustejovsky and Amber Stubbs. 2012. *Natural Language Annotation for Machine Learning: A Guide to Corpus-Building for Applications*. O'Reilly Media, Inc.

Ines Rehbein, Merel Scholman, and Vera Demberg. 2016. Annotating discourse relations in spoken language: A comparison of the PDTB and CCR frameworks. In *Proceedings of the 10th International Conference on Language Resources and Evaluation (LREC 2016)*, pages 1039–1046, Portorož, Slovenia. European Language Resources Association (ELRA).

Marine Riou. 2015a. *The Grammar of Topic Transition in American English Conversation. Topic Transition Design and Management in Typical and Atypical Conversations (Schizophrenia)*. Ph.D. thesis, Université Sorbonne Paris Cité.

Marine Riou. 2015b. A methodology for the identification of topic transitions in interaction. *Discours. Revue de linguistique, psycholinguistique et informatique. A journal of linguistics, psycholinguistics and computational linguistics*, (16).

Hannah Rohde, Alexander Johnson, Nathan Schneider, and Bonnie Webber. 2018. Discourse coherence: Concurrent explicit and implicit relations. In *Proceedings of the 56th Annual Meeting of the Association for Computational Linguistics (Volume 1: Long Papers)*, pages 2257–2267, Melbourne, Australia, July. Association for Computational Linguistics.

Sara Tonelli, Giuseppe Riccardi, Rashmi Prasad, and Aravind Joshi. 2010. Annotation of discourse relations for conversational spoken dialogs. In *Proceedings of the Seventh International Conference on Language Resources and Evaluation (LREC'10)*, Valletta, Malta, May. European Language Resources Association (ELRA).

Maarten van Gompel and Martin Reynaert. 2013. FoLiA: A practical XML format for linguistic annotation – a descriptive and comparative study. *Computational Linguistics in the Netherlands Journal*, 3:63–81, Dec.

Bonnie Webber, Rashmi Prasad, Alan Lee, and Aravind Joshi. 2016. A discourse-annotated corpus of conjoined VPs. In *Proceedings of the 10th Linguistic Annotation Workshop held in conjunction with ACL 2016 (LAW-X 2016)*, pages 22–31, Berlin, Germany, August. Association for Computational Linguistics.

Bonnie Webber, Rashmi Prasad, Alan Lee, and Aravind Joshi. 2019. The Penn Discourse Treebank 3.0 annotation manual. Technical report, University of Edinburgh.

Nianwen Xue, Qishen Su, and Sooyoung Jeong. 2016. Annotating the discourse and dialogue structure of SMS message conversations. In *Proceedings of the 10th Linguistic Annotation Workshop held in conjunction with ACL 2016 (LAW-X 2016)*, pages 180–187, Berlin, Germany, August. Association for Computational Linguistics.

Frances Yung, Vera Demberg, and Merel Scholman. 2019. Crowdsourcing discourse relation annotations by a two-step connective insertion task. In *Proceedings of the 13th Linguistic Annotation Workshop*, pages 16–25, Florence, Italy, August. Association for Computational Linguistics.